Networks and Religion

Social scientists who study religion generally believe that social networks play a central role in religious life. However, most studies draw on measures that are relatively poor proxies for capturing the effects of social networks. This book illustrates how researchers can draw on formal social network analysis methods to explore the interplay of networks and religion. The book's introductory chapters provide overviews of the social scientific study of religion and social network analysis. The remaining chapters explore a variety of topics current in the social scientific study of religion, as well as introduce a variety of social network theories and methods, such as balance theory, ego network analysis, exponential random graph models, and stochastic actor-oriented models. By embedding social network analysis within a social scientific study of religion framework, *Networks and Religion* offers an array of approaches for studying the role that social networks play in religious belief and practice.

Sean F. Everton is a professor in the Defense Analysis Department at the US Naval Postgraduate School (NPS). Prior to joining NPS in 2007, he served as an adjunct professor at both Santa Clara and Stanford Universities. Everton earned his PhD in Sociology from Stanford University and wrote his dissertation on the causes and consequences of status on venture capital firm performance. He has published in the areas of social network analysis, sociology of religion, economic sociology, and political sociology. He specializes in the use of social network analysis to disrupt dark networks (e.g., criminal and terrorist networks).

Structural Analysis in the Social Sciences

Mark Granovetter, editor

The series Structural Analysis in the Social Sciences presents studies that analyze social behavior and institutions by reference to relations among such concrete social entities as persons, organizations, and nations. Relational analysis contrasts on the one hand with reductionist methodological individualism and on the other with macro-level determinism, whether based on technology, material conditions, economic conflict, adaptive evolution, or functional imperatives. In this more intellectually flexible structural middle ground, analysts situate actors and their relations in a variety of contexts. Since the series began in 1987, its authors have variously focused on small groups, history, culture, politics, kinship, aesthetics, economics, and complex organizations, creatively theorizing how these shape and in turn are shaped by social relations. Their style and methods have ranged widely, from intense, long-term ethnographic observation to highly abstract mathematical models. Their disciplinary affiliations have included history, anthropology, sociology, political science, business, economics, mathematics, and computer science. Some have made explicit use of social network analysis, including many of the cutting-edge and standard works of that approach, whereas others have kept formal analysis in the background and used "networks" as a fruitful orienting metaphor. All have in common a sophisticated and revealing approach that forcefully illuminates our complex social world.

Recent Books in the Series
Brea L. Perry, *Egocentric Network Analysis: Foundations, Methods, and Models*
Darisu Mehri, *Iran Auto: Building a Global Industry in an Islamic State*
Navid Hassanpour, *Leading from the Periphery and Network Collective Action*
Cheol-Sung Lee, *When Solidarity Works*
Benjamin Cornwell, *Social Sequence Analysis*
Mariela Szwarcberg, *Mobilizing Poor Voters*
Luke M. Gerdes, ed., *Illuminating Dark Networks*
Silvia Domínguez and Betina Hollstein, eds., *Mixed Methods in Studying Social Networks*
Dean Lusher, Johan Koskinen, and Garry Robins, eds., *Exponential Random Graph Models for Social Networks: Theory, Methods, and Applications*
Sean F. Everton, *Disrupting Dark Networks*
Wouter de Nooy, Andrej Mrvar, and Vladimir Batagelj, *Exploratory Social Network Analysis with Pajek*
Noah E. Friedkin and Eugene C. Johnsen, *Social Influence Network Theory*
Zeev Maoz, *The Networks of Nations: The Evolution and Structure of International Networks, 1815–2002*
Martin Kilduff and David Krackhardt, *Interpersonal Networks in Organizations*
Ari Adut, *On Scandal: Moral Disturbances in Society, Politics, and Art*
Robert C. Feenstra and Gary G. Hamilton, *Emergent Economies, Divergent Paths*
Eiko Ikegami, *Bonds of Civility: Aesthetic Networks and the Political Origins of Japanese Culture*

Networks and Religion

Ties That Bind, Loose, Build Up, and Tear Down

SEAN F. EVERTON
US Naval Postgraduate School–Monterey, CA

CAMBRIDGE
UNIVERSITY PRESS

University Printing House, Cambridge CB2 8BS, United Kingdom

One Liberty Plaza, 20th Floor, New York, NY 10006, USA

477 Williamstown Road, Port Melbourne, VIC 3207, Australia

314–321, 3rd Floor, Plot 3, Splendor Forum, Jasola District Centre, New Delhi – 110025, India

79 Anson Road, #06–04/06, Singapore 079906

Cambridge University Press is part of the University of Cambridge.

It furthers the University's mission by disseminating knowledge in the pursuit of education, learning, and research at the highest international levels of excellence.

www.cambridge.org
Information on this title: www.cambridge.org/9781108416702
DOI: 10.1017/9781108241748

© The United States Government 2018. This work is not subject to copyright protection within the United States of America. 2018

This publication is in copyright. Subject to statutory exception and to the provisions of relevant collective licensing agreements, no reproduction of any part may take place without the written permission of Cambridge University Press.

First published 2018

Printed in the United States of America by Sheridan Books, Inc.

A catalogue record for this publication is available from the British Library.

Library of Congress Cataloging-in-Publication Data
Names: Everton, Sean F., author.
Title: Networks and religion : ties that bind, loose, build up, and tear down / Sean F. Everton, US Naval Postgraduate School–Monterey, CA.
Description: New York : Cambridge University Press, 2018. | Series: Structural analysis in the social sciences
Identifiers: LCCN 2018017825 | ISBN 9781108416702
Subjects: LCSH: Interpersonal relations – Religious aspects. | Social networks.
Classification: LCC BL626.33 .E94 2018 | DDC 204/.2–dc23
LC record available at https://lccn.loc.gov/2018017825

ISBN 978-1-108-41670-2 Hardback
ISBN 978-1-108-40407-5 Paperback

Cambridge University Press has no responsibility for the persistence or accuracy of URLs for external or third-party internet websites referred to in this publication and does not guarantee that any content on such websites is, or will remain, accurate or appropriate.

To Deanne, Tara, and Brendan

Contents

List of Figures	*page* x
List of Tables	xiii
Preface	xv
Acknowledgments	xxii

PART I INTRODUCTION — 1

1 The Surprising (at Least to Some) Persistence of Religion   3
   1.1 Introduction   3
   1.2 Empirical Anomalies   5
   1.3 Religion as Rational Choice   13
   1.4 Religious Economies   22
   1.5 A Cultural Sociology of Religion: Subcultural Identity Theory   34
   1.6 Summary and Conclusion   42
   1.7 For Further Reading   44

2 Social Network Analysis: A Brief Introduction   47
   2.1 Introduction   47
   2.2 Misconceptions   50
   2.3 Assumptions   52
   2.4 Terms and Concepts   59
   2.5 Social Network Data   74
   2.6 Collecting Social Network Data   80
   2.7 Summary and Conclusion   83
   2.8 For Further Reading   83

PART II TIES THAT BIND — 85

3 Recruitment and Conversion   87
   3.1 Introduction   87
   3.2 Moonies, Mormons, and More   89
   3.3 Why Do Networks Matter?   95
   3.4 Excursus: Statistical Models for Social Network Data   97

	3.5	Summary and Conclusion	111
	3.6	For Further Reading	112
4	Commitment and Conformity		114
	4.1	Introduction	114
	4.2	Homophily and Commitment	116
	4.3	Mobility and Commitment	122
	4.4	Community and Commitment	125
	4.5	Commitment and Conformity	128
	4.6	Summary and Conclusion	130
	4.7	For Further Reading	131
PART III TIES THAT LOOSE			135
5	Diffusion and Innovation		137
	5.1	Introduction	137
	5.2	Archeological Networks and the Diffusion of Rabbinic Judaism	139
	5.3	Student Networks and the Spread of the Protestant Reformation	145
	5.4	Denominational Networks and Women's Ordination	148
	5.5	Summary and Conclusion	166
	5.6	For Further Reading	166
6	Politics and Community		169
	6.1	Introduction	169
	6.2	Social Capital and Social Networks	171
	6.3	Social Networks and Civic Engagement	173
	6.4	Congregational Networks and Political Activism	174
	6.5	Excursus: Church and State Separation and Civic Engagement	188
	6.6	Summary and Conclusion	191
	6.7	For Further Reading	191
PART IV TIES THAT BUILD UP			195
7	Networks and Tradition		197
	7.1	Introduction	197
	7.2	Church and Sect	199
	7.3	Church, Sect, and Cult: Independent Religious Movements	206
	7.4	Ego Networks and Religious Tradition	212
	7.5	Summary and Conclusion	219
	7.6	For Further Reading	220
8	Health and Happiness		222
	8.1	Introduction	222
	8.2	Networks and Adolescent Health and Happiness	225

8.3	Networks and Life Satisfaction	230
8.4	Networks and Suicide	232
8.5	Epidemics, Networks, and the Rise of Christianity (with Robert Schroeder)	238
8.6	Summary and Conclusion	248
8.7	For Further Reading	249

PART V TIES THAT TEAR DOWN — 251

9 Conflict and Cohesion — 253
    9.1 Introduction — 253
    9.2 Cohesion and Conflict: Zablocki's Urban Communes — 255
    9.3 Conflict and Cohesion: Sampson's Monks — 263
    9.4 Conflict and Creativity: Collins's Philosophical Networks — 269
    9.5 Summary and Conclusion — 286
    9.6 For Further Reading — 286

10 Radicalization and Violence — 288
    10.1 Introduction — 288
    10.2 Group Polarization and Religious Radicalization — 290
    10.3 Peoples Temple, the Armed Islamic Group, and the Branch Davidians — 295
    10.4 Violent Anabaptists — 302
    10.5 Summary and Conclusion — 312
    10.6 For Further Reading — 314

PART VI CONCLUSION — 315

11 Lessons Learned: The End of the Beginning — 317
    11.1 Introduction — 317
    11.2 Ethics and Social Network Research — 319
    11.3 Summary and Conclusion — 321

Appendix A: Glossary of Terms — 323
Appendix B: Defining Religion — 332
Appendix C: SNA Software — 335
References — 339
Index — 383

Figures

P.1	Count of articles using network-related terms by year	page xvi
1.1	Religious adherence rate, 1776–2000	9
1.2	Predicted rate of attendance by degree	17
1.3	Religious attendance by Herfindahl index	26
1.4	Religious attendance by religious regulation	30
2.1	Illustrative link analysis diagram	51
2.2	Illustrative social network analysis diagrams	53
2.3	Strong and weak ties	55
2.4	Hypothetical social network	61
2.5	Sampson monastery, liking time 3	62
2.6	US interdenominational network, 1985	63
2.7	US denomination and ecumenical organization network, 1985	64
2.8	Sampson monastery, liking time 3 with community detection	69
2.9	Sixteenth-century Anabaptist leadership network (degree centrality)	70
2.10	Hypothetical social network (brokers and bridges)	71
2.11	Sixteenth-century Anabaptist leadership network (brokers and bridges)	72
2.12	Counts of ties	75
2.13	Hypothetical ego network	76
2.14	Whole network	78
2.15	One-mode network: Sampson monastery, liking time 3	78
2.16	US denomination and ecumenical organization two-mode network, 1985	79
3.1	Potential converts' ties to members and nonmembers	90
3.2	The CRTN: preexisting, post-joining, and operational ties	100
3.3	The CRTN: future, present, and past, 1989–2004	102
4.1	Blau Space	117
4.2	Niche edge effect	118

List of Figures

4.3	Niche overlap effect	119
4.4	Geographic mobility and church membership	124
5.1	Proximal point analysis network of cities in the Roman Empire, 200 CE	140
5.2	Maximum distance network of cities in the Roman Empire, 200 CE	141
5.3	Similarity network of cities in the Roman Empire, 200 CE	143
5.4	Interdenominational network, 1915	153
5.5	Interdenominational network, 1925	154
5.6	Interdenominational network, 1935	155
5.7	Interdenominational network, 1945	156
5.8	Interdenominational network, 1955	157
5.9	Interdenominational network, 1965	158
5.10	Interdenominational network, 1975	159
5.11	Interdenominational network, 1985	160
6.1	Congregational political activism by religious tradition and year	176
6.2	Comparison of congregational political activism and social service	180
6.3	Percentage of congregations offering social services by religious tradition and year	187
7.1	Church–sect continuum	201
7.2	Conservative Protestant upward mobility odds compared to other religious traditions	205
7.3	Hypothetical ego networks	214
7.4	Hypothetical ego networks shaded by religious affiliation	214
7.5	Average number of congregational ties by religious tradition, 2006 PALS	215
7.6	Reported network size by religious tradition, 2006 PALS	216
7.7	Average congregational ego network density by religious tradition, 2006 PALS	217
8.1	Church membership by suicide rates, 1980	235
8.2	Hypothetical association between integration/regulation and suicide protection	238
9.1	Predicted probability of commune disbanding by emotional cathexis	260
9.2	Simplified model predicting commune disbanding	262
9.3	Heider's person-other-object (P-O-X) triple	263
9.4	Balanced social network	265
9.5	Sampson's novices, three clusters	267
9.6	Sampson's novices, four clusters	268
9.7	Islamic and Jewish philosophers, Spain, 900–1235	272
9.8	Medieval Christian philosophers, 1000–1200	276
9.9	Medieval Christian philosophers, 1200–1335	279

9.10	Medieval Christian philosophers, 1335–1465	282
9.11	Medieval Christian philosophers, 1465–1600	285
10.1	A simple model of group radicalization	291
10.2	Social networks and group radicalization	292
10.3	Granovetter's forbidden triad	293
10.4	Religion, social networks, and group radicalization	294
10.5	Anabaptist leadership network	307

Tables

P.1	Social scientific study of religion topics by chapter	*page* xxi
1.1	Unconventional beliefs of religious nones	11
1.2	Highest education degree attained by attendance rate	16
1.3	Interaction of religious regulation with religious participation and pluralism	32
1.4	Embattled Christians, by tradition	41
2.1	Summary of Milgram's small world studies	65
3.1	Preexisting social ties among CRTN group members	99
3.2	Estimated QAP coefficients predicting tie formation in CRTN post-joining network	101
3.3	Micro-configurations found in undirected networks	106
3.4	ERGM estimates of tie formation in CRTN post-joining network	107
3.5	Goodness of fit statistics of tie formation in CRTN post-joining network	108
3.6	Auto-logistic actor attribute ERGM estimates on the fate of CRTN members	110
4.1	Church attendance and participation levels	130
5.1	Easter teachers who moved to the United States after 1965	138
5.2	Crosstab of denominational type and ordination policy: actual (expected) counts	162
5.3	Estimated effects of covariates on denominations granting full clergy rights to women	164
6.1	Political activities of religious congregations (percent)	175
6.2a	Estimated coefficients of various political activities on select independent variables	183
6.2b	Estimated coefficients of various political activities on select independent variables	185
6.3	Types of church and state separation	190
7.1	Sociocultural tension by theological tradition	202
7.2	Network density by theological tradition	207

List of Tables

7.3	Education of select American religious groups	209
7.4	Network density by theological tradition including Mormons	211
7.5	Generalized structural equation model predicting ego network density	218
8.1	Adolescent religious ideal types	226
8.2	Select behaviors and attitudes of US adolescents, ages 13–17, by religious ideal type	227
8.3	Social and organizational ties of adolescents, ages 13–17, by religious ideal type	229
8.4	Stark's hypothetical city: the effect of epidemics on counts of pagans and Christians	242
8.5	Stark's hypothetical city: likelihood of tie survival	243
8.6	Simulated hypothetical city: final status	245
8.7	Stark's hypothetical city: likelihood of tie survival	246
8.8	Stark's hypothetical city, average number of ties between Christians and pagans	247
9.1	Emotional cathexis and commune turnover and disintegration rates	256
9.2	Logistic regression predicting commune disbanding	258
9.3	Generalized structural equation model predicting commune disbanding	261
9.4	Error score of the Sampson network over time	269
9.5	Average normalized centrality scores by philosophical rank	274
9.6	Number of clusters identified by Doreian-Mrvar and Louvain algorithms	277
9.7	Comparison of Louvain and Doreian-Mrvar clusters, 1000–1200	277
9.8	Comparison of Louvain and Doreian-Mrvar clusters, 1200–1335	280
9.9	Comparison of Louvain and Doreian-Mrvar clusters, 1335–1465	283
9.10	Comparison of Louvain and Doreian-Mrvar clusters, 1465–1600	284
10.1	Measures of Anabaptist leadership network interconnectedness, 1530–1540	308
10.2	Estimated coefficients of stochastic actor-oriented models	309
10.3	Estimated coefficients of coevolution stochastic actor-oriented models	312
11.1	Summary of SNA topics and methods by chapter	320

Preface

This is a book about networks and religion.[1,2] Social scientists who study religion generally agree that social networks play a central role in religious life (Everton 2015b).[3] We are reasonably confident, for instance, that social ties not only facilitate the recruitment of individuals to faith communities (Lofland and Stark 1965; Sageman 2004; Smilde 2005; Snow, Zurcher, and Ekland-Olson 1980; Stark and Bainbridge 1980a; Stark and Wang 2015; Vala and O'Brien 2007) but also pressure people to conform to the community's accepted norms and behavior (Adamczyk and Felson 2006; Bott 1957; Coleman 1990; Finke and Stark 2005; Granovetter 1992, 2005), sometimes leading marginal church members to participate even when they have little or no desire to do so (Ellison and Sherkat 1995, 1999). It also appears that people with ties to a religious group's core are far less likely to leave than are those without such ties (Popielarz and McPherson 1995; Stark and Bainbridge 1980a). Social networks also play a role in diffusing religious ideas and practices with the wider world (Chaves 1996; Collar 2013a, 2013b; Kim and Pfaff 2012), as well as leading people to volunteer, vote, become politically active, and donate their time and money to both secular and religious charities (Beyerlein and Chaves 2003; Beyerlein and Sikkink 2008; Greeley 1997b; Lewis, MacGregor, and Putnam 2013; McClure 2015; Merino 2013; Schwadel et al. 2015). Congregational networks also play a key role in the health and happiness of their members. In particular, there is a positive association between religion and physical and mental health, and many social scientists believe that much of this is attributable to the networks in which people of faith are embedded (Brashears 2010; Ellison and George 1994; Lim and Putnam 2010; Smith 2003d; Smith and Denton 2005). Finally, some social network patterns are more likely to give rise to conflict and

---

[1] Portions of this and the following section previously appeared in Everton (2015b).
[2] The views expressed in this book are those of the author and do not reflect the official policy or position of the Department of Defense or the US government.
[3] In this book, I adopt a substantive definition of "religion." See Appendix B.

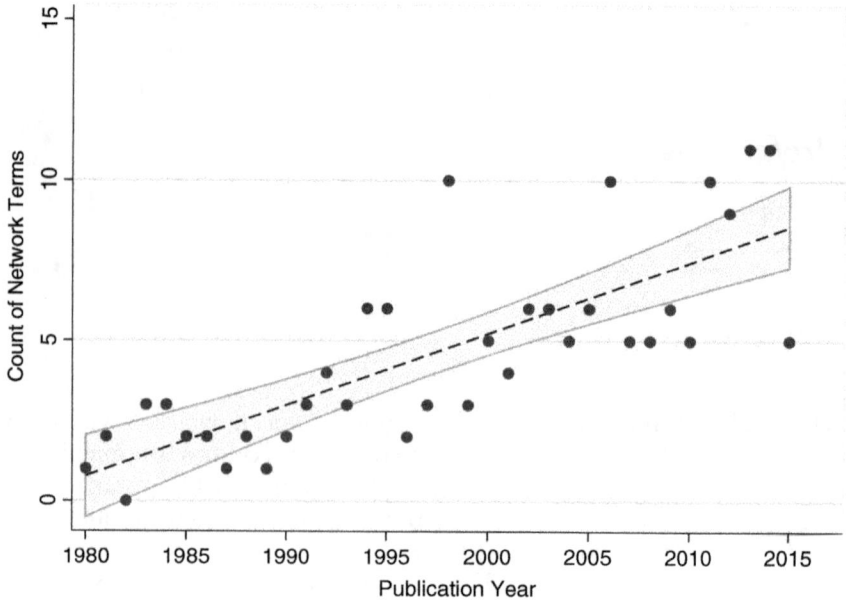

Figure P.1 Count of articles using network-related terms by year

violence than are others. Available evidence suggests that not only can very dense religious networks lead to internal conflict (Zablocki 1980), but they can also be a primary cause lying behind radicalization and violence (della Porta 2013; Everton 2016; Hafez 2003, 2004; Hall 1987, 1995; Sageman 2004; Tabor and Gallagher 1995; Wright 1995).

The appeal to social networks as a mechanism for explaining religious belief and behavior has steadily increased over the past few decades as well. This increase is captured in Figure P.1, which presents a count of the number of articles that include terms related to networks in either their titles or abstracts.[4] Unfortunately, most of these studies have drawn on measures that are relatively poor proxies for capturing network effects (Everton 2015b). In particular, they often infer ties from surveys that ask questions such as: "How often do you see, write, or talk on the telephone with your friends?" "How many close friends do you have in this congregation?" "Tell me if you agree with the following statement: My congregation feels/felt like family to me." "To what extent did you talk to people in your religious congregation?" and so on. Questions such

---

[4] For these counts, only articles from the *Journal for the Scientific Study of Religion*, *Review of Religious Research*, and *Sociology of Religion* were included. These were chosen because historically they have been the primary journals for publishing articles concerned with the social scientific study of religion.

as these cannot fully capture the social context in which religious beliefs and practices are embedded. As Cheadle and Schwadel (2012:1198) note, "[M]ost quantitative research on American religion is now based on surveys of unconnected individuals, with the result that the social context of religion is obscured." This is not to suggest that this is the desired state of affairs of social scientists who study religion. Indeed, it almost certainly is not, but their hands are "tied by design and method" (Cheadle and Schwadel 2012:1199). That is why one of the primary motivations behind this book is to introduce formal social network methods (and data) to social scientists who want to more fully explore the interplay of networks and religion but are unfamiliar with the tools and methods for doing so.

Social Network Analysis and the Study of Religion

Curiously, those most qualified to study networks and religion, namely social network analysts, have shown little interest in doing so. This may reflect an assumption that religious belief and practice is becoming increasingly rare – an assumption that, we will see in Chapter 1, has very little empirical support. Or, it could reflect, as Christian Smith (2010) argues, an anti-religious bias among network theorists. In one of the more impressive rants to ever appear in a footnote, at least in terms of its length and breadth, Smith (2010:273–276) notes that theology, religion, and faith repeatedly appear in the writings of network theorists but seldom in a positive way; instead, they use religion as a straw man against which they pit their own theoretical musings. For example, Bruce Mayhew and Stephan Fuchs draw analogies between religious faith and what they disparagingly call essentialist sociology: "The essentialist ... is locked into a view of reality that has the character of religious conviction" (Mayhew 1981:633); "Unlike religions, science is forward looking, not backward. A science cares for itself, not some social cause" (Fuchs 2001:7). Similarly, Donald Black writes, "The value of science has been amply demonstrated during the past several centuries. What are its competitors? Religion? Metaphysics? Folklore?" (Black 2002:105). And Harrison White traces social science's obsession with the individual to Christian theology:

> Most present social science theories can be seen as exegesis on Enlightenment myths. These in turn took their presuppositions from Christian theology. Thus, the Enlightenment was formed by, even as it fought against, a theology of the soul, and the social sciences as its progeny remain enmeshed in the same presuppositions.
> (White 1992:23–24)

After noting that these critiques are theologically and historically uninformed,[5] Smith (2010:276) speculates that network structuralists are hostile to things religious because Christianity and the social sciences have been rivals in the realm of higher education. There was a time when mainline and evangelical Christianity "held controlling positions of higher education, early science, publishing, and reform movements," but they have since been supplanted by more secular actors:

> Psychology displaced pastoral counseling, anthropology displaced missionaries, social work displaced the social gospel, and sociology displaced theological ethics and moral reform movements. That experience resulted in the construction over the twentieth century of American colleges and universities as havens of secularity in a broader society still largely "awash in a sea of faith" ... It also established the social sciences ... as the structural and therefore symbolic rivals of religion. In which case, discursive work aimed at strengthening the superior authority of social science ... will naturally underscore the contrast between its scientific and reliable knowledge and the superstitions and errors of religious faith.
>
> (Smith 2010:276)

Regardless of whether Smith's characterization of network structuralism is accurate, network analysts do appear to have little or no interest in exploring the interplay of networks and religion. A review of presentations at Sunbelt, the annual meeting of the International Network of Social Network Analysis, from 2001 to 2014, found that in less than 1 percent of the papers presented did the term "religion" or one associated with religion (e.g., Christianity, Judaism, Jew, Muslim, spiritual, scripture, clergy) appear in the title or abstract. Moreover, very few articles concerning religion have appeared in the pages of the three primary social network journals – *Social Networks, Connections,* or the *Journal of Social Structure* – and the *SAGE Handbook on Social Network Analysis* (Scott and Carrington 2011) includes no chapters on networks and religion. In fact, religion is not even mentioned in the index.[6] Because it is unlikely

---

[5] For instance, Smith notes that the notion of the soul, which some network analysts equate with atomistic human action, derives from Greek philosophy and not Judaism or Christianity. He also points out that Christian orthodoxy's relational ontology (i.e., the doctrine of the Trinity) is such that "if network structuralism were to find an isomorphic counterpart in any religious worldview, then Christianity should be a naturally prime candidate" (Smith 2010:275).

[6] Sociologists of religion often treat social networks as an afterthought as well. A review of five leading introductory texts to the sociology of religion (Christiano, Swatos, and Kivisto 2016; Davie 2013; Emerson, Mirola, and Monahan 2011; McGuire 2002; Roberts and Yamane 2012) turned up no mention of social networks in the table of contents or the indexes. As we will see, however, many sociologists of religion have a profound interest in the interplay of networks and religion.

Preface xix

that all social network analysts are uninterested in the role that social networks play in religious belief and practice, another motivating factor for this book is to introduce the social scientific study of religion to those interested in studying networks and religion, as well as provide an overview of some of the latest scholarship on the topic. Each of the substantive chapters also extend previous research with new analyses.

Organization of the Book

The book is organized topically. The first two chapters serve as an introduction. Chapter 1 introduces readers to the social scientific study of religion, while Chapter 2 provides an overview of social network analysis (SNA). Readers familiar with either one (or both) may want to skip ahead to the more substantive chapters. My sense is that most readers will be familiar with either one or the other but not both. The next eight chapters provide substantive looks at many of the ways in which social networks and religion interact. They are broken down into four sections (two chapters each) corresponding to the book's subtitle. The first two chapters consider the ways in which social networks bind people to faith communities, both in terms of recruitment (Chapter 3) and of commitment (Chapter 4). We will see that social ties not only draw people into faith communities but also play a key role in keeping them from leaving. Chapter 3 also takes time to introduce readers to some of statistical models developed specifically for social network data. Chapters 5 and 6 examine various ways in which social networks help diffuse religious beliefs and practices, as well as connect people to the larger society so that they are more likely to be civically engaged. The next two chapters explore the degree to which network structure can vary and contribute to the well-being of people of faith. More specifically, Chapter 7 examines how the density of peoples' networks varies in terms of religious tradition (i.e., church, sect, and new religious movements), while Chapter 8 delineates how social networks affect the happiness and health of people of faith. The final two substantive chapters consider how social networks can lead to conflict and violence. Chapter 9 examines how conflict between groups can lead to internal cohesion (i.e., network density), as well as creativity, while Chapter 10 shows how network density and isolation can increase the likelihood that a group will radicalize and sometimes engage in violence. Each of the first ten chapters includes a "For Further Reading" section for readers who want to pursue the chapter's topics in more depth. A concluding chapter summarizes some of the book's findings and considers ethical issues unique to social network research, while the three appendixes provide readers with a glossary, a brief discussion concerning definitions of religion, and an overview of software available for social network analysis.

Four communities of interest should find this monograph useful. The first of these are social network analysts who are interested in gaining a greater understanding of the social scientific study of religion and how researchers have explored the interplay of networks and religion. As I noted earlier, there has been very little formal social network analysis of religious belief and practice; thus, it is likely that most network researchers are relatively unaware of existing research. The book should also find an audience among social scientists of religion who are interested in sharpening their SNA skills. Although this book will not include worked examples, such as those found in de Nooy et al. (2011) and Everton (2012a), a companion website does,[7] which will enable those who are interested to learn "how" to do formal SNA. Third, social scientists of religion may also be interested in including a network analysis text in their graduate and undergraduate classes. Because the worked examples are pushed to the companion website, the book should not prove to be too daunting for undergrads, while the availability of worked examples can provide additional "meat" to graduate level classes. Table P.1 summarizes how this proposed book could be incorporated into a social science (or sociology) of religion class. Finally, students who are looking for a text that not only introduces them to SNA but also applies it to a specific phenomenon would undoubtedly find this book helpful. It is often easier to learn a new methodological discipline when it is set within a particular context.

[7] See https://www.seaneverton.com/networks-and-religion

Table P.1 *Social scientific study of religion topics by chapter*

Part	Chapter	Short Title	Social Network Analysis Topics & Methods	Church & Sect	Gender	Health	New Religious Movements	Politics & Conflict	Race & Ethnicity	Secularization	Social Class	Theory
Introduction	1	Religion's Surprising Persistence	N/A				X			X		X
Introduction	2	What Is SNA?	Assumptions, Concepts, Data Collection	X								X
Ties That Bind	3	Recruitment & Conversion	Structural Location, QAP, ERGMs, ALAAMs				X	X				
Ties That Bind	4	Commitment & Conformity	Homophily, Influence						X			
Ties That Loose	5	Diffusion & Innovation	Diffusion, Archeological Networks		X		X		X			
Ties That Loose	6	Politics & Community	Social Capital, Hypernetworks					X	X			
Ties That Build Up	7	Networks & Tradition	Density, Ego Networks	X			X					
Ties That Build Up	8	Health & Happiness	Closure, Topography, Simulation			X				X		X
Ties That Tear Down	9	Conflict & Cohesion	Topography Centrality, Balance, Subgroups					X			X	
Ties That Tear Down	10	Radicalization & Violence	Topography, Closure, SAOMs, Coevolution					X				
Conclusion	11	Lessons Learned	N/A									

Acknowledgments

I first became aware of the interplay between networks and religion after Chuck Powers of Santa Clara University asked if I had read Rodney Stark's *The Rise of Christianity* (1996a). I had not, so I picked it up and in the first chapter read about his and John Lofland's (1965) classic study of people converting to the Moonies. This began what became a life-long fascination with social networks, so when I landed at Stanford University in the fall of 1999, I joined (thanks to the prodding of one of my classmates, Jen van Stelle) Mark Granovetter's "Networks of Silicon Valley" working group at Stanford University. Within a couple of weeks, Mark assigned me the task of using existing software packages to visualize social networks, a task that not only resulted in the writing of a visualization manual for the working group (Everton 2004) but helped further my own interest in SNA. Mark ultimately became my advisor, and to say that his influence on my own work has been profound would be an understatement. That said, he should not be held responsible for any of the conclusions I draw in the pages that follow.

In addition to those already mentioned, the manuscript has benefited from the suggestions of, conversations with, and encouragement from several individuals, in particular John Arquilla, Mike Aspland, Ron Breiger, Chris Callaghan, Mark Chaves, Alan Cole, Randall Collins, Dan Cunningham, Dave and Pat Elliot, Mark Ensor, Jeanne Farrington, Karen Flaherty, Ann Gallenson, Larry Iannaccone, Soong Kang, Gordon Landale, Gordon McCormick, Ian McCulloh, Kevin McFeely, Phil Murphy, Nancy Roberts, Alan Schauer, Rob Schroeder (Rob, in fact, coauthored one of the book's sections with me – see Chapter 9), Kristin Tsolis, and Shelley Wessels, not to mention the students who suffered through the first two iterations of my "Networks and Religion" class as I worked out the organization and presentation of material. The work of several social network analysts and social scientists of religion have influenced much of what follows. They are too numerous to mention here, but you will find them listed in the "For Further Reading" sections that close each chapter. Feedback I received from my initial article exploring networks and religion (Everton 2015b), in particular from editor James Moody and two reviewers, was also quite helpful. I also benefited from the comments of two reviewers of the book's proposal and a handful of sample chapters; they offered valuable suggestions on how the manuscript could be improved. Several individuals from Cambridge University Press were also quite helpful at different stages of the process: Robert Dreesen, Cambridge's Senior Commissioning Editor in Politics and Sociology; Meera Seth, Editorial Assistant; Joshua Penney, Content Manager; and Sue Costello, whose copyediting caught numerous errors and greatly improved the book's readability.

Finally, I would not have been able to write this book without the support of my mom (Mary Ellen), wife (Deanne), and children (Brendan and Tara).[8] In particular, Deanne, Tara, and Brendan put up with the hours I spent on writing and rewriting this manuscript, not to mention the books and journals lying haphazardly around the house, and it is to them that I dedicate this book.

---

[8] Unfortunately, my dad (Harold) passed away in the Spring of 2015.

Part I

Introduction

1

The Surprising (at Least to Some) Persistence of Religion

1.1 Introduction

For more than twenty-five years the theoretical physicist, John Polkinghorne, taught mathematical physics at the University of Cambridge, where he explored the finer details of quantum theory and played a role in discovering the quark (Polkinghorne 2002; Wikipedia 2016b). He also spent time at Princeton, Berkeley, Stanford, and the European Organization for Nuclear Research (CERN). In recognition of his work, in 1974 he was elected Fellow of the Royal Society of London for Improving Natural Knowledge, commonly known as "The Royal Society" and probably the oldest and most prestigious scientific society in the world.[1] Then, in 1979 he stunned many of his scientific colleagues when he resigned his position in order to study theology. After he was ordained into the Anglican priesthood, he served as a curate (assistant pastor) in Bristol, a vicar (head pastor) in Blean (Canterbury), and finally as the Dean of Trinity Hall Chapel in Cambridge (Wikipedia 2016b). However, he is probably best known for his work as a theologian, specifically, his writings on the intersection of science and religion (Polkinghorne 1983, 1986a, 1986b, 1998, 2003, 2011).

Polkinghorne's religious faith may strike some as an anomaly, but it is not. Religious belief among scientists is greater than many realize (Iannaccone, Stark, and Finke 1998; Ecklund and Scheitle 2007; Gross and Solon 2009), a fact not lost on the late evolutionary biologist Stephen J. Gould, who once remarked, "Either half my colleagues are enormously stupid, or else the science of Darwinism is fully compatible with conventional religious beliefs – and equally compatible with atheism" (Gould 1992:118). Nevertheless, for years many social scientists believed that science and religion were incompatible and assumed that as societies become increasingly scientific (e.g., more education, technology,

---

[1] See https://royalsociety.org.

democracy, etc.), they would become increasingly secularized and religious devotion would decline. Some, such as the anthropologist Anthony Wallace (1966), believed religion would disappear completely. Others, such as the sociologists Peter Berger (1967, 1969), a Lutheran, and Robert Bellah (1967), an Episcopalian, saw religion as declining in importance but not disappearing altogether. In particular, they saw more sectarian forms of religion (e.g., the beliefs and practices of groups such as evangelical Protestants, conservative Catholics, and Orthodox Jews) as only surviving in society's backwaters, far removed from the corrosive effects of Harvey Cox's secular city (1966), whereas more generalized and inclusive forms (e.g., mainline Protestantism, Reform Judaism) would become increasingly influential or at least hold their own.

That has not happened. Although mainline Protestantism is in decline (Kelley 1972; Campolo 1995; Finke and Stark 2005; Putnam and Campbell 2010), sectarian forms of religion continue to thrive (Smith et al. 1998; Johnson 2011), not only in rural areas, but also in cities (Neitz 1987; Smith et al. 1998). Moreover, although religious belief and practice has declined in the West (Franck and Iannaccone 2014), in other parts of the world it appears to be on the rise (Maoz and Henderson 2013; Stark 2015) and is unlikely to disappear any time soon (see, e.g., Berger 1999; Micklethwait and Wooldridge 2009; Stark 1999; Atran 2010; Barrett 2011; Toft, Philpott, and Shah 2011; Fox 2015). Christianity is growing rapidly in the global South (Jenkins 2006), Russia has experienced a religious revival (Greeley 1994; Froese 2008), and Christians now outnumber communists in China (*The Economist* 2014). To be sure, Europe remains the poster child of secularization, and in recent years there has been an increase in the proportion of Americans who report no religious affiliation (religious "nones") (Pew Forum on Religion & Public Life 2012). However, it is unlikely that Europe was ever as religious as many assume it to have been (Strauss 1975; Thomas 1991 [1973]; Greeley 1993; Stark and Iannaccone 1994; Butler 2010), and of the approximately 20 percent of Americans who in 2012 reported no religious affiliation, 18 percent considered themselves religious, 30 percent had a religious or mystical experience, 33 percent believed that religion was somewhat or very important, 37 percent considered themselves spiritual but not religious, 41 percent prayed weekly or more, and 68 percent believed in God. It may be difficult to categorize such individuals, but "irreligious" and "secular" they are not.[2] Unchurched is not the same as irreligious. Moreover, these numbers do not reflect religious nones who hold paranormal beliefs (Bader, Baker, and Mencken 2017). According to

---

[2] Baker and Smith (2015) break the religiously unaffiliated into three broad categories: nonaffiliated believers (11 percent), agnostics (6 percent), and atheists (3 percent). To this they add a fourth category: culturally religious (8 percent), namely those who claim a religious affiliation but rarely if ever attend religious services.

the *2014 Chapman Survey of American Fears*,[3] 70.06 percent believe in at least one of the following: (1) fortune tellers can foresee the future, (2) astrology impacts their life and personality, (3) houses can be haunted, and (4) dreams can foretell the future.

Religion's surprising persistence has led many social scientists of religion to rethink much of the received wisdom concerning religion's demise, and this chapter provides an overview of some (but not all) of the current thinking regarding the role of religion in modern society. It begins with a summary of recent challenges to the standard secularization story. It then discusses three theoretical traditions that have emerged out of this new paradigm: religion as rational choice, the religious economies model, and subcultural identity theory. These, of course, do not exhaust all current social scientific theorizing about religious belief and practice. However, they have proven to be fairly influential, and as we will see in later chapters, they often draw on social network theories to explain religious outcomes. It is also important to note that they are not necessarily incompatible with one another. Social scientists often draw on more than one in explaining and exploring religious phenomena. Thus, while some of the advocates of these three theoretical traditions might be reluctant to admit it, the concepts and explanations of these theories are sometimes quite similar.

1.2 Empirical Anomalies

Western Europe's low religious attendance rates are often held up as evidence in support of increasing secularization. This, however, assumes that European attendance rates are substantially lower now than they were several centuries ago, a proposition that is highly debatable. Scholars are increasingly challenging the belief that medieval Europe was characterized by widespread religious devotion (Stark and Iannaccone 1994). Consider, for example, the fact that the Roman Catholic Church's Fourth Lateran Council of 1215 passed a series of reforms that sought to require that the laity confess and receive communion once a year. Not once a week. Not once a month. *But once a year.* It is unlikely that the Church would have passed such reforms if at the time Western Europe had been characterized by widespread piety (Greeley 1993). It was this lack of piety, in fact, that was one of the motivating forces lying behind the Protestant Reformation. However, in spite of the best efforts of Martin Luther, John Calvin, Ulrich Zwingli, and others, it appears that the Protestant Reformation had a limited impact. Sixty years after Luther

---

[3] The data are available for download at the Association of Religion Data Archives (ARDA): www.thearda.com/Archive/Files/Descriptions/CSAF2014.asp.

nailed his 95 theses to the Wittenberg door, visitations (i.e., inspections) of Lutheran parishes found that church attendance was poor and morals were worse. As one inspector reported:

> Those who do come to church walk out as the pastor begins his sermon. Parents withhold their children from catechism classes and refuse to pay school fees. Domestic servants leave their jobs rather than let themselves be sent to service. No wonder that blasphemy, fornication, adultery, drunkenness and gambling abounded ... Churches are half empty while taverns are full.
> (Strauss 1975:49)

One pastor reported that he often left church without having preached the catechism because no one showed up to hear him, and in another village only 20 out of 150 parishioners regularly attended church (Strauss 1975:49). In Saxony there was such widespread contempt for the church that groups of men would gather just outside the church "to drink brandy and sing bawdy songs," while people, what there were of them, worshipped inside (Strauss 1975:50). Similarly, the parish of Liebe "could not produce a single parishioner who could correctly answer the question, 'Who is our redeemer?'" and when criticized, the local pastor denied he was to blame: "It's the people's fault ... They don't go to church" (Strauss 1975:53). Other visitation reports "suggest that standards were little better in some Calvinist areas of Germany and in the Dutch Republic, as well as in much of rural England, Scotland, and Ireland" (Parker 1992: 45–46). The lack of devotion is even more stunning considering that many Lutheran countries passed laws making worship attendance mandatory (Stark 2017a).

Late medieval Britain is especially instructive. The British historian Keith Thomas (1991 [1973]:189) once noted "that the hold of orthodox religion upon the English people" was never complete:

> Indeed, it is problematical as to whether certain sections of the population at this time had any religion at all. Although complete statistics will never be obtainable, it can be confidently said that not all Tudor or Stuart Englishmen went to some kind of church, that many of those who did went with considerable reluctance, and that a certain proportion remained throughout their lives utterly ignorant of the elementary tenets of Christian dogma.
> (Thomas 1991 [1973]:189)

When people did show up, they often "jostled for pews, nudged their neighbors, hawked and spat, knitted, made coarse remarks, told jokes, fell asleep, and even let off guns" (Thomas 1991 [1973]:191). In Cambridge, a man "was charged with indecent behavior in church in 1598 after 'his most loathsome farting, striking, and scoffing speeches' had occasioned in 'the great offense of the good and the great rejoicing of the bad'" (Thomas 1991 [1973]:192). And although preaching was popular among the educated, it was not among the poor who, according to one report, headed straight for the alehouse when the preacher headed for the pulpit (Thomas 1991 [1973]:191). In fact, it is likely that the poorest classes never became regular church attendees (Thomas 1991 [1973]:190).

Eighteenth-century English church attendance rates tell a similar story. One visitation report indicates that in 1738, thirty parishes in Oxfordshire drew a combined total of 911 people at the four major Christian festivals – Easter, Ascension, Pentecost, and Christmas – less than 5 percent of the total population in those thirty parishes (Stark and Iannaccone 1994:243). Since it is likely that some parishioners attended more than a single festival, the actual attendance rate was probably even lower. Moreover, Rodney Stark and Laurence Iannaccone (1994:243) found that although British church membership rate was lower in 1980 (15.2 percent) than it was in 1900 (18.6 percent), it was higher in 1980 than it was in 1800 (11.5 percent). To be sure, these rates are low when compared to current rates in the United States (discussed later in this chapter), but they are hardly evidence of a decline in British religious belief from the eighteenth and nineteenth centuries.[4] Instead, they suggest a more nuanced story, one that recognizes that religious participation appears to fluctuate from time to time and place to place, and the task of social scientists is to uncover the underlying causes of these fluctuations.

Germany and England were not unique among European countries. Many medieval Europeans found Christian belief and practice unappealing (Greeley 1993). As the Yale historian, Jon Butler, notes:

> The European laity did not need the American wilderness to elicit waves of spiritual indifference. A third of Antwerp's adults failed to claim any religion in 1584; in France, if 90 percent of adults took Easter communion, only 2 to 5 percent attended mass weekly; in Hertfordshire in 1572, a reformer complained that on Sunday, "a man may find the churches empty, saving the minister and two or four lame, and old folke: for the rest are gone to follow the Devil's daunce."
>
> (Butler 2010:205)

---

[4] In September 2017, Britain's National Centre for Social Research reported that 53 percent of Britons claimed no religious affiliation. Some seized upon this to claim that unbelievers constituted more than half of the British population (see, e.g., Turner 2017). However, as in the American case, the absence of religious affiliation does not necessarily indicate someone is an unbeliever. In fact, a study released earlier in 2017 found that about 25 percent of Britain's religious nones say they pray, a similar percentage claims to be somewhat religious, and around 20 percent say they are open to the existence of God (*The Economist* 2017).

Indeed, "surviving evidence indicates a widespread inability on the part of the reformers – not just in one, but in several different countries – to create an acceptably pious laity within the first century of the Reformation" (Parker 1992:51).

This is not to suggest that medieval Europeans were irreligious. They almost certainly were religious. Both Gerald Strauss (1975) and Keith Thomas (1991 [1973]) note that at different times and places, one could find pockets of individuals deeply committed to the Christian faith. Moreover, as the philosopher Charles Taylor (2007) has argued, they lived in an "enchanted" world that was populated by spirits, demons, and moral forces, and it is likely that the Christian God functioned as a unifying factor of those beliefs. However, "by the standards of orthodoxy and devotion we take for granted today ... medieval Christians were not paragons of either orthodoxy or devotion" (Greeley 1993:15).

Medieval Europe is not the only piece of evidence that calls into question the standard secularization story. As noted earlier, worldwide religion appears to be on the upswing (Maoz and Henderson 2013; Stark 2015), and contemporary Russia and China are experiencing religious revivals (Greeley 1994; Froese 2008; *The Economist* 2014). What is perhaps more striking is that in the United States, a higher percentage of people are affiliated with communities of faith today than 200 years ago. Roger Finke and Rodney Stark (2005:23) have documented that in 1776 the church adherence rate was approximately 17 percent, but by the mid-nineteenth century it had doubled, and by the late twentieth century (1980) it had risen to about 60 percent, a level at which it remained at least until 2000 (see Figure 1.1).[5]

Finke and Stark's findings are consistent with the Middletown (i.e., Muncie, Indiana) studies of the 1970s, which followed up on the early twentieth-century studies of Robert and Helen Lynd (1929, 1937).[6] Researchers discovered that religion had not declined, but

---

[5] Adherence rates differ from affiliation rates in that the latter includes anyone who claims affiliation with a particular church, mosque, synagogue, etc., while the former includes only members of faith communities. In calculating the adherence rate, Finke and Stark (2005) adjusted for denominations, such as Baptists, whose youth are not considered members until they make a profession of faith (often around the age of twelve). Readers may be curious about the "gap" between the reported affiliation rate (approximately 80 percent) and the adherence rate calculated by Finke and Stark (approximately 60 percent). The gap may capture the proportion of individuals who claim an affiliation but seldom, if ever, attend religious services. The fact that the gap has decreased in recent years (in 1990 it was closer to 30 percent – see Hout and Fischer 2014) may simply reflect the fact that individuals who rarely attend religious services are increasingly telling pollsters that they have no religious affiliation.

[6] The Lynds concluded that religious life in Muncie was "less pervasive than it was a generation before" (Lynd and Lynd 1929:407, cited in Christiano, Swatos, and Kivisto 2016:61) although "neither they nor anyone else had done research on the community's religious life a generation previously" (Christiano, Swatos, and Kivisto 2016:61).

1.2 Empirical Anomalies

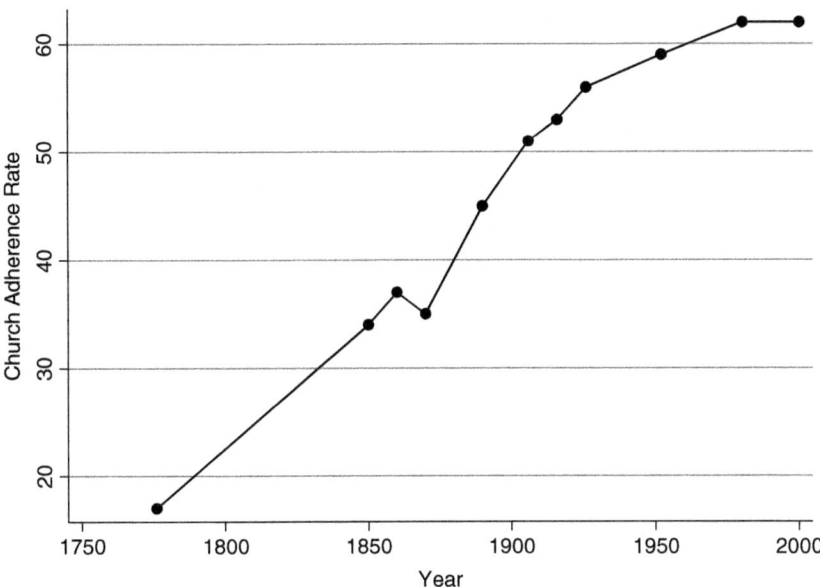

Figure 1.1 Religious adherence rate, 1776–2000 (adapted from Finke and Stark 2005:23)

had risen. They plotted the data of fifteen types of religious behavior from 1924 and 1978, and "only two pointed downward (which would indicate a secularization effect). Three more showed no trend, while the remaining ten ... displayed an upward curve, showing *greater religiosity* in Middletown in the 1970s than in the 1920s (Caplow 1982; Caplow, Bahr and Chadwick 1983)" (Christiano, Swatos, and Kivisto 2016:61).

To be sure, in recent years it appears there has been a decline in religious belief and practice in the United States. Church affiliation rates are on the wane (Pew Forum on Religion & Public Life 2012), as are attendance rates and levels of belief in God (Voas and Chaves 2016). However, it is unclear how we should interpret this decline. Robert Wuthnow (2007) argues that we can understand it as the result of a historically specific (and probably short-term) failure on the part of religious institutions to adapt to a changing life course trajectory by providing ministries relevant to contemporary young adults, suggesting that the decline could be temporary. And Michael Hout and Claude Fischer (2014) attribute the decline to a combination of a backlash against the political alignment of religious and political conservatives and an increased sense of autonomy among younger generations (but they did not, however, attribute the decline to secularization) (see also Putnam and Campbell 2010; Zuckerman 2014):[7]

> Once the American public began connecting organized religion to the conservative political agenda – a connection that Republican politicians, abortion activists, and religious leaders all encouraged (Domke and Coe 2008) – many political liberals and moderates who seldom or never attended services quit expressing a religious preference when survey interviewers asked about it.
>
> For sixty years now, young people have been raised to think for themselves; parents emphasize obedience less (Alwin 1990). The young people who emerge from that kind of socialization may evince a fair amount of conformity, but they put the individual in the center and leave little margin for any authority – scientific, religious, judicial, political – to dictate a worldview.
>
> (Hout and Fischer 2014:443, 444)

Moreover, we should not equate low levels of adherence rates with low levels in belief (Stark 2017a). Just because people no longer affiliate with conventional forms of religion, it does not mean they have ceased to believe. As we saw earlier, many of America's "religious nones" still pray, consider themselves religious, and believe in God. Moreover, some people simply trade in their old beliefs for new ones. This is illustrated in Table 1.1, which reports, by several Western European countries, levels of belief of religious nones in phenomena that, at least in the West, many would consider unconventional.[8] More precisely, it presents the percentage of respondents who either strongly agreed or agreed with the following statements:[9]

- I have my own way of connecting with God without churches or religious services.
- I believe in life after death.
- I believe in reincarnation – being reborn in this world again and again.
- I believe in the supernatural power of deceased ancestors.
- Good luck charms sometimes do bring good luck.
- Some fortune tellers really can foresee the future.

[7] Another possibility, suggested by an anonymous reviewer, is that we are in a period of social disorganization, which can have contradictory effects on religious belief and practice, eroding some traditional institutions while providing opportunities for new forms of organization. Put differently, social disorganization on the large scale can stimulate social organization on the small scale (Thrasher 1927). This could help explain the apparent growth of the emerging church movement (Marti and Ganiel 2014).
[8] Data are from the 2008 International Social Survey Program, which can be downloaded from the Association of Religion Data Archives (ARDA): www.thearda.com/Archive/Files/Descriptions/ISSP08.asp.
[9] Unfortunately, not all of the questions were asked in all of the countries.

Table 1.1 Unconventional beliefs of religious nones

Percent of Religious Nones Who

Country	Connect with God Outside of Church	Believe There Is Life after Death	Believe in Reincarnation	Believe in Supernatural Power of Ancestors	Believe in Power of Good Luck Charms	Believe in Fortune Tellers	Believe Faith Healers Channel God's Power	Believe in Astrology	Agree with One or More Statements
Austria	30.00	37.50	32.50	22.50	27.50	25.00	40.00	42.50	60.00
Belgium	14.85	21.78	15.84	7.92	—	—	—	—	31.68
Denmark	24.00	18.80	14.40	9.20	13.20	14.00	12.80	14.00	42.00
Finland	27.78	18.52	9.26	5.56	11.11	14.81	9.26	9.26	42.59
France	22.92	20.27	14.62	11.30	16.61	18.27	13.95	21.59	49.83
Germany	10.00	12.78	10.83	13.06	27.50	13.89	18.61	16.67	43.89
Ireland	27.59	34.48	27.59	17.24	44.83	44.83	24.14	37.93	75.86
Italy	17.14	2.86	14.29	5.71	—	—	—	—	22.86
Netherlands	35.45	42.73	21.36	21.14	19.55	25.23	22.05	16.82	69.55
Norway	12.21	25.95	19.08	12.21	12.21	20.61	4.58	11.45	44.27
Portugal	31.25	18.75	18.75	6.25	—	—	—	—	43.75
Spain	45.71	21.43	14.29	24.29	—	—	—	—	55.71
Sweden	22.32	21.43	8.93	11.61	—	—	—	—	38.39
Switzerland	54.39	43.86	29.82	15.79	36.84	28.07	26.32	36.84	85.96
United Kingdom	17.48	34.62	23.78	22.38	—	—	—	—	44.76
Average	23.49	26.29	17.22	15.07	20.16	19.55	17.27	18.23	53.85/50.48

Source: International Social Survey Program, 2008.

- Some faith healers do have God-given healing powers.
- A person's star sign at birth, or horoscope, can affect the course of their future.

As the table shows, unconventional beliefs among religious nones is relatively high, even in Western Europe. More than half of Europeans surveyed in 2008 who reported no religious affiliation stated that they agreed with at least one of the eight statements.[10] Put simply, many religious nones do not stop believing; they just start believing something else.

In short, while the standard secularization story predicts a unilinear decline in religion, the available evidence from Europe, Asia, and the United States suggests that over time religious belief and practice waxes and wanes. There have been (and probably will continue to be) times and places when religion has (is) quite vibrant, and there have been (and will continue to be) others when it was (is) not. Thus, one of the goals of social scientific theories of religion should be to identify those factors that lead to increases and decreases in religious belief and practice. As we will see, that is exactly what many of the new theories attempt to do.

None of this is to suggest that the world has not changed. Taylor (2007), for instance, argues that we do not live in the enchanted world of medieval Europe in which the belief in God or the gods was taken for granted. Instead, we live in a world in which belief is one option among many. In a similar vein, Stark and Iannaccone (1994:234–235), drawing on Jeffery Hadden (1987), argue that we no longer live in what they call a sacralized world – that is, a world in which "religious symbols, rhetoric, and ritual" permeate almost all aspects of life. Instead we live in a desacralized world where the "primary aspects of life" are not full of religious symbols and rhetoric, religious leaders are largely absent from "political occasions and ceremonies," and classrooms do not display religious symbols. Others, such as Randall Collins (1998) and Christian Smith (2003c), contend that what has changed is not that people have become any less religious; rather, that the "control of intellectual production" has been removed "from the authority of the church" (Collins 1998:573). Their perspective is similar to that of Mark Chaves (1994), Karel Dobbelaere (1999), and David Yamane (1997), who argue that secularization is best understood as a decline in religious authority; their contention is that we no longer live in a world in which religious institutions hold as much sway as they did in the past. Finally, scholars with an economic bent have argued that governments can "crowd out" religious

---

[10] Two averages are reported in the final column. The first represents the average of the countries where respondents were asked all eight questions; the second represents the average of the countries where respondents were only asked the first four. Either way, the average is above 50 percent.

goods and services (Gruber and Hungerman 2007, 2008). For instance, Anthony Gill and Erik Lundsgaarde (2004) found that government spending not only crowds out church charity, but it accounts for nearly half of the observed variation in church attendance. Interestingly, however, Raphaël Franck and Laurence Iannaccone (2014) discovered that increases in government spending on health, old age, and family services did not predict a decline in church attendance. Only increases in school spending did. However, this was not due to increased levels of educational attainment because their models included direct measures of educational attainment; Franck and Iannaccone (tentatively) concluded that increases in school spending increase governments' ability to shape the content of what schools teach.

All of these explanations possess a ring of plausibility, and they are not necessarily incompatible with one another. Our purpose here, however, is not to settle the secularization debate; there are a number of excellent discussions elsewhere in the literature (see, e.g., Smith 2003c; Gorski and Altinordu 2008; Emerson, Mirola, and Monahan 2011:69–74; Baker and Smith 2015; Fox 2015:16–38; Stark 2015; Christiano, Swatos, and Kivisto 2016:55–83). Rather, it is simply to note that the secularization story, which argues that modernization inevitably leads to a decline in religious belief and practice, has run into a host of empirical problems. More important, at least for our purposes here, is that the empirical failure of this story has led to the development of a new "paradigm" in the social scientific study of religion (Warner 1993), a paradigm in which a number of theoretical traditions vie to provide a better account of the data. It is to one of the more influential of these – religion as rational choice – that we now turn.

1.3 Religion as Rational Choice

The rational choice approach to the scientific study of religion is largely associated with the social scientists Rodney Stark, Roger Finke, Laurence Iannaccone, and William Bainbridge (see, e.g., Stark and Bainbridge 1980b, 1985; Iannaccone 1994b, 1997; Stark, Iannaccone, and Finke 1996, 1998). It traces its roots to the work of the sociologist George Homans (1950, 1958, 1961) and is heavily influenced by the human capital approach of Gary Becker (1976). Formally, it holds that people are rational actors who evaluate the costs and benefits of a given action and then act in order to maximize their net benefits (i.e., their utility). Less formally, it argues that people of faith respond to incentives just as they do in other aspects of life. Moreover, it has proved to be remarkably adept at explaining and understanding religious behavior, suggesting that "it is a good working hypothesis that should not easily be abandoned" (Granovetter 1985:506).

Nevertheless, critics of the rational choice approach have raised a number of objections. Many have noted that people do not always act in ways that maximize their utility. Consider, for example, volunteers who spend a week building houses for a Habitat for Humanity work project. One could argue that they are not maximizing their own utility but instead someone else's. This, however, is a very restricted understanding of utility. As a rational choice theorist would probably point out, people who act on behalf of deeply held norms or beliefs (e.g., God calls on us to aid those in need) receive rewards, many of which are emotional rewards, for doing so. Indeed, the emotional satisfaction Habitat for Humanity volunteers get from a week's worth of home building can be quite fulfilling. This may not fit the typical definition of utility, but it is rewarding nonetheless. In fact, the quest for emotional rewards may be the ultimate rational choice (Collins 1993). As Kevin Christiano, William Swatos, and Peter Kivisto note:

> The word *rational* is used in different ways. In philosophy, the rational side of human life is often posited over against the emotional side. This is not the use here. Emotional decision-making is also a part of the rational choice model. Let's say that you are shopping for a car and decide to buy the red one because you like the way it looks. The philosophical rationalist would say, "That's not a rational decision." For rational choice theory, it is: You are getting a *reward*, because the red car apparently will make you happier. Of course, later you may realize you made a bad or silly decision. That's not the point. The point is that you did think about the decision and decided to go with color as your ultimate criterion ... Rational choice theory says the same kinds of processes occur in religious decision-making – one person may join a church, say, for the wonderful music, another for the fellowship of the people involved, another may want to avoid going to hell, another finds the preaching style intellectually challenging, and so on. In rational choice theory, all of these decisions are rational in the sense that they are centered on the satisfaction of wants.
>
> (Christiano, Swatos, and Kivisto 2016:44)

Another critique is that rational choice theory implicitly assumes that individuals are autonomous human beings, unaffected by those around them, while in reality they are located in social networks that profoundly shape the choices they make (Ellison 1995). As we will see in Chapter 2, this is a primary assumption of social network analysis. People are not automatons. Their ties to others and the networks in which they are embedded affect them. However, rational choice theorists often take into account the effect that network ties have on various forms of religious behavior, such as the recruitment of new members (Lofland and Stark 1965; Stark and Bainbridge 1980a), the retention of existing members (Stark and Bainbridge 1980a), the diffusion of religious ideas and practices (Stark 1996a), and the enforcement of norms of behavior (Ellison and Sherkat 1995). Moreover, as the late Roger Gould once noted, "[T]he idea that individuals make interdependent decisions has been accessible to [rational choice theorists] in a formal way for over half a century ... in the form of game theory ... Blanket attacks on rational-choice theory for modeling individual behavior as if it takes place in a vacuum are therefore misplaced" (2003:240).

Critics also often point out that standard economic models assume perfect knowledge, but in most cases, people operate with imperfect information and, thus, their rationality is, at best, "bounded." Moreover, as Daniel Kahneman and Amos Tversky (Kahneman 2011; Kahneman and Tversky 1979; Tversky and Kahneman 1974, 1981) have noted, human beings seldom process information in the ways that standard economic models predict. While this is no doubt true, few, if any, rational choice theorists believe that people always act rationally. Instead, they regard the rational choice assumption as a simplifying one that analysts "may assert ... without for a moment believing that people always act logically, efficiently, or in accordance with their own self-interest" (Iannaccone 1997:27). Still, it is an important caveat to keep in mind. Although it is unwise to discard the rational actor assumption, by itself it does not account for all variations in religious behavior. Other factors, such as culture and social ties, play a role as well.

A final, but often unspoken, objection to the rational choice approach to studying religious behavior is the assumption that religious belief is irrational, that it is antithetical to a scientific worldview, and thus cannot be evaluated using a rational actor model. This has led many to argue that education and religious belief are inversely related and that religious belief and science are antithetical to one another. As the next section demonstrates, such arguments are ill informed.

Is Religion Irrational?

Table 1.2 presents results from the 2012–2016 General Social Surveys, which are bi-annual surveys conducted by the National Opinion Research Center (NORC).[11] The table cross-tabulates the reported frequency of worship attendance by highest degree earned. As one can see, the groups most likely to report that they never attend church are those who did not

---

[11] The data are from the Association of Religion Data Archives (www.thearda.com/Archive/GSS.asp).

Table 1.2 *Highest education degree attained by attendance rate*

	Highest Degree (Percent)				
	Left High School	High School	Junior College	College	Graduate School
Never	28.12	26.01	24.73	22.55	23.80
Less than once a year	4.45	6.83	7.10	5.54	6.28
Once a year	9.56	13.43	11.93	14.56	14.27
Several times a year	9.50	11.65	10.18	10.09	10.26
Once a month	8.11	6.02	7.13	6.76	6.42
Two or three times a month	10.29	8.25	8.27	9.48	7.69
Nearly every week	4.19	4.04	2.98	4.43	6.16
Every week	16.67	16.62	20.92	20.46	20.86
More than once a week	9.11	7.14	6.76	6.13	4.25

Source: General Social Surveys, 2012–2016.

graduate from high school, followed by those with only a high school diploma or an associate degree (i.e., junior college degree). By contrast, those who are most likely to say they attend worship services every week are those with associate, college, and graduate degrees, with more than 20 percent in each group reporting they attend church weekly. Only when reported worship attendance reaches more than once a week do we find those with less than a high school education report attending worship services at higher rates than others.[12]

Perhaps more revealing is the predicted rate of attendance based on the highest degree earned because it captures all of the attendance information in the table. After recoding reported attendance rates into days per year,[13]

---

[12] It is important to stress that the lack of attending church is not necessarily a sign of irreligiousness. J. D. Vance notes in *Hillbilly Elegy*, his memoir of growing up poor in Appalachia that although Christianity "stood at the center of [their] lives ... [they] never went to church." His grandmother, who was deeply religious, "couldn't say 'organized religion' without contempt. She saw churches as breeding grounds for perverts and money changers. And she hated what she called the 'loud and the proud' – people who wore their faith on their sleeve, always ready to let you know how pious they were" (Vance 2016:85).

[13] Those who said they attended church less than once a year were coded as attending a half day per year; those who said they attended church once a year were coded as attending one day per year; those who said they attended several times a year were coded as attending church six days per year; those who said that they attended once a month were coded as attending twelve days per year; those who said they attended two or three times a month were coded as attending twenty-four days per year; those who said they attended nearly every week were coded as attending thirty-six days per year; those who said they attended every week were coded as attending fifty-two times per year; and those

1.3 Religion as Rational Choice

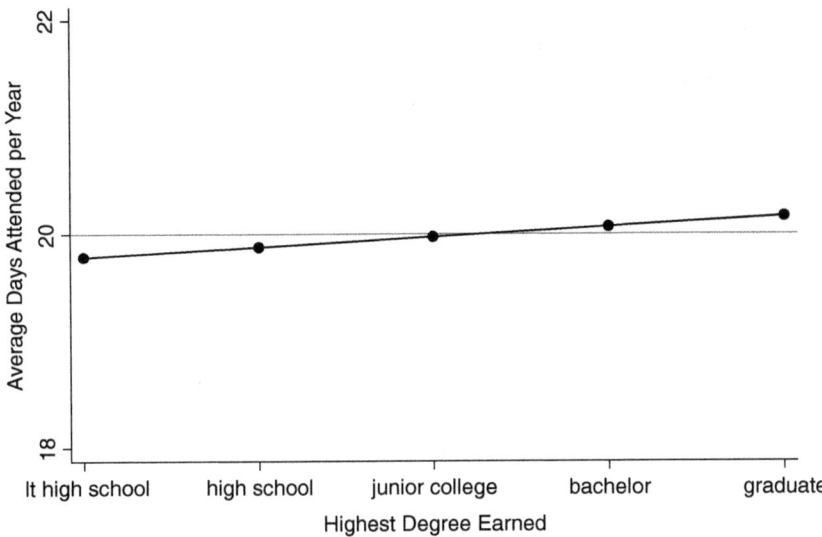

Note: 2012–16 General Social Survey

Figure 1.2 Predicted rate of attendance by degree

I estimated a Poisson model from which I calculated a predicted rate of attendance. The results are plotted in Figure 1.2. Notice that the predicted rate of yearly attendance increases somewhat with education level, ranging from those who did not complete high school attending worship services, on average, less than twenty times a year to those with a graduate degree attending worship services more than twenty times a year. The difference is not profound, but there is a distinct upward trend.

But what about the religious beliefs and practices of academics and scientists? As one might expect, academics and scientists tend to be less religious than the population as a whole. Iannaccone, Stark, and Finke (1998), for instance, found that professors and scientists are less likely to attend church regularly, to believe that the Bible is God's Word, or to pray regularly, and they are more likely to say they have no religion. Nevertheless, they also found that *a majority* consider themselves to be religious, report that they have a religion, say they believe in an afterlife, state that they feel close to God, and claim to attend worship services several times a year. A more recent study by Neil Gross and Solon Simmons (2009) uncovered similar results. While professors tend to be less religious than the population as a whole, they are still more likely to be religious than not:

who said they attended more than once a week were coded as attending seventy-eight times per year.

> To be sure, religion is no longer central to the official life of most nonreligiously affiliated colleges and universities, and on many campuses, there is overt hostility among some professors toward attempts at integrating the study of religion into the college curriculum, or toward going too far to accommodate students' religious views if these conflict with the demands of science or higher learning. But even at elite schools, there are more professors who are religious than who are nonbelievers, which suggests than in academe – as in American society more generally – secularization has entailed more the privatization of religious belief ... than its elimination.
>
> (Gross and Simmons 2009:124)

It is likely that selection effects are also at work here in that many people probably self-select into professions that either affirm their belief or unbelief. For example, Fred Thalheimer (1973) examined people's employment histories over time and concluded that college faculty are less religious, not because of their training, but because they tend to be less religious before they enter graduate school. Similarly, Elaine Ecklund and Christopher Scheitle (2007) found that being raised in a religious household was one of the strongest predictors of whether or not a professor was religious, suggesting that prior religiosity, and not the level of education, matters more. Moreover, most of the variation in the religiosity of academics remains unexplained, suggesting that there are processes at work "by which, at different historical junctures, those from religious backgrounds – who may be more inclined to retain their religious upbringing throughout their lives, regardless of their career choices – come to be selectively incorporated into or steered out of different kinds of academic careers" (Gross and Simmons 2009:123–124).

Finally, the fact that scientists are more likely to be religious than not may surprise some, especially those familiar with psychologist James Leuba's (1916) survey of prominent scientists listed in *American Men of Science*. Leuba asked respondents to select one of the following statements "concerning belief in God."

> a. I believe in a God to whom one may pray in the expectation of receiving an answer. *By "answer," I mean more than the subjective, psychological effect of prayer.*
> b. I do not believe in God as defined above.
> c. I have no definite belief regarding this question. (Leuba 1916:225)

To say that Leuba's standard for belief in God (i.e., response "a") is strict would be an understatement. Many would regard it as a belief characteristic of fundamentalists (Stark 1999). In fact, it is likely that most mainline

Protestant clergy would be unable to affirm it. Nevertheless, 42 percent of the respondents selected the "fundamentalist" option. Moreover, when his study was replicated in the 1990s (Larson and Witham 1998), the results were statistically unchanged (39 percent). In other words, over an eighty-year period, there was no decline among scientists holding a fundamentalist belief in God – certainly not what many believe to be true about religion and science.

Why Are Strict Churches Strong?

At first glance, the rapid growth of strict churches also presents a problem for rational choice theory. Why would someone join a "high-cost" church when plenty of "low-cost" alternatives are available? Why would people join a church that requires them to spend fifteen to twenty hours per week at church when they can join one that only requires that they only spend one hour? Moreover, membership in strict churches often "invites ridicule and persecution," and it sometimes limits "chances for social and economic advancement," as well as bars "access to apparently innocent pleasures" (Shulevitz 2005) (e.g., celebrating Halloween). So, why do strict churches thrive? Some dismiss this type of piety as a form of social pathology (e.g., cognitive dissonance), but others, such as Iannaccone (1994b), do not and argue that it is perfectly rational for people to join a strict church.

Iannaccone (1994b) builds on the work of Dean Kelley (1972), who in the 1970s made a compelling case as to why conservative churches were growing while mainline Protestant churches were not. Kelley, who worked for the National Council of Churches (which is populated primarily by mainline Protestant denominations), argued that conservative churches were more successful because they placed higher demands on their members, which raised commitment levels and made the worship and membership experience more meaningful. The emphasis on demands is important here, for as Kelley (1986:xvii) noted in the preface to a later edition of his book *Why Conservative Churches Are Growing*, his preferred title was "Why Strict Churches Are Strong" because his main point was that it is strictness, not conservativeness per se, that leads to higher levels of commitment. In Kelley's view, liberal churches were capable of being strict, and the fact that most were not was beside the point.

Iannaccone argues that strictness "works" because it eliminates free riding, and this leads to an increase in the net benefits of membership (Iannaccone 1997:35). In religious communities, free riders are those who show up for and benefit from worship services but only contribute marginally to the services themselves. Iannaccone believes that free riding undermines the collective activities of groups such as faith communities because it reduces the average level of participation, enthusiasm, energy, and so on. In strict groups, though, only those who are fully committed to the group join or at least stick around for the long term. This leads to an increase in the average level of participation, which in turn leads to higher levels of enthusiasm and energy. Religion, here, is seen as a "commodity" that congregations produce collectively. The satisfaction that individuals derive from worship does not depend just on how much they contribute to the worship service, but also on how much other people contribute. If only half of the congregation sings, then there is a high probability it will sound appalling, which means that the worship experience will be less than what it would have been if everyone sang. Moreover, in high commitment churches, people are expected to take care of one another and are sanctioned if they do not. Thus, when congregants are sick, not only will the pastor visit them, but so will other church members. They may bring them meals. They may help take their kids to school. And if a congregant is so sick that his or her family is financially at risk, church members will often see to it that the family lands on its feet.

Of course, not everyone joins strict churches. Those who are "most likely to join are those with the least to lose" (Iannaccone 1994b:1200). Individuals with few secular opportunities are more likely to join strict churches than are individuals with plenty of secular opportunities. To take a somewhat extreme example: an out-of-work farmer is far more likely to join a strict group such as the Amish than is a successful investment banker. Iannaccone notes that a corollary of this is that strict groups become attractive to more people during periods when secular opportunities decline (e.g., during economic recessions) than when secular opportunities are on the rise. He also points out that when the secular opportunities for a *specific group of individuals* decline, strict groups become more attractive to that specific group. This may help explain why oppressed groups are often attracted to sectarian forms of religion.

Churches can get too much of a good thing, though. There are limits to strictness. Too much drives "away all current and future members" (Iannaccone 1994b:1202) because the benefits no longer outweigh the costs of belonging. Consequently, churches must strike a balance between strictness and leniency; otherwise they will wither and possibly die. Striking a balance can be tricky, though – churches can choose the wrong areas in which to be strict and in which to be lenient. Consider, for example, the Roman Catholic Church,

> which has had a hard time holding on to members in Europe and attracting men to the priesthood in America. Traditionalists blame the church's difficulties on the reforms of Vatican II, which allowed the Mass to be said in the vernacular and priests and nuns to shed their otherworldly clothes. [Others] blame

church officials' refusal to yield to popular opinion on contraception and celibacy.

(Shulevitz 2005)

Iannaccone believes both may be right. "The Catholic church may have managed to arrive at a remarkable, 'worst-of-both-worlds' position," he writes, "discarding cherished distinctiveness in the areas of liturgy, theology, and lifestyle, while at the same time maintaining the very demands that its members and clergy are least willing to accept" (Iannaccone 1994b:1204).

In an interesting application of strictness theory, Stark (1996a) argues that one of the reasons why early Christianity, or at least certain branches of it, succeeded where other religious movements failed is because it demanded high levels of commitment from its followers. By doing so, Stark believes it produced benefits that were enjoyed by the Church as a whole. For example, we know that the early Christians enjoyed longer life expectancies than did non-Christians and may have had higher survival rates during the plagues that struck the Roman Empire during the first three centuries of the Common Era, and it is likely this was because the Church required its members to care for others (1996a:73–93) (see Chapter 8). Moreover, Stark believes, for the reasons outlined by Iannaccone, the worship services of the early house churches probably "yielded an immense, shared emotional satisfaction" (Stark 1996a:188). Thus, although the early Church was costly, it was still a bargain:

> Because the church asked much of its members, it was thereby possessed of the resources to give much. For example, because Christians were expected to aid the less fortunate, many of them received such aid, and all could feel greater security against bad times. Because they were asked to nurse the sick and dying, many of them received such nursing. Because they were asked to love others, they in turn were loved. And if Christians were required to observe a far more restrictive moral code than that observed by pagans, Christians – especially women – enjoyed a far more secure family life.
>
> (Stark 1996a:188)

Summary

The rational choice approach to modeling religious behavior is rooted in the belief that people of faith respond to incentives, including those associated with religious belief and practice, just as their secular counterparts do. More importantly, it does not regard people of faith as ignorant zealots. Instead, it assumes that they are no less rational than anyone else.

To be sure, professors and scientists are somewhat less religious than the average man or woman on the street, but that does not change the fact that academics and scientists are religious. They may not be so in a conventional sense, but they are religious nonetheless.

We now turn to an examination of the religious economies approach. This easily could have been included with the discussion of rational choice theory since most rational choice theorists also look to religious markets to help explain religious behavior. A key assumption of rational choice theory is that peoples' preferences are relatively stable. This means that rational choice theorists are seldom "content to explain ... changes [in behavior] with reference to changed tastes, norms, or beliefs," but instead they seek "to model behavioral changes ... as optimal responses to varying circumstances – different prices, incomes, skills, experiences, technologies, resource constraints, and the like" (Iannaccone 1997:27). This leads them to model religious behavior as rational responses to the opportunities and constraints present in religious markets. However, because nonrational choice theorists often draw on the logic of the religious marketplace, it makes more sense to keep religious economies analytically distinct and discuss it separately.

1.4 Religious Economies

At its most basic level, the religious economies approach is quite simple. It assumes that just as there are markets for commercial goods, there are markets for religious goods where various firms (i.e., religious institutions such as churches, synagogues, and mosques) seek to attract and retain customers (Stark and Bainbridge 1985; Iannaccone 1994a, 1997; Stark and Finke 2000a; Stark 2001b). Its central argument is that, all else being equal, church participation is inversely associated with the level of state regulation.[14] Put differently, net of other factors, the less that governments involve themselves in the religious lives of their citizens, the more vibrant religious belief and practice will be. Why? One reason is because less regulation generally means there will be a greater supply of religious firms (i.e., churches, synagogues, temples, mosques, etc.), which encourages competition and favors more "efficient" religious firms over less efficient ones. Religious markets reward religious producers that meet peoples' needs and punish those that do not. Put somewhat differently, faith communities that provide people with a high rate of return (i.e., meeting their spiritual, psychological, and social needs) on their investment (i.e., time, money, behavioral demands, etc.) tend to thrive, while

---

[14] For convenience purposes, throughout this chapter and the rest of the book the term "church" is used as a blanket term to refer to all communities of faith, not just Christian communities of faith.

those that do not, tend to wither and sometimes die. Adam Smith (1965: 740–741), the founder of modern economics, was one of the first to point this out and argued on behalf of what some call the "lazy monopoly" hypothesis. He contended that self-interest motivates clergy just as much as it does any other producer of consumable goods. He noticed a difference between the clergy of religious groups that hold a monopoly in the religious market and those of groups that have to compete for their followers. Clergy in competitive situations were more likely to exert a lot of effort to recruit new followers than were clergy in noncompetitive situations.

An interesting application of the lazy monopoly theory is Gill's (1994, 1998) examination of the rise of Latin American liberation theology, which emerged in the 1960s and 1970s. Associated primarily with the Roman Catholic Church, liberation theology holds that God has a preferential option for the poor (Guttierez 1973) and tends to focus more on social justice than on eternal salvation. Its proponents, often Roman Catholic priests, have been openly critical of Latin America's authoritarian military regimes, which they saw as causing and perpetuating the abject poverty found in many parts of Latin America. Not surprisingly, this led to a backlash, including the assassinations of several church leaders, such as Archbishop Oscar Romero (Brockman 2005) and six Jesuit priests at the Central American University in San Salvador (Cerna and Ignoffo 2014). What Gill noticed was that the Catholic Church embraced liberation theology in some Latin American countries but not in others. In some, the Church hierarchy adopted a distinctively anti-authoritarian position, while in others it did not. What he found was that liberation theology was much more likely to be embraced by the Catholic Church in countries where it faced competition from religious and ideological alternatives, namely evangelical Protestants and "Spiritist" sects. In countries where evangelicals and spiritists had made inroads among poor Catholics, Church leaders were more likely to champion the rights of the poor and turn against authoritarian regimes than they were in countries where competition was minimal. This is not to suggest that the Catholic clergy's concern for the poor was disingenuous, but rather that structural factors, in this case, Protestant competition, made it more likely for this concern to be activated and embraced.

Not only does an increase in the supply of religious firms lead to more competition, but it also allows religious firms to target the specific niches within the religious market. This generally does not happen in situations where a single religious group controls the market. In such situations, the needs of many potential religious consumers go unmet, so they end up skipping worship. For example, in America the Metropolitan Community Church (MCC) was founded in order to provide worship and fellowship opportunities for gay and lesbian Christians, needs that were largely being unmet by Roman Catholic and Protestant churches. It is unlikely that the MCC would have been founded in a market controlled by a single group – for example, as the Roman Catholic Church did in medieval Europe prior to the Reformation. Instead, it needed a religious market that permitted and, in fact, encouraged religious choice.

Shifts in Supply

Most who embrace the religious economies approach tend to focus more on the supply side of the religious equation than on the demand side. At one time, social scientists would typically explain wild swings in religious participation by pointing to some variation in religious demand. For example, when religious participation declined, they would conclude there must have been a decline in demand for religious goods, and when it rose, they concluded there must have been an increase in the demand. The religious economies approach does not consider religious demand unimportant, but it argues that changes in the supply of religious goods generally provide a better explanation for swings in participation than do shifts in religious preferences. Indeed, Finke and Stark (2005) argue that the growth in affiliation rates in the United States from 1776 to 1980 was largely due to the deregulation of the American religious market, which led to a greater supply of churches that, collectively, did a better job of meeting the needs of people of faith. They note that complete separation of church and state did not occur with the adoption of the First Amendment of the US Constitution, which only prohibited Congress from establishing religion. Church and state separation at both the federal and state levels was not complete until the state of Massachusetts ceased to collect taxes on behalf of the Congregationalists in 1833, which, as Figure 1.1 suggests, coincides with the takeoff of the US adherence rate.

This emphasis on the supply side can be illustrated with the explosion of new religious movements in Japan following World War II. As Iannaccone, Finke, and Stark (1997) note, prior to the end of the war, the Japanese government strictly controlled religious activity. "Shinto shrines were subsidized; Shinto priests were government officials; the Japanese emperor was proclaimed to be a god; and participation in Shinto ceremonies was considered a matter of civic duty. [However,] Japan's defeat led to an immediate repeal of all laws controlling religion" (Iannaccone, Finke, and Stark 1997:357); the emperor was forced to renounce his divinity, the Shinto religion was disestablished, and a tremendous amount of religious freedom was granted. This led to an increased supply in the number of religions and an upsurge in the number of people involved in religious activity. For example, prior to 1945, only 31 religious groups were officially recognized, but by 1949, 403 new groups had been founded and 1,546 had been established through splits.

1.4 Religious Economies

During the same period, overall membership in nontraditional religions rose from 4.5 percent of the population in 1945 to more than 20 percent in 1975.

A reanalysis (Iannaccone, Finke, and Stark 1997:361–363) of what has been called the "Consciousness Reformation" (Glock and Bellah 1976; Wuthnow 1976), a period in the 1970s when there was a sharp increase in Asian-born and Asian-inspired religious movements, provides another example of the supply side approach. At the time, many sociologists turned to demand side explanations to account for the upsurge. Some, for instance, argued that a new religious consciousness had developed among "America's youth that challenged Western-style materialism, individualism, and rationalism" (Iannaccone, Finke, and Stark 1997:361), and so they searched for new types of religion. By contrast, Iannaccone, Finke, and Stark assert that changes in the supply of religion offer a better explanation. They note that after World War I, Congress passed several laws "that dramatically cut immigration from Asian countries and denied citizenship to Asians already in America" (Iannaccone, Finke, and Stark 1997:361). However, the 1965 Immigration and Nationality Act Amendments abolished these laws, and the number of Asian immigrants rose dramatically, from 20,000 in 1965 to 90,000 in 1970. During the same period, Asia's share of total American immigration rose from less than 5 percent to almost 25 percent in a little more than five years. Unsurprisingly, immigrants brought their religious traditions with them, and teachers of Eastern religions were among the immigrants. Thus, "it was not so much that Asian faiths had struck a new chord in the American counterculture as that their growth had been artificially thwarted until then. With the immigration barrier removed, normal religious trade reasserted itself" (Iannaccone, Finke, and Stark 1997:361). In short, while shifting demand may account for some of the growth in Asian religions, it is also likely that the increase in their supply, traced directly to the rise in Asian immigration, was also a major cause.

Empirical Support?

Most of the early empirical tests of the theory did not use measures of religious market regulation, primarily because they were unavailable, so researchers used proxies instead (see, e.g., Finke and Stark 1988; Iannaccone 1991; Stark, Finke and Iannaccone 1995; Finke, Guest, and Stark 1996; Olson 1998, 1999). The most common of these has been the Herfindahl index, which measures the level of religious pluralism in a particular locality. Formally, it is defined as

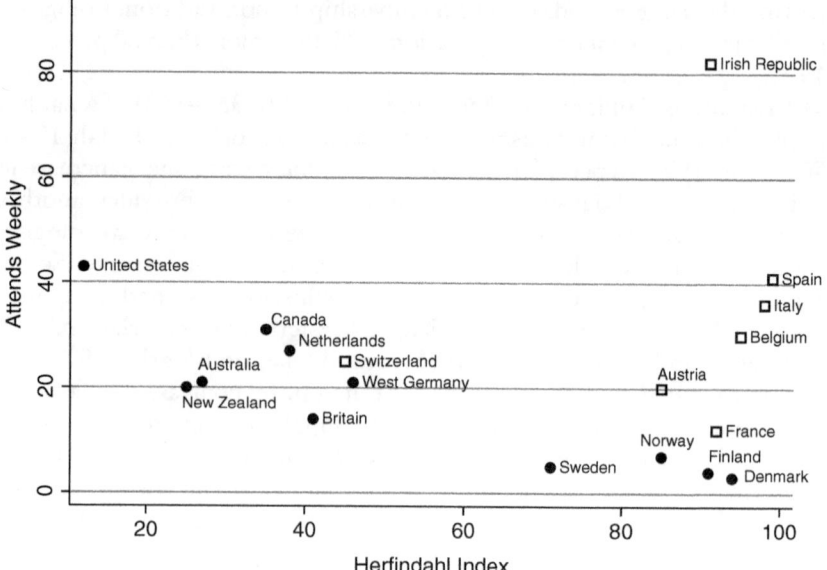

Figure 1.3 Religious attendance by Herfindahl index (using data from Iannaccone 1991:165).

$$H = \sum_{i=1}^{n} S_i^2$$

where S_i is the share of adherents in denomination i. An index of 1 indicates that all adherents belong to a single denomination (i.e., a monopoly), while an index approaching 0 indicates the presence of a large number of small denominations (i.e., greater pluralism).[15] For instance, Finke and Stark (1988) examined data on US cities in 1906 and, after controlling for the percentage of the population that was Catholic, found a positive relationship between the pluralism index and the adherence rate.

In a similar vein, Iannaccone (1991) analyzed weekly attendance rates in eighteen countries (fourteen European nations plus Canada, the United States, Australia, and New Zealand) and found a positive relationship between pluralism and predominantly Protestant countries but not between pluralism and Catholic countries. This is captured in Figure 1.3, which plots Iannaccone's data on religious attendance by the Herfindahl index. The twelve predominantly Protestant countries (i.e.,

---

[15] Some researchers subtract the index from 1, such that scores approaching 1.0 indicate a high level of pluralism and a score of 0.0 indicates a monopolistic situation.

1.4 Religious Economies

less than 50 percent Catholic populations) are represented by solid circles, while the six predominantly Catholic countries are represented by hollow squares. Clearly, a negative relationship exists between the Herfindahl index and weekly attendance in the twelve Protestant countries, but such a relationship does not appear to exist in the six Catholic countries. Iannaccone (1991:170–171) speculated that this could be due to two reasons. One was that Catholic national churches are more internally diverse than their Protestant counterparts, thus mitigating potential monopolistic effects. The other was that Catholic monopolies have not been subjected to the same level of state interference as have Protestant national churches. However, as Mark Chaves and David Cann (1992:278) point out, both of these reasons "imply that Catholic monopolies should have uniformly *high* levels of participation," but that clearly is not the case. "Weekly church attendance in heavily Catholic countries ranges from very low (12% in France) to very high (82% in Ireland)." We return to this apparent anomaly later, but for now it is worth noting that the Catholic countries with the highest rates of weekly attendance tend to be located in countries with low levels of *religious regulation*.

After Finke and Stark's initial publication, numerous researchers weighed in on the relationship between religious pluralism and religious participation. Some found a positive relationship between the two while others did not. In fact, in a review of the twenty-six articles published on the topic, Mark Chaves and Philip Gorski (2001) found that there was no consistent set of findings on the relationship. All of this research was seriously undermined when David Voas, Alasdair Crockett, and Daniel Olson (2002) demonstrated that constructing measures of both participation and pluralism from the same data introduced a mathematical bias that will produce a non-zero correlation between pluralism and participation even if no such correlation exists.[16] In particular, the Herfindahl index "has properties that can generate a correlation between religious pluralism and religious participation – properties related to the distribution of group sizes that are mathematical and not related to the substantive reasons hypothesized in the social scientific literature on religious pluralism and participation" (McBride 2008:89–90). Moreover, Michael McBride later showed that the pluralism-participation correlation is a function of the level of data (e.g., town, county, nation) and underlying supply and demand: "Supply and demand factors will vary differently across data from local markets than across data from aggregations of markets. Indeed, for this reason, it is possible to simultaneously obtain pluralism-participation correlations of opposite

---

[16] Iannaccone (1991:164) was aware of this problem, which is why he used different data sources to construct the two measures.

signs in market level (town or county) and aggregated (cross-national) data" (McBride 2008:95).

Not only does use of the Herfindahl index present a mathematical problem, but it also assumes, incorrectly, that deregulation and pluralism measure the same thing. That is, it assumes that increases in deregulation will always lead to greater levels of pluralism, but that is not necessarily the case. It is entirely possible for one or two firms to more than adequately meet a particular market's religious needs. The key is not how many firms are in the market but whether barriers to market entry exist. As Charles North notes, a single firm can only afford to be lazy if it is protected from competition.

> In standard economic theory, firms do not have the ability to be lazy or inefficient when they are the sole providers of a service. Rather, they can only afford to be lazy or inefficient when they are the sole firm in a market that is somehow sheltered from competition; dominant firms in unprotected markets are rarely lazy ... Dominant firms in various consumer industries ... must work hard to keep their customers from switching to other products and to keep other firms from entering markets. In the same way, dominant churches in unprotected markets must constantly work to keep their followers attached to and involved in the church lest new entrants come in and steal away their flocks. The implication ... is that a search for a correlation between pluralism and participation was ultimately doomed, regardless of the computational problems raised by Voas, Olson, and Crocket (2002).
>
> (North 2014:496)

It is also likely that in some markets where most people adhere to a single faith, the addition of churches from a different faith will not substantially impact the religious participation rate.

> Consider ... a hypothetical county in Utah in which most of the population ... prefers the combination of teaching and practices represented by the LDS Church. In such a place with fairly homogeneous demand, the outcome of unfettered competition in a religious economy is that most people would be Mormon, and they would not be easily attracted to a particularly charismatic Methodist preacher at the church down the street.
>
> (North 2014:496)

In other words, a religious market can become saturated, and once it does, the entry of additional churches may lead to an increase in pluralism, but it will not lead to an increase in the participation

1.4 Religious Economies

rate.[17] This is somewhat akin to Randall Collins's (1998) insight into the competition among intellectuals for attention space.[18] Collins contends that generally there is only room for three to six schools of philosophical thought, and if the number of schools grows too large, the weaker ones will eventually disappear.[19] To be sure, the intellectual space for religious schools of thought probably has room for more than six, but the dynamic is remarkably similar. In an uncrowded religious market, communities of faith can rush in to fill the void and successfully attract adherents. However, in an overcrowded market, the demise of some faith communities is almost certain.

Increasingly, social scientists have concluded that a better test of the religious economies hypothesis is to use measures of market regulation rather than of religious pluralism. In fact, that is exactly how Chaves and Cann reanalyzed Iannaccone's data, plotting weekly attendance by religious regulation. They constructed a six-point religious regulation scale based on whether or not in a given country

> (1) there is a single, officially designated state church, (2) there is official state recognition of some denominations but not others, (3) the state appoints or approves the appointment of church leaders, (4) the state directly pays church personnel salaries, (5) there is a system of ecclesiastical tax collection, and (6) the state directly subsidizes, beyond tax breaks, the operating, maintenance, or capital expenses for churches.
> (Chaves and Cann 1992:280)

Figure 1.4 captures the relationship between weekly religious attendance and religious regulation, and it is clear that a negative correlation between the two exists for all eighteen countries, not just the Protestant ones. Moreover, the relationship held up in a regression analysis after controlling for other factors, such as percent Catholic and the Herfindahl index. Interestingly, percent Catholic was just as strong a predictor of weekly attendance as was religious regulation, indicating that while religious regulation may in fact influence religious participation rates, so do other factors, including demand-side factors (Ammerman 1997; Sherkat 1997).

---

[17] Interestingly, Stark (1996a) makes a similar argument with regards to the Roman Empire's religious market, albeit in a slightly different context.
[18] Collins, in fact, occasionally refers to the attention space as a market. For example, in his examination of Chinese philosophical networks, he remarks that "Taoism and Buddhism began as market competitors which gradually settled into adjacent but overlapping niches" (Collins 1998:275), and notes that "the religious economy of the [Zen] monasteries, once so important in opening up the agrarian state-coercive structure of China, was now surpassed by a burgeoning market economy in the secular society of the Sung" (Collins 1998:297).
[19] We will examine Collins's thesis in more detail in Chapter 9.

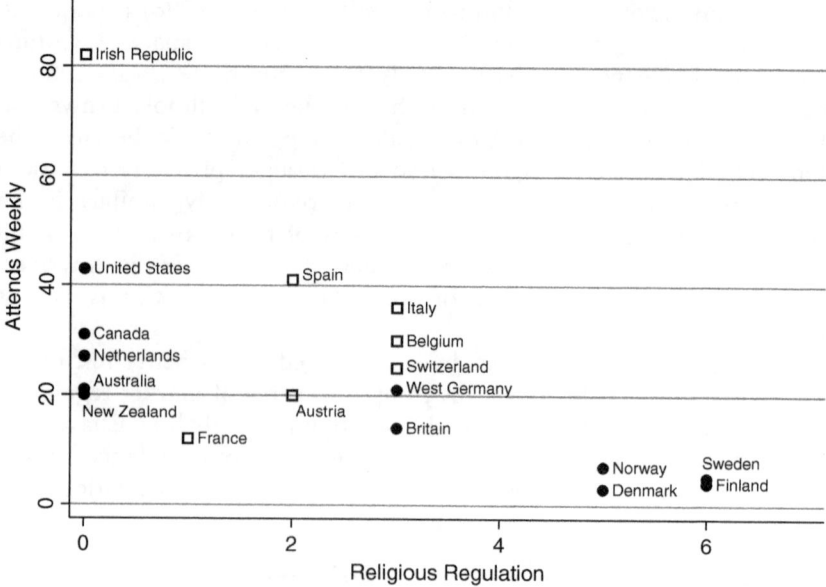

Figure 1.4 Religious attendance by religious regulation *(redrawn from Chaves and Cann 1992:284)*.

Most subsequent studies (Chaves, Schraeder, and Sprindys 1994; Barro and McCleary 2003, 2005; North and Gwin 2004; McCleary and Barro 2006a, 2006b; Fox and Tabory 2008) have found a negative relationship between regulation and participation. For instance, Mark Chaves, Peter Schraeder, and Mario Sprindys (1994) analyzed eighteen countries and found that, after controlling for social class, there was a negative correlation between state regulation and the percentage of Muslims who made a pilgrimage to Mecca (i.e., *hajj*). Charles North and Carl Gwin (2004) examined fifty-nine countries and found that higher levels of religious regulation were associated with lower religious attendance. They also controlled for the earliest date that each country provided formal legal protection of religious freedom and found that each decade of legal protection was associated with an increase in religious attendance of about 1.2 percentage points. Robert Barro and Rachel McCleary (Barro and McCleary 2003, 2005; McCleary and Barro 2006a, 2006b) conducted several studies and uncovered similar results. However, they included separate indicators of religious regulation and the presence of a state-sponsored church and found that state support of religion was associated with higher attendance, whereas the regulation of religious markets was associated with lower levels of attendance. And Jonathan Fox and Ephraim Tabory (2008), using one of the most sophisticated measures of religious regulation to date – Fox's Religion and State Project (RAS)[20] – examined eighty-one countries at several different points and found that greater religious regulation generally led to lower levels of religious attendance. They measured religious regulation on six different dimensions: (1) official support for religion, (2) general restrictions on some or all religions, (3) religious discrimination against minority religions, (4) religious regulation on most or all religion, (5) religious legislation whereby government enforces religious teachings through law, and (6) a composite measure of all five. All six were negatively associated with the likelihood of someone attending services at least once a month, and five out of six were negatively associated with the likelihood of someone attending services at least once a week.

An exception to these studies is the one by Matthew Swift (2012), which examined the relationship between religious attendance and several measures of religious regulation, including Fox's RAS data, as well as Grim and Finke's (2006) religious freedom indexes based on the US State Department's *International Religious Freedom Reports*. Swift's analysis included 208 countries, which to date is the largest number of countries. He found both positive and negative associations between various forms of religious regulation and religious attendance, but the measures of regulations tended to correlate with one another so that the net effect was essentially zero. However, when he limited his analysis to the smaller samples of earlier researchers, the results were similar. This suggests that the results of earlier studies may be limited to Western, predominantly Christian, countries. It is also possible that different types of regulations can affect religious participation in different ways. Some may lead to increases in participation, while others may lead to decreases. As we will see, recent research suggests this may, in fact, be true.

Discussion

In recent years, theorists have come to recognize that more sophisticated models of the interaction of religious markets are in order. McBride (2008, 2010), for instance, uses a game-theoretic approach that draws on a model by Harold Hotelling (1929) in order to evaluate the impact that regulation of both secular and religious activities has on religious participation and pluralism. His model demonstrates that, all else being equal, an increase in the population size of a (local) market would lead to an increase in both participation and pluralism. As he notes, however, everything else is seldom equal. For example, an increase in population could reflect improved secular economic opportunities, which are often negatively correlated with religious participation. Thus, he argues that if

---

[20] See www.religionandstate.org.

Table 1.3 *Interaction of religious regulation with religious participation and pluralism*

	Regulation of		
Market Entry	Alternative Activities	Religious Participation	Religious Pluralism
Low	Low	High	High
High	Low	Low	Low
High	High	High	Low

the correlation between population size and economic activity is weak or negative, "the positive effect of population size on pluralism and participation will outweigh the impact of counteracting effects, should there be any." However, if the correlation is strong, "then the negative impact [of secular opportunities] on participation is enough to generate the negative pluralism-participation correlation" (McBride 2008:98). Turning to the impact of regulation on religious participation and pluralism, he notes that there are two broad types of religious regulations: "those that hinder the entry of new religious groups and those that punish individuals for not participating in the privileged group" (McBride 2008:100). When both are low, it is likely that both religious pluralism and participation will be high. However, when one or both are high, then religious pluralism will always be low but participation will vary. Regulations that hinder market entry raise the costs of potential new religious firms, which if high enough, dampen religious participation and pluralism. Regulations that raise the cost of nonparticipation can also dampen religious pluralism, but they can lead to higher levels of religious participation if they make secular alternatives too costly.

> Governments throughout the world both historically and today have placed restrictions on secular activities thought to be substitutes for religious participation. Laws in modern Israel require shops to be closed on the Sabbath, and modern Islamic states have even stricter prohibitions on many different secular activities. By placing restrictions on secular substitutes for religious activity, the government decreases the opportunity cost of religious participation, thereby artificially increasing demand for religious participation. Evidence of this effect was found by Gruber and Hungerman (2008) in their study of the repeal of blue laws in the United States.
>
> (McBride 2008:100)

1.4 Religious Economies

McBride's conclusions are summarized in Table 1.3. In countries with little regulation of secular and religious activities, religious participation and pluralism are likely to be high. However, in countries where religious regulation is high but secular regulation is low, then both religious participation and pluralism will be low. And finally, in countries where the regulation of both secular and religious activities is high, religious participation will be high but pluralism will be low. This is hardly the clear-cut picture we began with at the beginning of this section.

Also complicating matters is Gill's (2005, 2008) analysis of the political origins of religious liberty. He notes, for example, that countries where a majority of the population is of one faith, it is likely there will be a state church. Why? As North (2014:498) notes, "First, religious organizations whose adherents are a high percentage of a population will prefer more regulation, primarily to uphold monopoly status. Second, political actors will choose to embrace specific religious organizations when doing so helps them maintain social control and preserve their positions of political power." In other words, in countries where a particular faith, say, the Roman Catholic Church, dominates, political leaders will often believe it is in their interest to institutionalize such faiths. And if such a faith is thriving (i.e., high rates of participation), the causal arrow may point in the other direction; in other words, in some situations high levels of religious participation lead to the formation of a state church. Gill's analysis suggests that non-longitudinal cross-sectional analyses may be inadequate to capture the interplay of the church, state, and religious participation. To this end North and Gwin (2014) analyzed a sixty-five-year panel of thirty-one predominantly Western countries. Drawing on a Hotelling model similar to McBride's, they found that, consistent with Gill, "governments are most likely to establish a state religion in countries with homogeneous populations" (North and Gwin 2014:1). They also discovered "that state religions undermine the overall religiosity of the population in religiously pluralistic countries, and that religious freedom increases religious attendance and stimulates increases in religious pluralism" (North and Gwin 2014:1).

In short, the relationship between religious regulation, pluralism, and participation is far more complex than the early religious economies models suggested, but given how most social scientific theories develop and grow, that is hardly surprising. Nevertheless, it does appear that after controlling for the factors mentioned earlier, religious regulations, at least those that place barriers to the entry of new religious suppliers into the market, can negatively affect religious participation levels.[21] However, regulations that raise the cost of not participating in the dominant group

---

[21] The historian Nile Green (2014) has drawn on the religious economies approach in order to help explain the expansion of Islam.

may have a similar effect. Perhaps more importantly, the religious economies approach should take into account the effect of social networks on market behavior (Ellison 1995). While this has occurred in the field of economics (Banerjee et al. 2013; Granovetter 2005; Jackson 2008, 2014), it has yet to exert much influence on the religious economies approach.

The fact that pluralism and participation can coexist challenges one of the most cherished beliefs held by many secularization theorists, namely, that pluralism is the enemy of religion. Berger (1967) and others argued that a religion can only survive when its beliefs and practices go relatively unchallenged, when it is located in a society where virtually everyone adheres to the same beliefs and practices, when it exists under what Berger called a "sacred canopy." Berger believed that pluralism undermined the plausibility of religious worldviews by relativizing them, so that believers no longer took their religious worldviews for granted. Some theorists have sought to explain why pluralism is not the enemy of religion. Perhaps the most notable of these are Christian Smith and his colleagues, who argue that "far from undermining the strength of religion, we propose that the cultural pluralism and social differentiation of modern society provide an environment within which well-adapted religious traditions ... can flourish" (Smith et al. 1998:90). It is to their "subcultural identity theory of religious strength" that we now turn.

1.5 A Cultural Sociology of Religion: Subcultural Identity Theory

As in other social science fields, the social scientific study of religion has experienced a cultural turn (Swidler 1986; Wuthnow 1989; Chaney 1994; Nash 2001; Smith 2003a), in that it "is renewing a long-standing emphasis on meaning, identification, and moral order" (Edgell 2012: 248). Although there are several variants of this turn in the social scientific study of religion, such as the role of institutional fields (Chaves 1996; Wilde et al. 2010), the experience of lived religion (Ammerman 1987; Cadge 2004), and the drawing of symbolic boundaries (Smith et al. 1998; Edgell, Gerteis, and Hartmann 2006), here we focus on Christian Smith's (2003b; Smith et al. 1998) "subcultural identity theory," in part because it has exerted a tremendous influence on the field, but also because it explicitly addresses why religious belief and practice continues to thrive in the modern world.

Subcultural identity theory argues that our primary drive in life is not utility maximization but rather the search for meaning and belonging. It holds that we are, at heart, moral, believing animals who are trying to make sense of the world around us (Smith 2003a). According to Smith, we do not do this in the midst of a vacuum; instead we do so by identifying

1.5 A Cultural Sociology of Religion

with (i.e., believing in) an overarching narrative or story of the world that helps us interpret and make sense of that world. He argues that "for all our science, rationality and technology, we moderns are no less the makers, tellers, and believers of stories that make sense of our existence, history and purpose than were our forebears at any other time in human history" (Smith 2003a:64). As Robert Bellah puts it in another context:

> That even the narratives of early childhood are organized through relationships that are in some sense logical warns us against assuming that narrative, or symbolic representation generally, is "irrational." Art, music, poetry, and narrative are not just effusions of feeling. They are all forms of thought and are in principle as deeply rational as mathematics or physics. It is easier for adults as well as children (even for theoretical physicists) to think narratively than it is to think conceptually, so it is not surprising that logical relationships are often expressed in narrative form.
> (Bellah 2011:36–37)

In fact, according to Smith, much of the debates that we witness today (e.g., over abortion, stem-cell research, policy toward the Middle East, etc.) are rooted in rival but not entirely compatible narratives. This is not to imply that people do not respond to incentives. They do, but they do so as moral, believing animals. As Smith notes, people "are inescapably normative and moral (as well as instrumentally pleasure-seeking) creatures" (Smith et al. 1998:90).

Subcultural identity theory emerged out of a study of American evangelicalism (Smith 2000; Smith et al. 1998) that sought to explain why religion, in general, continues to thrive in pluralistic societies (a theory of religious persistence) and why some groups (in this case, evangelicalism) thrive in pluralistic societies while others (e.g., mainline Protestantism) do not (a theory of religious strength). As suggested earlier, it is a reaction, in part, to Berger (1967, 1969), who argued that pluralism is not conducive to religious belief and practice. Thus, before turning to why Smith believes pluralism can be religion's friend, or at least the friend of some religious traditions, we will briefly consider Berger's sacred canopy theory.

Peter Berger's Sacred Canopy

Berger argued that the plausibility of what we regard as real (i.e., our worldview) depends largely on the social support – that is, the consensus – it receives. When that support erodes, so does our confidence in our worldview. This is true of religious beliefs. According to Berger, religious beliefs depend on social support in order for them to retain their plausibility. As long as there is widespread social support for a particular way of looking at the heavens – a sacred canopy, so to speak – then that way of looking at the heavens remains plausible. When that support erodes, however, the plausibility of a religious worldview begins to fall apart. This was not an issue in premodern societies, according to Berger. That is because almost everyone belonged to the same religious tradition; it was easy for people to believe because their beliefs were socially reinforced. Everybody held the same beliefs, so few people challenged the status quo. However, in modern societies, where particular religious traditions no longer receive the broad social support they once did, Berger believes that religion undergoes a plausibility crisis. That is because believers no longer take their religious worldviews for granted. Instead, they see them, including their own faith traditions, as different options competing for their allegiance. This led Berger to argue that highly distinctive religious traditions can only survive when they are sheltered from modernity's harmful effects, such as in rural America. That, however, is not what Smith and his colleagues found:

> Little in our findings suggest that American evangelicalism's vitality is due to any social or geographic distance from modernity ... [E]vangelicals are – almost always *more* than most other Americans – voting in political elections; working hard to educate themselves about social and political issues; lobbying elected officials; participating in public protests and demonstrations; talking with nonbelievers about their faith; getting involved in local community organizations; giving money to help the poor; defending a biblical worldview in intellectual circles; and struggling with the public issues of racism, abortion, and educational policy. Here are people who appear quite engaged with the people, institutions, and concerns of the pluralistic, modern world.
>
> (Smith et al. 1998:75)

Moreover, in terms of education and income, Smith and his colleagues discovered that evangelicals were hardly distinguishable from other groups. Except for mainline Protestants, their average level of education was higher than members of other groups, including those identifying as not religious. In terms of average yearly income, they earned more than fundamentalists, theological liberals, members of other religious faiths, and those with no religion, and slightly less than mainline Protestants and Catholics (Smith et al. 1998:77–78). Finally, evangelicals were "only slightly less likely than nonreligious Americans to live in more urban areas ..., and they [were] less likely than either fundamentalists, mainline Protestants, or liberals to reside in [rural counties]" (Smith et al. 1998:79).

The question, of course, is why? Why are groups, such as American evangelicals, thriving in a pluralistic world that regularly challenges their worldviews? Smith's short answer is that religious traditions can survive in pluralistic societies when they embed themselves in subcultures (i.e., groups) that offer collective identities that provide followers with a clear sense of meaning and belonging in the world (Smith et al. 1998:118–119). His longer answer requires a bit more elaboration.

Why Religion Survives in Pluralistic Societies

Smith argues that we satisfy our drive for meaning and belonging by locating ourselves "within social groups (or subcultures) that sustain distinctive, morally orienting collective identities" (Smith et al. 1998:90), something that religious traditions are well positioned to do. Most of us belong to one or more subcultures, and these, according to Smith, are what provide us with worldviews that help us make sense of our world. Put simply, our identities are not formed in isolation from other human beings but through our interaction with them. However, constructing and maintaining these identities are not easy, and for groups to succeed at this task they need to draw distinct boundaries between who is in and who is out. "Social groups know who they are in large measure by knowing who they are not" (Smith et al. 1998:91). Thus, groups that maintain an optimum level of distinctiveness between themselves and other groups are more likely to enjoy success than those who are unable to maintain such distinctiveness. Smith acknowledges that there are parallels here with Iannaccone's strictness theory, but he believes that strictness cannot account for all of the vitality we see in movements such as American evangelicalism.

Smith also argues that modern religious believers "can establish stronger religious identities and commitments on the basis of individual choice than through ascription" (Smith et al. 1998:102). Older theories, such as Berger's, saw choice as relativizing religion: because we could choose to believe or not to believe, this was seen as making religious belief an option, not a given, thus making religious belief weaker. Subcultural identity theory argues just the opposite: in modern societies, such as the United States, choice strengthens a person's faith because it increases his or her level of commitment. "For moderns – perhaps especially modern Americans – the ultimate criteria of identity and lifestyle validity is individual choice. It is by choosing a product, a mate, a lifestyle, or an identity that one makes it one's very own, personal, special, and meaningful – not 'merely' something one inherits or assumes" (Smith et al. 1998:103).

Smith also holds that modern pluralism probably actually benefits religion because it encourages the formation of distinct subcultures, including religious subcultures. To borrow from the language of religious economies, pluralism allows groups to target different niches in the cultural market, thus providing people with a greater choice of groups in which they can locate themselves.

> Cities, these quintessentially modern places, in fact do not produce the kind of rationalized, integrated uniformity that we might expect to erode distinctive religious beliefs and practices. To the contrary, cities promote cultural and institutional diversity, distinction, and unconventionality. Demographically and instructionally, they positively nourish the kinds of strong subcultures that are needed to sustain particular religious beliefs and practices, both traditional and innovative."
>
> (Smith et al. 1998:111)

New York City is a case in point. An ongoing study by Tony Carnes (2015) has documented the tremendous religious diversity that can be found in the city's five boroughs.

Finally, Smith contends that modernity may "actually increase religion's appeal" because it "creates social conditions which intensify the kinds of felt needs and desires that religion is especially well-positioned to satisfy" (Smith et al. 1998:116). This is a variation of deprivation theory, which we will consider in greater detail in conjunction with our discussion of religious conversion in the next chapter. For our purposes here, it is sufficient to note that deprivation theory argues that people join particular groups because they suffer from some sort of deprivation – economic, social, political – that the group addresses. Thus, people who suffer economically in this world will join a religion that promises them eternal bliss in the next, or those who suffer from ill health will join a religion that promises them good health.

Why Some Religions Thrive

The preceding arguments help explain why religion continues to survive in pluralistic, modern societies. We now consider why Smith believes some groups thrive while others do not. We begin by returning to what we noted in the previous section, namely, that in order for groups to thrive they need to draw distinct boundaries between themselves and other groups. Creating distinct boundaries helps separate "insiders" from "outsiders," which, in turn, helps us identify who we are as individuals and the groups to which we belong (and do not belong). Evangelical Protestants, for instance, draw symbolic boundaries between themselves from both non-Christians and non-

1.5 A Cultural Sociology of Religion

evangelical Christians. When they use the term "Christian," they are generally not referring to all Christians – instead, they generally have in mind other evangelicals who hold certain beliefs. Smith et al. (1998:125) quotes an evangelical woman who told him, "I wouldn't identify myself with someone who doesn't recognize Jesus as the son of God, as both divine and human, or with those who don't see Scripture as the basis of authority." Similarly, evangelicals distinguish themselves from non-Christians by speaking about the difference between themselves and "the world" out there. As one Baptist put it:

> Christians should look for every opportunity to show they are different. One way to set ourselves apart is by bowing our heads and praying at lunch. When you go out on a business lunch, say "excuse me," and bow your head and pray. It says to people something is different. I think Christians need to look for opportunities to live a Christian life where people see that you are different.
> (Smith et al. 1998:126)

Smith also contends that individuals and groups define what they believe to be true in relation to "specific, chosen reference groups" (Smith et al. 1998:104). In other words, we do not evaluate the validity of our beliefs based on the norms of outsiders but rather on the norms of people whose opinions we value – that is, people who are part of our group. Whereas older theories argued that religious pluralism relativizes religious belief because it provides us with a wide array of religious choices, subcultural identity theory argues that we tend to ignore the opinions and beliefs of negative reference groups because we do not value their opinions. Instead, we value the opinions of those we know. The exception to this is that negative reference groups can reinforce what we "do *not* believe," who we "do *not* want to become," and how we "do *not* want to act" (Smith et al. 1998:105). This leads Smith to argue that we do not need "sacred canopies," just "sacred umbrellas:"

> Canopies are expansive, immobile, and held up by props beyond the reach of those covered. Umbrellas, on the other hand, are small, handheld, and portable – like the faith sustaining religious worlds that modern people construct for themselves. We suggest that, as the old, overarching canopies split apart and their pieces of fabric fell to the ground, many innovative religious actors caught those falling pieces of cloth in the air and, with more than a little ingenuity, remanufactured them into umbrellas. In the pluralistic, modern world, people don't need macro-encompassing sacred cosmos to maintain their religious beliefs. They only need "sacred

umbrellas," small, portable, accessible relational worlds – religious reference groups – "under" which their beliefs can make complete sense.

(Smith et al. 1998:106)

Finally, Smith contends that in a pluralistic context, intergroup conflict can strengthen in-group identity and solidarity. This is in contrast to earlier theories that held that conflict weakens religious belief, arguing that as religious believers come into contact with other people who espouse conflicting views and values, religious believers would eventually revise or abandon their own beliefs and practices as a means of resolving this conflict. Research has found, however, that conflict with relevant out-groups actually builds in-group strength. External conflict helps build internal cohesion. Thus, battles over school prayer, gay and lesbian rights, whether the Ten Commandments can be displayed in government buildings, and so on actually strengthen, rather than weaken, the groups engaging in the conflict. And Smith argues that in the United States, evangelicals are an embattled group, as illustrated by the lament of a Presbyterian woman:

> Christians are not treated too nicely. I'm thinking of two Chief Justices who are Christians, who spoke up and voted against certain things. Then in the *Washington Post* there were columns after columns laughing about their decision on these cases. I think Christians are mocked and made fun of by mainstream America. I have even experienced that opposition personally from friends, in subtle ways, thinking me very odd to prefer to go to a church activity over a movie.
>
> (Smith et al. 1998:141)

Table 1.4, which is adapted from Smith et al. (1998:139), captures this sense of embattlement. More than members of other religious groups, evangelicals perceive that people of faith in general, and Christians in particular, are under attack by the wider American culture, in particular the mass media, feminists, and public schools. Ironically, however, it is this sense of being under attack that strengthens the beliefs and commitments of American evangelicals.

Summary

In short, subcultural identity theory holds that religion continues to survive in the modern world because religion has created subcultures with collective identities that provide followers with a sense of meaning and belonging. It also argues that religious groups that

Table 1.4 *Embattled Christians, by tradition**

	Evangelicals	Fundamentalists	Mainline	Liberals	Catholics	Nonreligious
Christian values are under serious attack today	91%	87%	80%	69%	—	—
View as hostile to own values and morals						
Mass media	77%	72%	59%	46%	49%	42%
Feminists	67%	57%	40%	24%	30%	24%
Public schools	57%	52%	36%	27%	19%	20%
We are seeing the breakdown of American society	94%	94%	88%	87%	83%	68%

Note: Religious Identity and Influence Survey. Data downloaded from the *Association of Religion Data Archives*, www.TheARDA.com. Percentages recalculated by author.
Source: Smith et al. 1998:139.

engage with and maintain clear boundaries between themselves and others are more likely to thrive in pluralistic societies than those that do not. Moreover, theologically conservative groups tend to emphasize their distinctiveness, whereas liberal groups generally do not – that is, theologically conservative groups tend to enjoy success whereas more theologically liberal ones do not. This is not to suggest that it is impossible for theologically liberal churches to create meaning and identity. However, it is difficult to do so without drawing distinct boundaries about who is in and who is out, and that often cuts against the theological beliefs of mainline and liberal Protestants.

1.6 Summary and Conclusion

In this chapter, we have explored some of the theories that have arisen in reaction to the empirical challenges to the standard secularization story that social scientists and philosophers have embraced for some time. Although they reflect different perspectives, they all implicitly accept that religion will continue to maintain an ongoing presence in modern life. Indeed, cognitive scientists of religion, such as Scott Atran (2002, 2010), Justin Barrett (2004, 2011), Jesse Bering (2011), Pascal Boyer (2001), and Robert McCauley (2011), have all noted that believing in God, gods, or some higher power is something that comes quite naturally (i.e., it is cognitively easy) to human beings, similar to learning a language.[22] To be clear, they are not arguing that being irreligious is somehow unnatural or abnormal, a critique made by some (see, e.g., Zuckerman 2014:72–74). Rather, they are simply arguing that because believing in God, the gods, or a higher power comes easily, there will always be a proportion of the population inclined toward things religious.[23] Whether such belief manifests itself in attendance at temple, synagogue, or church will depend on other factors (e.g., how compelling worship services are at local congregations; the level of religious freedom; the demands and/or pull of other activities, such as club sports, that play on Sundays; and so on). Moreover, within a particular society certain religious traditions will thrive while others will not, reflecting the interaction of various groups with their external environment. Still, it is likely that there is an upper limit to how many people actively pursue a religious

---

[22] The cognitive science of religion is an emerging field and populated by scholars from a variety of fields. For instance, Atran and Boyer are anthropologists, Barrett and Bering are psychologists, and McCauley is a philosopher. For a helpful overview, see James Jones's (2016) recent book.

[23] Bering, Boyer, and Atran are atheists, so it is unlikely they believe that a lack of belief is unnatural.

1.6 Summary and Conclusion

life. As we saw earlier, even with belief levels and reported affiliation rates around 90 percent, the US church adherence rate has never climbed much higher than 60 percent (Finke and Stark 2005). Thus, it is perhaps better to assume that the future of religion will be one of variation. There will be periods of time when it will be quite high, and there will be periods of time when it will be quite low, but it will not be going away any time soon.

The cognitive sciences have also uncovered evidence that human beings are naturally relational. For example, a number of psychologists have argued that the human psyche does not develop in isolation but in relation to others (Klein 1948; Kohut 1971; Greenberg 1991). Their theories contend "that since other people are necessary to satisfy basic human needs, the seeking out of others is a primary human activity" (Kadushin 2012:59). More recently, the neuropsychologist Matthew Lieberman (2013) has drawn on functional neuroimaging (fMRI) to demonstrate that our brains are wired to connect with others. Similarly, numerous nineteenth- and twentieth-century philosophers have argued, albeit in different ways, that the sphere of the interhuman lies at the foundation of being human in this world.[24] The best known treatment is Martin Buber's *I and Thou* (1937), but several others have explored this sphere as well (see, e.g., Marcel 1951; Sartre 1956; Husserl 1960; Levinas 1969; Merleau-Ponty 1974; Theunissen 1984; Farley 1990).

Thus, we should not be too surprised that a social science – social network analysis – has emerged that focuses on the relational aspects of the human condition. As we will see in the next chapter, some social network analysts embrace rational choice theory in that they assume that individuals respond to incentives. These analysts differ from some rational choice theorists, however, in arguing that such incentives are largely a function of the networks in which we are embedded. Social network analysts also explore the functioning of markets. Their primary insight is that markets are not composed of atomized individuals who are unaffected by their interactions with others, which is why they argue that all economic action is also social action (Granovetter 1985, 2017). Ron Burt (1992a, 1992b), in fact, argues that people and firms who take advantage of market imperfections, in particular those in positions of brokerage, tend to be more successful than those who do not. The same can probably be said of religious markets as well. It may be true that, all else being equal, efficient congregations will out-compete less efficient ones, but it is also likely that some are better positioned to leverage their structural location than others. Thus, we cannot explain success solely in terms of market forces. Finally, social network analysts have developed metrics and algorithms for not only detecting subgroups but also for estimating the level to which they are connected to or isolated from other groups. Thus, social network analysis may provide a method (or methods) that

---

[24] The term "interhuman" is a translation of Martin Buber's term, *Zwischenmenschlichte*, which is sometimes translated "between." See Farley (1990:32).

subcultural identity theorists can use for quantifying the level at which religious groups maintain distinct boundaries between themselves and the outside world.

1.7 For Further Reading

The literature on the social scientific study of religion is voluminous. Luckily, several excellent introductions exist, such as *Sociology of Religion: Contemporary Developments* (2016) by Kevin Christiano, William Swatos, and Peter Kivisto; *The Sociology of Religion: A Critical Agenda* (2013) by Grace Davie; *Religion Matters: What Sociology Teaches Us about Religion in Our World* (2011) by Michael Emerson, William Mirola, and Susanne Monahan; *Religion: The Social Context* (2002) by Meredith McGuire; *Religion in Sociological Perspective* (2012) by Keith Roberts and David Yamane; and *The Future of Religion* (1985) by Rodney Stark and William Bainbridge.

Monographs that are technically not introductions can sometimes be just as helpful. Falling into this category are *The Churching of America* (2005) by Roger Finke and Rodney Stark; *The Plot to Kill God* (2008) by Paul Froese; *Rendering unto Caesar* (1998) by Anthony Gill; *Moral, Believing, Animals* (2003) and *Religion: What It Is, How It Works, and Why It Matters* (2017) by Christian Smith; *American Evangelicalism* (1998) by Christian Smith et al.; and *The Rise of Christianity* (1996) and *Why God? Explaining Religious Phenomena* (2017) by Rodney Stark. There are, of course, the classics: Peter Berger's, *The Sacred Canopy* (1967) and *A Rumor of Angels* (1969); Emile Durkheim's, *The Elementary Forms of the Religious Life* (1965); and Max Weber's, *The Sociology of Religion* (1963) and *The Protestant Ethic and the Spirit of Capitalism* (1996 [1905]). Readers may also find the following essays helpful:

- Christopher G. Ellison and Darren E. Sherkat. 1995. "Is Sociology the Core Discipline for the Scientific Study of Religion?" *Social Forces* 73(4):1255–1266.
- Laurence R. Iannaccone. 1994. "Progress in the Economics of Religion." *Journal of Institutional and Theoretical Economics* 150(4):737–744.
- Darren E. Sherkat and Christopher G. Ellison. 1999. "Recent Developments and Current Controversies in the Sociology of Religion." In *Annual Review of Sociology*, vol. 25, edited by K. S. Cook and J. Hagan. Palo Alto, CA: Annual Reviews Inc., pp. 363–394.
- R. Stephen Warner. 1993. "Work in Progress toward a New Paradigm for the Sociological Study of Religion in the

1.7 For Further Reading

United States." *American Journal of Sociology* 98 (5):1044–1093.
- Robert Wuthnow. 1986. "Sociology of Religion." In *Handbook of Sociology*, edited by N. J. Smelser and R. S. Burt. Beverley Hills, CA: Sage, pp. 473–509.

Much has been written on religion's persistence. Some of it is quite scholarly, but others are written for a more popular audience. Here are a few that readers may find helpful:

- Justin L. Barrett. 2011. *Cognitive Science, Religion, and Theology*. West Conshohocken, PA: Templeton Press.
- Peter L. Berger. 1996. "Secularism in Retreat." *The National Interest* (Winter):3–12.
- Mark Chaves. 1994. "Secularization as Declining Religious Authority." *Social Forces* 72(3):749–774.
- Karel Dobbelaere. 1999. "Towards an Integrated Perspective of the Processes Related to the Descriptive Concept of Secularization." *Sociology of Religion* 60 (3):229–247.
- Jonathan Fox. 2015. *Political Secularism, Religion, and the State: A Time Series Analysis of Worldwide Data*. New York, NY: Cambridge University Press.
- Philip S. Gorski and Ates Altinordu. 2008. "After Secularization?" *Annual Review of Sociology* 34:55–85.
- Jeffrey K. Hadden. 1987. "Toward Desacralizing Secularization Theory." *Social Forces* 65(3):587–611.
- Robert McCauley. 2011. *Why Religion Is Natural and Science Is Not*. New York: Oxford University Press.
- John Micklethwait and Adrian Wooldridge. 2009. *God Is Back: How the Global Revival of Faith Is Changing the World*. New York: Penguin Press.
- Christian S. Smith (ed.). 2003. *The Secular Revolution: Power, Interests, and Conflict in the Secularization of American Public Life*. Berkeley, CA: University of California Press.
- Rodney Stark. 1999. "Secularization, R.I.P." *Sociology of Religion* 60(3):249–273.
- Monica Duffy Toft, Daniel Philpott, and Timothy Samuel Shah. 2011. *God's Century: Resurgent Religion and Global Politics*. New York, NY: W. W. Norton & Company Ltd.

Readers who are interested in exploring more about *rational choice theory and religion* should find Lawrence Young's edited book, *Rational Choice Theory and Religion* (1997), helpful. It contains chapters by Rodney Stark,

Larry Iannaccone, Roger Finke, Darren Sherkat, Nancy Ammerman, Michael Hechter, Randall Collins, and others. The following readings are also recommended:

- Christopher G. Ellison. 1995. "Rational Choice Explanations of Individual Religious Behavior: Notes on the Problem of Social Embeddedness." *Journal for the Scientific Study of Religion* 34(1):89–97.
- Laurence R. Iannaccone. 1994. "Progress in the Economics of Religion." *Journal of Institutional and Theoretical Economics* 150(4):737–744.
- Laurence R. Iannaccone, Rodney Stark, and Roger Finke. 1998. "Rationality and the Religious Mind." *Economic Inquiry* 36:373–389.

Young's volume also includes chapters that examine the *religious economies approach*. Other readings that readers may want to consider include the following:

- Roger Finke and Rodney Stark. 2005. *The Churching of America, 1776–2005: Winners and Losers in Our Religious Economy*, 2nd ed. New Brunswick, NJ: Rutgers University Press.
- Anthony J. Gill 1998. *Rendering unto Caesar: The Catholic Church and the State in Latin America*. Chicago, IL: University of Chicago Press.
- Laurence R. Iannaccone, Roger Finke, and Rodney Stark. 1997. "Deregulating Religion: The Economics of Church and State." *Economic Inquiry* 35(2):350–364.
- Michael McBride. 2008. "Religious Pluralism and Religious Participation: A Game Theoretic Analysis." *American Journal of Sociology* 114(1):77–106.
- Charles M. North. 2014. "Regulation of Religious Markets." In *The Oxford Handbook of Christianity and Economics*, edited by Paul Oslington. New York: Oxford University Press, pp. 489–511.

Finally, Christian Smith's subcultural identity theory is fleshed out in his study of American evangelicalism, *American Evangelicalism: Embattled and Thriving* (1998), although his *Moral, Believing Animals* (2003) is quite helpful too. He has recently updated his thoughts on religion in his *Religion: What It Is, How It Works, and Why It Matters* (2017). Readers may also benefit from John Evans's article, "The Creation of a Distinct Subcultural Identity and Denominational Growth," (2003) which summarizes Smith's approach and appeared in the *Journal for the Scientific Study of Religion* 42(3):467–477.

2

Social Network Analysis: A Brief Introduction

2.1 Introduction

Nicholas Christakis begins his widely viewed TED talk, *The Hidden Influence of Social Networks* (2010), with a story from when he was a hospice doctor at the University of Chicago in the 1990s. At the time, he was studying the "widower effect," which is the phenomenon of how, when someone who is married dies, the risk that his or her spouse will die within a year doubles. Christakis tells how he was caring for a woman who was dying from dementia and was being cared for by her daughter.

> [T]he daughter was exhausted from caring for her mother. And the daughter's husband, he also was sick from his wife's exhaustion. And I was driving home one day, and I get a phone call from the husband's friend, calling me because he was depressed about what was happening to his friend. So here I get this call from this random guy that's having an experience that's being influenced by people at some social distance."
>
> (Christakis 2010)

This led him to experience an epiphany:

> I suddenly realized two very simple things: First, the widowhood effect was not restricted to husbands and wives. And second, it was not restricted to pairs of people. And I started to see the world in a whole new way, like pairs of people connected to each other. And then I realized that these individuals would be connected into foursomes with other pairs of people nearby. And then, in fact, these people were embedded in other sorts of relationships: marriage and spousal and friendship and other sorts of ties. And that, in fact, these connections were vast and that we were all embedded in this broad set of connections with each other. So, I started to see the world in a completely new way and I became obsessed with this. I became obsessed with how it might

be that we're embedded in these social networks, and how they affect our lives.

(Christakis 2010)

Christakis is not the first to become obsessed with social networks. For some time, social scientists have explored the dynamics of the networks in which individuals are embedded. For instance, Georg Simmel (1955 [1908], 1971 [1908]), who is generally seen as the intellectual forebearer of what is now referred to as social network analysis (SNA) (Freeman 2004),[1] argued that in order to understand social behavior, we must study patterns of interaction, and he offered penetrating insights into the nature of secret societies (Simmel 1950b), the dynamics of dyads and triads (Simmel 1950a, 1950c),[2] and how increasing social complexity helped lead to the rise of modern individualism (Simmel 1955 [1908]). While Simmel's contributions continue to influence the discipline, SNA's emergence can be traced to two major strands of thought (Prell 2011; Scott 2013): the work of (1) social psychologists, such as Fritz Heider, Kurt Lewin, and Jacob Moreno (Heider 1946; Lewin 1951; Moreno 1953), and (2) social anthropologists, such as Siegfried Nadel (1957) and Alfred Radcliffe-Brown (1940). The former emphasized how organized patterns shape how we see and interpret the world, while the latter focused on the relationship between social patterns and social structure. Not only did these individuals influence the research of individuals such as Elton Mayo (1933, 1945; see also Roethlisberger and Dickson 1939), W. Lloyd Warner (Warner and Lunt 1941), John Barnes (1954), Elizabeth Bott (1957), and J. Clyde Mitchell (1969), but they laid the groundwork for SNA's formal development at Harvard in the 1960s and 1970s, which was led by the sociologist Harrison White and his students (e.g., Ronald Breiger, Kathleen Carley, Ivan Chase, Bonnie Erickson, Mark Granovetter, Michael Schwartz, and Barry Wellman). White, who also earned a PhD in theoretical physics, argued that sociology, in spite of its claim to study social phenomena, was beholden to individualistic forms of analysis based on the aggregated characteristics of individuals often aided by statistical analysis of survey data. This, he believed, was a mistake, and, along with his students, he developed an approach that drew on case studies that focused on social relations and the patterns that emerged from them. White's efforts did not occur in a vacuum. Other theoretical traditions also informed SNA's development, including graph theory (Harary 1953, 1969; Harary and Norman 1953; Lewis 2009), exchange theory (Cook and Whitmeyer 1992; Emerson 1972a, 1972b, 1976;

---

[1] To be sure, the work on social groups by Emile Durkheim (1984) and Ferdinand Tönnies (1957 [1855]) certainly anticipated much of what was to come.
[2] A dyad is a pair of actors with a tie between them. A triad is a set of three actors that may or may not have ties between them.

2.1 Introduction

Homans 1950, 1958, 1961), and research into the recruitment of individuals to religious and social movements (Gould 1991, 1993a; Lofland 1977; Lofland and Stark 1965; McAdam 1986, 1988b; Snow and Phillips 1980; Snow, Zurcher, and Ekland-Olson 1980).[3]

To say that the discipline has come into its own would be an understatement. Social network analysts have created their own organization (International Network for Social Network Analysis), launched their own journals (*Connections, Social Networks*, and the *Journal of Social Structure*), and produced a number of excellent monographs (see, e.g., Wasserman and Faust 1994; Knoke and Yang 2007; de Nooy, Mrvar, and Batagelj 2011; Prell 2011; Kadushin 2012; Borgatti, Everett, and Johnson 2013; McCulloh, Armstrong, and Johnson 2013; Robins 2015; Scott 2017). In recent years, economists have become increasingly interested in social networks, as have physicists and other scientists. This has led to an increased interest in SNA, attracting researchers from a wide array of different disciplines and generating a number of highly creative studies (see, e.g., Barabási and Albert 1999; Kleinberg 1999, 2000; Watts 1999a, 1999b, 2003; Buchanan 2001, 2002; Barabási 2002; Girvan and Newman 2002; Bramoullé and Kranton 2006; Onnela et al. 2007; Jackson 2008, 2014; Easley and Kleinberg 2010). In fact, Linton Freeman (2006), one of the architects of the SNA software package UCINET (Borgatti, Everett, and Freeman 2002), recently argued that social network analysis has become, in a Kuhnian (Kuhn 1970) sense, a normal science in that its practitioners work out of common set of assumptions and practices, something quite common in the hard sciences but relatively rare in the social sciences.[4]

What is social network analysis? Briefly put, it is a collection of theories and methods that assumes that the behavior of actors (whether individuals, groups, or organizations) is affected by (1) their ties to others and (2) the networks in which they are embedded, what Granovetter (2017:19) refers to as the relational and structural aspects of network embeddedness. Rather than viewing individuals (and groups and organizations) as unaffected by those around them, SNA assumes that interaction patterns affect what actors do, say, and believe. Although some interactions are random, many are not. Actors tend to interact with similar others, and repeated interaction can lead (among other things) to the emergence of social formation at various levels (e.g., individual, group, institutions, and nations) that can be the object of SNA in their own right. SNA differs

---

[3] The story, of course, is far more complex than this brief overview. For a more detailed account, see Linton Freeman's book, *The Development of Social Network Analysis* (2004), and his 2011 follow-up essay (Freeman 2011). John Scott's (2017) nontechnical introduction is also quite helpful.

[4] Freeman is not the first to make this argument. Norman Hummon and Kathleen Carley (1993) made a similar point about a decade earlier.

from more traditional approaches (i.e., variable-based) in that the latter tends to focus on actors' attributes (e.g., gender, race, education), whereas SNA focuses on how interaction patterns affect behavior. It notes that while attributes typically do not vary across social contexts, most interaction patterns do, suggesting that interaction patterns are just as (or perhaps more) important for understanding behavior than are attributes.

> A woman who holds a menial job requiring little initiative in an office may be a dynamic leader of a neighborhood association and an assertive PTA participant. Such behavioral differences are difficult to reconcile with unchanging gender, age and status attributes, but comprehensible on recognizing that people's structural relations can vary markedly across social contexts.
> (Knoke and Yang 2007:5)

Consequently, a primary goal of SNA has been to develop metrics that help analysts gain a better understanding of a particular network's structural features. It has been used successfully to explain varieties of behavior largely because it forces researchers "to think in terms of constraints and options that are inherent in the way social relations are organized" (Raab and Milward 2003). Most of the remainder of this chapter introduces readers to SNA's basic terms, concepts, and assumptions. First, however, we briefly discuss some of the misconceptions surrounding SNA. Then we consider its core assumptions before turning to a discussion of its basic terms and concepts. Where appropriate we note the implications these may have for the social scientific study of religion. This is followed by an overview of the different types of social network data and a brief discussion as to how social network data are collected.

2.2 Misconceptions

Social network analysis is sometimes confused with social networking and social media. Often when people learn they are going to learn social network analysis, they think that they are going to be taught how to mine data from social media sites such as Facebook and Twitter. The two are not the same, however. SNA is a collection of theories and methods that have been developed to understand the structure of social networks, whereas social media is user-generated content that can include text, pictures, videos, connections among users, and links to websites. Analysts can extract network data from social media platforms and subsequently use SNA to understand those social media networks (e.g., followers in a user-to-user Twitter network), but that is different.

2.2 Misconceptions

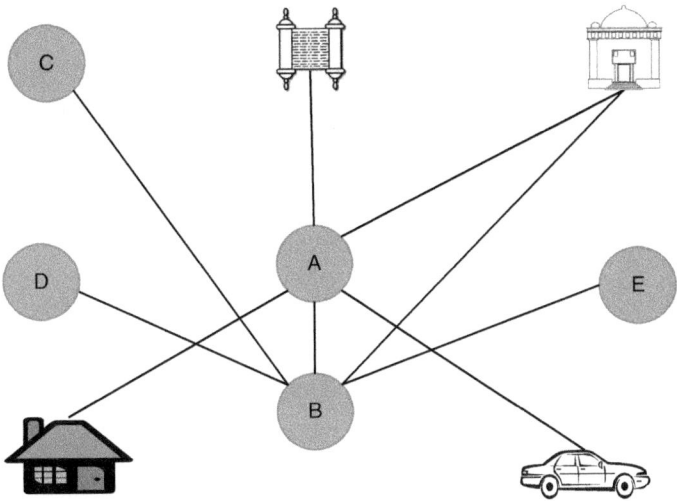

Figure 2.1 Illustrative link analysis diagram

The fact that social media content is often relational and can therefore lend itself to SNA has only added to the confusion.

How some use the term "network" can also be confusing. Some use it to refer to decentralized, informal, and/or organic types of organizations (Burns and Stalker 1961; Powell 1990; Powell and Smith-Doerr 1994; Podolny and Page 1998; Ronfeldt and Arquilla 2001). This distinction can be useful in some contexts, but within the world of SNA, all organizations are seen as networks. Some may be more hierarchical than others, but they are still networks (Nohria 1992), which is why social network analysts have developed algorithms that measure the degree to which a particular network is hierarchical (see, e.g., Davis 1979; Krackhardt 1994; de Nooy, Mrvar, and Batagelj 2005:205–212).

Finally, SNA is sometimes confused with link analysis, a related but distinct methodology that, like SNA, examines the relational patterns of various objects. Although there are similarities between the two, a basic difference is that while link analysis diagrams often include different types of objects (e.g., individuals, cars, cell phones, etc.) and the ties between them, social network diagrams only include ties between similar types of objects. Take, for example, a link analysis diagram where two individuals (A and B) each have links to five other objects, but the objects to which they have ties differ from one another (Figure 2.1). In this example, person A is linked to person B as well as a scroll, a synagogue, a house, and a car, whereas person B is linked to four individuals (A, C, D, and E) and a synagogue. While both have five ties, we cannot meaningfully compare the number of ties of these two individuals because they are tied to different types of objects.

By contrast, in SNA actors have ties to similar objects, making direct comparison of the numbers of ties meaningful. This is illustrated in Figure 2.2, where in the upper panel, individuals A and B each have five ties to five other individuals, and in the lower they have five ties to five different churches. In both cases, A's ties are comparable to B's because the ties are to the same type of object. Of course, social network analysts are interested in more than the count of an actor's ties, but other social network analysis algorithms generally assume that ties are between similar types of objects.

2.3 Assumptions

Most social network analysis theories and methods are built on a common set of assumptions (Wasserman and Faust 1994; Azarian 2005; Knoke and Yang 2007; Christakis and Fowler 2009):

- Actors and their related actions are interdependent – rather than independent – with other actors
- Ties between actors are conduits for the transfer or flow of various types of material and/or nonmaterial goods or resources (e.g., funds, beliefs, trust, enmity, etc.)
- Social structures are seen in terms of enduring patterns of ties between actors
- Repeated interactions between actors give rise to social formations that take on a life of their own, follow their own logic, and cannot be reduced to their constituent parts even though they remain dependent upon those parts
- Actors' location in the social structure (i.e., its structural location) impacts their beliefs, norms, and observed behavior
- Social networks are dynamic entities that change as actors, subgroups, and ties between actors enter, form, leave, or are removed from the network

Interdependence of Actors

SNA assumes that actors do not make decisions autonomously; instead they are substantially influenced by the behavior and choices of other actors. This assumption differs substantially from a "pure" rational choice perspective where actors act independently of those with whom they interact.[5] Studies

---

[5] As we saw in the previous chapter, however, rational choice theories seldom hold such a pure assumption.

2.3 Assumptions

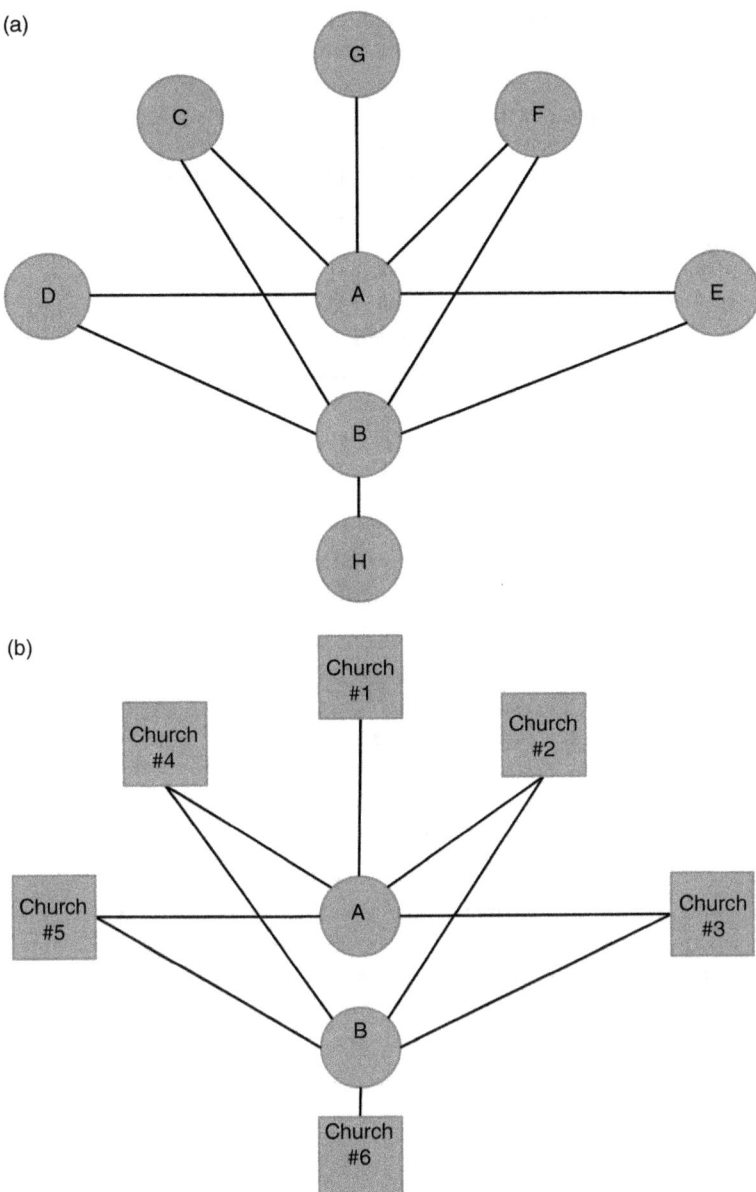

Figure 2.2 Illustrative social network analysis diagrams

such as Solomon Asch's (1951, 1955) social conformity experiments, Stanley Milgram's (1974) obedience to authority experiments, and Philip Zimbardo's (1972; Zimbardo, Maslasch, and Haney 2000) prison experiment all highlight how the networks in which actors are embedded influence their behavior. They suggest that far from acting independently of those around them, people do just the opposite. In the face of peer pressure, Asch's student subjects chose to go along with the crowd even when the correct answer was obvious. Milgram's subjects made choices in the presence of authority that they probably would not have done in a different context. And in just a few days, Zimbardo's guards devolved into a surprising level of brutality that foreshadowed the Abu Ghraib prison debacle almost thirty years later (Wikipedia 2015a).

Individuals are not the only actors that are influenced by other actors. For example, John Meyer, Woody Powell, and Paul DiMaggio (and their numerous collaborators) have demonstrated that groups, corporations, and nation-states are no more likely to act autonomously than are individuals (see, e.g., Meyer and Rowan 1977; DiMaggio and Powell 1983; Powell and DiMaggio 1991; Meyer et al. 1997; Frank, Hironaka, and Schofer 2000). The more they interact with one another, the more alike one another they become over time. They do this not necessarily for instrumental reasons, but in order to maintain their legitimacy in the eyes of other similar actors (DiMaggio and Powell 1983).

> When an organizational practice or structure becomes commonly understood as a defining feature of a "legitimate" organization of a certain type, organizational elites feel pressure to institute that practice or structure. If there is a cultural norm that says, "In order for an organization to be a good organization, it must have characteristic X," organizations feel pressure to institute characteristic X.
>
> (Chaves 1997:32–33)

Indeed, as we will see in Chapter 5, during the twentieth century, religious denominations were far more likely to approve the ordination of women if they had a tie to a denomination that has already begun ordaining women (Chaves 1996).

Ties as Conduits

Another assumption is that ties (i.e., relations) between actors function as conduits for the flow of various types of material and nonmaterial "goods," such as information, feelings, financial resources, norms, diseases, opinions, and trust. Perhaps, the best known example of this is Granovetter's (1973, 1974) study of how people found their present jobs. He discovered that when it came to finding jobs, people were far more likely to use personal contacts than other means. Moreover, of those who found their jobs through personal contacts, most of those contacts were weak (i.e., acquaintances) rather than strong ties (i.e., close friends). Why? Because our weak

2.3 Assumptions

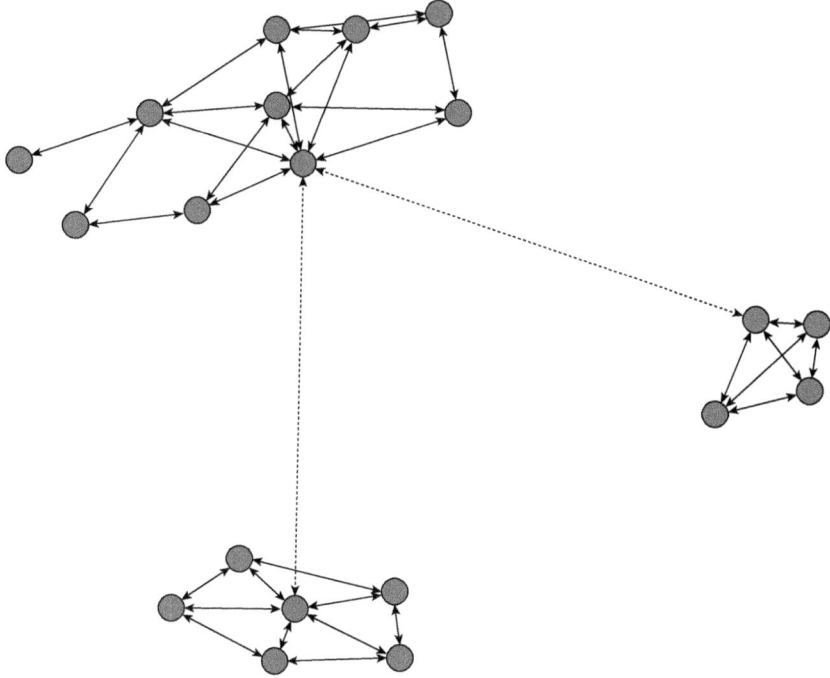

Figure 2.3 Strong and weak ties

ties are less likely to be socially involved with one another than are our strong ties. Thus, the set of people making up our network of acquaintances tends to be relatively sparse, while the set of people making up our network of close friends tends to be relatively dense. Consider the pattern of social ties suggested by this argument (Figure 2.3).[6] Most people will have a few close friends, most of whom know one another. They will also probably have several acquaintances, few of whom know one another. However, each of these acquaintances is likely to have close friends in their own right, so they are also likely to be embedded in tightly knit networks of their own but ones different from our original individual. According to Granovetter, weak ties are important in terms of the overall structure of a network because they form the crucial bridges that tie together densely knit clusters of people. In fact, without them, such clusters would not be connected at all.

This led Granovetter to argue that "whatever is to be diffused" – whether it is job information, influence, resources, trust, etc. – it "will reach a larger number of people, and travel a greater social distance (i.e., path length), when passed through weak rather than strong ties"

---

[6] Figure 2.3 was created in Pajek (Batagelj and Mrvar 2017).

(Granovetter 1973:1366). Because of this, actors with few weak ties are more likely to be "confined to the provincial news and views of their close friends" (Granovetter 1983:202). Moreover, groups or communities whose members lack weak ties will find it more difficult to mobilize on behalf of a goal. For example, comparing two attempts of community organizing, one that succeeded and one that did not, Granovetter (1973: 1373–1376) argued that a key difference between the two was that the unsuccessful one lacked the weak ties it needed in order to bind its various social circles together. This left it severely fragmented – something that it could not overcome.

This is not to imply that strong ties are of little or no value. Feelings of trust and solidarity are more likely to be shared across strong ties than weak ones. Thus, while weak ties provide individuals with access to information and resources beyond those available in their immediate social circles, strong ties have greater motivation to be sources of support in times of uncertainty (Krackhardt 1992). In fact, people with numerous strong ties are more likely to be happier and enjoy better health, which is a primary reason why frequent churchgoers tend to live longer: They are much more likely to be embedded in networks consisting of numerous strong ties (see Chapter 8).

Social Structure and Emergent Social Formations

Social scientists frequently refer to the concept of social structure. By this term, they usually have in mind the enduring patterns of behavior and relationships within social systems (e.g., roles) or the social institutions and norms that have become embedded in social systems in such a way that they shape behavior. Social structures "constrain who is present, where they stand, what they can do, and how they are related to each other. This structure is as real as the buildings that people occupy" (Turner 2006:88). However, while social structure may be as real as the buildings that people occupy, it is notoriously difficult to capture empirically, which is one reason why many find SNA attractive. SNA conceptualizes social structures in terms of enduring patterns of ties between actors. Thus, it provides a method for systematically and empirically studying the causes and consequences of social structure.

Most social network analysts also hold that repeated interactions between actors (e.g., individuals) can give rise to emergent social formations (e.g., groups, formal organizations, nations) that follow their own logic and cannot be reduced to or explained by their constituent parts even though they remain dependent upon those parts (Clayton and Davies 2006; White 2008). Examples of emergence abound in the physical world, such as the combination of hydrogen (H) and oxygen (O) into water (H_2O) (Smith 2010:27). And much like water, such emergent social

2.3 Assumptions

formations cannot be reduced to or explained entirely by their underlying actors, although they are still dependent upon them. Instead, they take on a life of their own, which means that actors of all types and levels – whether they are individuals, groups, churches, denominations, or nations – can be examined using SNA without the need to examine the lower-level actors of which they are comprised.

Structural Location: Beliefs, Norms, Intentions, Behavior, and Identity

Emergent social formations have the potential to exert what is referred to as downward causation, which is why SNA assumes that actors' attitudes, beliefs, intentions, behavior, and even their identities are largely determined by their location in the social structure. This assumption is at odds with what many moderns believe to be true:

> Humans come to believe in a world full of continuous, neatly bounded, self-propelling individuals whose intentions interact with accidents and natural limits to produce all of social life ... Closely observed, however, these same humans turn out to be interacting repeatedly with others, renegotiating who they are, adjusting the boundaries they occupy, modifying their actions in rapid response to other peoples' reactions, selecting among and altering available scripts, improvising new forms of joint action, speaking sentences no one has ever uttered before, yet responding predictably to their locations within webs of social relations they themselves cannot map in detail.
> (McAdam, Tarrow and Tilly 2001:131)

As we will see in the next chapter, research has repeatedly found that people who are located structurally (i.e., socially) close to a particular movement, religious or otherwise, are much more likely to join that movement than are those who are not (Lofland and Stark 1965; Snow, Zurcher, and Ekland-Olson 1980; McAdam 1986, 1988b; Sageman 2004; see also Stark 1996a:13–21; Stark and Bainbridge 1980a). In other words, people tend not to join groups randomly. Instead, they are more likely to join those groups where they already know someone than those where they do not.

Dynamic Social Networks

Finally, social network analysis assumes that networks are dynamic. They are always changing as actors enter and leave the network and as ties form and dissolve. They can grow or shrink in size, become more or less fragmented, or increase or decrease their level of centralization. Groups of actors may cluster together at some points in time and not in others, and actors that were central at one point may become less so later (and vice versa). To make matters more complicated, actors also move from one geographic location to another, which can potentially affect a network's operations. Historically, longitudinal network data have been difficult to come by, and methods for examining them undeveloped. Indeed, Stanley Wasserman and Katherine Faust's classic *Social Network Analysis: Methods and Applications* makes little mention of longitudinal networks. Only the book's final chapter discusses the importance of developing good and easy-to-use methods for examining longitudinal network data (Wasserman and Faust 1994:730–731).

Luckily, longitudinal network data are becoming more common. Much of the analysis to date has been largely descriptive, but in recent years social network analysts have developed a number of different approaches for teasing out patterns and processes from longitudinal data (Doreian and Stockman 1997; Breiger, Carley, and Pattison 2003; Snijders 2005; Snijders, Bunt, and Steglich 2010; Steglich, Snijders, and Pearson 2010; de Nooy 2011; McCulloh and Carley 2011). As appealing and promising as these models are, as of yet most do not fall into Wasserman and Faust's "easy-to-use" category and often require specialized software. In Chapter 10 we will see an example of these more advanced methods when we examine the evolution of the sixteenth-century Anabaptist leadership network, a portion of which became involved in one of the more violent episodes during the Protestant Reformation: the Münster Rebellion.

Summary: Social Networks, Human Agency, and Culture

The priority that social network analysis places on relations between actors over individual attributes inevitably leads to questions of human agency and culture. In short, does SNA leave room for free will and the effects of culture? Yes and no. Some versions do. Some do not. Mustafa Emirbayer and Jeff Goodwin (1994:1424–1436) have identified three social network paradigms to which most social network analysts adhere: structural determinism, instrumentalism, and constructionism. *Structural determinism* entirely ignores (or dismisses) the possible causal role that actors' beliefs, values, and commitments play in terms of social processes and historical change. The early writings of Harrison White (Boorman and White 1976; White, Boorman, and Breiger 1976) reflect this view, as do those of the early network theorist Bruce Mayhew (1980, 1981). As far as Mayhew was concerned, individuals are no more than biological machines, and human consciousness is irrelevant to understanding the social world.

By contrast *structural instrumentalism* does allow room for human agency but frames it solely in terms of rational choice, instrumental action, and utility maximization. Roger Gould's analysis of the Paris Commune (1991, 1993b) and Nan Lin's work on social capital (Lin 2001) are examples, as well as the work of many of the rational choice theorists we encountered in the previous chapter (see, e.g., Stark and Bainbridge 1980a; Stark 1991, 1996a, 1996b; Finke and Stark 1992; Iannaccone, Finke, and Stark 1997). Given that ample evidence exists supporting the premise that actors do respond to incentives (see, e.g., Becker 1976; Iannaccone 1995; Levitt and Dubner 2005; Berman 2009), this approach clearly improves on the previous one. Nevertheless, it is not without its critics.

Structural constructionism, like structural instrumentalism, takes seriously the role of human agency, but unlike structural instrumentalism, it sees actors as motivated by additional concerns, such as norms, values, cultural commitments, and collective and individual identities. David Knoke, for instance, argues that "a sophisticated understanding of ... action requires blending cultural, rational, and structural constraints in complex specifications for given substantive problems" (Knoke 1990:19). Doug McAdam's studies of Freedom Summer (McAdam 1986, 1988a, 1988b) illustrate this approach, as do the later writings of Harrison White (1992, 2008), with their emphasis on the importance of narratives, stories, and networks of meaning.

While social network methodologies tend to be agnostic on issues of structure, culture, and human agency, it often helps to make analytical distinctions between the cultural influences, normative commitments, and instrumental concerns of actors. Consider, for example, the issues surrounding the collection of kinship network data. What constitutes a kinship network in the West can differ considerably from what constitutes one in some Middle Eastern and Asian cultures. Thus, if an analyst were to code a Middle Eastern kinship network guided by Western assumptions, the resulting data could turn out to be utterly useless. Moreover, since instrumental ties may exert different effects on actors than cultural ties, it only makes methodological sense to account for them separately.

2.4 Terms and Concepts

Actors and Ties

As noted earlier, actors can come in all shapes and sizes (e.g., individuals, groups, synagogues, denominations, and nations). The same can be said of ties. They can vary in terms of type, strength, and directionality. Types of ties include (but are not limited to) ties of sentiment (e.g., friendship, acquaintance, like and dislike), biology (e.g., spouse, sibling, cousin), shared affiliation (e.g., members of the same church, mosque, synagogue, or ecumenical organization), communication (e.g., prayer chains, phone calls, email, tweets), and so on. Moreover, ties can vary from strong to weak (Granovetter 1973, 1974) although the cutoff between a strong and a weak tie is not always obvious (Krackhardt 1992), nor is the distinction between a weak tie and the numerous, random, and usually unrepeated encounters actors experience on a daily basis (Azarian 2005:37). Some ties have directionality (arcs) while others do not (edges); both capture the flow of resources from one actor to another, the communication between actors (e.g., actor A may repeatedly send emails to actor B, but B does not reciprocate), which actors seek advice from other actors (Krackhardt 1992), and so on. Finally, most actors are connected to others by multiple ties (see, e.g., the discussion of the Sampson monastery data in the following paragraphs); in fact, one of the challenges of SNA is determining which ties should be modeled.

Social Network

A social network is a finite set or sets of actors that share ties with one another (Wasserman and Faust 1994:21). Figure 2.4 depicts a hypothetical social network where the circles represent actors and the lines represent ties or relations.[7] As it illustrates, actors often cluster within relatively distinct subgroups. Moreover, some are embedded in the center of these subgroups while others are located more on the periphery, sometimes serving as bridges between subgroups.[8]

Social networks vary in size. Figure 2.5, for instance, presents a network map of the Sampson monastery data, which is a relatively small network (eighteen actors). The data were recorded by Samuel Sampson (1968), who spent a year in a Roman Catholic monastery in the late 1960s observing the social interactions among a group of novices (i.e., men preparing to join a monastic order). During his stay, a "crisis in the cloister" developed in reaction to the changes introduced by Vatican II; it resulted in the expulsion of four novices and the voluntary departure of several others.[9] Based on his observations, Sampson partitioned (i.e., sorted, divided) the novices into four groups: (1) the young Turks, (2) the loyal opposition, (3) the outcasts, and (4) the neutrals. The young Turks arrived later than the other novices and

---

[7] Figures 2.4 through 2.11 were created in R using either the *igraph* (Csárdi and Nepusz 2006) or the *sna* (Butts 2014) libraries.
[8] Generally, ties with direction are referred to as "arcs," whereas ties without direction are referred to as "edges."
[9] Vatican II was a conference of all the bishops and cardinals of the Roman Catholic Church who met from 1962 to 1965; it introduced numerous changes in order to modernize the Church (Finke and Stark 2005; Stark and Finke 2000b).

2.4 Terms and Concepts

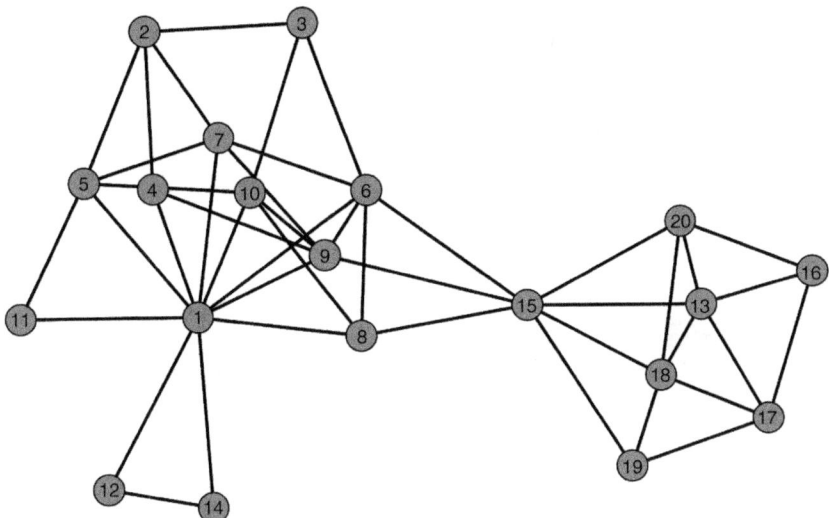

Figure 2.4 Hypothetical social network

questioned some of the monastery's practices, which were then defended by members of the loyal opposition, most of whom attended seminary together before arriving at the monastery. The outcasts were those who were not accepted into the larger group, and the neutrals were those who did not take sides in the debate. Sampson coded four types of ties of sentiment (i.e., like, dislike, esteem, disesteem). He had each novice rank his top three choices for each type of tie, although some offered tied ranks for their top four choices. All of the ties were recorded at a single time period, except for "liking," which were recorded at several. Note that not all of the ties were reciprocal (the arrows did not point in both directions). For instance, Ambrose indicated that he liked Winfrid, but Winfrid apparently did not feel the same way.

Figure 2.6 presents a somewhat larger network, the 1985 US interdenominational network where actors are denominations (e.g., the Episcopal Church) and the ties between them indicate that they share at least one common ecumenical affiliation (e.g., the National Council of Churches, the National Association of Evangelicals).[10] As one can see there are two main clusters. Unsurprisingly, one consists primarily of mainline Protestant denominations and the other primarily of evangelical Protestant denominations. Nevertheless, there are a handful of denominations with ties to both groups – the Church of the Brethren, the Baptist General Conference, and the Evangelical Church – and, as such, are lying

---

[10] Network data graciously provided by Mark Chaves.

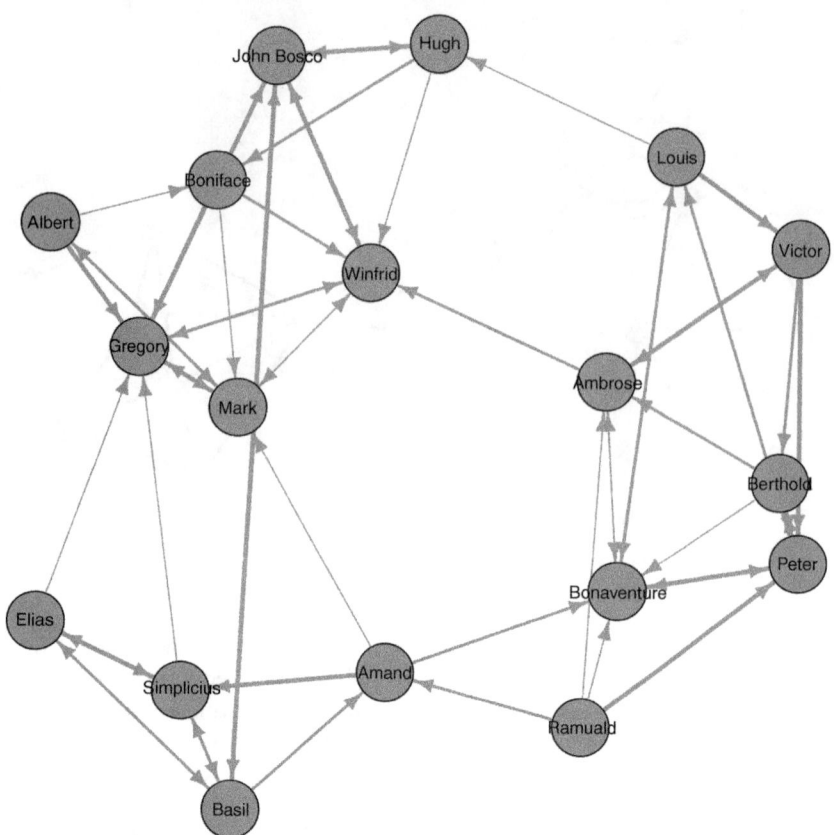

Figure 2.5 Sampson monastery, liking time 3

in a position of brokerage in the network (see "Brokers and Bridges" later in this chapter).

The networks in Figures 2.5 and 2.6 are what social network analysts call one-mode networks. One-mode networks consist of a single set of actors, such as people, groups, families, tribes, organizations, corporations, nation-states, etc. Two-mode networks differ from one-mode networks in that they either consist of two sets of different actors, or one set of actors and one set of events or affiliations. Examples of two-mode networks include membership in various organizations, attendance at particular events, employees at a particular company, and so on. Figure 2.7 presents an example of a two-mode network. It is the same denominational network as the one presented in Figure 2.6, except here both the denominations and ecumenical organizations (and the ties between them) are shown.

2.4 Terms and Concepts

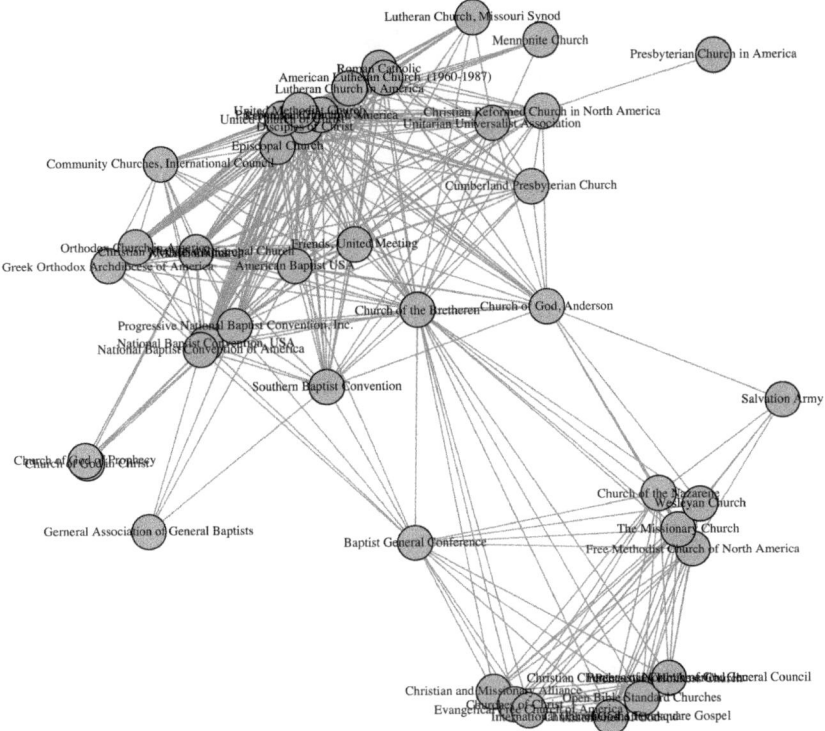

Figure 2.6 US interdenominational network, 1985 [author's analysis of data used in Chaves (1996)]

Path (and Path Distance)

A *path* is defined as a *walk* (i.e., a sequence of actors and ties) in which no actor between the first and last actor of the walk occurs more than once, whereas the *path distance* between two actors is the number of steps between the two actors. In Figure 2.4 you can trace a path from actor 9 to actor 19 through actor 15, and the path from actor 6 to actor 11 through actor 1. In both cases the distance between the actors is two (i.e., two steps). It is quite common for there to be numerous paths between actors. The shortest path between two actors is called the *geodesic*, and a network's longest geodesic is considered the network's *diameter*. Actors that can reach one another via a path are considered to be in the same *component*. Networks may have multiple components, and in such cases, they are considered to be *disconnected*. The smallest component that a network can have is a single actor with no ties to other actors. These single actors are referred to as *isolates*.

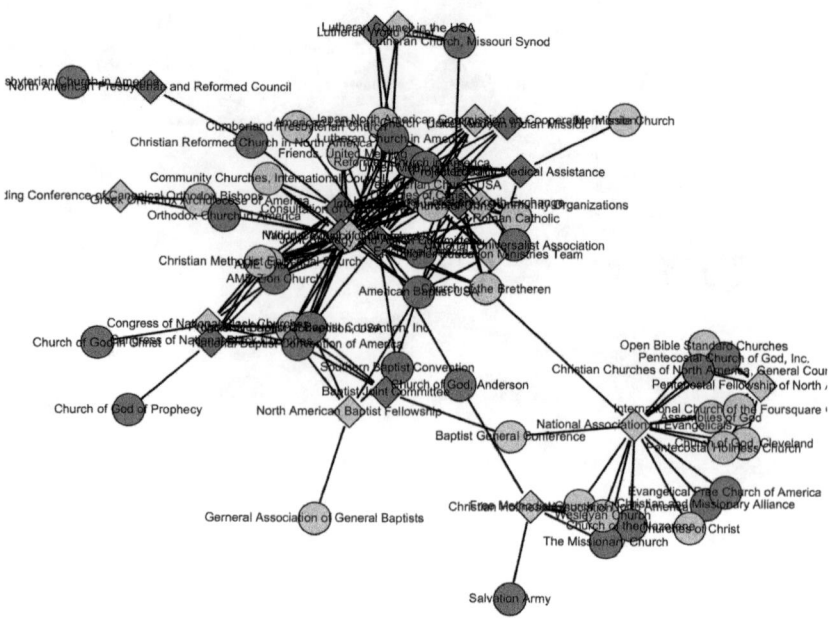

Figure 2.7 US denomination and ecumenical organization network, 1985 [author's analysis of data used in Chaves (1996)]

Perhaps the best known studies of path distance are the small world studies of Stanley Milgram and his colleagues (Milgram 1967; Travers and Milgram 1969; Korte and Milgram 1970), which sought to discover how far, on average, randomly selected individuals are from one another (in terms of path distance). Using a creative message-passing technique, Milgram sent a package to people living in Wichita (Kansas), Omaha (Nebraska), Boston (Massachusetts), and Los Angeles (California). The people living in Wichita were asked to send the packages to the wife of a divinity school student living in Boston. The people living in Omaha and Boston were asked to send the packages to a single target person: a stockbroker from Sharon, Massachusetts, who worked in Boston. And the people living in Los Angeles were asked to send the packages to one of eighteen target persons (all males, nine black, nine white) located around the country.

Table 2.1 presents the results of the studies. In the Nebraska study, 217 of the 296 starting persons actually sent the documents on to friends, but in the end only 64 of the 296 letters reached the target person, with an average path length of 5.2 steps.[11] Milgram did not publish the results

[11] Some question the validity of Milgram's studies since so many chains were not completed (Kleinfeld 2002). However, analysis suggests there was no systematic bias to the dropout

Table 2.1 *Summary of Milgram's small world studies*

Study	Starting Person (Location)	#	Target Person	Completed #	%	Path Length
Wichita	Wichita – random	60	Student's wife	3	5	~8.0
Nebraska	Nebraska – random	96	Boston stockholder	18	19	5.7
	Nebraska – stockholders	100	Boston stockholder	24	24	5.4
	Boston – random	100	Boston stockholder	22	22	4.4
Los Angeles	Los Angeles	270	White males (9)	88	33	5.5
	Los Angeles	270	Black males (9)	35	13	5.9
Totals		896		190	21	~5.5

from his Kansas study – it was more of a pilot study – but very few of the letters found their way to the target person. However, he did mention in a 1967 *Psychology Today* article that four days after he sent out the packages, an instructor at the Episcopal Theological Seminary in Boston approached the target person on the street. "Alice," he said, handing a package to her, "this is for you." Evidently, the package had initially been sent to a farmer, who then passed it on to an Episcopal priest in his hometown, who then sent it on to the instructor who taught at the Episcopal seminary in Boston, who then gave it to the target person. As it turned out, this was one of the shortest chains Milgram ever found – the number of intermediaries ranged anywhere from one to ten. The Los Angeles study was the largest: 540 individuals received packets, of which 123 reached the target person (21 percent) with an average path length of around 5.6 steps. Interestingly, however, where the target person was white, the chain was nearly three times more likely to be completed and the path length was almost one-half of a step shorter.[12]

When Milgram spoke to groups of people about his studies, he often asked them how many steps they thought it would take to get a letter from one place to another. They typically estimated the number to be in the hundreds. The result was closer to six, which is where the phrase "six degrees of separation" originates. And although the idea that any two individuals in the world are only separated by "six degrees of separation" is now a part of American culture, at the time of Milgram's study, most found the results quite surprising.

Topography

A network's topography can vary along several dimensions. For example, analysts can measure a network's *size* (the number of actors in a network), its *average distance* (the average length of the geodesics between all actors in a network), and its *diameter*. Two of the more common topographical measures are density and centralization.

---

rate, suggesting that the chain length was representative of the entire sample (White 1970). More recent small world studies have returned similar results (Dodds, Muhamad, and Watts 2003; Watts, Dodds, and Newman 2003). For instance, Jure Leskovec and Eric Horvitz (2007) examined a data set of instant messages composed of 30 billion conversations among 240 million people and found the average path length among Microsoft Messenger users was six.

[12] Granovetter (1973) analyzed the chains where white senders were to send the packet to a black target. He found that when the packet was first passed from a white individual to a black individual, the chain was much more likely to be completed if it passed through a weak tie rather than a strong one. "In 50% of the instances where the white described this Negro as an 'acquaintance,' the chain was ultimately completed; completion rate fell to 26%, however, when the white sent the booklet to a Negro 'friend.' ... Thus, weaker interracial ties can be seen as more effective in bridging social distance" (Granovetter 1973:1368–1369).

2.4 Terms and Concepts

Density captures the interconnectedness of a network and is equal to the ratio of actual ties to possible ties. Unfortunately, the formal measure of density is inversely related to network size (i.e., all else being equal, the density of larger networks tends to be lower than the density of smaller networks). Thus, social network analysts often turn to alternative measures for capturing a network's interconnectedness, such as average degree centrality, the clustering coefficient, and cohesion/fragmentation. *Centralization* measures the extent to which a network is centralized around a single actor or handful of actors. Multiple centralization measures exist, and they vary in terms on which centrality measure is used (see the description of basic centrality measures in the following paragraphs). The standard centralization measure, which is typically called network centralization, calculates a variance score based on the difference between each actor's centrality score to the highest centrality score in the network. An alternative measure (variance/standard deviation) calculates a variance score based on the difference between each actor's centrality score to the average centrality score in the network. For both, the greater the level of variance, the higher the degree of centralization.

Dense networks typically consist of numerous strong ties and very few weak ones, while sparse networks are just the opposite. The former are sometimes referred to as provincial networks, while the latter are referred to as cosmopolitan (Everton 2012a, 2012b), and existing research suggests that networks that lie somewhere between the two extremes (suburban networks?) are more effective or resilient than those that do not (Pescosolido and Georgianna 1989; Uzzi 1996; Uzzi and Spiro 2005). Indeed, in Chapter 8, we will see that individuals whose networks are neither too dense nor too sparse are much less likely to commit suicide than those whose networks are closer to the extremes. Similarly, studies indicate that networks that are neither too centralized nor too decentralized are more effective than those that lie on the extremes. Why? On the one hand, a high level of centralization can provide organizations with substantial command and control over their operations, but it can make them slow to adapt to a changing environment. On the other hand, organizations that are highly decentralized may be able to change course quickly, but they may lack the command and control needed to get everyone on the same page.

For example, Rodney Stark (1996b) has found that religious movements that maintain a balance between topographical extremes are more likely to survive (and thrive) beyond the first generation. He notes that it is crucial for religious movements to be sufficiently dense (i.e., strong internal attachments) in order to reinforce norms and monitor behavior but not so much that they cut themselves off from the surrounding society.

They also must be centralized enough that their leaders possess sufficient authority to exert influence over their movements, but not to such an extent that nonleaders are motivated to work on the group's behalf. He holds up the Church of Jesus Christ of Latter-day Saints (i.e., LDS, Mormon Church) as an example:

> It would be wrong to stress only the hierarchical nature of LDS authority and its authoritarian aspects, for the Latter-day Saints display an amazing degree of amateur participation at all levels of their formal structure. Moreover, this highly authoritarian body also displays extraordinary levels of participatory democracy – to a considerable extent the rank-and-file Saints are the church. A central aspect of this is that among the Latter-day Saints to be a priest is an unpaid, part-time role that all committed males are expected to fulfill.
>
> (Stark 2005:125)

Subgroups (Clusters, Subnetworks)

A major focus of SNA is to identify subgroups of actors "among whom there are relatively strong, direct, intense, and/or positive ties" (Wasserman and Faust 1994:249). As with network topography, there are numerous methods for identifying clusters of actors although all assume that ties between subgroup members should be more numerous than ties between members of other groups. Figure 2.8 presents the same Sampson monastery data we saw in Figure 2.5, except that here what is called a community detection algorithm has been used to identify subgroups within the network. Although in this case we probably did not need an algorithm to sort the novices into distinct groups, identifying subgroups is often not as straightforward as it is here, which is why clustering algorithms can be quite valuable. The most common are components (weak and strong), cliques, k-cores, community detection algorithms, and factions. As we will see in Chapter 9, there are also algorithms for taking into account positive and negative ties. See Appendix A for discussion of these.

Centrality

Most social networks contain people or organizations that are more central than others, and because of this, they enjoy better access to resources and are in better positions to spread information. Social network analysts have identified several measures of centrality, each

2.4 Terms and Concepts

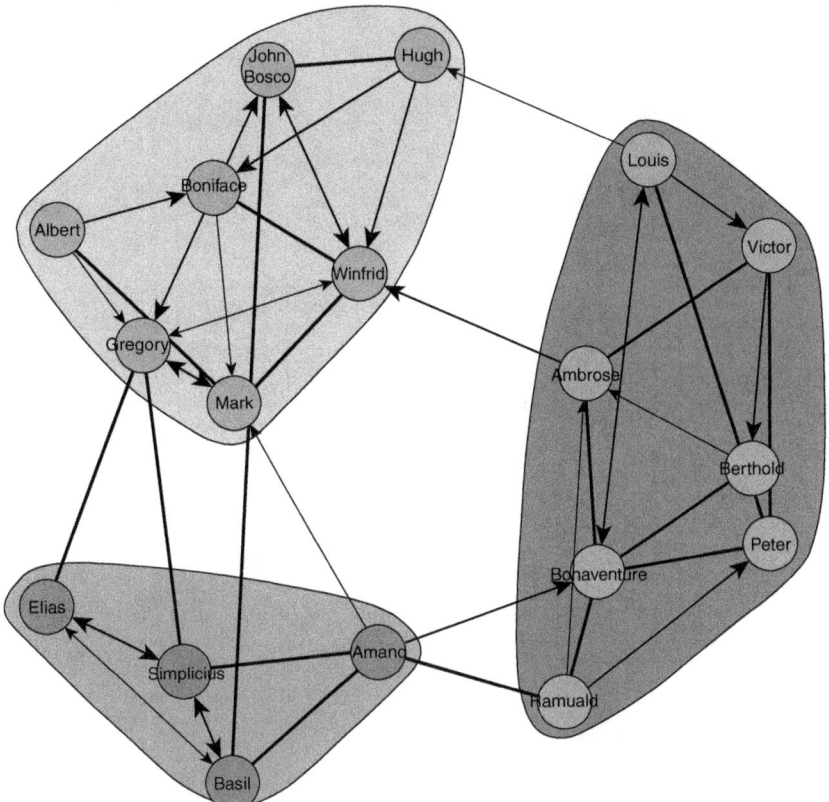

Figure 2.8 Sampson monastery, liking time 3 with community detection

based on different assumptions of what it means for an actor to be central. Four of the more common measures are

- degree centrality, which is a count of the number of an actor's ties
- closeness centrality, which measures, on average, how close (in terms of path distance) each actor is to all other actors in a network
- betweenness centrality, which measures the extent to which each actor lies on the shortest path between all other actors in a network
- eigenvector centrality, which assumes that ties to highly central actors are more important than ties to peripheral actors, so it weights an actor's summed ties to other actors by their centrality

70 Social Network Analysis: A Brief Introduction

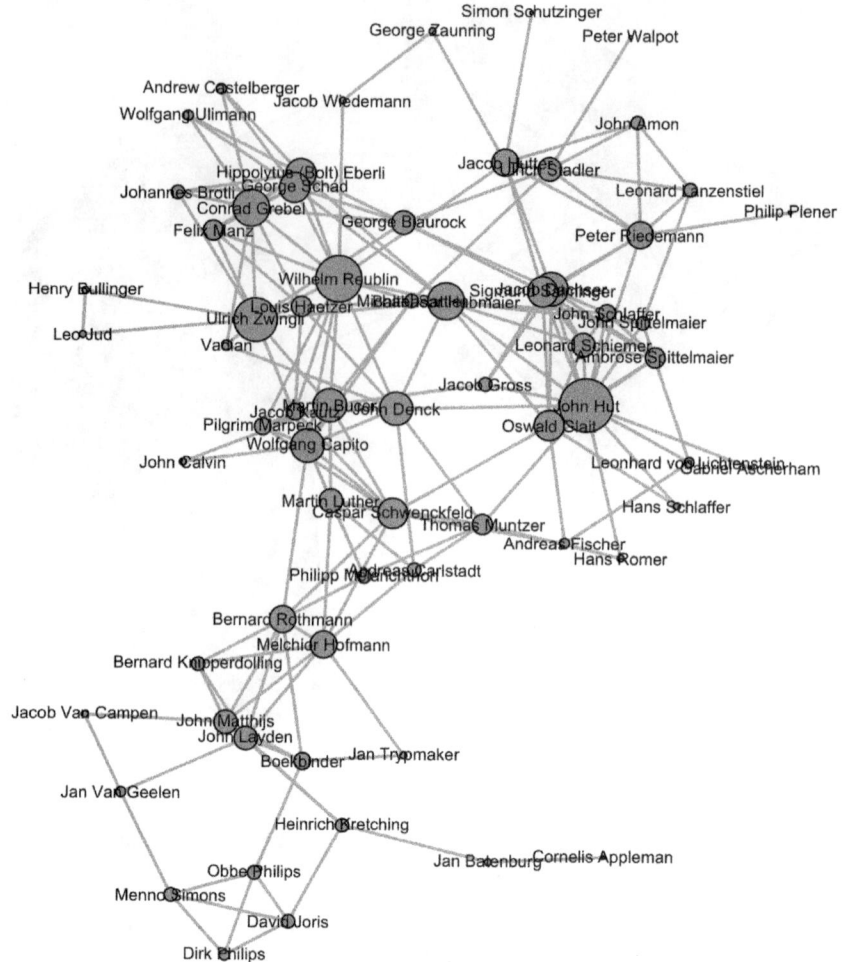

Figure 2.9 Sixteenth-century Anabaptist leadership network (degree centrality)

Figure 2.9 presents a sixteenth-century Anabaptist leadership network where the size of each node varies in terms of its degree centrality. As it illustrates, some Anabaptist leaders had far more ties than did others. John Hut, in particular, stands out, but there are others, such as Balthasar Hubmaier and Oswald Glait, who had numerous connections. Another actor included in the network, Ulrich Zwingli, was not an Anabaptist, but he had a profound influence on the Anabaptist movement, which is why he is included in the network. Perhaps most interesting is how peripheral Menno Simons is in the network since one of the most prominent

2.4 Terms and Concepts

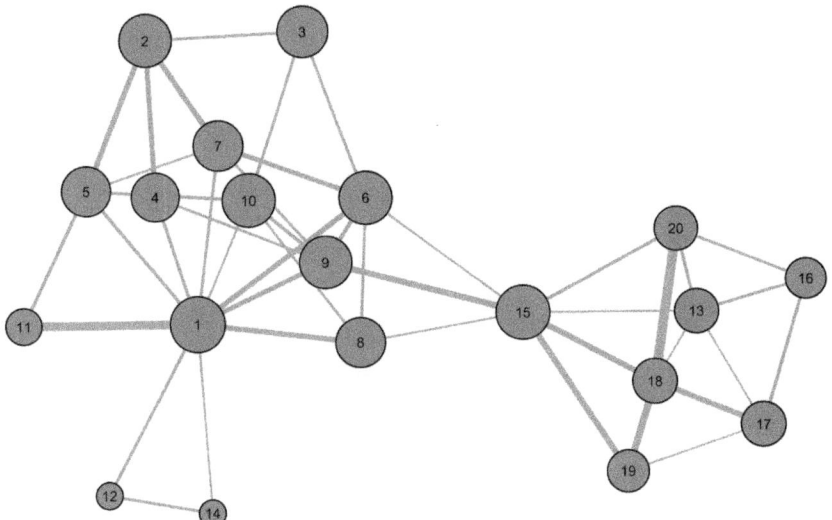

Figure 2.10 Hypothetical social network (brokers and bridges)

Anabaptist groups in existence today takes its name from him (i.e., the Mennonites).

Brokers and Bridges

Bridges are ties that span gaps in a social network; brokers are actors that sit aside such bridges. Both can be seen as being in a position to control the flow of resources through a network. In terms of Figure 2.4, the edges between actor 15 and actors 6, 8, and 9 could all be considered bridges, whereas the four actors themselves would be considered brokers. That said, because actor 15 sits aside all three bridges while the other three actors sit aside only one, actor 15 is clearly in more of a position of brokerage than are actors 6, 8, and 9. Indeed, if actor 15 left the network, it would fragment into two separate networks. Rather than trying to guess who are brokers and what ties are bridges, numerous algorithms have been designed to detect them.

Figure 2.10 presents the network from Figure 2.4, except now the size of the node reflects Ronald Burt's (1992b) structural holes measure, perhaps the best known brokerage measure, and the width of the ties reflects edge betweenness centrality, a metric that is sometimes used to detect bridges between clusters. The larger the node, the more brokerage potential it possesses, and the thicker the tie, the more likely it is a bridge. Here we can see that actor 15 possesses considerable brokerage potential, but it appears that the tie to actor 9 is more crucial than the ties to actor 6

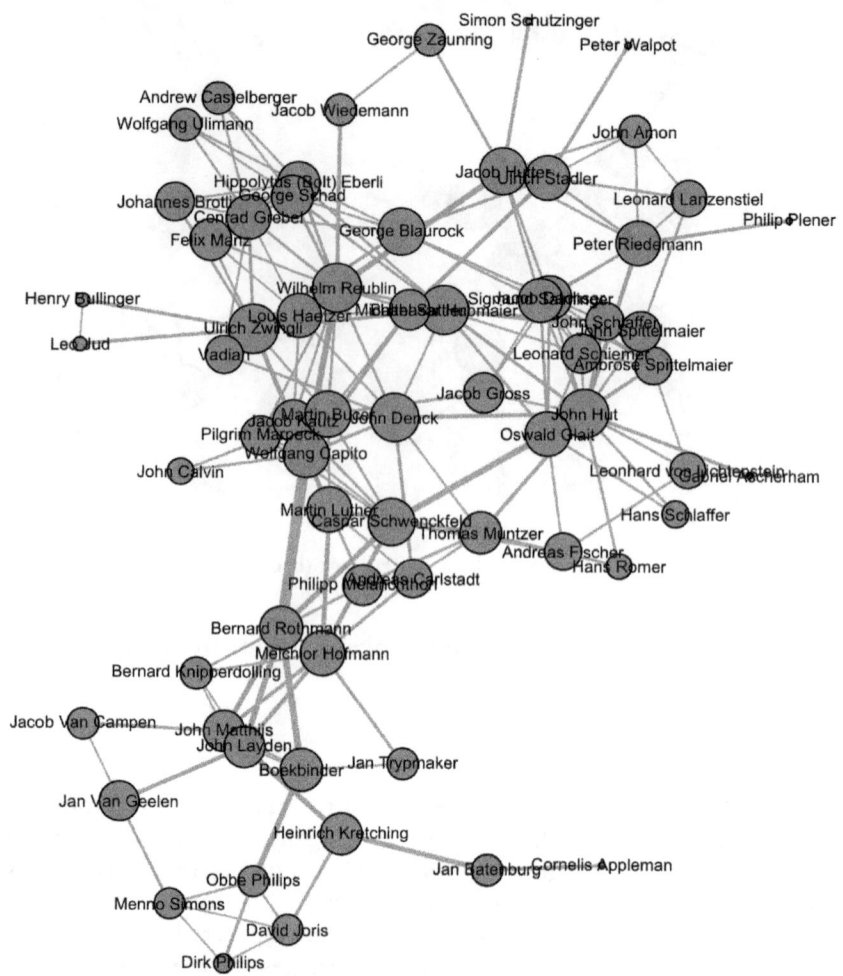

Figure 2.11 Sixteenth-century Anabaptist leadership network (brokers and bridges)

and actor 8. Actor 1 is also in a position of brokerage, primarily because of his or her ties to actors 12 and 14.

A similar analysis of the sixteenth-century Anabaptist leadership network is presented in Figure 2.11. Here again, the larger the node (betweenness centrality), the more brokerage potential it possesses, while the thicker the tie (edge betweenness), the more likely it is a bridge. Looking for a combination of larger nodes lying next to thicker ties, it appears that Oswald Glait and Caspar Schwenckfeld may have functioned as brokers in this leadership network.

2.4 Terms and Concepts

Roles and Positions

Social network analysts typically analyze network data in one of two ways: (1) a relational or social connectivity approach or (2) a positional approach (Emirbayer and Goodwin 1994). The former focuses on the direct and indirect ties among actors and seeks to explain behavior and social processes in light of those ties (Emirbayer and Goodwin 1994:1419). By contrast, the positional approach seeks to identify structurally equivalent actors – that is, actors who may or may not have ties with one another but who hold a similar position within a particular social network (e.g., the pastors of different congregations, the chairs of religious studies departments in different academic institutions, the heads of different denominations, and so on). This approach assumes (among other things) that structurally equivalent actors are likely to behave in similar ways regardless of whether a tie exists between them.

Structurally equivalent positions can be observed by looking at the actors to whom a particular is connected (e.g., a pastor interacts with congregants; the chair of a religious studies department interacts with graduate students, other professors, chairs of other departments, and university administrators; the head of a denomination interacts with other denominational officers and various ecumenical organizations). "The relevant issue from this point of view is the specific 'position' or 'role' that a set of actors occupies within the system as a whole. Any such set is termed a 'block'" (Emirbayer and Goodwin 1994:1422), and the process by which such blocks are identified is referred to as blockmodeling (White, Boorman, and Breiger 1976). Analysts have developed a number of different types of algorithms for identifying structurally equivalent actors (e.g., structural equivalence, automorphic equivalence, regular equivalence) and multiple algorithms within each of these types.

Explanatory Social Network Analysis: QAP, ERGMs, and SAOMs

Social network methods can be roughly sorted into two broad categories: exploratory and explanatory. Exploratory methods are those that can help analysts identify central actors, highlight aspects about a network's structure, locate subgroups, illuminate brokers and bridges, and find structurally equivalent actors. Although these methods are quite common and useful, they only help analysts describe network data. They do not allow us to understand the underlying causes of observed patterns and trends. By contrast, explanatory methods are more focused on verification of the findings that arise from exploratory and qualitative analyses. One way to think about it is that exploratory analyses can assist us in developing hypotheses, whereas explanatory approaches, such as QAP, ERGMs, and SAOMs, can help us test them.

Because social network data are seldom random and they "violate" (by definition) the assumption of observational independence, social network analysts have developed various models that account for the uniqueness of social network data. The three most common are quadratic assignment procedure (QAP), exponential random graph models (ERGMs), and stochastic actor-oriented models (SAOMs). QAP is similar to standard regression models, except that it uses a method analogous to bootstrapping in order to estimate standard errors and statistical significance. ERGMs and SAOMs are more unique in that they examine how an observed social network is a function of underlying patterns of ties (e.g., dyads, triangles, etc.). ERGMs are generally used for social network at a single point in time,[13] while SAOMs are designed for longitudinal data. We consider QAP and ERGMs in Chapter 3, and SAOMs in Chapter 10.

Attributes

While social network analysis focuses primarily on the pattern of ties between actors, most social network analysts do not completely ignore attribute data, which are characteristics of individual actors. If the actors in a network are individuals, then attribute data include things such as gender, race, ethnicity, years of education, income level, age, etc. If the actors are organizations, then attribute variables can be those that indicate size (e.g., number of members), age, type (e.g., denomination), and so on. And if the actors are countries, then attribute variables would include measures such as GDP per capita or population size. Centrality measures (once calculated) are attributes of actors as well. Sometimes the boundary between attributes and affiliations can be somewhat fuzzy. As a general rule, something is an affiliation if two actors' participation in it indicates a relationship (e.g., membership in an ecumenical organization), but it is also possible for an affiliation to function as an attribute as well.

2.5 Social Network Data

Social scientists have drawn on three types of network data in their studies of the interplay of religion and social networks: counts of network ties, ego network data, and whole network data. The first, counts of network ties, is the most common, but it does not

---

[13] Temporal ERGMS, known as TERGMs, are increasingly being used with longitudinal social network data.

2.5 Social Network Data

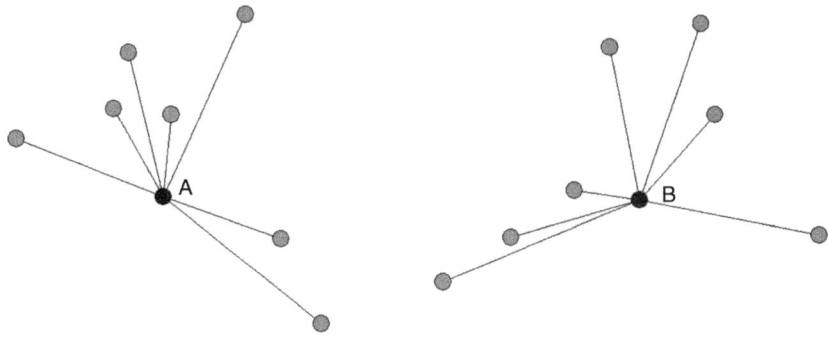

Figure 2.12 Counts of ties

adequately capture the networks in which individuals are embedded. The second, ego network data, represents an improvement over a simple count of ties but still has limitations. The last, whole network data, is the ideal type of data, but it is the most time-consuming to collect.

Counts of Ties

The most common form of network data used by social scientists studying religion is counts of ties. These counts are typically gathered through surveys with questions such as "How many of your close friends attend the same church (temple, synagogue) as you?" Unfortunately, such questions fail to capture the social context in which religious beliefs and practices are embedded. We do not know, for instance, whether any of a respondent's close friends have ties with one another. For example, in Figure 2.12 it is entirely possible that some of A's friends (gray nodes) are connected (tied) to one another.[14] The same may also be true of B's friends. Moreover, it is possible (probable) that the level of interconnectedness of A's friends differs from the level of interconnectedness of B's friends. With only counts of ties, however, there is no way to know.

As a consequence "most quantitative research on American religion is now based on surveys of unconnected individuals, with the result that the social context of religion is obscured" (Cheadle and Schwadel 2012:1198). This is not to suggest that scholars are necessarily happy with this state of affairs, but their hands are "tied by design and method" (Cheadle and Schwadel 2012:1199). The use of ego network data improves this situation somewhat.

---

[14] Figures 2.12 through 2.14 were created using NetDraw (Borgatti 2011).

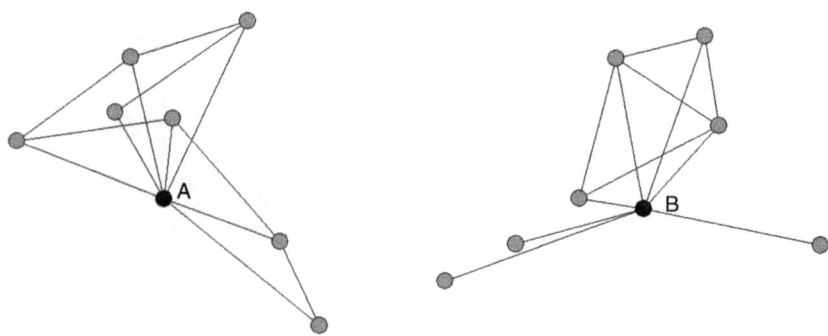

Figure 2.13 Hypothetical ego network

Ego Networks

An ego-centered approach focuses on an actor (typically termed "ego"), the set of actors (i.e., alters, neighbors) that have ties to the actor, and the ties among ego's alters. There are generally two ways of obtaining ego network data. One way is to use whole network data (see the discussion in the next section) and then extract the ego networks of an actor or set of actors. The other is to survey a random sample of individuals from whom ego network data are then collected. Each person surveyed is generally asked for a set of contacts (Burt 1984, 1985) using questions such as "Looking back over the last six months, who are the people with whom you discussed matters important to you?" After providing a list of contacts, he or she is then asked about the ties (if any) between the contacts (e.g., do they know one another, do they attend the same church, are they friends, and so on), as well as various attributes of the alters (e.g., gender, race, education level, etc.). This yields a data structure similar to that displayed in Figure 2.13. Note that these are the same actors as those in Figure 2.12 but now we can see the ties between A's and B's close friends. At a glance, we can see that A's ego network is denser than B's ego network.

Still, ego network data are limited because we do cannot know if there are connections between A's ego network and B's ego network. Moreover, the only properties that can be studied are the size (number of ego's connections), the density (the extent to which ego's contacts are tied to one another), the strength of ties connecting ego to his or her connections, and the brokerage potential between ego and his or her connections (Prell 2011).[15] Moreover, as several recent studies have documented (Fischer

---

[15] See, however, the recent paper by Pavel Krivitsky and Martina Morris (2017) that uses a class of ERGMs designed for ego network data, which allows researchers to draw inferences concerning ego's unobserved network.

2.5 Social Network Data

2009; Paik and Sanchagrin 2013; Eagle and Proeschold-Bell 2015), ego network data can be sensitive to interviewer effects. Ideally, social scientists will collect and use whole network data when studying religion, but unfortunately whole network data are the most difficult and-time consuming to collect. Although ego network data possess some limitations, they do lend themselves to certain types of analyses. Borgatti, Everett, and Johnson (2013:270) note that ego network research can be broken down into two broad camps: one focused on social capital and one focused on social homogeneity. The former examines how success is a function of the resources and support that an individual's ties provide him or her, while the latter explores how actors' ties influence their attitudes and behavior. One of the attractive features of ego network data is that if the data are collected through a randomly sampled survey, the results can be generalized to the larger population.

Whole Networks

Whole network data (also known as full data, complete data) includes, at least in theory, all relevant actors, as well as all relevant ties between actors. Figure 2.14 presents a complete or whole network. Whole network data improve on ego network data because they not only include ties among ego's alters, but also because they include ties among egos and the alters of different egos. Thus, we can see where A and B are embedded within the network. In this case, A lies in the center of the network while B lies on the periphery.[16] Moreover, this is the type of data for which most social network analysis algorithms are designed. The primary drawback, however, is the time and difficulty involved in collecting such data.

Whole social network data have traditionally been recorded in matrices. Figure 2.15 presents an example of a one-mode network, the Sampson monastery data at "liking" time 3.[17] One-mode networks always result in square matrices because each actor appears as both a row and a column.

Figure 2.16 presents an example of a two-mode network; it is the US denominational network featured in Figure 2.7, except here it is for the year 1955. As noted earlier, two-mode networks differ from one-mode networks in that they either consist of two sets of different

---

[16] This can have profound effects on religious behavior and practice. As we will see in Chapter 4, for instance, Emerson and Smith (2000) found that peripheral members of a mixed race congregation (in this case, white members) were far more likely to leave than central ones (in this case, black members), a finding consistent with previous research of volunteer organizations (e.g., Popielarz and McPherson 1995; Stark and Bainbridge 1980a).
[17] Figures 2.15 and 2.16 were created using UCINET 6 (Borgatti, Everett, and Freeman 2002).

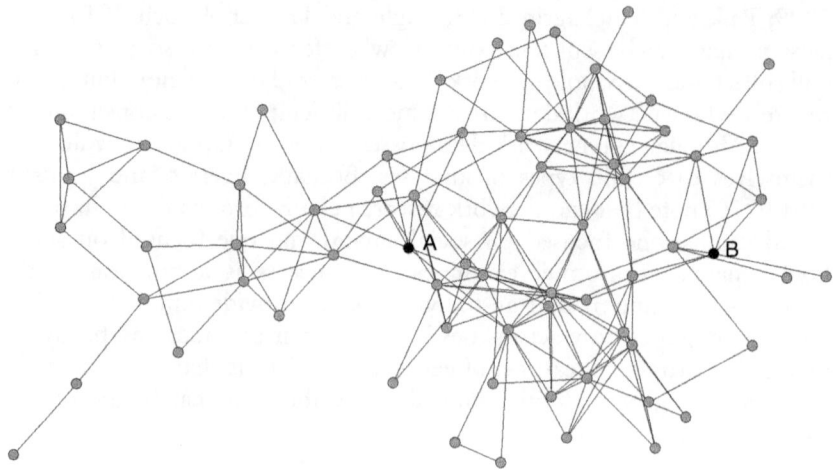

Figure 2.14 Whole network

		1 Ramuald	2 Bonaventure	3 Ambrose	4 Berthold	5 Peter	6 Louis	7 Victor	8 Winfrid	9 John Bosco	10 Gregory	11 Hugh	12 Boniface	13 Mark	14 Albert	15 Amand	16 Basil	17 Elias	18 Simplicius
1	Ramuald	0	1	1	0	3	0	0	0	0	0	0	0	0	2	0	0	0	0
2	Bonaventure	0	0	1	0	3	2	0	0	0	0	0	0	0	0	0	0	0	0
3	Ambrose	0	1	0	0	0	0	3	2	0	0	0	0	0	0	0	0	0	0
4	Berthold	0	0	2	0	3	0	0	0	0	0	0	0	0	0	0	0	0	0
5	Peter	0	3	0	1	0	2	0	0	0	0	0	0	0	0	0	0	0	0
6	Louis	0	2	0	0	0	0	3	0	0	1	0	0	0	0	0	0	0	0
7	Victor	0	0	1	2	3	0	0	0	0	0	0	0	0	0	0	0	0	0
8	Winfrid	0	0	0	0	0	0	0	0	3	2	0	1	0	0	0	0	0	0
9	John Bosco	0	0	0	0	0	0	0	1	0	0	2	0	0	0	3	0	0	0
10	Gregory	0	0	0	0	0	0	0	2	3	0	0	1	0	0	0	0	0	0
11	Hugh	0	0	0	0	0	0	1	3	0	0	2	0	0	0	0	0	0	0
12	Boniface	0	0	0	0	0	0	0	2	0	3	0	0	1	0	0	0	0	0
13	Mark	0	0	0	0	0	0	0	1	0	3	0	0	0	2	0	0	0	0
14	Albert	0	0	0	0	0	0	0	0	0	3	0	1	2	0	0	0	0	0
15	Amand	0	2	0	0	0	0	0	0	0	0	0	0	1	0	0	0	0	3
16	Basil	0	0	0	0	0	0	0	3	0	0	0	0	0	2	0	0	1	2
17	Elias	0	0	0	0	0	0	0	0	0	1	0	0	0	0	0	2	0	3
18	Simplicius	0	0	0	0	0	0	0	0	0	1	0	0	0	0	0	2	3	0

Figure 2.15 One-mode network: Sampson monastery, liking time 3

actors, or one set of actors and one set of events or affiliations. Two-mode networks rarely result in square matrices since the number of actors in the different modes is seldom the same. Here, the rows are denominations and the columns are ecumenical organizations.

2.5 Social Network Data

#	Organization	1	2	3	4	5	6	7	8	9	10	11	12	13	14	15	16	17	18	19	20	21	22
1	Advent christian church	0	0	0	0	0	0	0	0	0	0	0	0	0	0	0	0	0	0	0	0	0	0
2	AME church	0	0	1	1	0	0	0	0	1	0	0	0	1	0	0	0	0	0	0	0	1	1
3	AME zion church	0	0	1	1	0	0	0	0	1	0	0	0	1	0	0	0	0	0	0	0	1	1
4	American Baptist Associat	0	0	0	0	0	0	0	0	0	0	0	0	0	0	0	0	0	0	0	0	0	0
5	American Baptist USA	0	1	0	0	1	0	1	1	0	1	0	0	1	1	0	0	1	0	0	1	0	0
6	Assemblies of God	0	0	0	0	0	0	0	0	0	0	1	0	0	0	0	1	0	0	0	0	0	0
7	Baptist Bible Fellowship	0	0	0	0	0	0	0	0	0	0	0	0	0	0	0	0	0	0	0	0	0	0
8	Baptist General Conferenc	0	0	1	0	0	0	0	0	0	0	0	0	1	0	0	0	0	0	0	0	0	0
9	Baptist Missionary Associ	0	0	0	0	0	0	0	0	0	0	0	0	0	0	0	0	0	0	0	0	0	0
10	Bible way of our Lord Jes	0	0	0	0	0	0	0	0	0	0	0	0	0	0	0	0	0	0	0	0	0	0
11	Christian and Missionary	0	0	0	0	0	0	0	0	0	0	1	0	0	0	0	0	0	0	0	0	0	0
12	Disciples of Christ	0	0	0	1	1	0	1	1	0	1	0	0	1	0	0	0	1	0	0	1	0	0
13	The Christian Congregatio	0	0	0	0	0	0	0	0	0	0	0	0	0	0	0	0	0	0	0	0	0	0
14	Christian Methodist Episc	0	0	1	1	0	0	0	0	1	0	0	0	1	0	0	0	0	0	0	0	1	1
15	Christian Reformed Church	0	0	0	0	0	0	0	0	1	0	0	0	0	0	0	1	0	0	0	0	0	0
16	Church of God, Huntsville	0	0	0	0	0	0	0	0	0	0	0	0	0	0	0	0	0	0	0	0	0	0
17	Church of God, Anderson	1	0	0	0	0	0	0	0	0	1	0	0	0	0	0	0	0	0	0	0	0	0
18	Church of God, Cleveland	0	0	0	0	0	0	0	0	0	0	0	0	0	0	0	0	1	0	0	0	0	0
19	Church of God in Christ	0	0	1	0	0	0	0	0	0	0	0	0	0	0	0	0	0	0	0	0	0	0
20	Church of God in Christ I	0	0	0	0	0	0	0	0	0	0	0	0	0	0	0	0	0	0	0	0	0	0
21	Church of God of Prophecy	0	0	0	0	0	0	0	0	0	0	0	0	0	0	0	0	0	0	0	0	0	1
22	Church of the Brethren	0	0	0	0	1	1	0	1	0	1	0	0	1	1	0	0	1	0	0	1	0	0
23	Church of the Nazarene	1	0	0	0	0	0	0	0	0	0	0	0	1	0	0	0	0	0	0	0	0	0
24	Churches of Christ	0	0	0	0	0	0	0	0	0	0	0	0	0	0	0	0	0	0	0	0	0	0
25	Churches of God, General	0	0	0	0	0	0	0	0	0	0	0	0	0	0	0	1	0	0	0	0	0	0
26	Community Churches, Inter	0	0	0	1	0	0	0	0	0	0	0	0	0	0	0	0	0	0	0	0	1	0
27	Conservative Baptist Asso	0	0	0	0	0	0	0	0	0	0	0	0	0	0	0	0	0	0	0	0	0	0
28	Cumberland Presbyterian C	0	0	0	0	0	0	0	0	0	0	0	0	1	0	0	0	0	0	0	0	0	0
29	Episcopal Church	0	0	0	1	1	0	1	1	0	1	0	0	1	0	0	0	1	0	0	1	0	0
30	Evangelical Covenant Chur	0	0	0	0	0	0	0	0	0	0	0	0	0	0	0	1	0	0	0	0	0	0
31	Evangelical Free Church o	0	0	0	0	0	0	0	0	0	0	0	1	0	0	0	1	0	0	0	0	0	0
32	Free Methodist Church of	1	0	0	0	0	0	0	0	0	0	0	0	1	0	0	0	0	0	0	0	0	0

Figure 2.16 US denomination and ecumenical organization two-mode network, 1985

Boundaries and Ties

An important concern in social network study is which actors and ties to include in the network. Sometimes the boundary between who is in and who is not is relatively clear. Often it is not. Edward Laumann, Peter Marsden, and David Prensky (1983, 1989) note that researchers adopt various approaches for determining the boundaries of their networks. The goal should be "to find a set of actors with relatively good separateness from the rest of the world" from which we can draw reasonable conclusions (Erickson 2001:317). This is far easier said than done, however. Some researchers adopt the "vantage point of the actors themselves ... [and] the network is treated as a social fact only in that it is consciously experienced ... by the actors composing it" (Laumann, Marsden, and Prensky 1983:20). Thus, actors and their ties are only included to the extent that other actors consider them to be part of the network (Knoke and Yang 2007:15). Others impose an a priori framework based on the analyst's theoretical concerns (Wasserman and Faust 1994; Knoke and Yang 2007). "For example, a researcher might be interested in studying the flow of computer messages among researchers in a scientific specialty. In such a study, the list of actors might be the collection of people who published papers on the topic in previous years. The list is constructed for the analytical purposes of the researcher, even though the scientists themselves might not perceive the list as constituting a distinctive social entity" (Wasserman and Faust 1994:32). Analysts often refine these two approaches by focusing on certain features of a network, such as the attributes of actors (e.g., membership in a group), types of relations (e.g., friendship, business), or participation in events (e.g., study group, choir) (Laumann, Marsden, and Prensky 1983:22).

2.6 Collecting Social Network Data

Social network analysts collect social network data in a variety of ways. The most common are questionnaires, interviews, direct observation, and written records (Wasserman and Faust 1994:45–54).[18] More recently, access to "big data" has opened up new opportunities for social network analysts.

Questionnaires

Questionnaires are a common method for collecting social network data, especially when actors are individuals. They contain questions about whom people consider to be their friends, to whom do they go for advice, with whom they regularly communicate (e.g., talk face-to-face, email, telephone), and so on. Such data can be recorded either symmetrically or asymmetrically. Say, for instance, actor A considers actor B to be a friend, but B does not consider A to be a friend. In such a case, researchers can either record the data as Krackhardt did (i.e., asymmetrically) by placing a "1" in the "A–B" cell of the matrix and a "0" in the "B–A" cell of the matrix, or they can record it symmetrically by placing a "0" in both cells under the assumption that a friendship tie only exists if both actors indicate that they consider the other to be a friend. Analysts use various formats for collecting social network data using questionnaires; they fall under three broad categories: (1) roster vs. free recall, (2) free vs. fixed

---

[18] For a more in-depth summary of methods for collecting social network data, see Prell (2011:68–74).

choice, and (3) ratings vs. complete rankings (Wasserman and Faust 1994:45).

Roster vs. Free Recall. Sometimes analysts present each respondent with a complete roster of the actors in the network or allow the respondents to generate a list of names. Rosters can only be used when researchers know the members in the network prior to gathering data (Wasserman and Faust 1994:46). This, of course, raises the network boundary issue discussed earlier: how do researchers know a priori which actors belong to a network and which ones do not? When working with a self-contained organization (e.g., a small high technology start-up), this is sometimes relatively obvious (at least for the purposes of the study), but it is not always so clear-cut. In the latter case, it is usually advisable to use the free recall approach.

Free vs. Fixed Choice. In some network designs, analysts tell respondents how many other actors they are to nominate on a questionnaire (e.g., "Name five people with whom you have regular contact"); at other times, they are not presented with any such constraints as to how many nominations they can make (e.g., "Name everyone with whom you have regular contact"). The former (fixed choice) can underestimate the size or density of a network and produce misleading results.

Ratings vs. Complete Rankings. Finally, sometimes analysts ask respondents to rate or rank the ties in terms of strength among all actors in the network (Wasserman and Faust 1994:48). Ratings can be either dichotomous (e.g., ties are either present or absent) or valued (e.g., respondents choose one of a few possible categories for the strength of each tie). Rankings differ in that each actor is asked to rank his or her ties to every other actor in the network. This latter approach becomes increasingly difficult as the size of the network increases.

Interviews

Social network analysts sometimes use interviews (either face-to-face or over the phone). Interviews can prove useful for mapping the networks, but given the limitations of human recall, these should probably be supplemented with other methods (e.g., direct observation, written records).

Direct Observation

Another way to record data is to have an observer record all interactions that take place among actors in the network (Wasserman and Faust 1994:49). Dan McFarland (2004) used this approach to record student interaction patterns at two different high schools. An obvious drawback to this approach is that in some situations interactions can be so numerous and occur so closely together that it becomes next to impossible to record all interactions. Moreover, those being observed often alter their behavior when they are aware that their interactions are being recorded (Roethlisberger and Dickson 1939).

Written Records

Written records can be valuable sources of relational data. Emails, memos, historical records, and church membership and committee rolls are just a few examples of sources from which one can determine ties among individual actors. At the organizational level, written records indicating joint ventures, interlocking directorates (i.e., where the same individual sits on the boards of two different companies), and membership in the same trade association may indicate ties, while records indicating the trade of manufactured goods or the exchange of diplomats may indicate ties between countries. Mark Chaves (1996, 1997) drew on various church almanacs and denominational reports in order to determine what denominations were affiliated with which ecumenical organizations.

Big Data

The recent advent of big data has opened up new vistas for social network analysts. In particular, researchers have data pulled from social media sites, such as Facebook and Twitter, and then structured the data in terms of actors and ties in order to offer researchers opportunities for exploring the effects of social networks. For example, Lu Chen, Ingmar Weber, and Adam Okulicz-Kozaryn (2014) collected data on more than 250,000 Twitter users who listed their religious preference in order to examine the geographic distribution of people of faith and patterns of homophily.

Other Approaches

These are not the only approaches to collecting social network data. They are simply the most common. Other forms of data collection include cognitive social structure data, experiments, diaries, and small worlds (Wasserman and Faust 1994:51–54). When collecting cognitive social structure data, researchers ask respondents for their perception of other actors' network ties (e.g., "Who is friends with whom?") (Krackhardt 1987a). Social network analysts sometimes use experiments to observe the behavior of a set of actors in experimentally controlled environments (Bavelas 1950; Emerson 1962). Sometimes they have respondents keep diaries in order to maintain a record of those with whom they interact (Wasserman and Faust 1994:54). And finally researchers will use variations on small world network design (Milgram 1967; Travers and

Milgram 1969) to estimate how many steps (i.e., degrees of separation) a respondent is removed from a randomly chosen target (Watts 1999a; Watts, Dodds, and Newman 2003).

2.7 Summary and Conclusion

This chapter has provided an overview of social network analysis, how it differs from other analytic approaches, the basic terms and concepts that it employs, and the key assumptions that underlie much of the work of social network analysts. The following chapters will not always draw explicit ties between these assumptions and the analyses being highlighted, but the connections will be there. This chapter has also explored the related issues of culture and human agency and the degree to which (if at all) they affect human behavior. Finally, it has introduced the various types (i.e., ego network and whole network data) and modes (one-mode, two-mode) of social network data, as well as the various methods researchers use to collect such data.

2.8 For Further Reading

For exploring the history of social network analysis, Linton C. Freeman's, *The Development of Social Network Analysis: A Study in the Sociology of Science* (2004) is invaluable, as is his 2011 follow-up chapter "The Development of Social Network Analysis – with an Emphasis on Recent Events," which appears in *The SAGE Handbook of Social Network Analysis*, edited by John Scott and Peter J. Carrington (2011). There are a number of excellent introductions to social network analysis. The "SNA bible" is, of course, Stanley Wasserman and Katherine Faust's, *Social Network Analysis: Methods and Applications* (1994), which the attentive reader will note is cited repeatedly in this monograph. However, there are a number of more recent texts that cover contemporary developments in the field:

- Stephen P. Borgatti, Martin G. Everett, and Jeffrey C. Johnson. 2013. *Analyzing Social Networks*. Thousand Oaks, CA: Sage Publishing – an excellent introduction that is especially valuable for users of UCINET.
- David Knoke and Song Yang. 2007. *Social Network Analysis*, 2nd ed. Thousand Oaks, CA: SAGE Publications.
- Wouter de Nooy, Andrej Mrvar, and Vladimir Batagelj. 2011. *Exploratory Social Network Analysis with Pajek*, rev. and expanded ed. Cambridge: Cambridge University Press – an

introduction that features worked examples from the software package, Pajek.
- Charles Kadushin. 2012. *Understanding Social Networks: Theories, Concepts, and Findings*. Oxford: Oxford University Press – written by one of the leading theorists in the field.
- Ian McCulloh, Helen Armstrong, and Anthony Johnson. 2013. *Social Network Analysis with Applications*. New York, NY: Wiley – an introduction that includes worked examples from the social network analysis package Organizational Risk Analyzer (ORA).
- Christina Prell. 2011. *Social Network Analysis: History, Theory and Methodology*. London: SAGE Publications – includes excellent discussion of recent developments.
- Garry L. Robins. 2015. *Doing Social Network Research: Network-based Research Design for Social Scientists*. London: SAGE – a book by one of the developers of the PNet suite of programs that estimates exponential random graph models (ERGMs) that focuses on the how to conduct social network research.
- John Scott. 2017. *Social Network Analysis*, 4th ed. London: SAGE – a classic that is now in its fourth edition.

As with the scientific study of religion, monographs that are not technically introductions can sometimes be just as helpful. Here are a few:

- David Easley and Jon Kleinberg. 2010. *Networks, Crowds and Markets: Reasoning about a Highly Connected World*. New York: Cambridge University Press.
- Sean F. Everton. 2012. *Disrupting Dark Networks*. New York: Cambridge University Press.
- Matthew O. Jackson. 2008. *Social and Economic Networks*. Princeton, NJ: Princeton University Press.
- David Knoke. 1990. *Political Networks: The Structural Perspective*. Cambridge: Cambridge University Press.
- David Knoke. 2012. *Economic Networks*. Cambridge: Polity Press.
- Nan Lin. 2001. *Social Capital*. Cambridge: Cambridge University Press.
- Zeev Maoz. 2011. *Networks of Nations: The Evolution, Structure, and Impact of International Networks, 1816–2001*. New York: Cambridge University Press.

Part II

Ties That Bind

3

Recruitment and Conversion

3.1 Introduction

C. S. Lewis (1898–1963), the Oxford and Cambridge don who specialized in the study of medieval and Renaissance literature, is probably best known as the author of the *Chronicles of Narnia* (1950–1956), a series of seven books that have sold more than 100 million copies and have been successfully adapted for television and the screen. Lewis, however, was also a popular Christian apologist whose books, such as *Mere Christianity* (1942a), *The Screwtape Letters* (1942b), and *The Problem of Pain* (1940), became bestsellers. Indeed, Lewis's Christian writings became so popular that he was featured on the September 8, 1947, cover of *Time* magazine with the caption "His Heresy: Christianity." Lewis did not come by his Christian faith easily, however. He later remarked that when he "gave in, and admitted that God was God, and knelt and prayed ... that night [he was probably] the most dejected and reluctant convert in all England" (Lewis 1966 [1955]:228–229). Although Lewis had been born into a religious family, by the age of fifteen he considered himself an atheist. He attended Oxford, where he won a triple first, that is, highest honors in three areas of study (Greek and Latin literature, philosophy and ancient history, and English). He was "elected a Fellow of Magdalen College, Oxford, where he worked... from 1925 to 1954"; then in 1954 he accepted "the newly founded chair of Mediaeval and Renaissance Literature at Cambridge University (Magdalene College)," where he remained until his retirement in 1963 (Wikipedia 2014a). Lewis's interest in Christianity was rekindled, in part, by his reading of the works of the Scottish author, poet, and minister, George McDonald, but it was primarily his discussions with his close friends and fellow Oxford colleagues J. R. R. Tolkien and Hugo Dyson that eventually brought him back to the faith. In fact, it was after a long discussion and late-night walk with Tolkien and Dyson that he became England's "most dejected and reluctant convert."

Lewis's experience is not unusual. Research has repeatedly found that people are far more likely to join, convert, or be recruited by groups if they have a social tie with someone who is already a member of the group (Lofland and Stark 1965; Snow, Zurcher, and Ekland-Olson 1980; Stark and Bainbridge 1980a).[1] The fact that social ties appear to play a key role in the conversion process presents a challenge to deprivation theories of conversion, which argue that people convert in order to solve a problem (e.g., alcoholism, divorce, drug addiction) or to address a particular need (e.g., lack of wealth, status, health). Although these theories offer "obvious" explanations for why people convert, they are often problematic. For instance, one might argue that since "Christian Science promise[s] to restore health, converts must disproportionately be drawn from among those with chronic health problems, or at least those who suffer from hypochondria" (Stark 1996a:15). However, it is equally probable that "only people with excellent health could long hold to the Christian Science doctrine that illness was all in the mind" (Stark 1996a:15). Or again, some may attempt to explain the explosive growth of Latin American evangelicalism as a response to Latin America's grinding poverty, but the problems that Latin American evangelicalism "purportedly addresses – addictive behavior, violence, gender conflict, and unemployment – are much more widespread among Latin America's poor than among its evangelical membership, and ... do not ... distinguish between those who convert and those who do not" (Smilde 2005:761). It is because of issues such as these that the social network perspective places greater weight on the role that network ties play in the conversion process than it does on the beliefs and practices of the groups that people join.

This chapter begins with an overview of many (but not all) of the studies that have examined the role that social ties play in the process of conversion. Since most social scientists agree that network ties play a role in the conversion process but often disagree as to the why and how (Marwell, Oliver, and Prahl 1988; Diani 2002; Gould 2003; Passy 2003; Smilde 2005), the following section examines research that has taken up this debate. In the chapter's final section, we will use some network data that includes information on ties formed prior to and after joining a group in order to introduce three statistical models that have been developed specifically for analyzing social network data: (1) quadratic assignment procedure (QAP) models, (2) exponential random graph models (ERGMs, also known as p* models), and (3) auto-logistic actor attribute models (ALAAMs).

---

[1] This chapter uses the terms "conversion" and "recruitment" interchangeably.

3.2 Moonies, Mormons, and More

Probably the first study to highlight the link between social ties and conversion was John Lofland and Rodney Stark's (1965; see also, Stark 1996a:13–21) study of people converting to the Unification Church (more commonly known as the Moonies), a worldwide religious movement founded by the Rev. Sung Yun Moon in 1954. When Lofland and Stark decided to study the process of conversion, they searched for a group to which conversion would represent a radical leap, as opposed to a more mundane one, such as a Baptist becoming an Episcopalian. They eventually settled on a local Unification congregation that had begun in Eugene, Oregon, and then moved to the San Francisco Bay area. The congregation was founded by Young Oon Kim, who was a university professor in Korea before coming to the United States as a missionary. When she first arrived in the United States, she spoke at a number of public events, but these yielded no converts. Instead, her first three converts were close friends who she got to know after she became a lodger with one of them. Next, some of the women's husbands joined, who were then followed by their friends from work. The next converts "were old friends, relatives, or people who first formed close friendships with one or more members in the group" (Stark 1996a:16). As Stark later noted, when he and Lofland began observing, the group "had never succeeded in attracting a stranger" (Stark 1996a:16). Lofland and Stark observed a number of people who were sympathetic to the group's doctrines, but ultimately they did not join because of their numerous ties with people who disapproved of the Moonies. They also observed others who initially found the group's doctrines unappealing but later became full-fledged members. Stark recalls one who was genuinely "puzzled that such nice people could get so worked up about 'some guy in Korea' who claimed to be the Lord of the Second Advent. Then, one day, he got worked up about the guy too" (Stark 1996a:20). In the end, Lofland and Stark concluded that the people who ultimately joined the Moonies tended to be those whose ties to group members exceeded those to nonmembers (Stark 1996a:16).

Figure 3.1 illustrates the role of social ties in the conversion process identified by Lofland and Stark. Imagine that individuals A and B have ties to both members (M) and nonmembers (N) of a particular religious group. However, A has ties to six nonmembers and only two members, while B has ties to six members and two nonmembers. According to Lofland and Stark, B is far more likely than A to join the group because B's ties to group members outnumber his or her ties to nonmembers, while A's do not. Note also that in the network map, which was created using the *sna* R package (Butts 2014), B is structurally located much closer to the

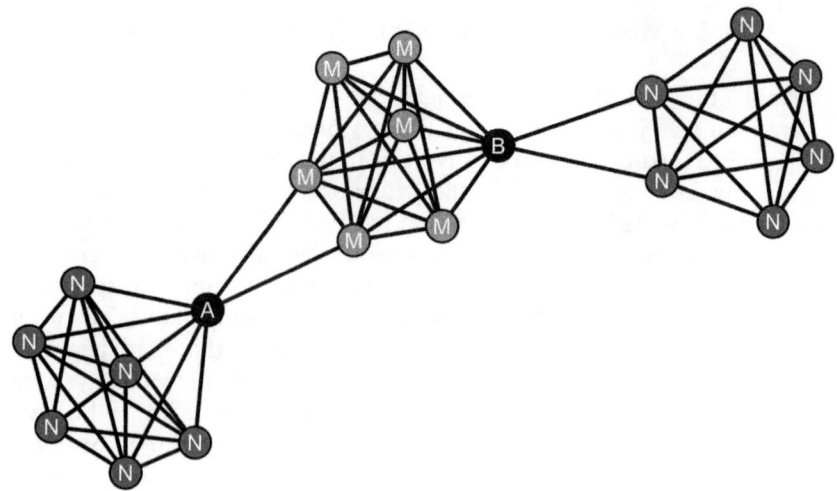

Figure 3.1 Potential converts' ties to members and nonmembers

religious group than is A. This is because B's six ties to members of the religious group pull him closer to the group than do A's two ties. Thus, another way to think of this dynamic is that people who are located socially (i.e., structurally) proximate to groups are far more likely to join than are those who are located socially distant. To be clear, social ties are not the only factor Lofland and Stark identify as leading someone to undergo a conversion. Indeed, they detail seven steps, and only the last three concern social ties.

In another study, Rodney Stark and William Bainbridge (1980a) looked at the role that social ties play in the recruitment of new members to the Mormon Church. The Mormon Church, it turns out, keeps detailed records of their missionary efforts, and Stark and Bainbridge were provided with data for all missionaries in the state of Washington during 1976 and 1977 (Stark and Bainbridge 1980a:1386). The church recruits members in a variety of ways: missionaries go door-to-door, they follow up on referrals, and they meet potential recruits in the homes of other Mormons. Although door-to-door visitation is probably the most common (and visible) means of recruitment, Stark and Bainbridge found that this method was highly unsuccessful: only 0.1 percent (1 out of 1,000) of non-Mormons contacted in this way ultimately joined the Mormon Church. By contrast, referrals provided a somewhat higher rate of success (7 percent for covert referrals and 8 percent for overt referrals), and when someone set up an appointment with the missionaries, the recruitment rate was even higher (34 percent). The church experienced its highest rates of success, however, when missionaries met potential recruits in the homes of other Mormons. In those instances, the rate was close to 50 percent. Of course, the potential recruits were not random passers-by invited in from the street; they were individuals with whom church members had previously formed close ties. In fact, Stark and Bainbridge note that an article in the Mormon Church's official magazine provided detailed instructions on how to recruit new members, and a recurring theme was the importance of building close personal ties with non-Mormons. It explicitly stated that members should downplay or avoid discussing religion while forming these ties. Only later were members to bring up the fact that they were Mormons (Stark 2005:79–80).

> Another way of looking at these findings is that missionaries do not serve as the primary instrument of recruitment to the Mormon faith. Instead, recruitment is accomplished primarily by the rank and file of the church as they construct intimate interpersonal ties with non-Mormons and thus link them into a group network.
>
> (Stark and Bainbridge 1980a:1387–1388)

Shortly after Stark and Bainbridge's study appeared, David Snow and his colleagues (Snow, Zurcher, and Ekland-Olson 1980) published the results of a study that examined several movements – some religious, some not – and found that successful social movements recruit primarily through ties with kith-and-kin networks. All of the groups they studied, save one, recruited more than 50 percent of their current members through either of such networks. Several, in fact, recruited more than 90 percent. The lone exception was the Hare Krishnas, which only recruited 3 percent. Why? Because the Hare Krishnas demanded exclusive participation from members and required them to sever all extra-movement ties. Thus, it had few, if any, social ties outside of the group through which to recruit, and as such was "structurally compelled to concentrate its recruitment efforts in public places" (Snow, Zurcher, and Ekland-Olson 1980:796). This almost certainly helps explain, at least in part, its relatively small size and suggests that successful movements (both religious and nonreligious) must maintain open social networks in order to grow.

Similarly, Doug McAdam's (1986) analysis of those who participated in the 1964 Freedom Summer campaign to register as many African-American voters as possible in Mississippi found that network ties were a key component distinguishing those who chose to participate and those who did not.[2] McAdam's analysis included information on (1) those who had applied to participate, been accepted, and chose to go (i.e.,

---

[2] Although this is not an example of people converting to a religious movement, it is one of the few studies that had data on both those who chose to participate and those who did not. Thus, it is worth highlighting here.

participants); (2) those who had applied, been accepted, and chose not to go (i.e., no-shows); and (3) those who applied but were rejected. He found that the participants and the no-shows shared similar attitudes and values, but where they differed was in terms of biographical availability and network ties. In terms of biographical availability, most of the students who participated had few commitments that otherwise would have prevented them from volunteering: only 10 percent were married, most were older than twenty-one, and most came from relatively well-to-do families, so they did not have to work summer jobs. With regards to the social ties, McAdam discovered that many volunteered based on their ties to others, many of which were formed through earlier participation in civil rights organizations. He found that 90 percent of the volunteers had already participated in various forms of activism, and nearly two-thirds had a friend who had volunteered. In fact, participants were three times as likely as no-shows to have friends who also went to Mississippi:

> The volunteers were already linked to the civil rights community. Whether these links took the form of organizational memberships, prior activism, or ties to other applicants, the volunteers benefited from greater "social proximity" to the project than did the no-shows. In fact, nothing distinguishes the two groups more clearly than this contrast. Biographical availability and attitudinal affinity may have been necessary prerequisites for applying, but it was the strength of one's links to the project that seem to have finally determined whether one got to Mississippi or not.
> (McAdam 1988a:65)

A final example comes from Marc Sageman's (2004) analysis of what he calls the global Salafi jihad (GSJ), namely those groups, such as al-Qaeda, that target the United States and its Western allies because they see them as preventing the establishment of a true Islamic state. In conducting his analysis Sageman collected social network and attribute (i.e., sociodemographic) data on 172 members of the GSJ. He only included Islamic terrorists who specifically target the far enemy in their pursuit of establishing an Islamic state. This led him to eliminate all non-Muslim terrorists, as well as Muslim terrorists fighting against their own governments. He was well aware that "drawing these boundaries removes many terrorists from consideration," but he was concerned "that an overly inclusive sample [might] obscure important factors that might help us to understand this phenomenon" (Sageman 2004:61). Because his sources of information were all in the public domain (e.g., press, Internet, and scholarly articles; documents and legal proceedings; government documents; and subject matter experts), he acknowledged that they are not a representative sample of all those involved in the GSJ. In some cases, information on known GSJ members was simply unavailable, and as he notes, there is often a journalistic and scholarly bias toward "leaders, people they can investigate, and unusual cases" (Sageman 2004:66–67). In recent years he has sought to distance himself from his original analysis (Sageman 2017:6); nevertheless, many of his results have been corroborated by other studies (see e.g., Kreuger 2008; Berman 2009; Bergen 2015), suggesting that his data are somewhat representative. What Sageman found was that most of the terrorists he studied came from middle-class backgrounds, had attended secular grade schools, were not terribly religious as children, and had attained a higher level of education than the average person from their respective countries of origin. More importantly, at least for our purposes here, he discovered that although factors such as anger at US policies increased the potential pool of GSJ recruits,[3] it was primarily those with ties to the GSJ who joined. In particular, he found that approximately 68 percent of those who joined had preexisting friendship ties (acquaintance, close friend) with someone in the GSJ or who joined with them,[4] 14 percent had kinship ties (relatives, nuclear family), and 8 percent had discipleship ties (teacher, religious mentor). After eliminating overlapping ties, Sageman calculated that 83 percent of the GSJ either had preexisting ties to individuals already involved in the GSJ or joined with a group of friends or relatives.

Numerous other studies have uncovered similar results. Kox, Meeus, and 't Hart (1991), for instance, cited fourteen studies (in addition to their own) that highlighted the important role that social ties play in the recruitment process. Similarly, Mears and Ellison (2000) found that those most likely to participate in New Age groups or activities were those who were embedded in interpersonal networks composed of other New Age devotees, and studies of religious switching (see e.g., Sherkat and Wilson 1995) have highlighted the importance of social ties in either facilitating or preventing someone from joining another faith (or no faith at all). It also appears that social ties can have an indirect impact on recruitment. In a study of conversion to Venezuelan evangelicalism, David Smilde (2005) found that just being in the presence of evangelicals could lead someone to convert. This generally occurred in one of two ways: either through the modeling of the evangelical life or the creation of an environment in which nonmembers developed an interest in evangelicalism (Smilde 2005:774):

---

[3] As we will see in Chapter 7, religious movements, especially new religious movements, often recruit disproportionately from the middle and upper classes. However, as one reviewer noted, people who join often experience strain (Merton 1938; Smelser 1962), which can be defined as "a lack of integration or a contradiction between elements of a cultural system that people feel should be intimately connected and mutually supporting" (Stark and Bainbridge 1987:217). In fact, the first step in the Lofland-Stark conversion model "suggests strain theory" (Stark and Bainbridge 1987:202).

[4] Sageman (2004:112) noted that many joined the GSJ in small clusters of friends.

In none of these cases did the person appear preoccupied by coming into line with the beliefs of their spatially present evangelicals. Rather, either through modeling or by changing ecological conditions, spatially present evangelicals exposed these respondents to evangelical meanings and practices that came to make sense to them in their lives.

One of the more statistically sophisticated (albeit indirect) tests of this dynamic is Cheadle and Schwadel's (2012) analysis of tie formation among adolescents. Using a coevolution stochastic actor-oriented model (SAOM) (Snijders, Bunt, and Steglich 2010; Steglich, Snijders, and Pearson 2010) in order to separate the effects of influence (i.e., socialization) and selection (i.e., homophily), Cheadle and Schwadel found that both socialization and homophily had an impact on various religious outcomes. In particular, after controlling for various effects, including whether adolescents formed friendship ties with those sharing the same religion (or non-religion), adolescents were still influenced by their friends' religious beliefs and behavior. Put somewhat differently, adolescents were influenced into "bringing [their] religious behavior into alignment with that of [their] friends and family" (Stark 1996a:17); these results are consistent with the studies outlined earlier in this chapter.

To be sure, there are exceptions to the rule. In China, for instance, where public proselytizing is forbidden and direct contact with potential converts is discouraged, China's illegal house churches do recruit a substantial number of its members outside of their social networks. They often "rely on door-to-door proselytizing in the countryside, cultural performances embedded with religious messages in the cities, and one-on-one conversations when the opportunity arises" (Vala and O'Brien 2007:79). Interestingly, it appears that in such a context, social ties are more important later in the recruitment process:

> Social networks may sometimes matter less for drawing a person into a movement's orbit, than for completing a conversion. Conversion (and its maintenance) may require encapsulation in a network of believers, but that often occurs long after initial exposure, when newcomers to Bible study find their time quickly fills with group worship and prayer activities, and countervailing influences weaken. Attraction is the first order of business for Chinese Protestants, and evangelists have become skilled at finding ways to make Christianity attractive through "contact events" like Christmas plays that broadcast the pleasures of religious participation and "demonstration events" that relieve feelings of powerlessness through acts of healing. These events spark interest and open the door to further engagement.
>
> (Vala and O'Brien 2007:88)

Nevertheless, when they are available, network ties do facilitate recruitment to China's illegal house churches. Indeed, Rodney Stark and Xiuhua Wang found that 90 percent of rural Chinese Christians "had their initial contact with Christianity through interpersonal ties: through acquaintances, family members, or neighbors" (Stark and Wang 2015:105).

3.3 Why Do Networks Matter?

In recent years, social scientists have challenged the social network perspective on conversion. In particular, they note that although it is clear that social networks matter, why and how they matter is unclear (Marwell, Oliver, and Prahl 1988; Diani 2002; Gould 2003; Passy 2003; Smilde 2005). Some have noted, for instance, that although we know that most people who join a movement have a preexisting tie to the movement, we seldom know how many people who had preexisting ties to the group failed to join:

> Almost invariably, the studies of movement recruitment start by surveying activists after their entrance into the movement. But showing that these activists were linked to the movement by some preexisting network tie does not prove the causal potency of that tie. No doubt there are many others who also had ties to the movement but did not participate in its activities.
> (McAdam and Paulsen 1993:641–642)

This can lead to the implicit conclusion that social ties have an almost deterministic effect, but as McAdam found, not everyone who had a tie to the Freedom Summer campaign ended up participating. Thus, it is important to emphasize that the social network perspective does not claim that most or all of those who have ties to a particular faith community will join. In fact, it is likely that most will not. Instead, it simply argues that people who have ties to a church, synagogue, mosque, or temple are more likely to join than those who do not have such ties.

Closely related to this is the critique that the social network perspective on conversion often leaves little or no room for human agency. It has typically rested "on a default conceptualization of human beings acted upon by networks rather than acting on them and through them" (Smilde 2005:758) and has ignored (or dismissed) the possible causal role that actors' beliefs, values, and commitments play in terms of social processes and historical change. Addressing this concern, Smilde (2005), in his analysis of converts to Venezuelan evangelicalism, uncovered a handful of cases in which network location (and the corresponding social ties) functioned as a mediating factor between individual motivations and conversion. Ties clearly had an impact, but "the respondents themselves created that impact as part of a conscious project of change." They "did not necessarily see that a change in network location would lead to conversion in particular. But they did correctly perceive that, in more general terms, it would facilitate a project of change" (Smilde 2005:789).

Finally, Roger Gould (2003) highlighted the important fact that ties that lead to conversion are unlikely to be "symmetric" in terms of power and influence. He correctly noted that a symmetric tie between a member and a nonmember is no more likely to lead to participation by the latter than nonparticipation by the former. Before taking up Gould's critique directly, however, it is important to note that few of the studies on recruitment and conversion have argued that ties between members and nonmembers were symmetric in nature. For instance, Lofland and Stark (1965) concluded that the networks in which future converts were embedded were asymmetric in that their ties to members *exceeded* their ties to nonmembers. Similarly, Stark and Bainbridge (1980a) argued that as the church's rank and file formed ties with non-Mormons, the latter became increasingly embedded in a network *disproportionately constituted* by Mormons. Nevertheless, Gould raised a valid concern, and Smilde's (2005) analysis of converts to Venezuelan evangelicalism is one of the few studies to specifically address it. For example, Smilde tells of one convert who "returned to his family in the interior from military service to find that the majority of them had converted to evangelicalism and attended the evangelical church across the road from their home. They no longer would go to parties and social occasions with him. So when they invited him to attend a young adults' program at their church, he gladly went and ended up converting as well" (Smilde 2005:768). Smilde also noted several other cases which at first glance appeared to reflect a symmetric relationship, but closer examination revealed asymmetries that privileged conversion to nonconversion:

> In five cases a respondent converted through spatial ties to a romantic interest ... Here we can ask Gould's question: Why did the network tie lead the man to convert instead of the woman to discontinue her participation? Gould argues that, frequently, social movement participation in itself can provide additional value to the relationship, thereby outweighing the alternative of nonparticipation. In each of these five cases either the relationship was new or the couple was experiencing relationship problems. Given evangelicalism's strong association with family and conjugal relationships among adherents (Brusco 1995; Smilde 1997), participation likely added value to these new or troubled ties.
>
> In my fieldwork, evangelicals who lived with nonevangelicals tend to engage the latter in a low-intensity but persistent way by continually providing evangelical conceptualizations of the

situations and dilemmas the nonevangelical confronts. This requires response from the nonevangelical, who develops a repertoire of ways to deflect the confrontation. The equilibrium is often broken when a moment of sickness, mishap, or misfortune arises that tips the interpretive balance of power toward the evangelizer, who inevitably provides an evangelical analysis of the nonevangelical's misfortune. The meaning system gains life for the evangelized, and he assents to adopting that system (Brusco 1995).

(Smilde 2005:769)

Sometimes the asymmetries did favor nonconversion, however. Smilde found that ties with (nonevangelical) families of origin often prevented conversion because evangelicalism threatened the norms and values of Venezuelan culture. He tells, for instance, of a father who broke down and cried after his son converted because he would no longer drink with him. Of the sixty cases he analyzed where the individuals lived with their nonevangelical families, there were only five conversions, four of which led to considerable conflict between the converts and their respective families (Smilde 2005:776).

In short, then, social ties are not everything. Indeed, we know that individuals who are deeply embedded in (and content with) a particular religious community typically do not join a new one. We have also learned that "religious movements do best in places where there is the greatest amount of secularization – for example, in places with low rates of church membership such as the west coasts of the United States and Canada, and northern Europe" (Stark 1996a:54). That is why the "Moonies quickly learned that they were wasting their time at church socials or frequenting denominational student centers. They did far better in places where they came in contact with the uncommitted" (Stark 1996a:19). Thus, while social ties play an important role in the conversion process, they are not the only factor that leads people to join a new faith community. Of course, this was something Lofland and Stark noted back in 1965.

3.4 Excursus: Statistical Models for Social Network Data

Like many other forms of empirical analysis, social network analysis is often concerned with whether the observed features of a network reflect genuine causal processes or have occurred randomly. However, statistical inference with social network data differs from standard statistical models in at least two important ways. One is that standard statistical models are designed with random samples in mind so that researchers can generalize their results to the population at large. However, because social network researchers typically analyze networks that (at least in theory) include all nodes and ties (i.e., whole, complete, or full networks), there is no need to generalize. A second is that standard statistical models assume the independence of observations, but as we noted in Chapter 2, a key assumption of SNA is that observations (i.e., actors) are interdependent and thus influence one another. Thus, when analyzing social network data, we should not use standard approaches for testing hypotheses, such as whether actor centrality is a function of a particular attribute (e.g., education, gender, race) or that one set of network ties (e.g., friendship) is a function of another set (e.g., religious affiliation). Instead, we should turn to models specifically designed for social network data.

One model, known as the quadratic assignment procedure, or QAP (Krackhardt 1987b), is similar to bootstrapping in that it entails the random rearrangement of a network's rows and columns thousands of times in order to calculate a sampling distribution of statistics that can then be compared to the statistics generated by the observed (i.e., actual) network. If the observed statistics differ significantly from the randomly generated ones, we can conclude that the observed statistics could not have occurred by random chance and are "statistically significant." For example, when calculating the correlation between two networks, the first step is to compute the correlation coefficient between corresponding cells. Next, the rows and columns (together) of one of the networks are randomly permuted (i.e., rearranged) and the correlation is recalculated. This step is carried out hundreds or thousands of times in order to compute the proportion of times that a random measure is larger than or equal to the observed measure calculated in the first step. A low proportion suggests that a correlation between networks is unlikely to have occurred by chance and thus considered statistically significant.[5] A similar approach is used when regressing a dependent network on a series of independent networks. First, using standard multivariate regression techniques, the coefficients are estimated across the corresponding cells of the dependent and independent networks. Then, the rows and columns of the dependent matrix are randomly permuted, and the regression coefficients are reestimated. As before, this second step is repeated numerous times in order to compute the proportion of time the randomly generated statistics are larger than or equal to those generated in the first step. Once again, a low proportion is interpreted to mean that the results could not have occurred by random chance. Finally, the same approach is used when calculating the correlation or regression of attribute data (e.g., centrality

---

[5] More precisely, if an estimated coefficient differs from the mean of the randomly generated distribution by 1.96 standard deviations, there is only a 5 percent chance that the estimated coefficient could have occurred randomly. Put in the language of statistical significance, $p < .05$.

3.4 Excursus: Statistical Models for Social Network Data

Table 3.1 *Preexisting social ties among CRTN group members*

	Number	Percent
Preexisting tie with:		
Acquaintance	195	53.28
Friend	177	48.36
Nuclear family	53	14.48
Relative	34	9.29
Teacher	19	5.19
Religious leader	71	19.40
At least one preexisting tie	307	83.88
No preexisting ties	59	16.12
Total	366	100.00

and education level). In the first step, a correlation or standard multivariate regression is estimated across corresponding values of the dependent and independent attributes; in the second, the elements of the dependent attribute data are randomly permuted numerous times, and the distribution of randomly generated results is compared to the actual results to see if the latter is likely to have occurred by random chance.[6]

To illustrate, we use social network data from 1989 to 2004 on a religiously inspired terrorist group. The researchers who originally gathered the data later concluded that the data were a poor reflection of reality, which is why we will refer to the group as the Chimeric Religious Terrorist Network (CRTN). Nevertheless, the network data do possess properties (in particular, data on ties formed before and after people joined the group) that allow us to demonstrate the basics of the QAP model, as well as other models considered later in this section. Table 3.1 presents data regarding the percentage of group members recruited through preexisting ties (83.88 percent). As the table indicates, of the 307 (out of 366) individuals who had a preexisting tie, 261 had an acquaintance and/or friendship tie, and 111 had both. Interestingly, group members had more preexisting acquaintance ties (i.e., weak ties) than friendship ties (i.e., strong ties), which could lead one to conclude that weak ties exerted more "pull" than strong ties. However, since most of us have more weak than strong ties (Granovetter 1973; Burt 1992a, 1992b), that is not necessarily the case. We cannot know this for certain without data on members' ties outside of the group, but it is probably an assumption worth holding until evidence suggests otherwise.

Figure 3.2 presents network maps of the data. The top panel includes only preexisting ties between group members, the middle adds the ties that

---

[6] For an excellent discussion of testing hypotheses using permutation methods, see Borgatti et al. (2013:125–138).

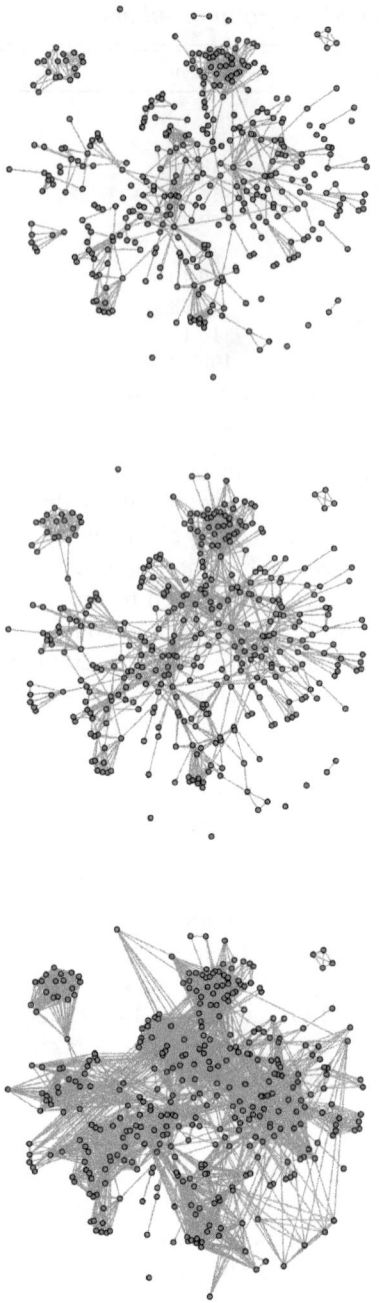

Figure 3.2 The CRTN: preexisting, post-joining, and operational ties

3.4 Excursus: Statistical Models for Social Network Data

Table 3.2 *Estimated QAP coefficients predicting tie formation in CRTN post-joining network*

	Model 1	Model 2	Model 3	Model 4
Intercept	0.007***	0.009***	0.007***	0.004***
Shared place of birth	0.044***			0.026***
Preexisting ties		0.122***		0.110***
Indirect preexisting ties			0.091***	0.085***
Adjusted R2	0.014	0.016	0.024	0.045

Note: *** = $p < 0.001$

formed after people joined, and the bottom adds ties between individuals who worked together on the same operation. As the top panel illustrates, most people had a preexisting tie to some member of the network. There are very few isolates. Moreover, as the middle and bottom panels illustrate, group members formed more ties after they joined, but these were in addition to and not substitutes for their preexisting ties. Figure 3.3 presents the network over time. Moving from left to right and top to bottom, the graphs present the network in 1989, 1992, 1995, 1998, 2001, and 2004. At each of these time points, the white nodes indicate individuals who have yet to join (future members), the gray nodes indicate those who have joined (current members), and the black nodes indicate those who have left (past members), either because they were killed or captured. As the upper left panel indicates, most of the nodes are colored white, which indicates that in 1989 the majority of people who became involved in the group had yet to join. Interestingly, little had changed three years later (upper right panel). By 1995 (middle left panel), however, the CRTN had grown considerably. More nodes are colored gray than white. We can also see that a handful of group members were no longer in the network (black colored nodes), most of whom had been captured after a relatively unsuccessful attack. By 1998 (middle right panel) almost everyone had joined (there are few white nodes), and a few more had been captured or killed. This trend continues through 2001 and 2004 (lower left and right panels, respectively) such that by 2004 there are few remaining members of the group.

Table 3.2 presents the estimated coefficients for testing whether direct and indirect preexisting ties had a positive effect on post-joining tie formation.[7] In particular, it regresses the post-joining tie network on the preexisting tie and the indirect preexisting tie networks,[8] as well as

---

[7] All QAP models were estimated with the social network analysis package, UCINET (Borgatti, Everett, and Freeman 2002).
[8] The preexisting tie network consists of ties between individuals who did not share a direct tie with one another but did share a tie with a common friend, acquaintance, relative, family member, teacher, or religious leader. Indirect ties were identified by squaring the

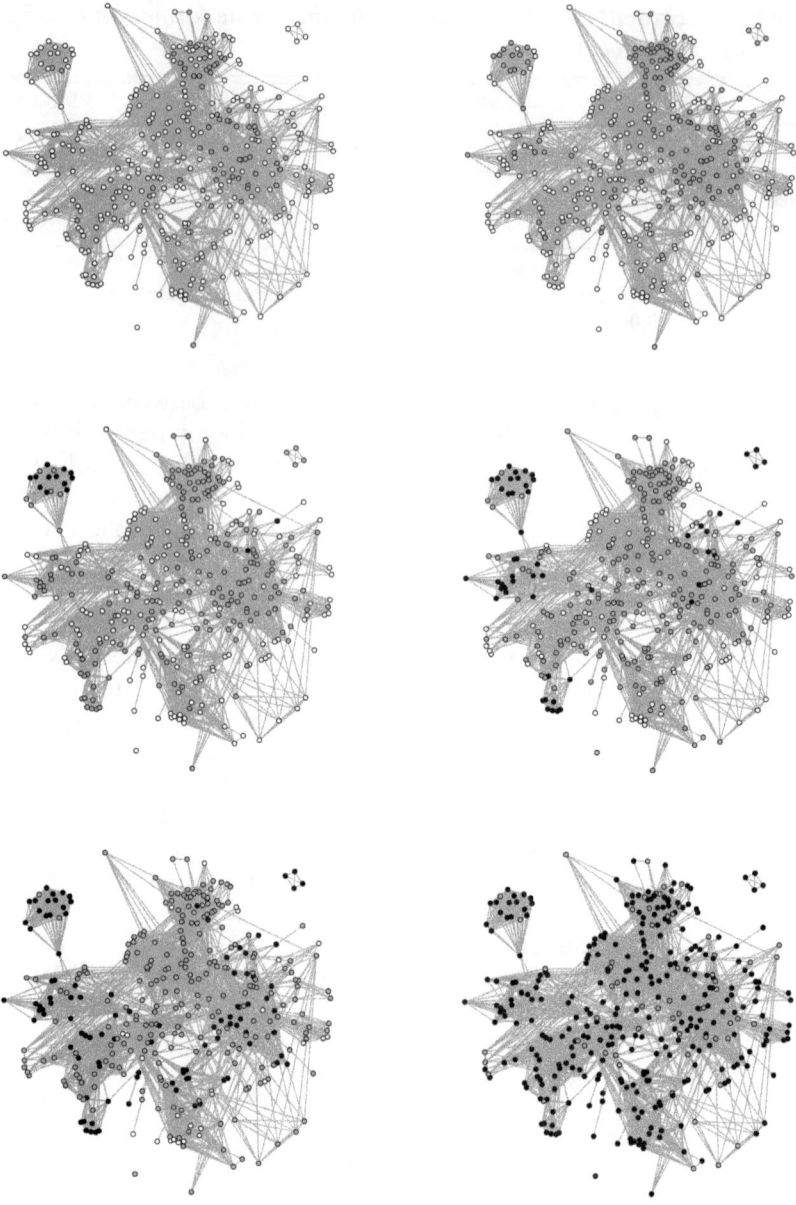

Figure 3.3 The CRTN: future, present, and past, 1989–2004

original network matrix, which yields a network of all indirect ties between pairs of actors of path length two. However, because this can include pairs of actors that also had a direct tie in the preexisting network, those pairs of actors with both preexisting ties and indirect ties of path length two were recoded to "0," yielding an indirect network consisting of ties between pairs of actors that did not share a preexisting tie.

3.4 Excursus: Statistical Models for Social Network Data

controlling for whether two members share a common birthplace.[9] As the coefficients indicate, all three independent variables exert a positive and statistically significant effect on tie formation among CRTN members after they joined the network, with preexisting ties exerting the largest effect. However, as the adjusted R2 indicates, together they account for only 4.5 percent of the observed tie formation in the post-joining network, suggesting that other factors are at work.

Exponential Random Graph Models

One of the weaknesses of QAP models is that they cannot control for endogenous properties of the observed (dependent) network itself. That is one of the motivations lying behind the development of exponential random graph models (ERGMs, also referred to as p* models). ERGMs provide analysts with a method for examining the internal (endogenous) and external (exogenous) social processes that give rise to a network's observed patterns at the macro level (Robins et al. 2007; Lusher, Koskinen, and Robins 2013; Harris 2014). They "are designed to predict the probability of tie formation in an observed network, while incorporating properties of the network itself as well as an array of covariates pertaining to the network actors and sets of ties among them" (Papachristos, Hureau, and Braga 2013:427). ERGMs assume that observed social networks are built upon local patterns of ties, sometimes called micro-configurations, that are a function of local social processes, such that "actors in the network form connections in response to other ties in their social environment" (Lusher, Koskinen, and Robins 2013:1). These models are similar to the general linear models found in standard statistical packages (in particular, logistic regression models), except that they include important modifications in order to account for the dependencies between observations (Robins et al. 2007; Lusher, Koskinen, and Robins 2013; Harris 2014).

The basic approach for estimating an ERGM is to hypothesize which endogenous social processes gave rise to a particular network's global properties, and then to build a model that takes these and other factors into account. Local processes are operationalized in terms of the various micro-configurations found within a network (e.g., edges, stars, open and closed triads, etc.), whereas exogenous factors, such as race, gender, religious affiliation, and age, are modeled in order to capture various social selection processes, such as homophily or status. For example, analysts may hypothesize that actors who share a particular attribute

---

[9] A shared place of birth matrix was created using UCINET (Borgatti, Everett, and Freeman 2002) such that if two individuals were born in the same place, a "1" was included in their common cell and a "0" otherwise.

are more likely to form ties with one another than those who do not, or they may test whether actors who score high in terms of a particular attribute (e.g., age, tenure) are more (or less) likely to form ties than those who do not. The key is to build a model that takes into account both endogenous and exogenous processes because what lies behind tie formation is not always clear. Take, for example, the presence of a large number of triangles (closed triads) in a friendship network:

> This pattern could be produced by a direct propensity for triadic closure. However, by concentrating ties with attribute categories, assortative mixing can also create more triangles than in a random network. Variation in sociality can also produce this pattern, as a network with few active and many less-active persons will have more triangles than one with the same ties distributed randomly. A single population-level signature can thus be produced by processes operating at the individual, dyadic, or triadic levels.
>
> (Goodreau, Kitts, and Morris 2009:104–105)

Estimating an ERGM is essentially a two-step process. The first step is to build a model that includes a mix of micro-configurations and attributes that yield fitted parameter values and allow the model to converge. A t-ratio for each parameter value is calculated by taking the difference between the actual count of a micro-configuration (e.g., triads) and the average count of the micro-configuration from a large sample of graphs that were simulated using the parameter estimates and then dividing this difference by the simulation standard error (Lusher, Koskinen, and Robins 2013). When the absolute value of all of the t-ratios in the model are less than 0.10, the model is considered to have converged, and when a parameter's absolute value is greater than twice the size of the estimated standard error, it is considered statistically significant (Wang et al. 2014:22). The goal "is to find a small set of configurations which capture the properties we are interested in and which yield reasonable parameter values that converge" (Borgatti, Everett, and Johnson 2013:142). The next step is to see if the fitted parameters adequately account for the remaining micro-configurations that were not included in the model. If not, then the ERGM needs to be reestimated with a different set of parameters and the process starts anew.

We illustrate how to estimate an ERGM using the same network data that was in the QAP models discussed earlier.[10] We begin by first estimating a model that only includes the micro-configurations of the post-joining

---

[10] ERGMs can be estimated using either the PNet suite of programs for ERGMs (Wang, Robins, and Pattison 2009b) or the R statnet package (Handcock et al. 2003). Here the MPNet (Wang, Robins, and Pattison 2014) package was used.

3.4 Excursus: Statistical Models for Social Network Data

network, after which we will add covariates that capture the presence or absence of preexisting ties, as well as shared place of birth. In a sense, we are treating the micro-configurations as control variables in order to see whether the other variables have an effect above and beyond the local processes captured by the micro-configurations. Such an approach is not always the case. In fact, it is probably more common for the endogenous factors to be the variables of interest (see, e.g., Goodreau, Kitts, and Morris 2009; Gondal and McLean 2013). Table 3.3 lists some of the configurations (and their interpretation) that can be found in undirected networks, such as the CRTN post-joining network.[11] Lusher et al. (2013:174) "suggest that a good starting point for models for undirected networks is to include an edge, alternating star, alternating triangle, and alternating 2-path parameters ... In short, models should include at least a density parameter (edge), as well as control for degree distribution (star parameters) and closure (triangle parameters)."

That is the essentially the approach we adopt in model 1 (Table 3.4), except that it includes parameters for isolates and isolated edges. Also, rather than including an edge configuration in the model itself, we fixed the density of the network, which can help models to converge.[12] As you can see, all of the parameter estimates in the first model are statistically significant. However, the goodness of fit (GOF) statistics (Table 3.5) indicate that the fitted parameters do not adequately account for all of the configurations present in the network. For example, there are 390 triangles in the post-joining network, but the average number in the simulated networks is approximately 293, which yields a t-ratio of 4.939.[13] As a rule of thumb, GOF t-ratios should be less than 1.96, which indicates that the actual and simulated parameters are not statistically significantly different from one another (Wang et al. 2014:24).[14] However, the t-ratios of fitted parameters should ideally be closer to 0.10 or less, and as we can see, that is certainly not the case here. More striking is the GOF statistics for the non-fitted parameters. The actual number of 2-, 3-, 4-, and 5-stars, 4-cycles, and alternating star triangles differ significantly than one would predict from the micro-configurations fitted in the first model. Table 3.5 also includes several global measures of model fit: the standard deviation and skewness of the degree distributions, the global clustering coefficient (which measures the extent to which

---

[11] Directed networks include far more possible configurations.
[12] This is not a concern since the edge statistic in ERGMs is analogous to the intercept in standard regression models and not typically interpreted.
[13] The GOF t-ratio equals the actual count less the mean estimated count divided by the associated standard deviation (see Lusher, Koskinen, and Robins 2013:165–166, 179–185).
[14] In other words, in terms of goodness of fit, we want the difference between the actual and estimated number of configurations to be statistically insignificant from one another. Those that are, are indicated by a "#."

Table 3.3 *Micro-configurations found in undirected networks*

Configuration (Parameter)	Graphic	Interpretation	Configuration (Parameter)	Graphic	Interpretation
Isolate	•	Isolated actor			
Edge		Propensity of two actors to form ties	Isolated edge		Isolated dyad
2-star		Propensity to form ties with others; a measure of popularity	Alternating two-path		Propensity to form ties with alters of same actor
3-star		Measure of popularity; note: 2-stars are nested in 3-stars	Triangle		Triadic closure (friends of friends of friends)
4-star		Measure of popularity; note: 2- and 3-stars are nested in 4-stars	Alternating triangle		Nested triadic closure
5-star		Measure of popularity; note: 2-, 3-, and 4-stars are nested in 5-stars	Four-cycle		Cyclic closure
Alternating star		Measure of popularity; note: lower-order stars are nested in higher-order stars	Alternating edge triangle		Propensity or potential for brokerage

3.4 Excursus: Statistical Models for Social Network Data

Table 3.4 *ERGM estimates of tie formation in CRTN post-joining network*

	Model 1	Model 2	Model 3	Model 4
Structural (endogenous) effects				
Triangle	0.238*	−0.142	−0.020	−0.217*
Isolates	−0.969*	−0.385	−0.632	−0.124
Isolated edges	−2.356*	−2.097*	−2.194*	−2.020
Alternating star	0.435*	0.097	0.241	−0.038
Alternating triangle	1.530*	1.648*	1.596*	1.641*
Alternating two-path	−0.042*	−0.015	−0.025*	−0.010
Actor relation effects				
Shared place of birth		0.893*	0.827*	0.670*
Dyadic covariates (exogenous)				
Preexisting ties			1.115*	1.334*
Indirect preexisting ties		0.880*		1.075*
Mahalanobis distance	17,453	3,993	−673	1,663

* Statistically significant effect

a network has high and low areas of density), and the Mahalanobis distance. The GOF for the first three is measured similarly to the other configurations present in the network, and as the t-ratios in the table indicate, the fitted model does not adequately account for these network patterns either. The Mahalanobis distance is an overall measure of model goodness of fit used by the PNet suite of programs that takes into account the covariance of the included statistics (Wang, Robins, and Pattison 2009a). Smaller Mahalanobis distances indicate a better fit of the data (Wang et al. 2014:24), and as we can see, the Mahalanobis distance for the first model is substantially larger than for models 2 through 4. Thus, we can conclude that although the first model converged and all of its parameters were statistically significant, it does not adequately account for the network's global properties.

Model 2 adds two covariates to the model: a variable indicating whether two members share a common place of birth[15] and the indirect preexisting tie network.[16] Both of the estimated parameters of these covariates are statistically significant (although some of the other parameters no longer are), and their inclusion substantially improves the fit of the model as measured by the Mahalanobis distance. However, the results

---

[15] In two cases, place of birth was unknown. Rather than eliminating the actors from the dataset and losing valuable network information, the mode category (Algeria) was used.
[16] When estimating ERGMs, it is unnecessary to convert shared attributes into a matrix before estimating the model. Moreover, ERGMs allow for analysts to test the direct effect of an attribute (called the main effect) on tie formation, which is something that analysts are unable to do in a multivariate QAP model.

Table 3.5 Goodness of fit statistics of tie formation in CRTN post-joining network

	Count	Model 1 Mean	Model 1 t-ratio	Model 2 Mean	Model 2 t-ratio	Model 3 Mean	Model 3 t-ratio	Model 4 Mean	Model 4 t-ratio
Fitted Effects									
Triangle	390.000	292.992	4.939#	384.306	0.220	354.678	1.556	382.642	0.299
Isolates	60.000	51.916	1.171	58.159	0.261	55.773	0.597	58.026	0.300
Isolated edges	1.000	0.867	0.141	0.954	0.048	0.877	0.127	0.933	0.066
Alternating stars	1,694.108	1,662.693	1.889	1,686.796	0.345	1,670.977	1.082	1,686.373	0.381
Alternating triangle	688.729	642.478	1.306	676.719	0.498	662.147	1.099	679.455	0.422
Alternating two-path	3,710.422	3,519.806	1.348	3,699.021	0.079	3,566.400	1.002	3,710.847	−0.003
Shared place of birth	269.000			264.088	0.222	247.624	1.462	258.693	0.832
Preexisting ties	92.000					87.887	0.726	85.686	0.768
Indirect preexisting ties	192.000			175.891	1.067			181.627	0.863
Non-fitted effects									
Edges	671.000	671.000	NA	671.000	NA	671.000	NA	671.000	NA
2-star	4,809.000	4,007.649	3.825#	4814.219	−0.026	4,403.182	1.892	4,845.015	−0.161
3-star	18,969.000	10,248.571	6.346#	17,301.800	0.958	14,155.838	2.505#	17,535.699	0.774
4-star	81,266.000	22,372.916	10.773#	56,065.070	2.408#	43,479.641	3.086#	57,082.941	2.308#
5-star	349,389.000	42,350.301	18.446#	157,580.924	4.035#	124,831.344	3.587#	162,008.185	3.834#
4-cycle	1,665.000	569.462	9.703#	1,672.983	−0.033	1,195.457	2.385#	1,661.930	0.012
Alternating edge triangle	2,144.411	1,607.223	4.477#	2,163.018	−0.121	1,978.777	1.213	2,152.847	−0.056
Degree standard deviation	4.068	3.482	3.523#	4.069	0.135	3.781	1.848	4.089	−0.144
Degree skew	2.424	1.274	6.542#	1.999	2.246#	1.858	2.260#	2.004	2.624#
Global clustering	0.243	0.219	2.486#	0.240	0.013	0.242	0.151	0.237	0.565
Mahalanobis distance			17,453		3,993		−673		1,663

Note: # = poor GOF

presented in Table 3.5 indicate that there is a lack of goodness of fit in terms of three measures (alternating 4- and 5-stars and degree skew). Model 3 swaps the preexisting network for the indirect preexisting network, and as the Mahalanobis distance indicates, it improves upon the fit of model 2. However, the fitted parameters do not adequately account for five of the non-fitted effects: 3-, 4-, and 5-stars, 4-cycle, and degree skew. The final model includes both the preexisting and indirect preexisting network in the model, and while its Mahalanobis distance is larger than that of model 3, it better accounts for the non-fitted effects. Here, only three are inadequately accounted for.

These models suggest that after controlling for potential local processes in the post-joining network, all three factors – shared place of birth, preexisting ties, and indirect preexisting ties – had a positive effect in the formation of ties after people joined the CRTN, although preexisting ties have the largest effect of the three. These results are consistent with what we found earlier using QAP regression, but because we have taken into account endogenous structural effects, we can be more confident about the results. We could refine this analysis, of course. If we disaggregated the preexisting tie network in terms of friendship, acquaintance, family, relatives, teacher, and religious mentor ties, we could test whether prior ties of trust (i.e., strong ties) exert a greater influence on tie formation after people joined the network. If that was indeed the case, it may be evidence that CRTN consists of deeply embedded individuals who are unlikely to defect or betray the network (Stark and Bainbridge 1980a; Popielarz and McPherson 1995).

Auto-logistic Actor Attribute Models

While social scientists of religion may sometimes be interested in who forms ties with whom and why, many will be more interested in using social network models to help explain behavioral outcomes. That is, they will be interested in models where the dependent variable is an attribute not a tie. Auto-logistic actor attribute ERGMs, more commonly known as social influence models, are designed specifically for this purpose (Robins, Pattison, and Elliott 2001; Daraganova and Pattison 2013; Daraganova and Robins 2013). Unlike standard ERGMs which model network structure, social influence ERGMs allow analysts "to understand how individual behavior may be constrained by position in a social network and by behavior of other actors in the network" (Daraganova and Robins 2013:102). In particular, they model the distribution of behaviors (i.e., attributes) "across a fixed network of relational ties" (Daraganova and Pattison 2013:104).

Table 3.6 presents the results of regressing the fate (i.e., alive and free, captured or killed) of CRTN members on a series of independent

Table 3.6 *Auto-logistic actor attribute ERGM estimates on the fate of CRTN members*

	Alive and Free			
	Model 1	Model 2	Model 3	Model 4
Network position effects				
Attribute density	−1.888*	−1.947*	NA	−2.763*
Actor activity	−0.014	−0.008	−0.043	−0.033
Partner activity (contagion)	0.296*	0.289	0.289*	0.284*
Alternating triangle	−0.006	−0.009	−0.006	−0.005
Attribute only effects				
Religious background		0.169	0.169	0.135
Education level			0.093	0.159*
Year of birth			−0.019*	
Mahalanobis distance	53	53	33	43

	Captured or Killed			
	Model 1	Model 2	Model 3	Model 4
Network attribute effects				
Attribute density	1.882*	1.935*	NA	2.738*
Actor activity	−0.277*	−0.276*	−0.243*	−0.265*
Partner activity (contagion)	0.292*	0.284*	0.287*	0.300*
Alternating triangle	0.006	0.008	0.006	0.006
Attribute only effects				
Religious background		−0.169	−0.163	−0.127
Education level			−0.096	−0.157*
Year of birth			0.019*	
Mahalanobis distance	53	63	33	43

* Statistically significant effect

variables: whether the member was raised to be religious, level of education, and age (i.e., year of birth).[17] As with the standard ERGMs presented earlier, all of the models include network effects: in this case, network position effects. The first, attribute density, captures the baseline probability that the behavior is present and, as such, is akin to the intercept in standard statistical models. The second, actor activity, measures the dependence of the actor's behavior on the number of ties the actor has; a positive estimate indicates that actors with multiple ties are more likely to display the behavior.[18] The third, partner activity, refers to the number

---

[17] Data were missing in several cases for religious background (29), education level (76), and year of birth (25). Rather than drop these actors from the network and lose valuable network tie information, the mode of each category was used.

[18] Analysts can also model higher-order parameters (e.g., 2-star and 3-star; see Table 3.3), which allow for nonlinear dependence on the number of an actor's partners. These

of actor partners who display the behavior; if the parameter is positive, then the behavior is more likely if an actor's immediate neighbors display the behavior. The fourth, an alternating triangle, indicates whether the behavior is associated with network closure. Focusing first on the Mahalanobis distance, we can see that in terms of both dependent variables – whether the actor was "alive and free" or "captured or killed" at the time the researchers ceased collecting data on the CRTN – the third and fourth models provide a better fit of the data than do the first two models. GOF statistics like those presented for the earlier ERGM (Table 3.5) are not presented for these models since all eight adequately account for all of the fitted and non-fitted effects. However, in both cases it was difficult to get model 3, which includes year of birth as an independent variable, to converge unless the actor density parameter was dropped from the model and density was fixed as it was in the standard ERGM estimated earlier.

Summary

Although this brief illustration of estimating an ERGM may appear relatively straightforward, in practice ERGMs can be difficult to fit. Identifying a set of micro-configurations that yield reasonable parameter values that converge and adequately account for the remaining configurations in a network can be a time-consuming and sometimes frustrating experience that can be "more of an art than science" (Borgatti, Everett, and Johnson 2013:142). Nevertheless, ERGMs represent a major advance in the statistical modeling of social network data, and as methods improve for model estimation (see e.g., Koskinen et al. 2013), they will almost certainly become easier and less frustrating to model.

3.5 Summary and Conclusion

This chapter has examined the role that structural location plays in leading some people to join (convert to) religious movements. It began with an overview of many of the studies that have examined the role that social ties play in the process of conversion/recruitment, and then explored studies that have teased out how and why network ties are central to conversion/recruitment. The chapter concluded by noting that standard statistical models should not be applied to social network data because we are examining entire populations rather than random samples, and the

---

higher-order parameters were originally included in the model but were statistically insignificant and unnecessary for model convergence and thus were dropped from the estimated models.

observations, by definition, are not independent of one another. With this in mind, we considered three statistical models designed specifically for social network data: quadratic assignment procedure (QAP) models, exponential random graph models (ERGMs), and auto-logistic actor attribute models (ALAAMs). We will consider one additional statistical model designed for longitudinal data (stochastic actor-oriented model) in Chapter 10.

3.6 For Further Reading

Most of the pertinent literature on recruitment and conversion has been cited and discussed in this chapter. Some of the key studies are the following:

- Roger V. Gould. 2003. "Why Do Networks Matter? Rationalist and Structuralist Interpretations." In *Social Movement Networks: Relational Approaches to Collective Action*, edited by Mario Diani and Doug McAdam. Oxford: Oxford University Press, pp. 233–257.
- John Lofland and Rodney Stark. 1965. "Becoming a World-Saver: A Theory of Conversion to a Deviant Perspective." *American Sociological Review* 30:862–875.
- Doug McAdam. 1986. "Recruitment to High Risk Activism: The Case of Freedom Summer." *American Journal of Sociology* 92:64–90.
- Doug McAdam and Ronnelle Paulsen. 1993. "Specifying the Relationship between Social Ties and Activism." *American Journal of Sociology* 99:640–667.
- David Smilde. 2005. "A Qualitative Comparative Analysis of Conversion to Venezuelan Evangelicalism: How Networks Matter." *American Journal of Sociology* 111(3):757–796.
- David Snow and Cynthia Phillips. 1980. "The Lofland-Stark Conversion Model: A Critical Assessment." *Social Problems* 27:430–447.
- David A. Snow, Louis A. Zurcher, and Sheldon Ekland-Olson. 1980. "Social Networks and Social Movements: A Microstructural Approach to Differential Recruitment." *American Sociological Review* 45:787–801.
- Rodney Stark and William Sims Bainbridge. 1980a. "Networks of Faith: Interpersonal Bonds and Recruitment to Cults and Sects." *American Journal of Sociology* 85(6):1376–1395.

Two books are essential for learning about ERGMs: Jenine K. Harris's, *An Introduction to Exponential Random Graph Modeling* (Los Angeles:

3.6 For Further Reading

Sage Publications, 2014), and Dean Lusher, Johan H. Koskinen, and Garry L. Robins (eds.), *Exponential Random Graph Models for Social Networks* (New York: Cambridge University Press, 2013). The former uses the R statnet package, while the latter uses the PNet suite of programs. In addition, you may want to consider the following:

- Stephen P. Borgatti, Martin G. Everett, and Jeffrey C. Johnson. 2013. "Testing Hypotheses." In *Analyzing Social Networks*. Thousand Oaks, CA: SAGE Publications, pp. 139–145.
- Christina Prell. 2011. Appendix 2: Exponential Random Graph Modelling and Longitudinal Modelling through Siena. In *Social Network Analysis: History, Theory & Methodology*. London: SAGE Publications, pp. 238–248.
- Garry L. Robins. 2011. "Exponential Random Graph Models for Social Networks." In *The SAGE Handbook of Social Network Analysis*, edited by John Scott and Peter J. Carrington. London: SAGE Publications, pp. 484–500.

4

Commitment and Conformity

4.1 Introduction

When in 1974 Bill Hybels decided to start a church, one of the first things he did was survey the local community. He wanted to find out what people liked and disliked about "church." He heard things like, "Church is irrelevant to daily life," "It's boring and predictable," "Churches are always asking for money," and "I don't like being preached down to." Answers such as these led him to found what is now known as a "seeker-sensitive" church, one that seeks to make "church" more accessible and sensitive to the needs of "the unchurched" (Hybels and Hybels 1995). Hybels's experiment was a roaring success. The church he founded, Willow Creek Community Church, which is located west of Chicago, seats 7,000 people, attracts up to 15,000 worshippers on a given weekend, and has given birth to eight "regional" congregations in the Chicago area.[1] Willow Creek's success helped jumpstart the modern megachurch movement. It was not the first, but many of its innovations are now megachurch mainstays (Thumma and Travis 2007). In fact, it subsequently formed the Willow Creek Association, which is an international organization that holds conferences, offers support, and provides written and video resources to churches seeking to follow the Willow Creek model.[2]

A crucial aspect of the megachurch movement is its use of small groups. Willow Creek implemented small groups from the outset, believing that while large gatherings can be useful in some respects (e.g., worship), it is only in more intimate settings that people can gain a sense of community and deepen their commitment to others. He longed for a church where "the value of community is lifted up and [Christians] develop an increasing thirst for close relationships" (Hybels and Hybels 1995:191). That is why he structured Willow Creek so that it would be a church of small

---

[1] See www.willowcreek.org.
[2] The association is not a denomination but rather a network of churches with a similar approach to ministry. See www.willowcreek.com.

4.1 Introduction

groups rather than a church that offered small groups (Hybels and Hybels 1995:178).

The use of small groups is now widespread among megachurches. Megachurch leaders see them as crucial for connecting members (and potential members) into the life of the church:

> [They realized they could not] rely on chance interactions or informal networking to create social groups. Rather, they intentionally structure multiple ways for people to interact and form social ties. Exactly how many, and to what extent, megachurches use small groups varies depending on the individual church. Nevertheless, the effort to connect people and gather them into smaller groupings is now universal among megachurches.
> (Thumma and Travis 2007:48)

In fact, a recent study found that 79 percent of megachurches reported that they were "intentional about maximizing the number and variety of small groups they offer" (Thumma and Bird 2015:4–5). And the intuition of megachurch leaders about the effectiveness of small groups appears to be correct. The more intentional megachurches are about small groups, the more likely they are to report that their church's spiritual vitality is high (Thumma and Bird 2015:5).[3]

Connecting members (both actual and potential) is a key concern for most faith communities. The more that members are well-integrated into a congregation, the more likely they are to stay. We saw in the previous chapter that social ties play a key role in bringing people into faith communities. In this chapter, we will see that they also play a key role in keeping people from leaving. Take, for instance, Rodney Stark and William Bainbridge's (1980) study of a "doomsday" group, which believed that the end of the world was nigh. The group had formed primarily along kinship ties, and Stark and Bainbridge found that members who had direct ties to the group's leaders were less likely to leave (i.e., defect) than those who did not:

> Members who were direct kin of the leaders, only 14% quit. Of those who were related to kin of the leaders, but not directly to the leaders (e.g., in-laws), 25% defected. But of those who had no relatives in the group, two-thirds left prematurely. For those who had to abandon their families as well as their faith, defection

---

[3] Small groups are not the only strategy that megachurches use to raise the commitment levels of members. "Half the mega-churches also use Sunday School (with a median of 34% of members participating), three-quarters (79%) of them offer age-graded children and youth worship services concurrent with adult services, and a sizable majority (70%) use their building's informal spaces during service to reach those who might linger on the margins rather than actively participate in the services" (Thumma and Bird 2015:5).

was rare. But for those without familial ties to the group, defection was the rule!

(Stark and Bainbridge 1980a:1383)

Although this analysis was only of a single group, subsequent studies have uncovered similar dynamics, of which this chapter will explore a few. The chapter focuses on the factors that increase commitment among people of faith, with an emphasis on the role of social ties. It begins by examining how homophilic processes help explain why some groups members leave at greater rates than others (McPherson and Smith-Lovin 1987; Popielarz and McPherson 1995), as well as why interracial faith communities are more the exception than the rule (Emerson and Smith 2000). Next, it briefly considers how geographic mobility affects peoples' level of commitment; people on the move are much less likely to form ties with voluntary associations than are those who stay put (Welch and Baltzell 1984). The chapter then turns to an analysis of the Plowshares movement, a Roman Catholic antiwar group, which began in the 1980s and is still active today. Its ability to persist over a long period of time provides a case study that can help identify the mechanisms that better integrate members into groups and thus raise retention rates (Nepstad 2004, 2008). Finally, the chapter considers how social ties will sometimes "coerce" people into behaving in ways they would not if not for their ties. After providing an overview of how this can happen, it examines the rural Southern Black Church, which some have called a "semi-involuntary institution" because there is evidence that some people worship and participate, not because they want to, but because they would suffer sanctions if they did not (Lewis 1955; Nelson, Yokley, and Nelsen 1971; Nelsen and Nelsen 1975; Ellison and Sherkat 1995).

4.2 Homophily and Commitment

Peter Blau (1977, 1994) noted that although it would be ideal to analyze each and every tie among all individuals, it is impractical to do so when the number of individuals becomes too large, such as when we study entire populations. This led him to conclude that in such situations, we should focus on the opportunities of contact among the social positions that people occupy, which he located in terms of peoples' attributes (e.g., age, education, race, gender, occupational prestige). Drawing on the principle of homophily (Lazarfeld and Merton 1954), he argued that "the probability of two individuals sharing a network connection (i.e., friendship, kinship, etc.) is a direct function of their similarity in sociodemographic and spatial characteristics. That is, the more similar two people are, the more likely they are to share a network connection; in more

4.2 Homophily and Commitment

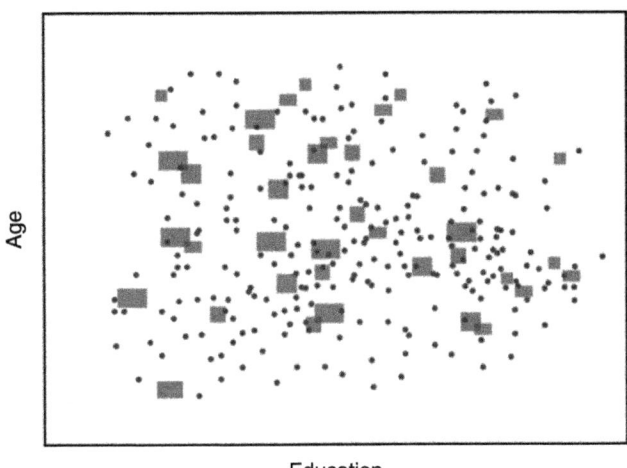

Figure 4.1 Blau Space *(adapted from figure 2 in McPherson, Popielarz, and Drobnic 1992:155)*

informal terms, birds of a feather flock together" (Rotolo and McPherson 2001:1101). As such, he adopted an approach that stands standard social network analysis on its head in that it uses peoples' attributes to infer their ties. It locates people in social space based on sociodemographic characteristics, and the more socially similar they are, the more likely they will form a tie.

Miller McPherson, along with his colleagues and students (McPherson and Ranger-Moore 1991; McPherson, Popielarz, and Drobnic 1992; Popielarz and McPherson 1995; McPherson and Rotolo 1996; Cress, McPherson, and Rotolo 1997; Mark 1998; Rotolo and McPherson 2001), have extended Blau's theory to the study of groups. They do so by locating individuals and groups in sociodemographic space, or what they sometimes refer to as "Blau Space" (McPherson and Ranger-Moore 1991; McPherson 2004; Brashears 2008). "In this space, people who are close to one another have a greater chance of knowing each other, interacting with one each other, or having other social network connections than people who are distant from one another" (McPherson, Popielarz, and Drobnic 1992:154). Figure 4.1 illustrates their approach. It presents sociodemographic space in terms of two dimensions: age and years of education (adapted from figure 2 in McPherson, Popielarz, and Drobnic 1992:155). Points represent individuals, and squares represent groups. McPherson and his colleagues have found that people located closer to a particular group in terms of sociodemographic space are not only more likely to join it, but those located closer to a group's sociodemographic center are more likely to remain with it for an extended period of time (see e.g., McPherson, Popielarz, and Drobnic 1992;

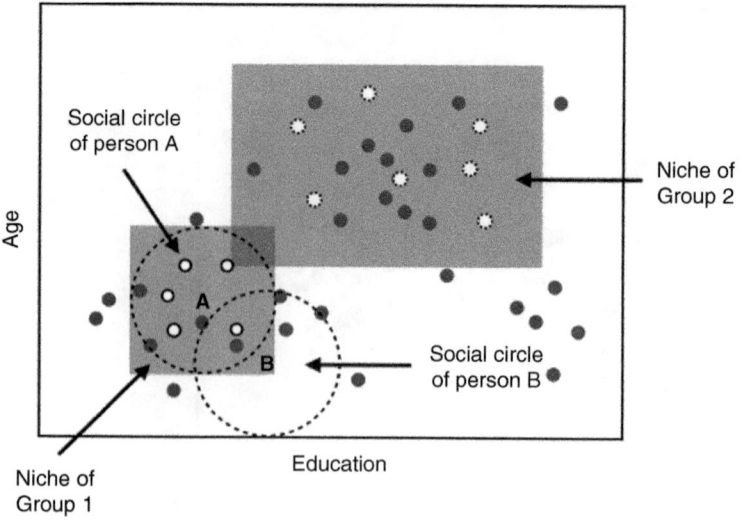

Figure 4.2 Niche edge effect *(adapted from figures 1 and 2 in Popielarz and McPherson 1995:700, 703)*

Cress, McPherson, and Rotolo 1997). Put differently, they found that groups are more likely to lose members located on the group's edge (i.e., its periphery) than they are those located at the group's center (i.e., the core). They call this the "niche edge, niche overlap" effect (Popielarz and McPherson 1995).

Niche Edge, Niche Overlap

Figure 4.2 illustrates the "niche edge" effect (adapted from figures 1 and 2 in Popielarz and McPherson 1995:700, 703). It presents a slice of sociodemographic space in which various individuals and two groups are located. The squares represent the groups; they differ in size because their niches in social space differ. A group "whose members are spread widely in social space ... is heterogeneous in member characteristics and is called a generalist," whereas a group that is "more restrictive in its membership in social space is [called] a 'specialist'" (Popielarz and McPherson 1995:700).[4] The white circles with a solid border indicate members of the group located in group 1, the white circles with a dashed border indicate members of group 2, and the dark gray circles represent individuals located in a group's niche but who are not members of the group. Now consider the two members of group 1 – A and B – and their

---

[4] Although Popielarz and McPherson do not consider religious groups in particular, it is likely that the strict churches we examined in the first chapter would be considered specialists, while more lenient churches would be considered generalists.

4.2 Homophily and Commitment

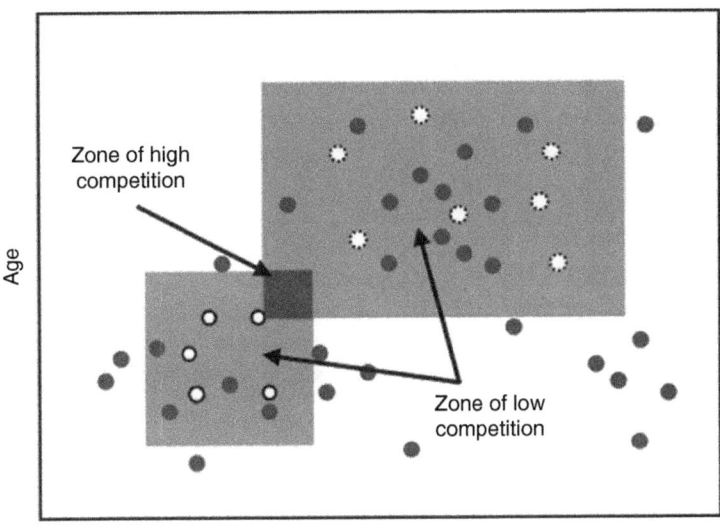

Figure 4.3 Niche overlap effect *(adapted from figure 3 in Popielarz and McPherson 1995:705)*

respective social circles (indicated by dashed lines). Their social circles reflect "the area of social space within which the homophily principle guarantees most of their network contacts lie" (Popielarz and McPherson 1995:702). As the figure suggests, A is located at the center of the group, and his or her social circle is located entirely in the group's niche. Thus, it includes current and potential members of the group and thus "reinforces membership in the group" (Popielarz and McPherson 1995:702). By contrast, B is located on the group's periphery, and his or her social circle includes several individuals located outside of the group's niche, and ties to such individuals can pull members away from and out of a group. That is why, according to Popielarz and McPherson, individuals located on the edge of a group's niche are more likely to leave than are those located at a group's center.

Now consider Figure 4.3 (adapted from figure 3 in Popielarz and McPherson 1995:705), which illustrates the niche overlap effect. It shows how the niches of two groups can (and often) overlap and thus compete for members. Individuals located in an area in social space where two or more groups recruit "are subject to the highest intergroup competitive pressure," and numerous "opportunities for organizational membership make their affiliation with any one group tenuous" (Popielarz and McPherson 1995:704–705). Put differently, members located in areas of social space where multiple groups compete for their time and money tend to leave groups at higher rates than do members located in areas where few or no groups overlap.

There is an implicit connection here with Mark Granovetter's (1973) weak and strong tie argument discussed in Chapter 2. In fact, in a related but separate study, McPherson, Popielarz, and Drobnic (1992) specifically tested for strong and weak tie effects. Unsurprisingly, they hypothesized that strong ties to other group members should increase the length of time that someone belongs to a group as compared to weak ties to group members. However, they also hypothesized that weak ties to nonmembers would decrease the length of time of group memberships more than would strong ties to nonmembers. Why? Because weak ties are more likely to connect people to distant parts of the social structure and expose them to different social worlds:

> If this line of argument is true, then weak ties will be more likely than strong ties to provide information not already known to ego. Weak ties outside the group open possibilities for new affiliations not available to an individual through strong ties because the strong ties are redundant.
>
> (McPherson, Popielarz, and Drobnic 1992:159)

They found support for the second hypothesis but not the first. All else being equal, strong ties did increase the time that individuals stayed with a group but not more so than weak ties. By contrast, weak ties to nonmembers increased the likelihood that someone would leave a group than did strong ties, providing evidence that weak ties are more likely to bridge social distance and introduce individuals to novel information.

Why Congregations Tend to Be Racially Homogenous

Few have challenged the Rev. Martin Luther King, Jr.'s (reported) remark that "11 AM on a Sunday morning is the most segregated hour in America," and apart from appeals to racist beliefs and behaviors, even fewer have been able to explain why that is so. Recently, however, sociologists Michael Emerson and Christian Smith (2000) have demonstrated that much of the racial homogeny found in America's faith communities can be attributed to factors other than white prejudice. Instead, they "argue that in the face of social and religious pluralism, the organization of religious pluralism, the organization of American religion drives religious groups toward internal similarity" (Emerson and Smith 2000:136). In a nod to the religious economies approach, they note that the competitive American religious marketplace has led religious groups to specialize and market themselves to a specific segment (niche) of the population, which means they tend to attract individuals quite similar to one another:

4.2 Homophily and Commitment

> In the process of competing, of developing niches and assuring internal strength, congregations come to be made up of highly similar people. Individual congregations tend to be made up of people from similar geographic locations, similar socioeconomic statuses, similar ethnicities, and, perhaps first and foremost, predominantly the same race.
> (Emerson and Smith 2000:142)

Drawing on subcultural identity theory, they also note that faith communities that draw distinct boundaries between themselves and others tend to do a better job of providing members with a sense of meaning and belonging. An unfortunate consequence of this is that the religious marketplace tends to favor internally similar congregations over dissimilar ones, which works against the formation of racially heterogeneous faith communities. They also argue that internally similar congregations are "less costly" to sustain and thus are at a competitive advantage over internally diverse ones:

> The key generalization is this: the cost of producing meaning, belonging, and security in internally diverse congregations is usually much greater – because of the increased complexity of demands, needs, and backgrounds, the increased effort necessary to create social solidarity and group identity, and the greater potential for internal conflict. Thus, *internally homogenous congregations more often provide what draws people to religious groups for a lower cost than do internally diverse congregations.*
> (Emerson and Smith 2000:145)

Moreover, they note that social psychological studies have repeatedly found that people tend to prefer to be with others like themselves, with race being a primary marker of similarity and difference.

> It does not matter that there is little or no biological basis for the perception that people are racially similar. If a society attaches importance to some characteristic, that society will come to see people with that characteristic as similar. Individuals then use those categories when choosing groups and other social associations.
> (Emerson and Smith 2000:145)

Finally, Emerson and Smith draw on the niche edge, niche overlap effect in order to explain why interracial faith communities are rare. To illustrate, they tell the (true) story of a Seattle church's unsuccessful attempt to establish an interracial faith community. The church was founded by an African American pastor just out of seminary, who prior to founding the church, visited white and black churches in the area, sharing with them his vision of an interracial church and asking for volunteers to be charter members. After a year of preparation, the church held its first public service, and the congregation was almost evenly split between blacks and whites (Emerson and Smith 2000:147). As the church grew, however, the congregation began losing its white members, and within three years, fewer than ten remained. The first few who left (all of whom were charter members) claimed they did so because they felt like outsiders and their opinions were not being heard. Regardless as to whether their perception of the situation was accurate, their decision to leave ultimately had a deleterious effect on the church's makeup:

> There were fewer within-church social network ties to keep whites there and recruit new white members. Whites leaving also meant an increasingly great number of social ties outside the church for the remaining whites, making the church less central for them, and making them feel increasingly like outsiders, and that their needs were not being met.
> (Emerson and Smith 2000:149)

In essence, those who were on the group's periphery were ultimately pulled away by ties to others outside of the niche, some of whom were members of competing faith communities, most likely the ones from which they originally came. Thus, in spite of the desire and commitment of the church's original members, macro forces over which they had little control helped push the congregation in a direction they did not want to go: toward racial homogeneity.

4.3 Mobility and Commitment

Niche edge and niche overlap effects are not the only drivers of commitment, or lack thereof. Another is geographic mobility. People who are constantly on the move are less likely to invest the time and energy needed to be active participants in voluntary associations, including religious ones.

> People who move to a new city, or from one suburb to another, must reaffiliate with a church, a fraternal lodge, a service club, and other such organizations. People who move often must reaffiliate often or let their memberships lapse. At the very least, there will be a natural lag time in reaffiliation, and some people will move again before this normal lag time is up, thus continuing to be unaffiliated. These effects of movement undoubtedly are greatly amplified in communities where large proportions of the population move often. In more stable communities, newcomers

4.3 Mobility and Commitment

are easily reconnected to a church or to other organizations by neighbors and fellow workers who are members. But to the degree that one's neighbors and fellow workers are themselves unaffiliated newcomers, the reconnecting process is impeded.

(Stark and Bainbridge 1985:94)

That is why one of the strongest predictors of congregational membership (and attendance) is population turnover. For instance, Robert Wuthnow and Kevin Christiano (1979) found that people who had recently moved were less likely to attend worship than people who had not, and Rodney Stark and William Bainbridge (1985) discovered a strong negative correlation between population turnover and church membership. This relationship is illustrated in Figure 4.4, which compares, at the state level, three measures of geographic mobility and church membership.[5] On the left are four maps of the United States, where the darker a state is shaded, the greater the presence of that particular variable in that state; on the right is that particular measure's correlation with church membership in 1990. For example, in the uppermost map, the state of Florida is a dark gray and the state of Louisiana is a light gray indicating that a larger percentage of people living in Florida had lived in different state in 1985 (five years previous) than had in Louisiana, and as you can see, there is a strong negative correlation between a state's church membership rate and the percent of a state's residents who lived in a different state in the preceding five years. The figure also shows that there is a strong, positive correlation between church membership rates and the percentage of those born in their state of residence and those who still lived in the same house they did five years before.

Michael Welch and John Baltzell argue that geographic mobility's effect occurs indirectly through an individual's social network. They estimated a path model that included measures of geographic mobility, social ties, a sense of belonging to their community, and church attendance (rather than church membership) rates, which suggests that geographic mobility inhibits church attendance rates "primarily by disrupting the established patterns of acquaintance ties individuals maintained within the communities in which they previously resided and by inhibiting the formation of new ties in their new communities of residence" (Welch and Baltzell 1984:89).

Another dynamic highlighted by the maps presented in Figure 4.4 is what is commonly referred to as religious regionalism, where some parts of the country are characterized by high levels of religious commitment (e.g., the South) and others just the opposite (e.g., the West). What is interesting is that these patterns persist in spite of the fact that people

---

[5] The maps were created using the MicroCase Analysis System (Wadsworth 2003) and its compiled dataset, "The Fifty States of the United States, 2006."

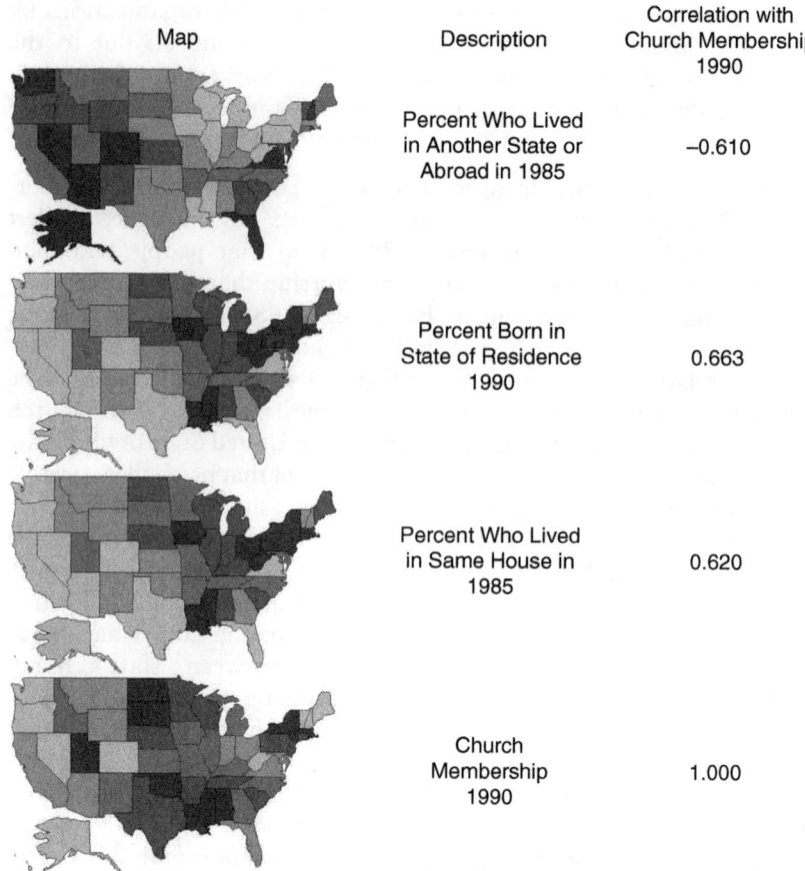

Figure 4.4 Geographic mobility and church membership

move from one part of the country to another. Thus, we hear stories about individuals moving from, say, Monterey, California, to Houston, Texas, and suddenly becoming more religious, as if there is "something about merely being in the South ... [that] leads one to have a stronger religious commitment" (Smith, Sikkink, and Bailey 1998:504). Similar stories could undoubtedly be told in reverse.

What accounts for religious regionalism? In an interesting application of multiagent modeling, Laurence Iannaccone and Michael Makowsky demonstrate that people tend to accommodate themselves to the culture in which they live. Religious regionalism is an emergent phenomenon that results from a combination of personal experience and social conformity. Because newcomers adapt to "their new social environment, ... a region can remain 'blue' despite a large influx of 'reds.' As newcomers change their colors, the West acquires 'accidental' atheists and the South gains 'accidental' enthusiasts" (Iannaccone and Makowsky 2007:2).

Does this mean that the negative correlation between geographic mobility and religious commitment is simply an artifact of religious regionalism? No. Iannaccone and Makowsky are clear that, all things equal, "residential mobility tends to reduce religious activity" (2007:3). However, their study does suggest that even if the mobility of individuals living in the West slows down or the mobility of those living in the South picks up, levels of religious commitment in the two regions will not change dramatically. It is as if the religious characters of the regions have been "written in stone" and nothing short of an act of God will cause them to change.

4.4 Community and Commitment

Given how macro forces such as homophily and mobility can make it difficult for groups to retain members, is there anything groups can do to improve retention rates? Yes. In particular, they can develop practices that not only help to embed members more deeply into their communities but also counteract those forces that threaten to entice people to leave. Sharon Nepstad's (2004) analysis of the Plowshares movement identifies several such practices. Building on the work of Doug McAdam's (1986) examination of the Mississippi Freedom Summer campaign, Nepstad examines how one group enhances commitment and limits group defection. As we saw in the previous chapter, McAdam argues that attitudes receptive to a movement's ideology are necessary (attitudinal affinity), but they are not enough for someone to join a group or movement. Potential activists also need to be "biographically available," that is, "relatively free from life responsibilities such as full-time employment and family obligations" (Nepstad 2004:44). And they need social ties to other activists in order to be pulled in. The Freedom Summer campaign only lasted for a short time, however, so the issue of long-term retention was not applicable. "Yet many movements endure for years, entail multiple campaigns, and have no clear end point. Under these circumstances, some participants inevitably become less committed or drop out completely" (Nepstad 2004:44). According to Nepstad, this occurs when peoples' convictions diminish, when their ties to the movement and its members weaken, when there is an increase in life responsibilities (i.e., biographical *unavailability*), when they burn out, and when their ties to people and organizations outside of the movement either disapprove of their activism or entice them to get involved in something else. The question for Nepstad is: What mechanisms can movements employ in order to counteract forces that undermine the commitment of their members?

For an answer, she turns to Plowshares, a pacifist movement associated with the Roman Catholic Left that engages in symbolic protests against war and nuclear proliferation. The movement takes its name from the prophet Isaiah who looked forward to the day when "swords would be beaten into plowshares" (Isaiah 2:4), and it traces its roots to Dorothy Day and the Catholic Worker movement. Its most famous members are the Berrigan brothers (Phil and Dan), Roman Catholic priests who engaged in a number of acts of civil disobedience. For example, on more than one occasion during the Vietnam War, they broke into draft board offices and poured blood over draft files, and in 1980 they, along with six others, broke into a Pennsylvania General Electric Nuclear Missile facility and damaged the nose cones of nuclear warheads. For this latter act, they became known as the "Plowshares Eight" because they claimed that by damaging nuclear warheads, they were symbolically beating swords into plowshares. It also formally gave birth to the Plowshares movement, which over the years has engaged in a number of antiwar and antinuclear protests around the world.

The movement itself is a loose network of activists and communities, the primary ones being Catholic Worker houses, which are located around the United States and throughout the world;[6] the Jonah House, which is located in Baltimore, Maryland (and founded by Phil Berrigan and his wife after they left their respective religious orders); and the Atlantic Life Community network, which is associated with Jonah House and organizes retreats for those involved in the antiwar movement. According to Nepstad, it is through participation in these three sets of communities that helps sustain member commitment and reduces the likelihood that members will leave. She notes that of the fifty-four Plowshare activists she surveyed, 81 percent had volunteered at a Catholic Worker house, 94 percent had attended an Atlantic Life Community gathering, and 97 percent had visited the Jonah House (Nepstad 2004:50). And these are not simply drive-by visits. Rather, activists, at least those who remain active, spend a considerable amount of time at one or more of these communities. "Nearly 60 percent have lived at a Catholic Worker house for more than a year and roughly 30 percent have lived at Jonah House for one or more years ... [and] almost three-quarters have participated in four or more Atlantic Life Community retreats; about one-third have been to 15 or more" (Nepstad 2004:55).

Why do these communities play such an important role? Nepstad identifies four important mechanisms that these communities employ.[7]

---

[6] According to the Catholic Worker website, there are currently 216 domestic (i.e., US) and 33 international houses/communities; see www.catholicworker.org/communities/directory.html.

[7] Although she does not reference the pertinent literature, Nepstad's conclusions are similar to those of cognitive anthropologists and organizational sociologists who study

4.4 Community and Commitment

First, through various rituals and cultural practices, they function as plausibility structures that help reinforce the convictions of activist members. In particular, they help maintain "activists' commitment to Plowshares goals and values" through communal practices such as "singing, prayer, and biblical reflection" (Nepstad 2004:51, 52). For example, at a 2002 retreat shortly after Christmas, leaders compared Herod and the slaughter of innocents (Mt. 2:13–23) to contemporary leaders and the unnecessary deaths of children in the Middle East, and they sang carols, such as "Silent Night," with alternative lyrics (Nepstad 2004:53):

> Silent night, holy night
> All is not calm
> All is not right
> Millions die from war and poverty
> Children living in misery
> Stop the violence, choose life
> Stop the violence, choose life

Second, participation in protest events organized by these communities help to deepen activist identity, which Nepstad argues derives not from identification with a particular ideology or political group but from action. Third, Plowshares communities help members remain biographically available for activism by providing material assistance and family support. This not only allows activists to take jobs that offer enough flexibility so that they can participate in protests but are often lower paying, but it provides them with the freedom to go to jail if necessary, a not uncommon occurrence for Plowshares activists (Nepstad 2004:57).

Finally, and what interests her most, participation in the Plowshares communities helps to strengthen the ties between activists. As we saw earlier, activists spend a considerable amount of time at one or more Plowshares houses or gatherings, and as Nepstad emphasizes, "ongoing contact is necessary to sustain these bonds over time" (2004:55). Put somewhat differently, participation helps embed activists deep in the center of the movement's niche rather than at its edge, thus increasing the likelihood they will stay.

While members of most faith communities do not face the same pressures that Plowshares activists do, most faith communities do struggle with member commitment retention and could probably adapt some of the practices that the Plowshares movement employs. In fact, one could argue that the megachurch small group model discussed at the outset of the chapter does just that. Small groups help reinforce beliefs, strengthen ties among members, and almost certainly deepen peoples' identity with

---

"communities of practice" (see e.g., Brown and Duguid 1991; Lave and Wenger 1991; Wenger 1998; Hundeide 2003).

the church. And given that many small groups are tailored for people in different parts of the life course (e.g., college and career, young families, singles, seniors, etc.), to a limited extent they help mitigate the effects of potential barriers to greater participation in the church.

4.5 Commitment and Conformity

What effect do social ties have on people who are already members of a group? Research has found that they are far more likely to conform when they are embedded in dense networks rather than sparse ones. One reason is that dense networks make it easier for groups to monitor the behavior of their members and prevent them from engaging in deviant behavior (Bott 1957; Coleman 1990; Granovetter 1992, 2005). For example, the perception that some individuals may not be fully committed to a group's beliefs can lead to gossip that can harm their reputations (Burt and Knez 1995). A second reason is that people are more likely to conform when they run the risk of losing their relationships to people they care about.

> When we are alone even the most respectable of us act in ways we would not were anyone present. People who have no relationships with family or close friends, or whose relationships are with persons far away, are essentially alone all the time. They do not risk their attachments if they are detected in deviant behavior because they have none to lose.
> (Finke and Stark 2005:35)[8]

And because people who are embedded in dense networks are probably more likely to possess ties they are reluctant to lose (i.e., strong ties) than are those embedded in sparse networks, social conformity tends to be more common in the former than in the latter. That is why frontier areas, like the Wild West, tend to be short on piety and long on deviance. People are constantly passing through on their way to somewhere else, which, as we have seen, makes it difficult for ties (and, by extension, institutions) to form (Finke and Stark 2005).

Amy Adamczyk and Jacob Felson uncovered similar dynamics with regards to adolescent coital debut (i.e., sexual intercourse for the first time). They found that it was less likely for adolescents who were embedded in dense social networks composed of religious friends.

---

[8] Philip Zimbardo makes a similar point. He writes, "When people feel anonymous in a situation, as if no one is aware of their true identity (and thus that no one probably cares), they can more easily be induced to behave in antisocial ways" (Zimbardo 2007:219).

4.5 Commitment and Conformity

> Adolescents [who] spend a lot of time with religious friends ... should become more attached to them and be exposed to more negative messages about extramarital sex. By having premarital sex, which violates religious precepts, teens ... jeopardize relationships with religious friends ... Likewise, in dense networks, adolescents should be more successful in monitoring each other's actions.
>
> (Adamczyk and Felson 2006:927, 929)

In other words, the greater the proportion that an adolescent's friends were religious, the greater the likelihood that he or she would conform to the teachings of his or her faith community (assuming, of course, that most faith communities discourage premarital sex), whether the adolescent did so because of monitoring by other members, because he or she feared losing ties to people he or she cared about, or a combination of both.

Rural Southern Black Church: A Semi-involuntary Institution?

The pressure to conform can sometimes lead marginal church members to participate even when they have little or no desire to do so. Take the Black Church, for example. Scholars have noted how it has historically served as the African American community's primary instrument of communication, entertainment, education, mutual aid, and, at least for males, a vehicle for upward mobility (DuBois 1969; Frazier 1974; Lincoln and Mamiya 1990; Caldwell, Green, and Billingsley 1992). This has led some to argue that it is something of a "semi-involuntary" institution in that some people attend worship services and participate in church activities not for religious rewards but in order to avoid the sanctions they would incur if they did not participate (Lewis 1955; Nelsen and Nelsen 1975; Nelson, Yokley, and Nelsen 1971:10). Many scholars also believe that this is truer for those living in the rural South than those living outside of it because, at least historically, those in the rural South have had access to fewer secular opportunities for achieving personal status and prestige (Nelsen 1988; Taylor 1988a, 1988b; Ellison and Sherkat 1990). This has led them to argue that not only should African Americans in the rural South display the highest rates of attendance, but they should also display the highest rates of intermittent attendance because those who do not want to attend but feel compelled to do so will only attend often enough in order to maintain their social standing within the community (Ellison and Sherkat 1995, 1999).

Using data from the 1979–1980 National Survey of Black Americans, Christopher Ellison and Darren Sherkat (1995) found that this was indeed the case (see Table 4.1). In the rural South 90.5 percent of respondents

Table 4.1 *Church attendance and participation levels*

	Rural South	Urban South	Non-South
Levels of Church Attendance			
Nearly every day	4.4%	4.7%	3.7%
At least once a week	35.6%	34.6%	29.9%
A few times a month	40.7%	30.5%	20.9%
A few times a year	9.8%	17.5%	21.3%
Less than once a year	4.6%	6.1%	13.3%
Not since age 18	4.9%	6.8%	11.1%
Levels of Participation in Other Church Activities			
Nearly every day	2.5%	2.8%	2.4%
At least once a week	18.2%	16.2%	14.8%
A few times a month	31.0%	18.7%	12.7%
A few times a year	15.7%	14.7%	12.3%
Never	32.7%	47.6%	57.7%

Source: Ellison and Sherkat (1995:1423)

indicated they attended church a few times a year or more, as compared to respondents in the urban South (87.1 percent) and non-South (75.6 percent). Moreover, the rates of intermittent attendance (i.e., attending church a few times a month) were far higher in the rural South (40.7 percent) than in the urban South (30.5 percent) and non-South (20.9 percent). Rates of participation in other types of church activities (presented in the second half of Table 4.1) reveal a similar pattern.

More directly related to this chapter's topic, Ellison and Sherkat's multivariate analysis found that the *frequency of contact with friends* was a statistically significant predictor of church attendance and participation for African Americans in the rural and urban South but not for those living outside of the South, suggesting that social ties have a conforming effect on religious behavior for African Americans living in the South. Moreover, the effect is larger in the rural South than it is in the urban South. These results, of course, do not irrefutably establish that the social networks of rural and urban southern African Americans lead some to participate in their local church when they otherwise would not (see, e.g., Hunt and Hunt 1999; see response by Ellison and Sherkat 1999), but the results are consistent with it.

4.6 Summary and Conclusion

Much of the literature on religion and social networks focuses on the important role that social ties play in terms of recruitment and conversion.

However, as we have seen in this chapter, social ties are instrumental for keeping people involved in their faith communities and movements. As the studies by Stark and Bainbridge (1980a), Popielarz and McPherson (1995), and Emerson and Smith (2000) show, members located at a group's periphery are much more difficult to keep from leaving than are those located at its center. Geographic mobility also makes it difficult for faith communities to retain members; people "just passing through" are less likely to invest time and energy in a local faith community. Thus, it becomes incumbent upon congregations to adopt practices similar to those identified by Nepstad (2004), at least if they wish to survive. As the final section on commitment and conformity highlights, however, there is a potential "dark side" to social ties. People deeply embedded in networks will often feel pressure to conform to beliefs and practices they may not fully embrace.

4.7 For Further Reading

Numerous studies have explored the dynamics of "Blau Space." A good place to start is with Peter Blau himself. He first outlined his theory in 1977 with his *Inequality and Heterogeneity*, and then later refined it in 1994 with *Structural Contexts of Opportunities*.[9] In the years since, Miller McPherson and his collaborators have produced a number of "Blau Space" studies, including the following:

- Brashears, Matthew E. 2008. "Gender and Homophily: Differences in Male and Female Association in Blau Space." *Social Science Research* 37:400–415.
- Cress, Daniel M., J. Miller McPherson, and Thomas Rotolo. 1997. "Competition and Commitment in Voluntary Memberships: The Paradox of Persistence and Participation." *Sociological Perspectives* 40(1):61–79.
- Mark, Noah. 1998. "Birds of a Feather Sing Together." *Social Forces* 77(2):453–485.
- McPherson, J. Miller. 2004. "A Blau Space Primer: Prolegomenon to an Ecology of Affiliation." *Industrial and Corporate Change* 13:263–280.
- McPherson, J. Miller, Pamela A. Popielarz, and Sonja Drobnic. 1992. "Social Networks and Organizational Dynamics." *American Sociological Review* 57(2):153–170.

---

[9] I have found Jonathan Turner's (1998:531–542) summary of Blau's theory to be quite helpful.

- McPherson, J. Miller, and James R. Ranger-Moore. 1991. "Evolution on a Dancing Landscape: Organizations and Networks in Dynamic Blau Space." *Social Forces* 70(1):19–42.
- McPherson, J. Miller, and Lynn Smith-Lovin. 1987. "Homophily in Voluntary Organizations: Status Distance and the Composition of Face-to-Face Groups." *American Sociological Review* 52(3):370–379.
- McPherson, J. Miller, Lynn Smith-Lovin, and James M. Cook. 2001. "Birds of a Feather: Homophily in Social Networks." *Annual Review of Sociology* 27:415–444.
- Popielarz, Pamela A., and J. Miller McPherson. 1995. "On the Edge or in Between: Niche Position, Niche Overlap, and the Duration of Voluntary Association Memberships." *American Journal of Sociology* 101(3):698–720.

Readers may also be interested in the R package, *Blaunet*, which has been designed specifically for analyzing Blau Space (Wang et al. 2015).

Undoubtedly, the best-known example of multiagent modeling is Thomas Schelling's (1971) classic on residential segregation, but to the best of my knowledge Iannaccone and Makowsky (2007) are the first to apply it to religious phenomena. Makowsky (2011a, 2011b, 2012) has continued to explore religious phenomena using multiagent models, which can be found at his website for those who are interested.[10]

Most of the literature on the use of small groups by megachurches is written by church insiders, but there has been some scholarly work on the topic. Robert Wuthnow (1993, 1994a, 1994b) was among the first to explore the phenomenon in his 1994 book, *Sharing the Journey*, along with a couple of companion articles that appeared in *The Christian Century* ("Small Groups Forge New Notions of Community and the Sacred") and *Christianity Today* ("How Small Groups Are Transforming Our Lives"). The research by Scott Thumma and his colleagues (see, e.g., Thumma and Travis 2007; Thumma and Bird 2015) is quite good, and David Eagle (2015) does a first-rate job placing today's megachurches in their historical context. Finally, the numerous studies by Mark Chaves and his colleagues/students (see, e.g., Chaves et al. 1999; Chaves 2004, 2006; Chaves and Anderson 2008, 2014) of congregational life in the United States are invaluable.

For those interested in exploring the role of the Black Church in the United States, W.E.B. DuBois's *The Souls of Black Folk* is considered

---

[10] www.michaelmakowsky.com/source-code/

a classic, and Eric Lincoln and Lawrence Mamia's *The Black Church in the African American Experience* offers a helpful perspective. Ellison and Sherkat's original 1995 article generated a minor debate, so readers may want to see Larry and Matthew Hunt's (1999) critique and Ellison and Sherkat's (1999) response. Finally, consult the numerous citations in Ellison and Sherkat's original article.

Part III

Ties That Loose

5

Diffusion and Innovation

5.1 Introduction

Abhay Charan De was born in Calcutta on September 1, 1896, into a Vaishnava family (i.e., devotees of the Hindu deity Vishnu).[1] Abhay Charan, whose name means "one who is fearless, having taken shelter at Lord Krishna's feet" (Wikipedia 2017c), was also called Nandulal because he was born on the day of Nandotsava, which celebrates Nanda, Krishna's father, and is a traditional festival in honor of Krishna's birth (Wikipedia 2017f). Abhay was educated at the prestigious Scottish Church College, which is the oldest continuously running Christian liberal arts and sciences college in India,[2] and to which, at least in the early twentieth century, many Vaishnava families sent their sons. He graduated in 1920, majoring in English, philosophy, and economics, but he rejected his diploma in response to Gandhi's independence movement. He married when he was twenty-two, had children, and for many years ran a pharmaceutical business. He met his first spiritual master, Bhaktisiddhanta Sarasvati Thakura, in 1922, and eleven years later he was formally initiated as one of his disciples. Beginning in 1950 he lived at a mandir (temple) in the town of Vrindavan, where he began writing his commentary and translation of the Bhagavata Purana, one of Hinduism's eighteen great Puranas[3] and "the source of many popular stories of Krishna's childhood told for centuries on the Indian subcontinent and of legends explaining Hindu festivals such as Holi and Diwali" (Wikipedia 2017b). In 1959 he became a sannyasin, that is, a renunciant, someone who cuts all ties with ordinary life (Ellwood and McGraw 2005:62, 521), and in 1965, at the age of sixty-nine, he traveled to the United States "to spread awareness and love of Krishna in the West" (Knott 1998:65). A year later he founded the International Society for

---

[1] Much of this opening section is based on the Wikipedia entry about Abhay Charan De, also known as A. C. Bhaktivedanta Swami Prabhupada (Wikipedia 2017f).
[2] See www.scottishchurch.ac.in.
[3] The Puranas are mythological texts composed from 300 CE to 900 CE that "refer to earlier events, often telling the stories of the gods and goddesses" (Knott 1998:16).

Table 5.1 *Easter teachers who moved to the United States after 1965*

Year	Name	Religious Tradition	Country
1965	Swami Bhaktivedanta	Hare Krishnas (ISKCON)	India
1965	Sant Keshavadas	Temple of Cosmic Wisdom	India
1965	Thera Bode Vinita	Buddhist Vihara Society	Sri Lanka
1968	Yogi Bhajan	Sikh Dharma	India/Pakistan
1969	Tarthang Tulku	Tibetan Nyingmapa	Tibet
1970	Swami Rama	Himalayan Institute	India
1971	Swami Satchidananda	Integral Yoga Institute	India
1971	Gurudev Chitrabhanu	Meditation International Center	India
1971	Maharaj Ji	Divine Light Mission	India
1972	Sun Myung Moon	Unification Church (Moonies)	Korea
1972	Shree Vesant Paranjpe	Fivefold Path	India

Source: Adapted from Melton, 1987:52

Krishna Consciousness (ISKCON), more commonly known as Hare Krishnas. It initially attracted a large following, and Swami Bhaktivendanta (as Abhay Charan was now known) was welcomed by Western scholars such as Harvey Cox of Harvard Divinity School. However, because of the restrictive recruitment practices that we examined in the third chapter, it is debatable how successful ISKCON has been in the intervening years.

Swami Bhaktivendanta was only one of several teachers from the East who moved to the United States and whose teachings attracted a following in the 1970s, especially among America's youth (see Table 5.1). As we saw in the first chapter, some scholars believed this signaled the development of a new religious consciousness, one that challenged Western-style materialism, individualism, and rationalism (Wuthnow 1976), while others, such as Gordon Melton, have argued that "the growth of the so-called new religions (primarily the old religions of Asia newly arrived in the West) can be traced to the movement of Eastern teachers to take up residency in the United States beginning in 1965" (Melton 1987:52) after a series of immigration laws banning immigration from several Asian countries were abolished (Iannaccone, Finke, and Stark 1997).

The former explanation constitutes a demand side explanation, while the latter is an example of a supply side one. However, it is also a diffusion story, and unsurprisingly religious beliefs and practices often diffuse across network ties. For example, jimi adams and Jenny Trinitapoli (2009:280) demonstrated that the social networks in which Malawi religious leaders are embedded influence the degree to which they are involved in HIV prevention and the types of strategies they employ, and Lené Levy-Storms and Steven Wallace (2003) found that

Samoan women who were well connected to their church-based networks were more likely to have or already have had a mammogram. In this chapter, we consider a handful of studies that have explored the diffusion of religion in depth. We begin by examining the spread of Rabbinic Judaism across the Roman Empire in the first few centuries of the common era. We first explore how archeologists have drawn on social network analysis tools and theories to examine ties among various localities. Next, we consider the study by Hyojoung Kim and Steven Pfaff (2012), who found that diffusion of the Protestant Reformation occurred through city-to-university ties with college students functioning as bridges between the two. Finally, we look at the diffusion of women's ordination across Protestant denominations; there we will see that ecumenical ties play a crucial role in determining whether a denomination ultimately begins to ordain women.

5.2 Archeological Networks and the Diffusion of Rabbinic Judaism

Archeologists are increasingly turning to social network analysis methods to analyze the connections between archeological sites (Knappett 2011; Brughmans, Collar, and Coward 2016). One of their biggest challenges is determining what constitutes a tie between two sites. Numerous approaches have been developed. Proximal point analysis (PPA) has been around the longest and is by far the simplest (Terrell 1997, 2010). It connects sites by linking each to its k nearest neighbors, typically three (Broodbank 1993:321). Its weakness lies in the fact that "it is indifferent to the limitations of travel technology" (Rivers 2017:133). Two sites can be close in terms of "how the bird flies," but they may be quite distant from one another in terms of travel time. Nevertheless, its simplicity makes it attractive, which is why if archeologists "know only one network model it is likely to be PPA" (Rivers 2017:133).

To illustrate PPA, consider Figure 5.1, which maps the thirty-two largest cities in the Roman Empire circa 200 CE analyzed by Stark (1996a, 2006), plus the city of Jerusalem.[4] All of the cities are white except Jerusalem, which is black. The top map plots just the cities themselves, whereas the bottom one links the cities together using PPA. Two details are worth noting. First, some cities, such as Jerusalem, have ties to more than three other cities. Why? Because although each city is only tied to its three closest neighbors, those neighbors may be tied to additional cities because they are among those cities' three closest neighbors. Take Jerusalem, for instance, which has five ties. Its three closest cities are

---

[4] Figures 5.1 through 5.3 were created in ORA NetScenes (Carley 2016).

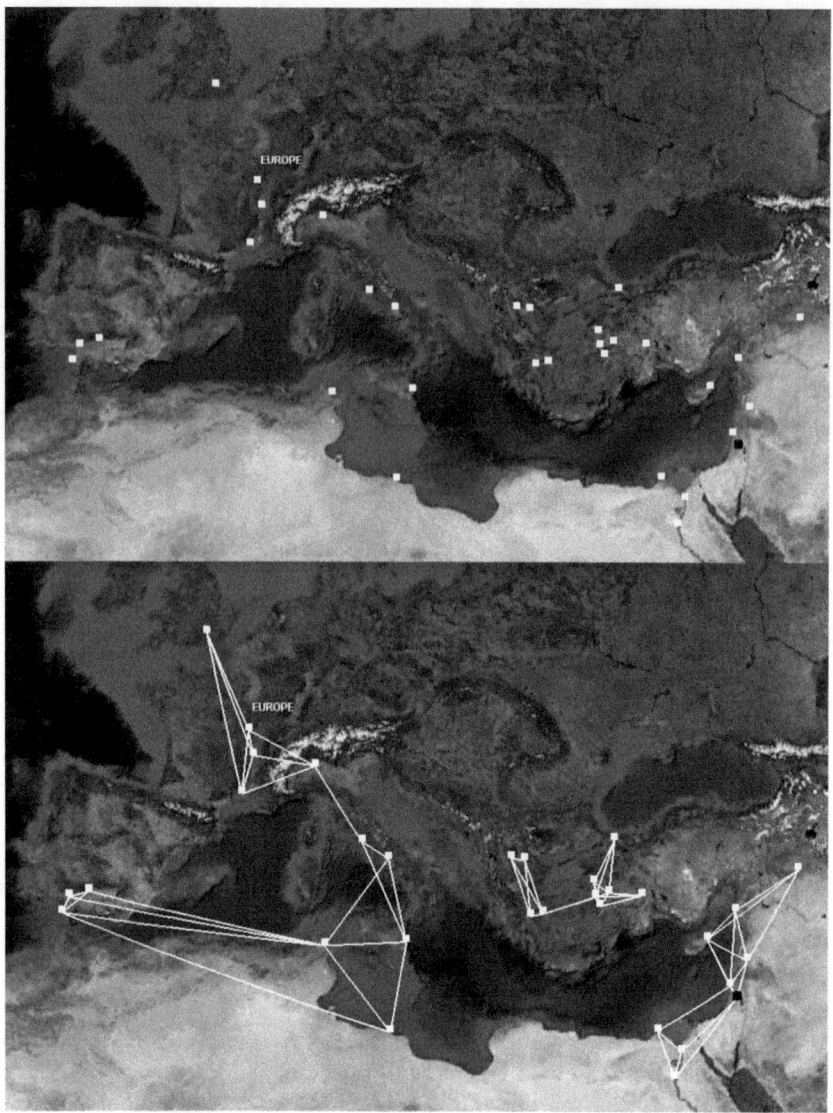

Figure 5.1 Proximal point analysis network of cities in the Roman Empire, 200 CE

Caesarea Maritima, Damascus, and Salamis. However, it is also one of the three closest cities to Memphis and to Oxyrhynchus. The second detail worth noting is that the network is disconnected. There are three distinct clusters unconnected with one another, suggesting that at least in this case, the PPA mapping of network ties among Rome's largest cities

5.2 Archeological Networks & Rabbinic Judaism

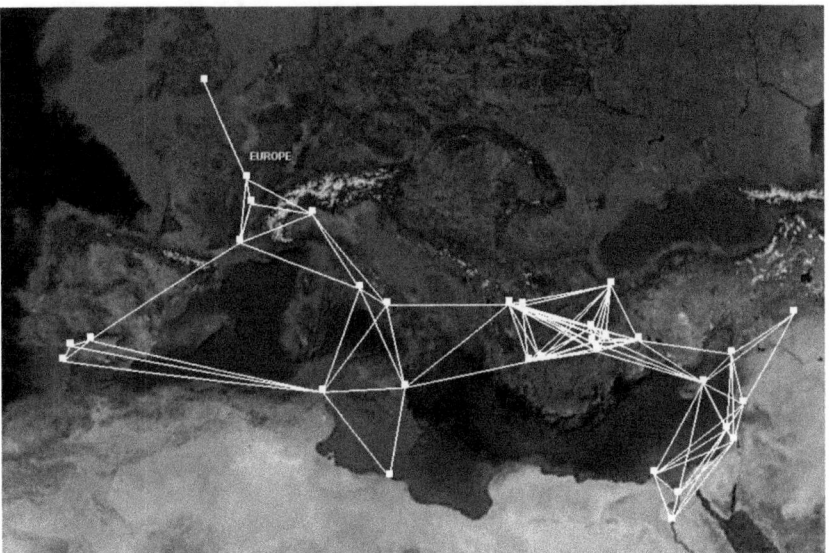

Figure 5.2 Maximum distance network of cities in the Roman Empire, 200 CE

inadequately accounts for the spread of Christianity. This highlights a potential limitation of PPA. By limiting links to a predefined number, it is possible to miss potential links between sites. One obvious solution would be to increase the number of k neighbors. Another is to assume that one or more sites (e.g., Jerusalem, Rome) have connections to all other sites; Anna Collar (2013a, 2013b) uses this approach to examine the diffusion of Rabbinic Judaism in the early Roman Empire (see the discussion in the next section).

Another method for connecting sites, known as maximum distance network (MDN), draws ties among sites within a specified distance (Evans 2017). Figure 5.2 illustrates this approach using the same data as before, except now two cities are tied together if they are within 450 miles of one another. In this case, the distance is Euclidean (i.e., "as the crow flies") but it does not have to be. As one can see, the network is connected, indicating that it might capture the potential paths early Christianity followed as it spread across the Roman Empire.[5] Variations on MDN include those where two sites have to be visible to one another in order for them to be linked (Brughmans, Keay, and Earl 2014), or where distance is weighted by estimated travel time. For instance, in "many ancient

---

[5] The distance of 450 miles was chosen in order to ensure that the graph would be connected. Obviously, a more rigorous analysis would choose a distance informed by relevant theoretical considerations.

situations, travel by land was considerably slower than by water, so a sea route could involve more kilometers but actually be faster and hence a true measure of separation" (Evans 2017:152).

A final method we will consider here links sites together based on the level of similarity between them (Peeples et al. 2016). For instance, archeologists may draw a tie between two sites if they discover Barbara Mills and her colleagues (2013a; 2013b; 2015) as part of the Southwest Social Networks (SWSN) Project.[6] They linked sites in terms of the similarities of ceramic ware assemblages. When calculating metrics such as degree and eigenvector centrality, they use the raw similarity scores, but when they generate network maps, they only link two sites if the level of similarity between them equaled or exceeded 75 percent (Mills et al. 2013a:5787, 5788).

To illustrate their approach, refer to Figure 5.3, which plots the same thirty-three cities as before, except here ties are drawn between cities based on their similarity level for four dimensions that Rodney Stark (2006) believes were positively associated with the Christianization of Roman cities: (1) the presence of a Diasporan Jewish community by 100 CE (Stark 2006:122), (2) the presence of a Cybelene temple by 100 CE (Stark 2006:93), (3) the presence of an Isis temple by 100 CE (Stark 2006:109), and (4) cities with a dominant Hellenic culture in 100 CE (Stark 2006:80). The top map ties cities together if they are similar on any of the four dimensions; the bottom only ties them together if their level of similarity exceeds 50 percent. In both, node size varies in terms of weighted degree centrality (i.e., the sum of the level of similarity).

These examples are, of course, somewhat contrived. They certainly do not claim to map the actual networks of the Roman Empire by which Christianity spread. Instead, they simply illustrate some of the methods archeologists use to recreate the social networks of ancient sites.[7] We now turn our attention to a bona fide archeological use of SNA – namely, Anna Collar's (2013a, 2013b) analysis of Rabbinic Judaism's diffusion across the Mediterranean in the early Roman Empire.

The Diffusion of Rabbinic Judaism

To map the social network of Diaspora Judaism (i.e., Jews who did not live in Jerusalem and were dispersed throughout the Roman Empire), Collar links Jewish epigraphs (inscriptions) using a modified version of proximal point analysis (PPA). In particular, she only draws ties between "finds that use Hebrew, Jewish symbols, or make explicit reference to Israel," (Collar 2013a:235; 2013b:205), and rather than connecting them

---

[6] Social network analyst Ronald Breiger helped with the research design of this project.
[7] For detailed examination of these and other methods, see the helpful discussions of Tom Evans, Carl Knappett, and Ray Rivers (Evans, Knappett, and Rivers 2009; Evans 2017; Rivers 2017).

5.2 Archeological Networks & Rabbinic Judaism 143

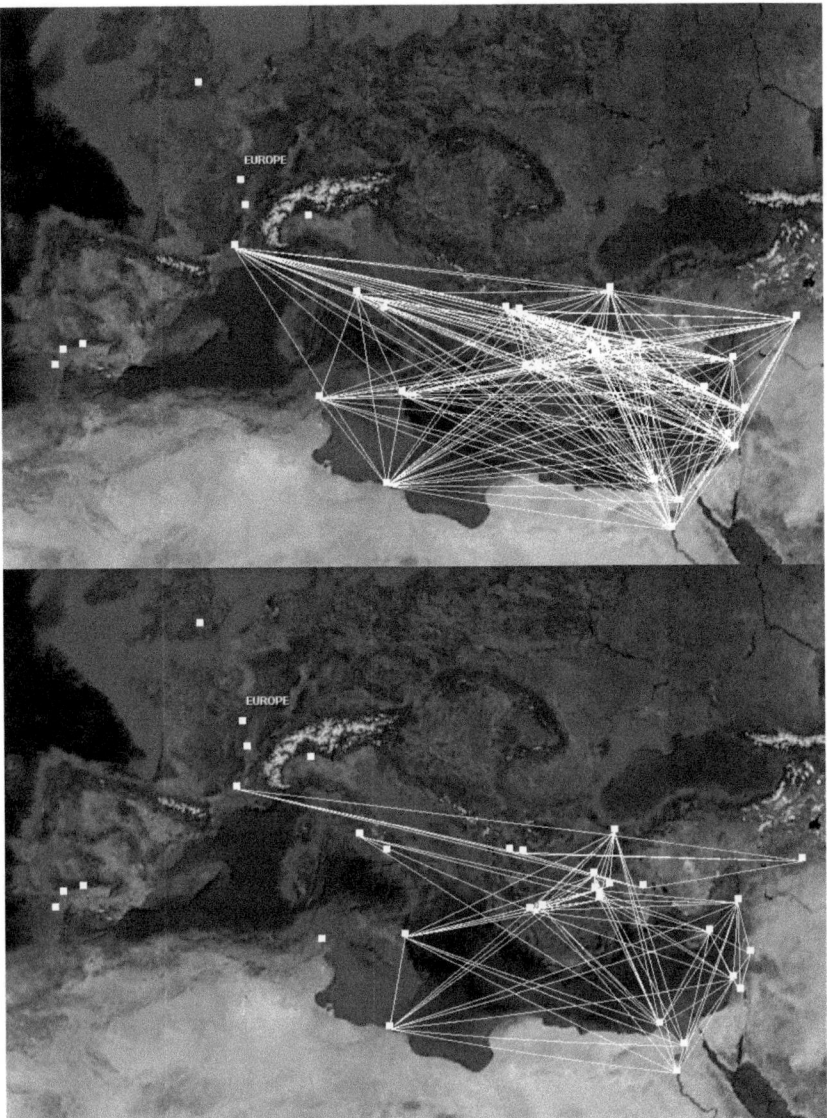

Figure 5.3 Similarity network of cities in the Roman Empire, 200 CE

to their three closest neighbors, she connects each one to Judaea plus one established connection, "except in later cases where there are three find spots close by" (Collar 2013b:212). "Although this skews the maps towards having very long-distance links and makes Judaea a heavy centre," Collar argues, it "creates a picture of more 'realistic' interaction patterns, the idea of rabbinic 'mission' to the Diaspora, in which places were first exposed to the reforms, and subsequent localized spread of information" (Collar 2013a:235). She then sorts her networks into four historical periods: (1) first–second century CE, (2) third century CE, (3) fourth century CE, and (4) fifth–sixth century CE. Because it is unclear how, if, and when communities declined, she assumes that "once a piece of epigraphic evidence is recorded, "Jews continued to be present" (Collar 2013b:212); the exceptions are Pompeii, which ceased to exist after it was destroyed by the eruption of Mount Vesuvius in 79 CE, and the Roman stronghold Dura Europus, which was covered in sand and eventually disappeared from sight after the Sassanians first captured and then abandoned it in 256–257 CE.

The resulting network maps yield an interesting pattern. In the first and second centuries, network connectivity is sparse, suggesting that there was minimal interaction between Jerusalem and the Jewish Diaspora. Things change dramatically with the third century and beyond as the network becomes increasingly interconnected. Collars believes this is not a coincidence but instead reflects the changes that ensued after the Romans destroyed the Second Temple in 70 CE during the First Jewish–Roman War (66–73 CE). She argues that prior to the Temple's destruction, which had possibly stood on Jerusalem's Temple Mount as far back as 518 BCE, Diaspora Jews did not overtly advertise their culture and identity because the Temple was the center of their religious life. After its destruction, however, things changed. The influence of Sadducees, whose identity was tied to the Temple, declined, while that of the rabbis, whose identity was not, increased. According to Collar, this led to a "widespread dissemination and adoption of explicitly Jewish names, symbols, and language" (Collar 2013a:230) through the ethnic network of the Jewish Diaspora across the Mediterranean world.

> The indicators found on Jewish monuments that reflect an increased awareness of a common Jewish practice, history, and behaviour include specifically Jewish symbols as referents to a universalized ritual and the religious calendar, and the use of Hebrew as a marker of education and a revived knowledge of the sacred texts, Torah, Jewish Law, and Jewish history. In addition, the increasing use of specifically Jewish name forms provides a subtle indication of the universal engendering of a more strongly defined Jewish identity, matched by the trend during the 3rd–4th centuries AD for individuals to define themselves as 'Jews' or, more often, as 'Hebrews'.
>
> (Collar 2013a:231)

Collar believes that it was strong, rather than weak, ties that played the key role in this diffusion. She contends "that the new religious authorities in Palestine used the highly influential strong-tie 'familial' connections of the ethnic network of the Diaspora to transmit the religious and social discipline of rabbinic Judaism" (Collar 2013a:230). She notes, however, that these ties had to be "re-activated" (Collar 2013b:180), suggesting they may have laid dormant for years, and one could argue that such ties, familial or not, could hardly be considered strong, at least not in the sense that the term is typically used today. Be that as it may, Collar does not dismiss the role that weak ties probably played. She believes that the weak (but ethnically strong) ties of missionaries and others were also important (Collar 2013a:242).

Finally, Collar notes that early Christianity, which consisted primarily of Jews in its formative years, almost certainly made use of the same ethnic network. It "was able to persuade and convert effectively both by utilizing the actual strong-tie familial network of the Jewish Diaspora, and by simultaneously manufacturing a new one for believers in Christ, whether Jew or gentile" (Collar 2013b:222). Here she echoes some of the arguments of Stark (1996a), who contends that the early Christian missionaries probably stayed with Diaspora Jewish families and friends when on the road, which probably led to some conversions among Diasporan Jews.[8] Like Stark, she believes, albeit for different reasons, that Diasporan Jews were "vulnerable to the religious innovations brought by people who preached change" (Collar 2013b:222). After the Temple's destruction and the persecution that followed the end of the Jewish-Roman war, Diaspora Jews came to embrace strong messianic hopes, and Christianity, which in its early years was one of many Jewish sects, had one to offer (Collar 2013a:244).

5.3 Student Networks and the Spread of the Protestant Reformation

The beginning of the Protestant Reformation is generally traced to October 31, 1517, when Martin Luther sent a letter to his bishop, Albert of Mainz, protesting the sale of indulgences. He enclosed a copy of his 95 theses, more formally known as the "Disputation of Martin Luther on the Power and Efficacy of Indulgences."[9] As some readers may be aware, the practice of selling indulgences is related to the Roman

---

[8] Since conversion is a function of face-to-face interaction, the fact that missionaries probably stayed with fellow Jews in all likelihood increased the probability that those with whom they stayed would convert. Stark further argues that because of this and other factors, the early Christian "mission to the Jews" was probably more successful than most scholars believe (Stark 1996a: chapter 3).

[9] The story that Luther nailed the theses to the door of the Wittenberg church may be apocryphal. It is attributed to Philipp Melanchthon, though he may not have been in Wittenberg at the time (Wikipedia 2017e).

Catholic doctrine of Purgatory, which holds that "there is an intermediate state between heaven and hell for people who die neither as saints" nor as unredeemable sinners. In Purgatory, souls are cleansed by "purging fires," which makes them fit for entry into heaven. Roman Catholics believe that the pope holds the "spiritual key to a 'treasury of merit'," which is a "superabundance of merit attained by Christ and the saints," and indulgences are certificates the pope issues by which he transfers "some of this merit" to repentant sinners. If such sinners perform "an adequate number of acts of penitence and devotion," a portion (or perhaps all) of their time in Purgatory can be remitted (Ellwood and McGraw 2005:326). Indulgences can also be obtained on behalf of another, living or dead. Luther believed that in his day the practice of selling indulgences was being abused. He argued that indulgences were being issued with little consideration for the remorsefulness of the penitents, but rather more for the funds that the Church was able to collect by issuing them. In fact, what probably triggered Luther to compose his 95 theses was when in 1516 the Church sent Johann Tetzel, a Dominican friar who was a papal commissioner for indulgences, to Germany to raise funds to rebuild St. Peter's Basilica in Rome. Tetzel had become notorious for granting indulgences in exchange for money. He reportedly remarked that "[a]s soon as the coin in the coffer rings, the soul from purgatory springs" (Wikipedia 2017e).[10]

What is surprising is that Luther's protest gained traction. He was certainly not the first to complain about corruption in the Roman Catholic Church. The Waldensians, which attracted a following in the twelfth and thirteenth centuries, and the Lollards and the Hussites, both of which were active in the fifteenth century, were highly critical of the commercialization of the Church. However, they did not meet with Luther's success; in fact, they were brutally suppressed by the Church and its secular allies (Becker, Pfaff, and Rubin 2016). Luther, however, was not suppressed, at least not initially. In fact, "his complaints were quickly echoed by lay and clerical interests alike throughout northern Europe, indicating that antipapal sentiments were deeply rooted well before the Reformation" (Rubin 2014:272).

All of which raises an important question: Why did Luther's protests gain purchase when others did not? Why did his ideas spread beyond Wittenberg? Numerous potential factors have been identified, such as the printing press (Rubin 2014), urbanization (Ozment 1975), military incursions by the Ottoman Empire, which forced the Holy Roman Empire to divert resources away from suppressing the Protestant Reformers (Iyigun 2015), the desire for political autonomy (Cantoni 2012), a dearth of

[10] At the time of his death in 1519, Tetzel had fallen into disrepute and was shunned by the public. When Luther heard that Tetzel was mortally ill and on his deathbed, he wrote to comfort him and bade him "not to be troubled, for the matter did not begin on his account, but the child had quite a different father" (Wikipedia 2017d).

shrines to saints (Pfaff 2013), a lack of monasteries (Pfaff and Corcoran 2012), and the absence of primogeniture laws (Ekelund, Hébert, and Tollison 2002).

The Spread of the Protestant Reformation

In a novel application of the network approach, Hyojoung Kim and Steven Pfaff uncovered evidence that the Protestant Reformation spread through city-to-university-to-city ties with students functioning as agents of diffusion between the two. "University students returning to their hometowns carried interpersonal networks that spanned beyond city boundaries and bridged structural holes separating dispersed cities" (Kim and Pfaff 2012:194). Not all universities played a key role, however. Only those that "committed themselves to clear ideological positions early on and sought to involve students in religious contention" did (Kim and Pfaff 2012:194). In particular, Kim and Pfaff found that, net of other factors, the university towns of Wittenberg and Basel, the respective intellectual homes of Luther and another key Protestant Reformer, Ulrich Zwingli, acted as "critical communities" (Kim and Pfaff 2012:190) through which the outside world was exposed to the Reformation's heterodox theology. The greater number of students that a city sent to Wittenberg and Basel, the greater the likelihood that the city would later institute reform by officially abolishing the Roman Catholic Mass. This effect was tempered by whether the local rulers supported reform. Students had greater success if territorial authorities either supported their efforts or actively opposed them. They "had much less success where territorial rulers handled them neither favorably nor antagonistically but with circumspection or opportunistic ambivalence" (Kim and Pfaff 2012:208). This may strike some as somewhat counterintuitive, but as Kim and Pfaff note, nascent social movements are helped not only by the presence of political opportunities (McAdam 1999 [1982]) but also by threats to their existence and moderate repression (Goldstone and Tilly 2001). They also found that the greater the number of students that a city sent to the orthodox university strongholds, Cologne and Louvain, the greater the likelihood the city would later reject reform. However, while the "Wittenberg and Basel students needed either clear support or clear opposition to mobilize insurgency effectively," the students from Cologne and Louvain consistently exerted a negative effect "across all types of princely patronage" (Kim and Pfaff 2012:209).

Interestingly, Kim and Pfaff also show that the presence of a printing press in a particular city had a negative effect on reform, but they warn that this should not be interpreted as evidence that the printing press played no role in the spread of the Reformation. They simply estimated the odds that the presence of printing presses would have on a city embracing reform. In fact, they note that although local authorities could easily control or censor what their local presses printed, "the larger book trade did not rely on local publishers; books were carried from place to place by preachers, peddlers, and merchants" (Kim and Pfaff 2012:205), which of course is another example of the diffusion of religious beliefs and practices across network ties.

5.4 Denominational Networks and Women's Ordination

Although many biblical scholars believe that Jesus treated (and regarded) women as equal with men (Borg 1987; Van Leeuwen 1990; Schottroff 1993; Witherington 1995; Ehrman 1999; Levine 2006), there "is little to suggest that Jesus was pushing social 'reform' in any fundamental way" since he believed that the world "and all its conventions were soon to come to a screeching halt, when the Son of Man arrived from heaven in judgment on the earth" (Ehrman 1999:190). Nevertheless, "his message had radically revolutionary implications" (Ehrman 1999:190) and could help explain why the early church, at least in some instances, embraced the equality of the sexes. Take, for example, the apostle Paul for whom women were often his "fellow ... evangelists and teachers" (Meeks 1983:71). In his letters, Paul refers to several women who were successful missionaries (e.g., Prisca, Junia), helped give birth to local house churches (e.g., Lydia, Nympha of Laodicea), and headed local congregations (e.g., Apphia in Colossae). In his letter to the Philippians, he holds up the work of two women, Euodia and Syntyche, who "contended" with him while laboring on behalf of the gospel (Phil. 4:2–3); in fact, he considers their authority to be so great that he urges them to put aside their differences so as to not endanger the Christian mission (Fiorenza 1994:169–170). And in his letter to the Romans, he entrusts to them Phoebe, who was a *diakonos* (i.e., deacon/minister) at the church at Cenchreae, and urges them to help her in any way she might require (Rom. 16:1–2).[11] According to Elizabeth Schüssler Fiorenza, women

> were among the most prominent missionaries and leaders of the early Christian movement. They were apostles and ministers like Paul, and some were his co-workers. They were teachers,

[11] Historically, when Paul used the term *diakonos* to refer to himself or another male leader, scholars translated it as "minister," "missionary," or "servant," but when he used it to refer to a woman, scholars translated it as "deaconess," which they interpreted as a servant of women but not of men. In doing so they projected "back into the first century the duties of deaconesses in later centuries ... However, Phoebe's 'office' in the church in Cenchreae is not limited by prescribed gender roles. She is not a deaconess of the women, but a minister of the whole church" (Fiorenza 1994:170).

preachers, and competitors in the race for the gospel. They founded house-churches and, as prominent patrons, used their influence for other missionaries and Christians.

(1994:183)

An obvious objection to such an assertion is Paul's pronouncement for women to remain silent and subordinate to men in the church (1 Cor. 14: 34–36). However, given the inconsistency of this compared to other teachings found in Paul's letters, it is likely that it either reflects the opposite of Paul's position and Paul is simply quoting it in order to refute it (Iannaccone 1982) or the verses were inserted by later editors who sought to "correct" Paul's teaching (Ehrman 2000:402).[12]

Regardless, women's equality within the Christian Church gave way to the patriarchal structures of Roman society, and it was not until the nineteenth century that Christian denominations in the United States began to once again recognize the right of women to be ordained. The first of these was the Congregationalists (1853), heirs of the Puritans and forerunners of today's United Church of Christ (UCC), and they were quickly followed by several other denominations, including the Advent Christian Church (1860), the Universalists (1863), the Unitarians (1871), the Salvation Army (1880),[13] the Church of God, Anderson, Indiana (1885), the Disciples of Christ (1888), the Methodists (1892), the National Baptist Convention (1895), and the African Methodist Episcopal Zion Church (1898), among others. In the years since, there has been a steady increase in the number of denominations that ordain women, although quite a few, including the Roman Catholic Church and the National Baptist Convention in America, still do not. In what follows we explore the diffusion of women's ordination in the United States. In particular, we will examine Mark Chaves's (1996, 1997) analyses which identified a number of potential factors that influenced denominations to begin ordaining women.

The Diffusion of an Institutional Innovation: Women's Ordination

In his study of women's ordination, Chaves (1996, 1997) draws heavily on the insights of the new institutionalism (Meyer and Rowan 1977; DiMaggio and Powell 1983; Meyer et al. 1997; Powell and DiMaggio 1991), which, as we saw earlier, holds that the more that institutions

---

[12] Arguing that the early church embraced the equality of women and men is not solely the province of theologically liberal biblical scholars. The evangelical organization Christians for Biblical Equality has published a number of studies that argue as such. See www.cbeinternational.org.
[13] In England, the Salvation Army ordained women beginning in 1865; they did not establish any "congregations" in the United States until 1880, however.

interact with one another, regardless of whether they are nation-states or corporations, the more like one another they will become. For example, John Meyer and his colleagues (1997:145–146) argue that if "an unknown society were 'discovered' on a previously unknown island," certain changes would almost certainly occur.

> A government would soon form, looking something like a modern state with many of the usual ministries and agencies ... Its people would be formally reorganized as citizens with many familiar rights, while certain categories of citizens – children, the elderly, the poor – would be granted special protection. Standard forms of discrimination, especially ethnic and gender based, would be discovered and decried ... Modern educational, medical, scientific, and family law institutions would be developed ... What would be unlikely to happen is also clear. Theological disputes about whether the newly discovered *Indios* had souls or were part of the general human moral order would be rare. There would be little by way of an imperial rush to colonize the island. Few would argue that the natives needed only modest citizenship or human rights or that they would best be educated by but a few years of vocational training ...
>
> Thus, without knowing anything about the history, culture, practices, or traditions that obtained in this previously unknown society, we could forecast many changes that, upon "discovery," would descend on the island under the general rubric of "development." Our forecast would be imprecise because of the complexity of the interplay among various world models and local traditions, but the likely range of outcomes would be quite limited. We can identify the range of possibilities by using the institutionalist theoretical perspective ... to interpret what has already happened to practically all of the societies of the world after their discovery and incorporation into world society.
>
> (Meyer et al. 1997:145–146)

To test the neo-institutionalist perspective with regards to women's ordination, Chaves (1996) estimated a series of event-history (survival) models that included a number of potential factors that could affect the likelihood that denominations would begin ordaining women, such as clergy shortages, theological beliefs, whether they are predominantly rural, black, or Southern, founding dates, denominational structures (e.g., decentralized or autonomous women's mission societies), and feminism's first (1880–1920) and second (1966–1983) waves. Using the *Yearbook of American and Canadian Churches*, he identified all the denominations that in 1992 had clergy, some degree of national-level organization, and more than 300 congregations.

5.4 Denominational Networks and Women's Ordination

Because many of these denominations were founded out of mergers, he traced their development backward over time in order to identify all precursors. This yielded a total of 100 denominations for which there was adequate data. Although these represented slightly less than 50 percent of all denominations, they include approximately 85 percent of all US church members. Of these, forty-four, plus the ones that resulted from mergers, approved of the ordination of women. He ended up dropping eight denominations from his analysis because they were born out of mergers between two or more denominations that had already begun ordaining women, so the mergers did not create any new entities that were at risk for beginning to ordain women. Thus, his final analysis was based on ninety-two denominations, of which forty-four sanctioned the ordination of women.

What did he find? On the negative side, Chaves found that sacramental denominations – that is, denominations that understand the celebration of communion as something more than a simple remembrance of a meal that Jesus held with his disciples shortly before his death – were more resistant to ordaining women than non-sacramental denominations. An example is the Episcopal Church, which is generally regarded as one of the more theologically liberal Protestant denominations, but it still did not get around to officially ordaining women until 1976. He also found that denominations that believe that the Bible is inerrant were less likely to ordain women than were those that do not. Some do, of course, such as the Baptist General Conference, which began ordaining women in 1918, but they were more the exception than the rule. Predominantly Southern denominations were also less likely to ordain women, but, somewhat surprisingly, predominantly black and rural denominations were neither more nor less likely to do so. Clergy shortages did not appear to have any effect either. On the positive side, younger denominations were more likely to ordain women, as were decentralized ones and those with autonomous women's organizations. The second, but not the first, wave of feminism also increased the likelihood that a denomination would begin ordaining women.

The largest effect Chaves found, however, was the one that directly captured the neo-institutionalist perspective: namely, network ties to prior adopters. Chaves considered two denominations to share a tie if they belonged to one or more of the same interdenominational organizations at eight points in time: 1915, 1925, 1935, 1945, 1955, 1965, 1975, and 1985. In the second chapter, we presented a network graph of the 1985 interdenominational network, and in Figures 5.4–5.11 we present network graphs of each time period. More important for our purposes here, however, is that Chaves found a positive association between the proportion of a denomination's interorganizational ties to prior adopters and the likelihood that it would begin ordaining women.

Whither Holiness and Pentecostal Denominations?

In his follow-up book Chaves (1997) addressed the possibility that Pentecostal and Holiness denominations were more likely to approve of women's ordination than other conservative Protestant denominations. To understand why this could be true, he argued that we need to consider the institutional world constructed by the fundamentalist denominations that formed in the early twentieth century. Chaves noted that they defined themselves, at least in part, over against the institutional world of liberal Protestantism. He argued that it would have been difficult for them to support women's ordination because they adopted antimodernism as a central defining identity, and in so doing, biblical inerrancy and opposition to women's ordination became primary symbols of this antimodern stance (Chaves 1997:101). Not all theologically conservative denominations developed within the institutional orbit of twentieth-century fundamentalism, however. The Holiness and Pentecostal traditions were two such examples. Although they embraced biblical inerrancy and other "fundamental" beliefs, historically, they have not been completely accepted by fundamentalist Protestants. Because of this, Chaves (1997: 112–116) argued that Pentecostal and Holiness denominations constructed separate institutional worlds and as such were not (and are not) as invested in fundamentalism's antimodernism, which made them less likely to oppose women's ordination. The Pentecostal and Holiness traditions also differed from twentieth-century fundamentalism in their understanding of how God's Spirit moves among believers. In particular, they hold that the gift of the Holy Spirit that arrived on the Day of Pentecost was received by both women and men, which has led some to argue that both women and men are called to preach and evangelize. Indeed, one of the largest Holiness denominations, the International Church of the Foursquare Gospel (also known as the Foursquare Church), was founded by a woman, Aimee Semple McPherson (Wikipedia 2017a), who for a time was probably the most popular evangelist in the United States.

To begin to explore whether Chaves's speculations were accurate, Figures 5.4 through 5.11 present the interdenominational networks from 1915 to 1985.[14] Denominations are represented by circles, interdenominational organizations by squares, Holiness and Pentecostal denominations are shaded black, and denominations that ordain women are labeled. As the figures indicate, from 1915 through 1935, only one denominational cluster forms and is comprised of those denominations that are members of the Federal Council of Churches. In 1945, a second cluster begins to form around a new ecumenical organization, the National Association of Evangelicals, which was founded in 1942. This

---

[14] Figures 5.4 through 5.11 were created in Pajek 5.01 (Batagelj and Mrvar 2017).

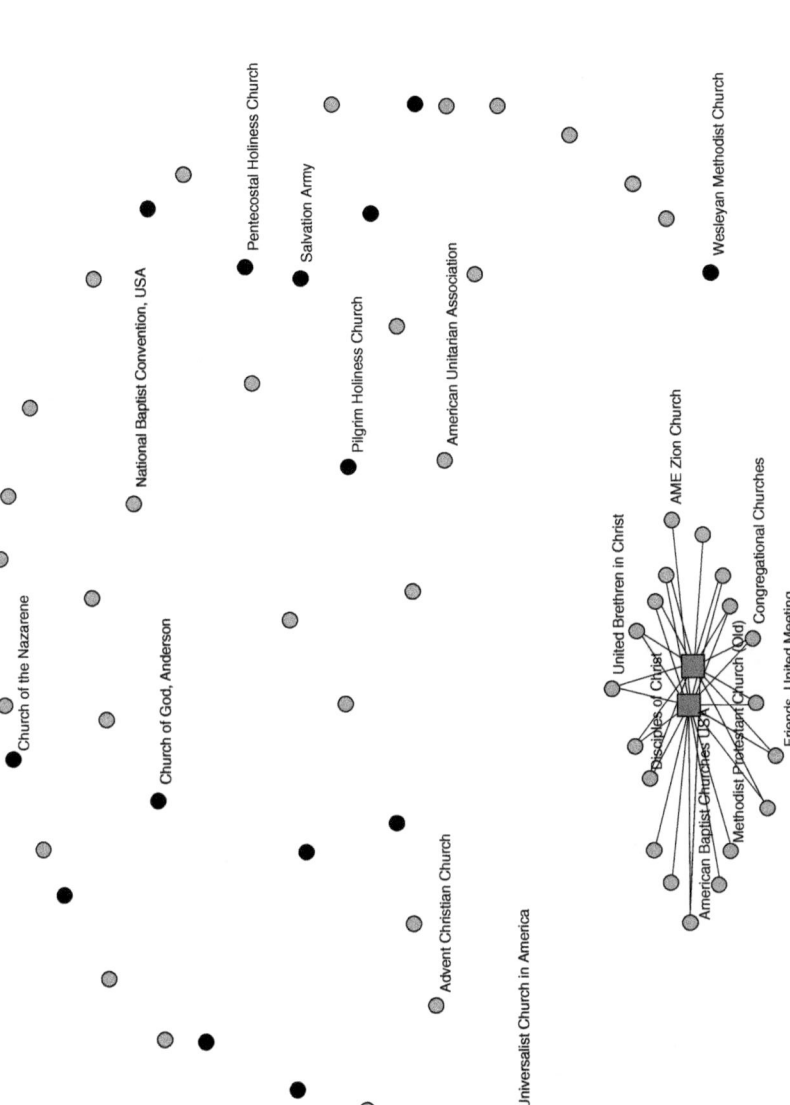

Figure 5.4 Interdenominational network, 1915 [author's analysis of data used in Chaves (1996)]

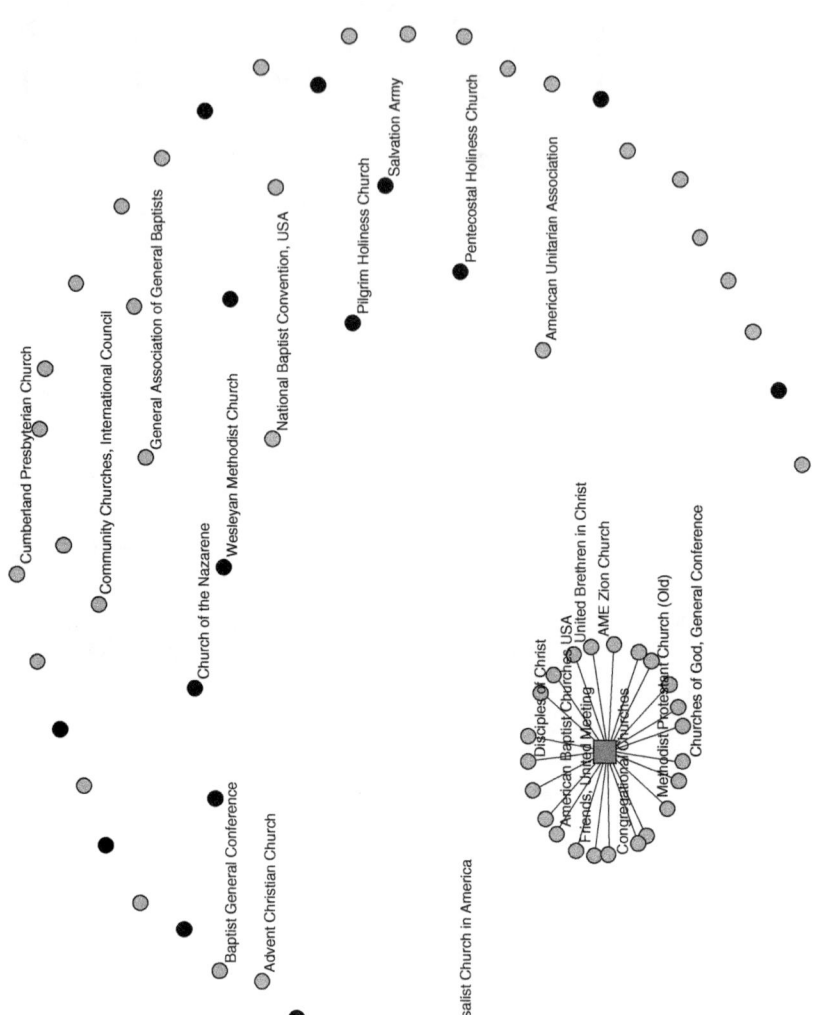

Figure 5.5 Interdenominational network, 1925 [author's analysis of data used in Chaves (1996)]

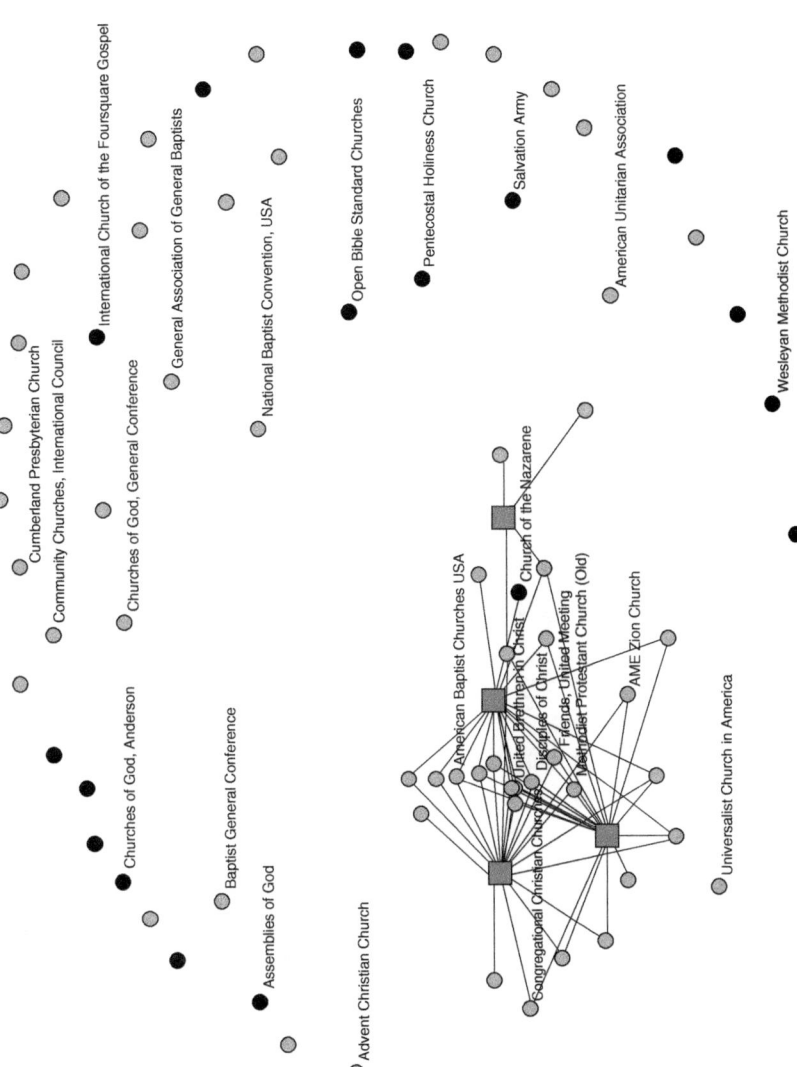

Figure 5.6 Interdenominational network, 1935 [author's analysis of data used in Chaves (1996)]

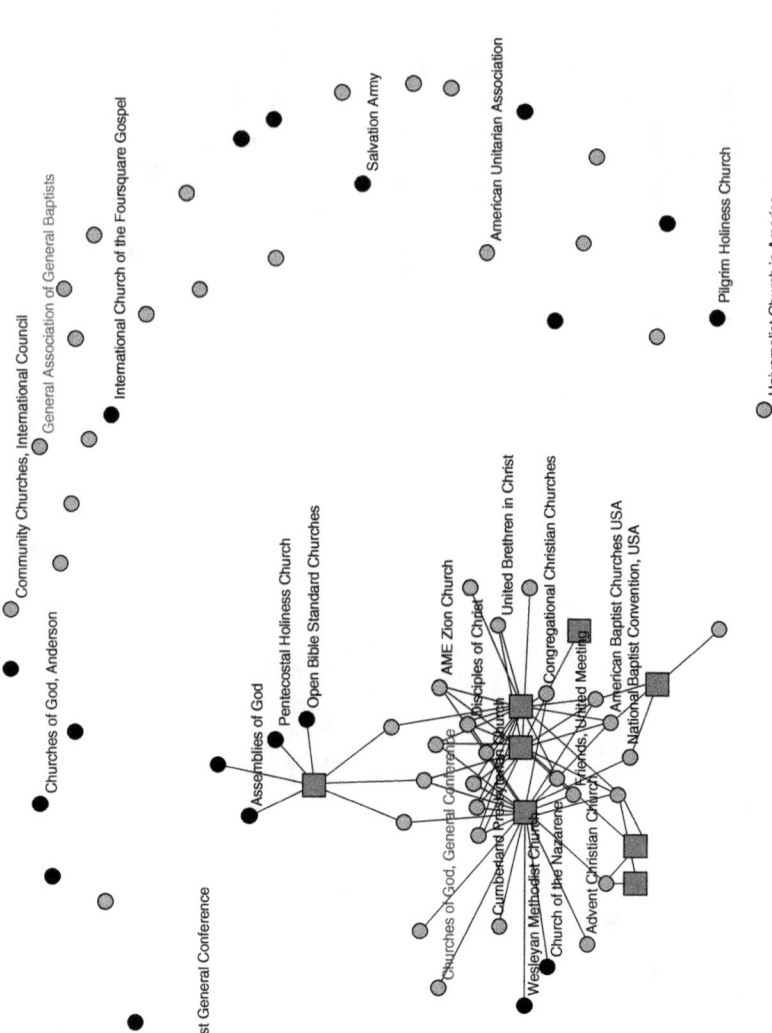

Figure 5.7 Interdenominational network, 1945 [author's analysis of data used in Chaves (1996)]

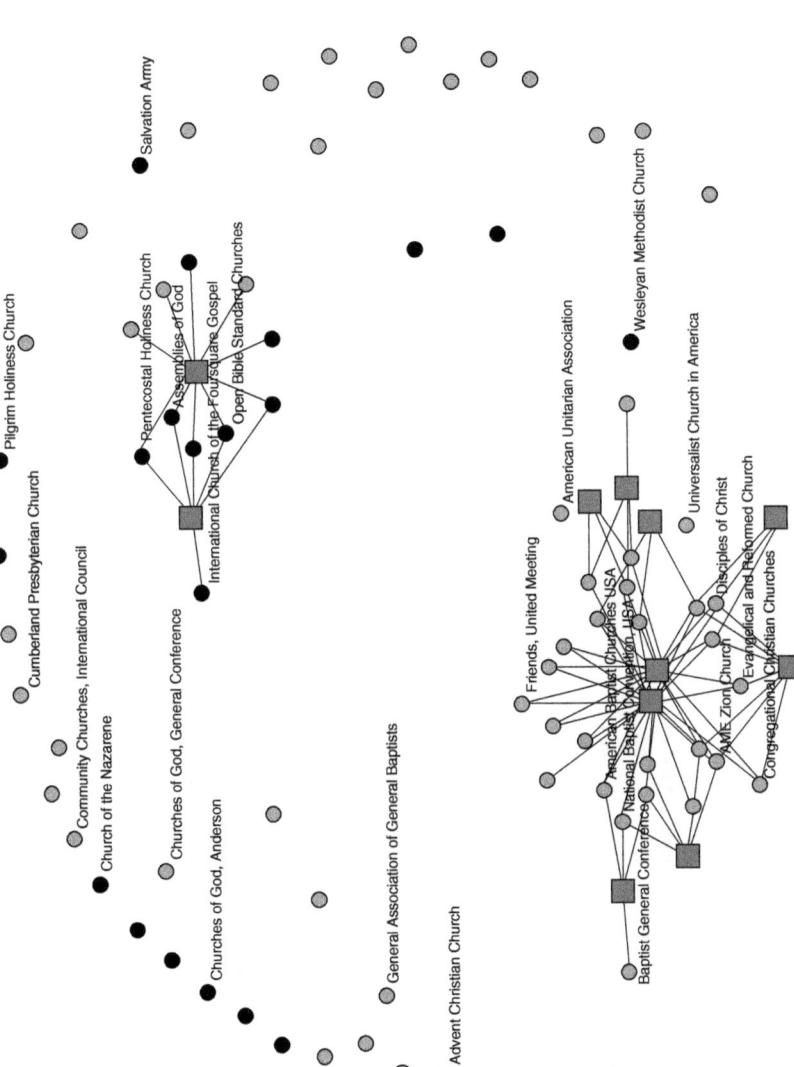

Figure 5.8 Interdenominational network, 1955 [author's analysis of data used in Chaves (1996)]

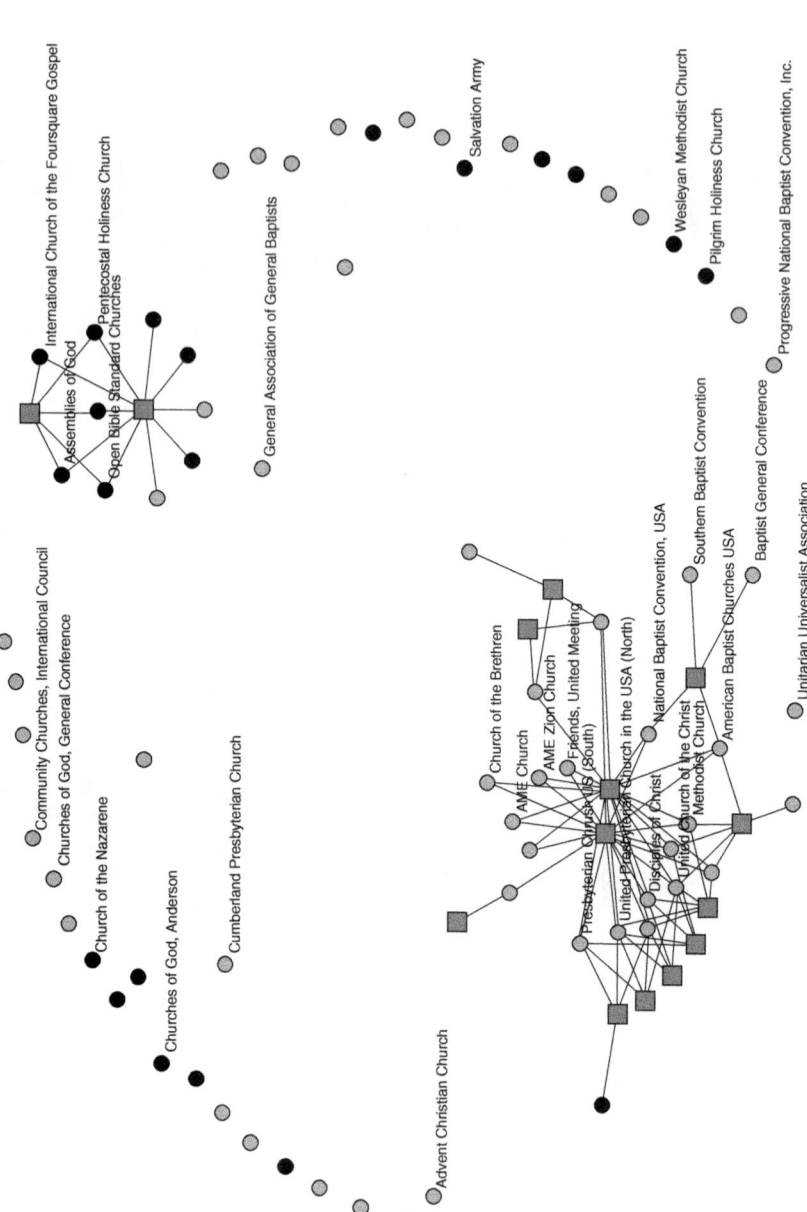

Figure 5.9 Interdenominational network, 1965 [author's analysis of data used in Chaves (1996)]

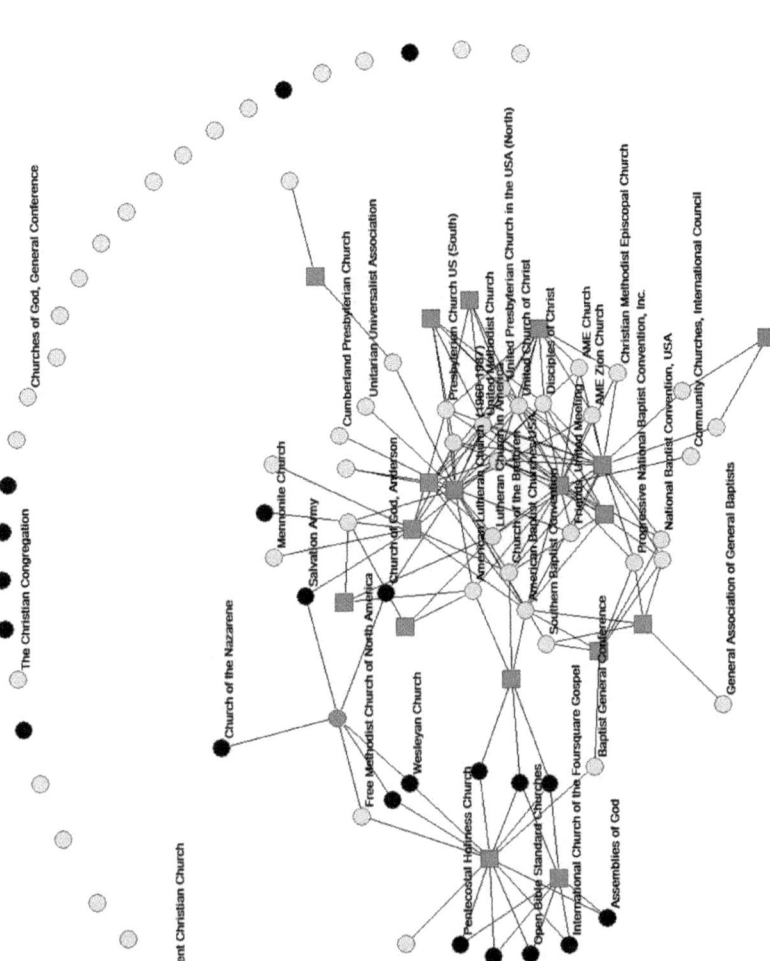

Figure 5.10 Interdenominational network, 1975 [author's analysis of data used in Chaves (1996)]

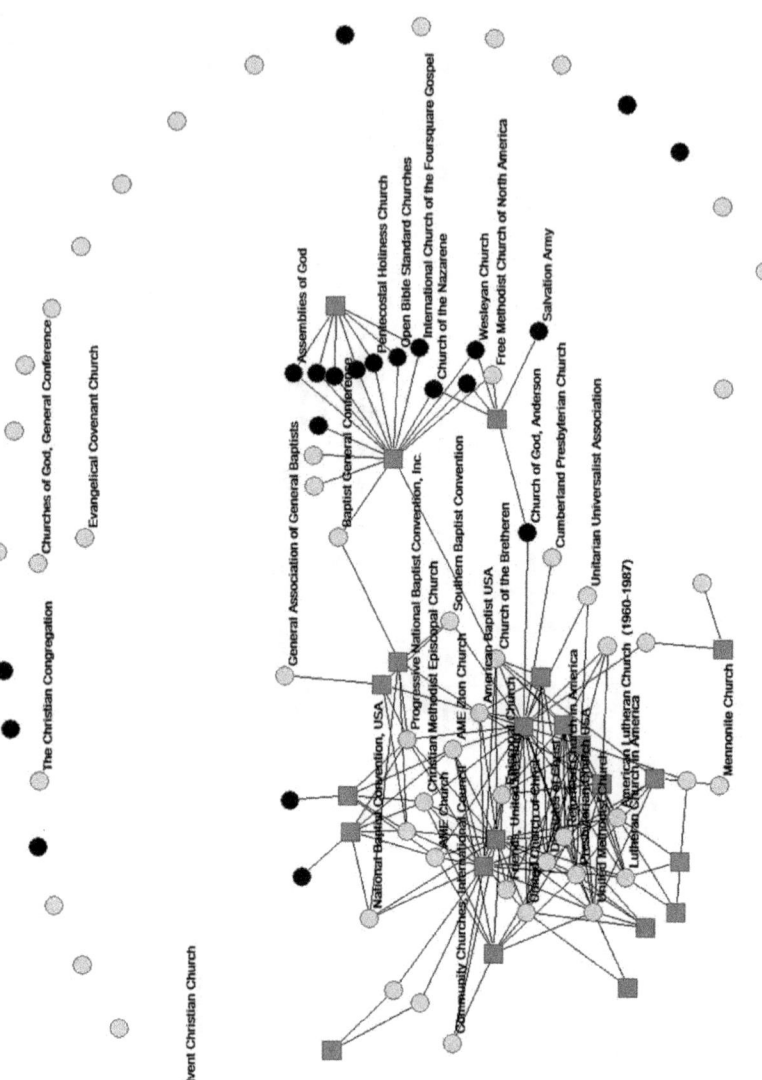

Figure 5.11 Interdenominational network, 1985 [author's analysis of data used in Chaves (1996)]

5.4 Denominational Networks and Women's Ordination

dual clustering pattern holds through 1985, but beginning in 1975 the two clusters, while remaining distinct, start to form ties between one another through a variety of "bridging" organizations, such as the Baptist Joint Committee and the International Society of Christian Endeavor.[15] Notice also that by 1985 very few of the ordaining denominations were isolated. In fact, only four of the thirty-four denominations that in 1985 approved of the ordination of women were. The rest have a tie to at least one ecumenical organization.

Two factors probably account for these patterns. One is social selection. Denominations theologically sympathetic to ordaining women are likely to join ecumenical organizations that approve of the ordination of the women, while denominations that oppose it are likely to join ecumenical organizations that do not. The second is social influence – that is, organizations that interact with one another tend to adopt one another's practices. This, of course, is the essence of the neo-institutionalist argument discussed earlier. The network maps highlight how many of the denominations that ordain women are either Holiness or Pentecostal denominations. As the crosstab presented in Table 5.2 suggests, a substantial difference may exist between Holiness and Pentecostal denominations and fundamentalist denominations. Here, fundamentalist denominations are those that embrace a strict form of biblical inerrancy; those coded as being part of the Holiness or Pentecostal tradition include only those that are not predominantly non-African American denominations, while all of the African American denominations are treated as a separate category. Any denomination not associated with the first four types are aggregated into the "other" category. It is notable that the actual number of denominations associated with the Holiness tradition that ordain women is substantially larger than the expected number of denominations, especially when compared to denominations classified as fundamentalist. This is not true of the denominations associated with the Pentecostal tradition; the actual number compared to the expected frequency is lower, suggesting that the Holiness tradition exerts something of an effect, while the Pentecostal tradition does not. Indeed, a simple logistic regression (not shown) that regresses denominations that ordain women on whether they are from the Holiness, Pentecostal, black, or other traditions (using fundamentalist as the comparison category) found that Holiness denominations are almost six times more likely than fundamentalist ones to ordain women, while Pentecostal denominations were just twice as likely (and the coefficient was statistically insignificant).[16]

---

[15] For the Baptist Joint Committee, see http://bjconline.org; for the International Society of Christian Endeavor, see www.endeavorministries.org.
[16] Results available upon request.

Table 5.2 *Crosstab of denominational type and ordination policy: actual (expected) counts*

		Denomination Type					Total
		Fundamentalist	Holiness	Pentecostal	Black	Other	
Ordain women	No	29.0 (21.6)	2.0 (3.9)	5.0 (4.9)	6.0 (5.4)	8.0 (14.2)	50.0
	Yes	15.0 (22.4)	6.0 (4.1)	5.0 (5.1)	5.0 (5.6)	21.0 (14.8)	52.0
Total		44.0	8.0	10.0	11.0	29.0	102.0

$X^2 = 12.339$, $p < 0.05$

A more robust test, of course, would be to estimate a survival model that replicates Chaves's original analysis but includes covariates indicating whether a denomination was associated with either the Holiness or Pentecostal traditions.[17] The results of such an analysis – both the estimated coefficients and their hazard (odds) ratios – are presented in Table 5.3. The first model includes the covariates Chaves included in his full model, while the second adds the Holiness and Pentecostal indicator variables. As briefly noted earlier, Chaves (1996: 856–862) included covariates that tested

- the effects of clergy shortages (i.e., when the number of clergy was less than the number of congregations)
- whether a denomination's constituency was largely southern (i.e., denominations with more than 50 percent of its congregations located in the South)
- whether a large portion of denomination's constituency lived in the rural United States (i.e., denominations with more than 60 percent of its congregations located in rural areas)
- whether a denomination's racial composition was predominantly African American
- the effects of each denomination's founding date
- the effects of the two waves of the women's movement (1880–1923; 1966–1983)
- the proportion of a denomination's ties to other denominations that had already begun ordaining women (i.e., prior adopters)
- whether a denomination was considered sacramental (i.e., Lutheran, Eastern Orthodox, Roman Catholic, or Episcopalian)

[17] Mark Chaves also shared the attribute data used in his 1996 analysis.

5.4 Denominational Networks and Women's Ordination

- whether a denomination embraced biblical inerrancy
- whether a denomination operated with a decentralized governing structure (polity)
- whether a denomination had or has an autonomous women's mission society

The data analyzed here include two additional denominations (and two additional ecumenical organizations), which is why the results in Table 5.2 reflect 102 denominations. Of these, seven were identified as resulting from mergers of two or more denominations that had already begun ordaining women; thus, the following analysis is based on ninety-five denominations, of which forty-five ordain women.[18]

Event history analysis allows researchers to incorporate aspects of previous life history and time-varying covariates in models of the time-dependent rate of occurrence of various life events (Tuma and Hannan 1984). The "general modeling strategy" assumes "there are data on a sequence of life events over time," and "observed events are regarded as realizations of a latent, random process of change that depends on covariates of theoretical interest," some of "which may change over time" (Zhou, Tuma, and Moen 1996). In event history analysis, the dependent variable is the "hazard rate," which is the rate (per unit of time) of movement from one state to another. Modeling time is of paramount importance when estimating event history models. On the one hand, it can be conceptualized in various ways, such as historical time, age, the duration since a previous event, birth cohort, and so on (Tuma and Hannan 1984: 190–195). On the other, the rate at which events occur (i.e., the hazard rate/function) can take different theoretical distributions, and survival models vary in order to take into account (or ignore) the shape of these distributions. The most popular model, the Cox proportional hazard model, makes no assumptions concerning the shape, while others, such as the exponential, Gompertz, Weibull, lognormal, and loglogistic regression models, do (Cleves et al. 2010). Here, we model time in terms of denominational age and estimate four different types of survival models: Cox, exponential, Gompertz, and Weibull.[19] The estimated results of all four models were quite similar, so Table 5.3 only presents the results of the Wiebull model because it yielded the lowest AIC and BIC scores. Because these results are from an entire (or close to an entire) organizational population rather than a random sample, standard rules of statistical inference do not apply. Thus, we focus on estimated effects that are either

---

[18] Following Chaves, all models include a dummy variable that equals 1 if before 1850 and 0 if afterward. They show a strong negative effect, which is not surprising, for as Chaves notes, no denomination ordained women prior to 1853.

[19] Models were also estimated using historical time (year) rather than age with no appreciable difference in the results. These are available upon request.

Table 5.3 *Estimated effects of covariates on denominations granting full clergy rights to women*

	Original Model (Chaves 1996)		Expanded Model	
	Coefficient	Hazard Ratio	Coefficient	Hazard Ratio
Internal rationalizing pressures				
Clergy shortage	−0.739	0.478	−0.741+	0.476+
Southern	−0.672	0.510	−0.610	0.543
Rural	0.498	1.645	0.664	1.942
Black	−0.682	0.506	−0.735	0.480
Institutional pressures outside of religious sphere				
Founding date	−0.003	0.997	−0.003	0.997
Feminism wave 1	0.402	1.495	0.297	1.346
Feminism wave 2	0.434	1.544	0.417	1.517
Institutional pressures inside religious sphere				
Ties to prior adopters	2.518***	12.399***	2.416***	11.201***
Sacramental	−1.602**	0.201**	−1.430*	0.239*
Biblically inerrant	−0.924*	0.396*	−0.969*	0.379*
Holiness			0.932+	2.539+
Pentecostal			0.312	1.365
Internal structure				
Decentralized	−0.229	0.795	−0.230	0.795
Autonomous women's mission society	0.481	1.618	0.615	1.849
Intercept	2.956		4.058	
Shape parameter	−0.729***		−0.725***	
AIC	232.161		233.949	
BIC	327.497		342.905	

* Total denominations = 95; total failures (ordaining events) = 45+ p < .10; * p < .05; ** p < .01; *** p < .001

statistically or substantively significant (McCloskey 1985; McCloskey 1995; Ziliak and McCloskey 2008). Following Chaves (1996:862), for the former we rely on traditional indicators of statistical significance (although we use robust regression to estimate the standard errors), while for the latter we identify effects where the hazard (odds) ratio is either greater than or equal to 2.00 or less than or equal to 0.50. we have bolded those effects that meet either or both of these thresholds for ease of identification.

The results of the first model are similar to but not identical to those of Chaves. In three instances the "direction" of the effect differs. For example, Chaves found a positive but statistically insignificant effect of clergy

5.4 Denominational Networks and Women's Ordination

shortages, while the models presented here find a substantively negative effect, suggesting that denominations experiencing clergy shortages are slower to ordain women. Interestingly, Chaves reestimated his model where he included a dummy variable that indicated whether a denomination ever experienced a clergy shortage. When this was included, the effect was negative and statistically significant. Chaves also found a positive and statistically significant effect for founding date, whereas the models presented in Table 5.3 do not in that they are slightly negative and statistically insignificant. This is unsurprising, however, since our models account for time (i.e., the clock) in terms of denominational age. Thus, any effect that founding date has is probably captured in terms of the baseline hazard rate. Indeed, when the founding date is dropped from the models, there is no appreciable change in the other coefficients. Finally, Chaves found a positive and statistically significant effect for denominational decentralization, whereas ours are negative but neither statistically nor substantively significant. The direction and significance of the coefficients in our models agree with Chaves's in terms of whether a denomination is southern, rural, black, sacramental, or inerrant. They also indicate positive effects for both waves of the feminist movement and the existence of autonomous women's mission societies, although Chaves found effects of the second wave of the feminist movement and the existence of an autonomous women's mission society to be statistically significant and we did not. Perhaps most encouragingly is that our estimated effect of ties to prior adopters is positive and substantively and statistically significant. Moreover, the size of our estimated effect (2.52) is virtually the same as the size of Chaves's estimated effect (2.69).

The differences between our models and those of Chaves are probably due to at least three factors. One is that there was a lot of missing data in terms of number of clergy, congregations (total, rural, and southern), and although we attempted to interpolate/impute the missing data in a similar method as Chaves, it is likely that we did not replicate his efforts identically. Second, the network data used in the models here include two additional denominations and two additional ecumenical organizations; plus, based on our own research, we adjusted the network matrices somewhat. Finally, the model used by Chaves accounts for time differently than those used here. As we have already seen, time is specifically accounted for in the models used here. By contrast, in his models Chaves included ten dummy variables measuring the age of each denomination and a continuous variable measuring historical year.

The estimated effects of the two models presented in Table 5.3 vary little from one another. In all cases the direction of the effects stay the same, and in only two cases is there a change in terms of statistical significance (clergy shortage) or substantive significance (predominantly black denomination). Of interest in the second model, of course, is the effect that including dummy variables for Holiness and Pentecostal beliefs has on the likelihood that a denomination will grant full clergy rights to women. As the table indicates, denominations from the Holiness tradition were significantly more likely to begin ordaining women, whereas denominations from the Pentecostal tradition were not. These results are consistent with those presented in Table 5.2. Why such a difference exists is unclear, given the level of similarity between the two traditions. It is worth noting, however, that the results suggest that Pentecostal denominations are far more likely to ordain women than are those that adhere to biblical inerrancy, which is a rough proxy for fundamentalist denominations that emerged in the early twentieth century. It is also worth pointing out that the inclusion of the Holiness and Pentecostal variables in the model somewhat reduces the effect of ties to prior adopters.

Summary

In short, then, our analysis has found support for the new institutionalist theory, which argues that the more that institutions interact with one another, the more they will behave like one another. In this case, the institutions were Christian denominations, the behavior was the sanctioning of women's ordination, and the form of interaction was co-participation in one or more ecumenical organizations. To be sure, the inclusion of variables that captured whether a denomination was part of the Holiness or Pentecostal traditions reduced the effect some, but the variables did not eliminate it.

5.5 Summary and Conclusion

The diffusion of innovations has long been of interest to social network analysts, but the use of network data to systematically study the spread of religious beliefs and practices has been rare. The study of women's ordination by Mark Chaves represents one of the few that have been conducted. One reason, of course, is the difficulty in collecting network data, especially for historical events, which is why the analyses of Kim and Pfaff as well as Collar are so helpful; they illustrate creative ways for collecting relevant social network data. Hopefully, others will step up to fill this "structural hole."

5.6 For Further Reading

The classic network study of diffusion is James Coleman, Elihu Katz, and Herbert Menzel's (1957, 1966) analysis of the adoption of a new drug (tetracycline) by physicians in four Illinois cities. They collected data on the first subscription of tetracycline by physicians, and asked each of the physicians to name three physicians whom they considered to be personal friends and three with whom they would choose to discuss medical matters. They found that doctors with more ties to other doctors were more likely to adopt the drug themselves than those with few or no ties. Others have reanalyzed the data, such as Ron Burt (1987), Peter Marsden and Joel Podolny (1990), David Strang and Nancy Tuma (1993), Thomas Valente (1995), and others. The limited quality of the network data, however, "make it a poor choice for studying adoption behavior" (Valente 2005:99). Of course, when researchers think of diffusion, Everett Rodgers often comes to mind. His *Diffusion of Innovations* (2003), which went through five editions, is considered a classic, and rightly so. For those interested in learning methods for using social network data to study diffusion, Thomas Valente's *Network Models of the Diffusion of Innovation* (1995) is a great resource, although readers may want to begin with his relatively short chapter, "Network Models and Methods for Studying the Diffusion of Innovations" in the edited book by Peter Carrington, John Scott, and Stanley Wasserman (2005). Along with some colleagues, Valente also recently developed an R package, *netdiffuseR* (Yon et al. 2017), which is specifically designed for the analysis of diffusion processes.

The use of social network analysis in archeology is a relatively new development. Much of the literature focuses on introducing archeologists to the basics of social network analysis (see, e.g., Brughmans 2010, 2013; Collar et al. 2015). Nevertheless, a number of studies, such as the Southwest Social Networks (SWSN) Project conducted by Barbara Mills and her colleagues (2013a; 2013b; 2015) noted earlier, are excellent illustrations as to how archeologists use social network analysis, and Tom Brughmans, Simon Keay, and Graeme Earl (2014) have drawn on ERGMs to analyze the pattern of visibility between settlements (it is also a nice introduction to ERGMs in general). Finally, the edited volume, *The Connected Past*, by Tom Brughmans, Anna Collar, and Fiona Coward (2016) is an excellent resource for those who want to learn more about archeological network analysis.

The number of studies of the Protestant Reformation is vast, and several works have hit bookshelves and journals in the last few years because the Reformation "celebrated" its 500-year anniversary in 2017. Sociologists still seem to be quite taken with Max Weber's, *The Protestant Ethic and the Spirit of Capitalism* (1996 [1905]), although there is little to no empirical support for the thesis (see, e.g., Tawney 1926; Becker 1997, 2009; Delacroix and Nielsen 2001; Sanderson, Abrutyn, and Proctor 2011). Social scientists would better spend their time attending to the paper by Sascha Becker, Steven Pfaff, and Jared Rubin (2016), which reviews and summarizes numerous studies that have examined the causes and consequences of the Protestant Reformation. Rodney Stark's *Reformation Myths* (2017a) serves as a helpful corrective to the many misconceptions people hold with regards to the Reformation. None of these works, of course, explore the role that social networks played in the spread of the Protestant Reformation (or the Counter-Reformation, for that matter). In addition to the paper by Kim and Pfaff explored earlier in the chapter, readers may want to consider the paper written by Luke Matthews and his colleagues, "Cultural Inheritance or Cultural Diffusion of Religious Violence? A Quantitative Case Study of the Radical Reformation" (2013), which explores the diffusion of violence among some Anabaptist groups during the Protestant Reformation. What makes this study so interesting is that the Anabaptists were the forerunners of today's Amish and Mennonites, groups that are known for their pacifism, not their violence. We will examine the data on the Anabaptists in more depth in Chapter 10.

6

Politics and Community

6.1 Introduction

On Thursday, December 1, 1955, Rosa Parks boarded a Montgomery, Alabama, city bus and sat in the last seat open in the bus's "colored section." A few stops later, the white section filled up, and a white man was left standing in the aisle. The bus driver asked Parks and three other African Americans to vacate their seats, which were located in the colored section's front row. All but Parks complied, and she was soon arrested for violating Montgomery's bus segregation law. It was not the first time Parks had refused to give up her seat; in fact, the driver who had her arrested in 1955 had kicked her off the bus twelve years before (Stark 2004). But for various reasons, this time was different (McAdam 1982). Her arrest set in motion a series of events that helped give birth to the civil rights movement. A local African American leader, E. D. Nixon, first posted bail for Parks and then called Jo Ann Robinson, an English professor at Alabama State University (a historically black university) and a member of Dexter Avenue Baptist Church, to tell her what happened. Robinson, who chaired the church's political affairs committee, called several other women who were both on the committee and the faculty at Alabama State, and together they drafted (and printed) a leaflet protesting Parks's arrest and calling on Montgomery's African American community to not ride the city's buses the following Monday. Robinson called E. D. Nixon back and told him what they were doing. He thought a boycott was a great idea and agreed to organize a meeting at her church on Friday, yet he called her new pastor, the Rev. Dr. Martin Luther King, Jr., just to make sure that it was okay.[1] It was. News of Parks's arrest and the upcoming meeting spread quickly. King phoned several of the ministers in town, Nixon reached out to many of Montgomery's civic leaders, and rank-and-file African Americans called family, friends, and neighbors. And "by early [Friday] afternoon the arrest of Mrs. Parks was becoming public knowledge. Telephones began to ring in almost rhythmic

---

[1] King joined Dexter Avenue Baptist Church as its pastor in the summer of 1954.

succession. By two o'clock an enthusiastic group had mimeographed leaflets concerning the arrest and the proposed boycott, and by evening these had been widely circulated" (King 1958:37).

Approximately fifty African American leaders attended the meeting, and they adopted a resolution that was essentially a condensed version of the leaflet drafted by Robinson and her colleagues. It urged Montgomery's African Americans on Monday to not "ride the bus to work, to town, to school, or any place," and if they worked, "take a cab, or share a ride, or walk." The resolution also invited them to "come to a mass meeting on Monday at 7:00pm, at the Holt Street Baptist Church for further instruction" (Branch 1988: 133).

Scholars have long recognized the important role that social networks play in connecting people to various types of collective action (see, e.g., McAdam 1982; Diani and McAdam 2003). The civil rights movement was no exception, and the Montgomery bus boycott is illustrative. News of Parks's arrest and the boycott spread primarily through social ties, most of which were church ties. As Rodney Stark notes:

> Jo Ann Robinson and her associates, who launched the initial call for a bus boycott, not only were friends and members of the same faculty but belonged to the same church. All served on the same political affairs committee of that church – and their pastor was none other than Martin Luther King, Jr. When E. D. Nixon organized a meeting of African American clergy at King's church, not only did he know all of them, but they all knew one another well. And every one of those mentioned above was well acquainted with the secretary of the Montgomery Chapter of the National Association for the Advancement of Colored People – Rosa Parks. Moreover, for most African Americans in Montgomery, the decision to join the boycott was not an individual act so much as it was a collective action by members of closely knit church groups.
>
> (2004: 600–601)

In this chapter, we examine why and how there are ties between religious networks and civic engagement. We begin by considering the concept of social capital, which has been developed in various ways by social theorists such as Pierre Bourdieu, James Coleman, and Robert Putnam. In particular, we explore why some social scientists believe there is a positive association between social capital and civic engagement and how faith communities are well positioned to foster the social networks seen as crucial to the development of social capital. Next, we examine studies that have helped to tease out the various mechanisms that lie behind the civic engagement of people of faith. Finally, we explore the degree to which congregations are civically engaged, both in terms of political activism as well as other types of community engagement. We also consider the potential effect that social networks play in congregational activism.

6.2 Social Capital and Social Networks

Although the concept of social capital no longer attracts the attention it did ten to twenty years ago (Putnam 1995a, 2000; Edwards and Foley 1997, 1998; Greeley 1997a; Portes 1998; Paxton 1999; Brinton 2000; Lin 2001; Lin, Cook, and Burt 2001; Putnam and Feldstein 2003), scholars and analysts still draw on the concept to explain various social and political outcomes (Field 2008). They generally understand social capital to be the quantity and quality of resources (i.e., individual, group, or community) that individuals can access through the various social networks in which they are embedded (Lin 1999, 2001). In other words, social capital inheres in the relations among and between persons, and like other forms of capital (e.g., cultural, human, physical) it facilitates productive activity (Coleman 1988, 1990). It involves more than the accumulation of social ties, however. It also involves "transforming contingent relations, such as those of neighborhood, the workplace, or even kinship, into relationships that are at once necessary and elective, implying durable obligations subjectively felt (feelings of gratitude, respect, friendship, etc.)" (Bourdieu 1986:249–250). Thus, ties between individuals need to also exhibit reciprocity, trust, and positive emotions (Paxton 1999:93, 95). Many believe that social capital increases the likelihood of attaining higher instrumental (e.g., higher paying jobs, earlier promotions) and expressive (e.g., better mental health, closer friendships) returns. Others argue that it also enhances the probability of participating in various types of collective action: civic engagement (e.g., voting, serving on committees), neighborhood crime watches, volunteering, and charitable giving, just to name a few (Koch et al. 2001; Putnam 1995b, 1996, 2000; Putnam and Feldstein 2003).

Pointing toward decreased voter turnout, declining membership in voluntary associations, and a drop in the level of trust that Americans have for one another, Robert Putnam has argued that America's social capital has fallen precipitously in recent years as Americans have become more individualistic,[2] and he sees this drop as threatening the long-term health of American democracy.[3] To counteract this decline, he believes

---

[2] Robert Bellah and his collaborators made similar arguments in their book *Habits of the Heart* (1985), as well as in their follow-up volume *The Good Society* (1991).
[3] Not all social scientists agree with Putnam (see, e.g., Greeley 1997c; Paxton 1999; Lin 2001). Paxton (1999), for example, has found only limited support for Putnam's thesis, and Lin (2001) argues that it is premature to declare that social capital in America is in

that voluntary associations need to play a crucial role, and he points to faith communities as America's most important form of associational life. Putnam does not regard all faith communities equally, however. He argues that some faith communities predominantly foster a form of social capital that turns individuals outward and generates a concern for others, while other types chiefly cultivate a form of social capital that turns individuals inward and only engenders concern for close friends. He calls the former "bridging social capital" and the latter "bonding social capital" and argues that theologically conservative faith communities are less likely to generate "bridging" social capital because they embrace exclusive theologies that prevent them from reaching out to the wider community. Although there is some evidence to support Putnam's argument, he may be mistaken. Research suggests that individualistic attitudes are actually more common among theologically moderate and liberal Christians than they are among conservative ones (Davis and Robinson 1996, 1999). To be sure, highly conservative faith communities, such as the Amish, do withdraw from American society, and conservative Protestants have historically visited the polling booth less often than others (Woodberry and Smith 1998). In general, however, contemporary evangelicals are just as likely as mainline Protestants to participate in civil society, and in some cases, they participate more (Smith and Sikkink 1999; Smith 2000).

Nevertheless, Putnam's notion of bridging and bonding social capital is useful and analogous to Mark Granovetter's (1973, 1983) theory of weak and strong ties. Recall that Granovetter found that people were far more likely to use their personal ties than they were other means when it came to finding jobs, and that most of those ties were weak rather than strong. He argued this occurred because our weak ties are less likely to be socially involved with one another than are our strong ties. Most of us have a handful of close friends, many of whom know one another; we also have numerous acquaintances, but only a few know one another. Thus, the set of people making up our network of acquaintances tends to be relatively sparse, while the set of people making up our network of close friends tends to be relatively dense. However, each of our acquaintances is likely to have close friends in their own right, so they are also likely to be embedded in tightly knit networks of their own. Weak ties are strong, according to Granovetter, because they form the crucial bridges that tie together densely knit clusters of people.

Strong ties can also be strong, however. Granovetter notes that feelings of trust and solidarity are more likely to be shared across strong ties than weak ones. Thus, while weak ties provide us with access to information

decline. It is possible that while participation in certain activities is declining, it is increasing in others.

and resources beyond those available in our immediate social circles, strong ties have greater motivation to be sources of support in times of uncertainty (see, e.g., Krackhardt 1992; Stark 2007). This suggests that our networks should consist of a mix of weak and strong ties. That is, they should not be local or provincial networks, consisting primarily of strong, redundant ties and very few weak ties; nor should they be worldly or cosmopolitan networks, consisting of numerous weak ties and very few strong ones (Everton 2012a, 2012b). Instead, they should be "suburban" networks, lying somewhere in between, not necessarily at the arithmetic mean, but rather at a "golden mean" (Aristotle 1998:36–43). This also suggests that the ideal type of social capital is neither bridging nor bonding, but rather some of both.

6.3 Social Networks and Civic Engagement[4]

Research suggests that religious social networks help facilitate various types of civic engagement, including volunteerism and political activism (Greeley 1997b; Merino 2013; McClure 2015; Schwadel et al. 2015). There is substantial evidence indicating that when it comes to charity and volunteerism, people of faith contribute more of their time and money than do their secular counterparts. And while much of this is to religious institutions (e.g., local synagogues, Habitat for Humanity), a substantial amount is to secular institutions. In fact, people of faith contribute their time and money *at rates higher than their secular counterparts* (Brooks 2006; Stark 2012). For example, Kraig Beyerlein and David Sikkink (2008) showed that individuals who attend church regularly were more likely to volunteer for 9/11 relief efforts than were those who did not (see also Beyerlein and Vaisey 2013). Similarly, Valerie Lewis, Carol Ann MacGregor, and Robert Putnam (2013) found that after controlling for religious tradition, religious attendance, number of friends, and sociability, religious social networks have a positive effect on volunteerism, informal giving, attendance at public meetings, participation in a political activity, and the number of political activities in which people participate. Interestingly, religious social networks do not appear to positively affect donating to a secular charity (although religious attendance does). None of this is to suggest that nonbelievers do not contribute their time and money to secular (and nonsecular) causes. They do. It is just that, on average, they do so at rates lower than people of faith (Regnerus, Smith, and Sikkink 1998; Stark 2012:114–120).

Why this is so is the subject of some debate, but most agree that social networks play a pivotal role. Just as social ties connect people to

---

[4] Portions of this section appeared in Everton (2015b:8).

communities of faith, they also link them to activities related to volunteerism and activism (Smith 1996). In fact, some argue that social ties matter more than religious beliefs (Becker and Dhingra 2001:329). This is something of a problematic assertion, however, since evidence suggests that beliefs help drive the types of ties people have and the networks in which they are embedded. For example, the social networks of theologically strict groups – that is, those whose beliefs place high demands on peoples' time, money, and behavior – tend to be denser than those of theologically lenient ones (Stark and Bainbridge 1985; Iannaccone 1994b), and as we have already seen, the topography of peoples' networks (i.e., the mix of strong and weak ties, whether they are provincial or cosmopolitan) may impact their level of political engagement.

6.4 Congregational Networks and Political Activism

Until recently little has been known about the degree to which religious congregations are civically engaged. Early attempts often drew conclusions based on the activity of clergy or rank-and-file members of congregations, but these were limited because there is often not a one-to-one correspondence between clergy, members, and their respective congregations. Some studies have attempted to correct this weakness by using churches as the unit of analysis, but until the advent of the 1998 National Congregations Study (NCS), a survey of US congregations that was repeated in 2006–2007 and 2012, nationally representative samples of congregations did not exist. Mark Chaves used a method known as hypernetwork sampling to collect these samples (Chaves et al. 1999). The basic premise lying behind this method is that a representative sample of organizations (or events) can be derived by randomly sampling people affiliated to such organizations and then having them nominate the particular organization with which they are affiliated. This approach was first introduced by Miller McPherson (1982) and has since been used to draw random samples of voluntary associations (McPherson 1983; McPherson and Smith-Lovin 1986, 1987; Popielarz and McPherson 1995), work establishments (Kalleberg et al. 1996; Knoke and Kalleberg 1994), and even protest events (Beyerlein et al. 2016).[5] For the NCS, respondents to the 1998, 2006, and 2012 General Social Surveys (GSS),[6] who said they attended religious services at least once a year, were asked to name the congregation they attended (Chaves et al. 1999; Chaves and Anderson 2008, 2014). This produced a random sample of

---

[5] The various studies that we considered in the fourth chapter that explored "Blau Space" used hypernetwork sampling to generate the sample of voluntary organizations.
[6] The GSS is an in-person survey of a nationally representative sample of noninstitutionalized English- or Spanish-speaking adults (Smith et al. 2013).

6.4 Congregational Networks and Political Activism

Table 6.1 *Political activities of religious congregations (percent)*

	1998	2006–2007	2012
Told people at worship services about opportunities for political activity within past 12 months	26.2	21.4	14.5
Have ever distributed voter guides	17.0	17.2	12.9
Have had a group, meeting, class, or event within the past 12 months to:			
Organize or participate in a demonstration or march in support of or opposition to some public issue or policy	9.2	8.3	12.5
Get people registered to vote	8.3	17.8	11.1
Discuss politics	6.4	6.3	5.8
Organize or participate in efforts to lobby elected officials of any sort	4.4	7.9	6.6
Have had someone running for office as a visiting speaker within the past 12 months	4.6	5.5	5.3
Have had an elected government official as a visiting speaker within the past 12 months	6.6	8.2	5.2
Participated in at least one of these activities	41.9	43.9	34.6
Unweighted number of congregations	1,234	1,506	1,331

Source: National Congregations Study 1998, 2006–2007, and 2012.

congregations, of which key representatives (e.g., priest, rabbi, minister, or other staff member or leader) were approached and asked about various aspects of their congregations, such as their size, the number of worship services held each week, the various groups active in their congregation, and of particular interest here, the various ways in which they engage their surrounding community.

Congregations and Political Activism

Table 6.1 expands upon an earlier analysis by Beyerlein and Chaves (2003) and presents data on the political activism of congregations in the United States in 1998, 2006–2007, and 2012. It indicates that, for the most part, the two most common forms of church activism are (1) telling people at worship about opportunities for political activity and (2) distributing voter guides.[7] Interestingly, though, both forms of activism appear to be in decline, except among Roman Catholic churches. Voter registration drives and organizing groups to demonstrate or march are the next most common forms of church activism. Voter registration drives were quite popular in 2006–2007, but in 2012 the percentage of churches

---

[7] When the type of voter guide is taken into account, as many churches distribute non-Christian-right voter guides as Christian-right voter guides. Roman Catholic, black Protestant, and mainline Protestant churches tend to distribute guides that do not come from Christian-right sources.

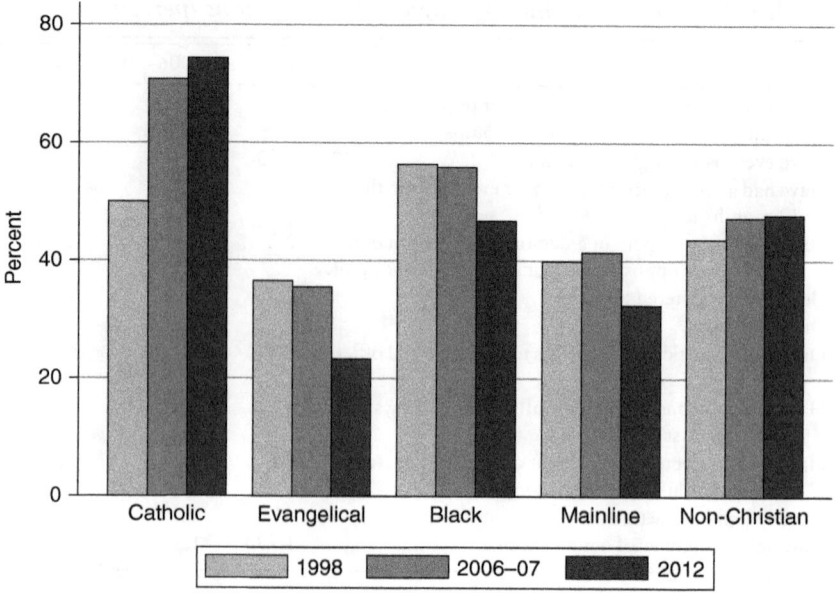

Figure 6.1 Congregational political activism by religious tradition and year

that engaged in this form of political activity dropped close to the 1998 level. The increase in organizing groups to march or demonstrate largely reflects the efforts of Roman Catholic congregations to express their concerns about abortion, same-sex marriage, and immigration (Everton 2015a). As the table indicates, other forms of political activity are far less common. Less than 10 percent of congregations formed groups to discuss politics or lobby government officials, or invited an elected official or someone running for office as a visiting speaker. These low levels do not hold for all religious traditions, however. Black Protestant congregations routinely invite individuals running for political office and government officials to speak at their worship services, an activity that dates back at least to the 1960 presidential race (Everton 2007). All told around 40 percent of congregations engaged in at least one of the activities listed in Table 6.1.

Figure 6.1 presents the percentage of politically active congregations (i.e., congregations that participated in at least one of the activities listed in Table 6.1), broken down by religious tradition. Although many assume that theologically conservative (i.e., evangelical) Christians are the most politically active religious group (see, e.g., Averill 1989; Robbins 1995; Martin 1996), that is not the case. Over the last decade and a half, Roman Catholic and black Protestant congregations have been the most

6.4 Congregational Networks and Political Activism

politically active (Beyerlein and Chaves 2003; Everton 2015a). In the late 1990s it was black Protestant congregations, but since the mid 2000s, it has been Roman Catholic ones. Moreover, both mainline and evangelical Protestant church activism has declined in recent years, although the drop in the latter's activism has been more precipitous.

What Figure 6.1 does not show is how congregations tend to specialize in how they get politically involved, emphasizing some forms of political activism over others. Some prefer to march and demonstrate while others gravitate to methods such as handing out voter guides or inviting candidates as guest speakers (Beyerlein and Chaves 2003; Everton 2015a). Roman Catholic congregations are the one exception. They participate in almost all forms of political activism. Indeed, the only form in which they do not engage is inviting political candidates and elected officials as visiting speakers (Everton 2015a). Moreover, as Figure 6.1 shows, Roman Catholic church activism appears to be on the upswing. In 1998, the percentage of Roman Catholic congregations that participated in at least one of the forms of political activity considered here was 50.0 percent; in 2006–2007 that percentage grew to 70.8 percent, and by 2012, it grew to 74.3 percent. Most of this jump can be traced to increases in handing out voter guides, organizing a demonstration or march, registering people to vote, and forming groups to discuss politics (Everton 2015a). Although the 1998 NCS did not include information about the issues motivating churches to become politically active, the second and third waves did, and they suggest that much of this activism is related to the issue of abortion, although Roman Catholic churches also mobilized or lobbied on behalf of other issues, such as poverty, same-sex marriage, and immigration reform (Everton 2015a).

When it comes to most forms of political activism, evangelical Protestant churches are surprisingly inactive. They are unlikely to tell people at worship about opportunities for political activity, organize a demonstration or a march, lobby elected officials, discuss politics, or invite elected officials or individuals running for office to speak (Everton 2015a). Instead, they tend to limit their political activities to handing out voter guides, but even in this regard, they lag behind Roman Catholic and black Protestant congregations (Everton 2015a). This relatively low level of political activism accords well with other research, such as that of Christian Smith (2000), who found that although most evangelicals believe they should be involved in politics, by this, most simply meant basic responsibilities and rights (e.g., voting). "Politics for the majority of evangelicals," Smith writes, "is not a trumpet call to take sides in the much-ballyhooed 'culture wars,' but a matter of basic citizen responsibilities and rights" (Smith 2000: 98). Those who did express a desire to impose their moral worldview on others represented only a small percentage of those Smith interviewed. In fact, they accounted for a smaller percentage than those who believed Christians should stay out of politics altogether. It could be possible that this latter group is exerting increasing influence over the evangelical movement as a whole, for as Figure 6.1 indicates, the percentage of politically active evangelical congregations has steadily declined from approximately 36 percent in 1998 to just 23 percent in 2012.

Black Protestant churches seldom form groups to discuss politics or lobby elected officials, and until recently, have not regularly participated in a demonstration or a march, which is surprising given its involvement in the civil rights movement; instead, they are more likely to tell people about opportunities for political activity, distribute voter guides, organize voter registration campaigns, and invite elected officials and political candidates as visiting speakers (Everton 2015a). This last activity has a long tradition in black churches and is probably its most visible form of political activism. For example, during the 2004 presidential campaign, John Kerry and John Edwards visited and spoke at numerous churches, and most were African American; the only time President Bush spoke at a church during the campaign, it also was an African American church (Everton 2007). Similarly, Bill Clinton and Al Gore visited and spoke at numerous black churches during the closing days of the 1992, 1996, and 2000 presidential campaigns (Ifill 1992:14); Andrew Young and Martin Luther King, Sr. took Jimmy Carter around to a number of black churches and had him meet with numerous African American clergy prior to the 1976 presidential election (Lincoln and Mamiya 1990: 215), and John F. Kennedy's campaign covertly distributed two million pamphlets at black churches on the Sunday before the 1960 election (Branch 1988). Black Protestant political activism is not limited to presidential campaigns. Anecdotal evidence suggests that it is common for African American political candidates to solicit the blessings of black pastors and ministerial associations. For example, Frederick Harris (1999:12–26) recounts Carol Mosely Braun's appearance before a gathering of African American ministers to help jumpstart her 1992 senatorial campaign, and Mary Sawyer's (1982) study of fourteen members of the Congressional Black Caucus found that thirteen received endorsements from pastors, ten received endorsements from ministerial bodies, ten spoke at black churches during their campaigns, and five received financial contributions from churches.

Mainline Protestant congregations score low on almost every form of political activity except for telling people at worship about political opportunities and for forming groups to discuss politics. However, there has been a slight increase in the percentage of mainline Protestant churches that demonstrated, marched, or lobbied in the previous year on behalf of one or more issues, three of which were more common than others: poverty, same-sex marriage, and immigration reform (Everton 2015a). The apparent low level of mainline Protestant church activism

6.4 Congregational Networks and Political Activism

could be misleading. As Robert Wuthnow and John Evans (2002) have documented, mainline Protestant political activism often occurs behind the scenes. For instance, all of the mainline Protestant denominations maintain offices in Washington, DC that represent (i.e., lobby on behalf of) the political interests of their respective denominations. Moreover, as Christian Smith (1996) noted in his study of the largely faith-based, peace movement that opposed President Ronald Reagan's policies in Central America, although local congregations tend not to demonstrate or march, they often serve as feeder organizations that funnel members into social movement organizations that do.

Finally, the political activism of non-Christian congregations is striking in that it is higher than the political activism of evangelical and mainline Protestant congregations and, at least in 2012, was higher than black Protestant congregations. Like other "traditions," they tend to specialize in how they are politically active (Everton 2015a). In particular, they are more likely to lobby elected officials, organize voter registration campaigns, or participate in a demonstration or march. In fact, they only lag behind Roman Catholic churches in terms of the latter. Be that as it may, we probably should not place too much stock in the results since the number of non-Christian congregations included in the NCS is relatively small. Plus, this is more of a catchall category than a particular religious tradition. Thus, more detailed analysis is in order before we can draw any definitive conclusions.

In all, approximately 40 percent of congregations participated in at least one of the activities listed in Table 6.1. Is this high or low? Figure 6.2, which compares the level of political activism of congregations with the level that they engage in or offer some type of social or human service (e.g., food assistance programs, home building or repair, etc.), suggests that it may be low.[8] As it indicates, the percentage of congregations offering social services is almost twice that of the percentage of congregations that are politically active. However, as Kraig Beyerlein and Mark Chaves have argued, when compared to other organizations whose primary purpose is not political, it is probably quite high:

---

[8] In the 1998 NCS survey, respondents (i.e., key representatives of congregations) were asked, "Has your congregation participated in or supported social service, community development, or neighborhood organizing projects of any sort within the past 12 months?" In the 2006–2007 and 2012 NCS surveys, respondents were asked an additional question if they answered "no" to that question: "Within the past 12 months, has your congregation engaged in any human service projects, outreach ministries, or other activities intended to help people who are not members of your congregation?" This identified 640 additional congregations (401 in 2006–2007 and 239 in 2012) that offered some sort of social service program. In order to compare congregations across all three waves, Figures 6.2 and 6.3 only include responses to the first question.

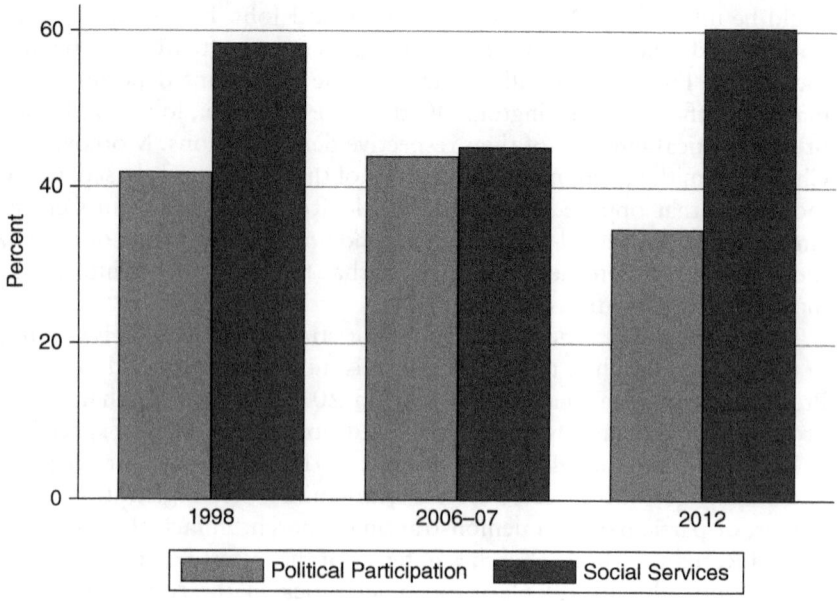

Figure 6.2 Comparison of congregational political activism and social service

We wonder if there is another set of organizations whose primary purpose is *not* political action, but where 41 percent of those organizations participate in some kind of political activity ... Weighted to only account for duplicate nominations, NCS data show that 37 percent of religious attenders were in congregations where opportunities for political activity were mentioned ... [By contrast] Verba, Schlozman, and Brady (1995:373, 558) showed that only 8 percent of contributors to or members of nonpolitical organizations and only 16 percent of people working full- or part-time being asked to be politically active in some way in these settings. It seems reasonable to conclude then, as Verba, Schlozman, and Brady (1995) do, that congregations lead the way among nonpolitical organizations when it comes to offering opportunities for political activity.

(Beyerlein and Chaves 2003:236)

Congregational Networks and Political Activism

It is difficult to determine the role that social networks may play in congregational political activism. The National Congregations Study surveys do not include direct measures of congregational social networks.

6.4 Congregational Networks and Political Activism

However, in an analysis of the political activism of mainline Protestant churches, Mark Chaves, Helen Giesel, and William Tsitsos (2002) identified thirty-eight congregational activities (i.e., responses to questions) captured in the 1998 NCS that could broadly be considered proxies for Putnam's notion of "bridging" social capital. They also offered empirical evidence that mainline Protestants outpaced other traditions engaging in these activities. Unfortunately, many of these questions were not asked in the 2006–2007 and 2012 surveys, and it is debatable whether all of them actually capture the effects of social networks. Nevertheless, one category, the social services category, may. It includes congregational participation in various social service programs in a number of areas, such as the provision of food, housing, clothing, health, and homelessness – activities that almost certainly help form bridges between congregations and the wider community.

Consequently, again building on the earlier analysis by Beyerlein and Chaves (2003), we estimated a series of multivariate logistic models that regress the various types of political activities summarized in Table 6.1 on a series of covariates, including a dummy variable indicating whether or not a congregation offered one or more social service programs.[9] Two sets of models were estimated because, as noted in footnote 8, the 1998 NCS survey asked respondents a single question regarding social service programs: "Has your congregation participated in or supported social service, community development, or neighborhood organizing projects of any sort within the past 12 months?" However, in the 2006–2007 and 2012 NCS surveys, they asked a follow-up question if respondents answered "no" to the first question: "Within the past 12 months, has your congregation engaged in any human service projects, outreach ministries, or other activities intended to help people who are not members of your congregation?" This identified 640 additional congregations (401 in 2006–2007 and 239 in 2012) that offered some sort of social service program. Thus, the first set of models includes all three waves of the NCS but only responses to the first question, while the second set only includes the last two waves but with responses to both questions. In addition to the social services dummy variable, both sets of models include covariates indicating wave year (with 1998 as the reference category),

---

[9] Aside from the region in which the congregation was located, all of the variables included in the models had cases of missing information. Following Beyerlein and Chaves (2003), we used multiple imputation (MI) as implemented in Stata 14 (StataCorp 2015a, 2015b) for those cases. MI has become an increasingly popular method for dealing with missing data (Rubin 1987, 1996; Schafer 1997; Carpenter and Kenward 2013) because it avoids many of the statistical pitfalls characteristic of other techniques for handling missing data (StataCorp 2015a:3–4). For this analysis, we generated twenty imputations for every case with missing information and estimated identical regression models for each of the twenty imputed datasets. These were then combined to produce estimated coefficients, standard errors, and levels of statistical significance.

religious tradition (with evangelical Protestant as the reference category), religious culture, congregational size and age, whether a congregation considered itself to be politically conservative, the percent of a congregation's members that were female, the percent of a congregation's members with at least a four-year college degree, the percent of a congregation's wealthy and poor members,[10] the percent of a congregation's members that were 60 years and older, the percent of a congregation's members that were 35 years and younger, whether a congregation was located in an urban area, whether it was located in the South, and whether it lacked a head pastor.[11]

The results are presented in Tables 6.2a and 6.2b and confirm much of what we saw in Table 6.1 and Figures 6.1 and 6.2. The year dummy variables indicate that, for the most part, congregational political activism was lower in 2012 than it was in 1998 or 2006–2007, the one exception being lobbying elected officials, where we saw a statistically significant increase from 1998. The religious tradition coefficients also confirm that Roman Catholic and black Protestant congregations were the most politically active congregations; both were more than twice as likely ($e^{0.753} = 2.12; e^{0.844} = 2.33$) to engage in some form of political activity than evangelical Protestant congregations. By contrast, evangelical Protestant congregations were just slightly more likely than mainline Protestants to be politically active ($e^{-0.239} = 0.787; 1/0.787 = 1.27$). The results also indicate that regardless of denominational affiliation, charismatic congregations were more politically active than non-charismatic ones. This could be "an echo of charismatic congregations' political mobilization by Pat Robertson's 1988 presidential campaign" (Beyerlein and Chaves 2003:241), or it could simply capture something about charismatic beliefs and practices that encourage civic engagement. The results indicate as well that congregational size was positively associated with political activity, while being located in the South and lacking a head pastor were negatively associated with it.

Of primary interest here, of course, is the effect that the offering of social service programs had on the political activity of congregations, and we can see that offering social service programs, on the whole, was positively associated

---

[10] The 1998 and 2006–2007 waves of the NCS asked, "What percent would you say live in households with income higher than $100,000 a year?" in order to identify the percentage of wealthy households in the congregation. The 2012 NCS raised the cutoff to $140,000 in order to identify wealthy households. Similarly, the first two waves of the NCS asked, "What percent would you say live in households with income under $25,000 a year?" in order to identify poor households. In 2012, the NCS raised the cutoff to $35,000.

[11] These covariates were selected in order to replicate, as much as possible, the initial study by Beyerlein and Chaves (2003). Unfortunately, some questions asked in 1998 were not repeated in either 2006–2007 or 2012 or both (e.g., whether a congregation's head clergy had at least a graduate degree), so they could not be included here.

Table 6.2a Estimated coefficients of various political activities on select independent variables

Independent Variables	All Political Activities		Offer Political Opportunities		Group to Demonstrate or March		Group to Lobby Elected Officials		Group to Discuss Politics	
	All Waves	2006–07, 2012	All Waves	2006–07, 2012	All Waves	2006–07, 2012	All Waves	2006–07, 2012	All Waves	2006–07, 2012
Year										
2006–07	−0.017		−0.291**		−0.050		0.297*		0.296*	
2012	−0.353***	−0.329***	−0.704***	−0.387***	0.210	0.124	0.346**	0.124	−0.000	−0.237*
Religious tradition										
Roman Catholic	0.753***	1.147***	1.026***	1.350***	1.768***	2.210***	1.759***	2.210***	0.466**	0.699***
Black Protestant	0.844***	0.860***	0.835***	0.971***	0.263	0.941***	0.774***	0.941***	0.881***	0.763**
Mainline Protestant	−0.239*	−0.284*	0.130	0.231	0.086	0.732**	0.495*	0.732**	0.921***	0.998***
Non-Christian	0.736***	0.892***	1.009***	1.336***	1.143***	2.227***	1.821***	2.227***	1.362***	1.436***
Religious culture										
Theological conservatism	−0.131	−0.157	−0.125	−0.222*	0.039	−0.047	−0.141	−0.047	−0.258*	−0.268
Charismatic	0.511***	0.567***	0.321**	0.397**	0.447***	0.337*	0.308*	0.337*	0.420***	0.587***
Social service programs offered	0.460***	0.529***	0.436***	0.391*	0.589***	0.737**	0.586***	0.737**	0.662***	0.514
Controls										
Size	0.285***	0.259***	0.079*	0.058	0.142***	0.075	0.135*	0.075	0.347***	0.328***
Age	0.002***	0.003**	0.001	0.001	0.002**	0.003**	0.003***	0.003**	0.002**	0.002
Political conservatism	0.027	0.039	0.049	0.134	−0.048	−0.187	−0.109	−0.187	−0.531***	−0.517***
% female	0.004	0.008	0.003	0.005	−0.003	0.013*	0.012*	0.013*	0.007	0.010

(continued)

Table 6.2a (*continued*)

Independent Variables	All Political Activities		Offer Political Opportunities		Group to Demonstrate or March		Group to Lobby Elected Officials		Group to Discuss Politics	
	All Waves	2006–07, 2012	All Waves	2006–07, 2012	All Waves	2006–07, 2012	All Waves	2006–07, 2012	All Waves	2006–07, 2012
% ≥ 4-year degree	0.001	0.004	0.003	0.004	0.006**	0.007*	0.007**	0.007*	0.010***	0.011***
% wealthy	-0.001	0.001	-0.002	0.000	-0.001	0.004	0.002	0.004	0.002	0.003
% poor	-0.001	0.000	-0.001	-0.002	0.004	-0.005	-0.003	-0.005	0.002	0.000
% ≥ 60 years old	-0.001	-0.001	-0.000	0.000	-0.003	-0.007	-0.003	-0.007	-0.003	-0.003
% ≤ 35 years old	-0.004	-0.004	-0.003	-0.002	0.005	-0.007	-0.003	-0.007	-0.003	-0.002
Urban	0.033	0.043	0.084	0.100	0.268*	0.260	0.298*	0.260	0.512***	0.506**
South	-0.177*	-0.129	-0.303***	-0.336***	-0.011	-0.169	-0.246*	-0.169	-0.381***	-0.338*
No head pastor	-0.734***	-0.730**	-0.549*	-0.620	0.011	-0.070	-0.092	-0.070	-0.417	-0.360
Intercept	-1.973***	-2.543***	-1.965***	-2.613***	-4.074***	-5.116***	-5.424***	-5.116***	-6.055***	-5.980***

Source: National Congregations Study 1998, 2006–2007, and 2012.

Table 6.2b Estimated coefficients of various political activities on select independent variables

Independent Variables	Candidate as Visiting Speaker		Government Official as Visiting Speaker		Group to Register People to Vote		Hand Out Voter Guides	
	All Waves	2006–07, 2012	All Waves	2006–07, 2012	All Waves	2006–07, 2012	All Waves	2006–07, 2012
Year								
2006–07	0.098		0.018		1.064***		-0.080	
2012	-0.242	-0.285	-0.295*	-0.251	0.603***	-0.397***	-0.256**	-0.174
Religious tradition								
Roman Catholic	-0.754**	-0.756*	-0.881***	-0.763***	0.326*	0.384*	0.223	0.714***
Black	2.136***	1.779***	0.891***	0.848***	1.381***	1.168***	0.423**	0.586***
Mainline Protestant	0.016	-0.425	-0.066	-0.069	-0.717***	-0.758***	-0.974***	-1.165***
Non-Christian	1.780***	1.500***	0.964***	0.934**	0.429	0.382	-0.267	-0.106
Religious culture								
Theological conservatism	-0.106	-0.230	-0.187	-0.230	0.001	-0.075	0.138	0.190
Charismatic	0.597***	0.668***	0.408**	0.439**	0.664***	0.659***	0.297**	0.268*
Social service programs offered	1.014***	1.108*	0.657***	0.901**	0.351***	0.154	0.276**	0.912***
Controls								
Size	0.335***	0.310***	0.402***	0.385***	0.356***	0.360***	0.172***	0.118**
Age	0.003	0.002	0.004***	0.004**	0.001	0.000	0.001	0.002*
Political conservatism	-0.133	-0.198	-0.249*	-0.177	-0.062	-0.065	0.261**	0.163
% female	0.001	0.009	0.005	0.006	0.002	0.003	0.003	0.006
% ≥ 4-year degree	-0.005	-0.003	0.001	-0.000	-0.001	-0.001	-0.002	-0.001
% wealthy	0.009	0.013*	-0.001	0.002	0.004	0.005	0.001	0.002

(continued)

Table 6.2b (*continued*)

Independent Variables	Candidate as Visiting Speaker		Government Official as Visiting Speaker		Group to Register People to Vote		Hand Out Voter Guides	
	All Waves	2006–07, 2012	All Waves	2006–07, 2012	All Waves	2006–07, 2012	All Waves	2006–07, 2012
% poor	0.005	0.005	0.002	0.002	0.004	0.002	−0.003	−0.004
% ≥ 60 years old	0.003	0.007	0.005	0.004	−0.002	−0.002	−0.000	−0.000
% ≤ 35 years old	−0.004	0.000	0.001	0.001	0.002	0.001	0.001	−0.000
Urban	0.145	0.182	0.159	0.162	0.193	0.100	0.100	0.082
South	0.252	0.366*	0.305**	0.244	−0.100	−0.011	−0.148	−0.017
No head pastor	−0.130	−0.482	−0.156	−0.114	−0.697*	−0.783*	−1.051***	−1.085**
Intercept	−6.595***	−7.301***	−5.794***	−6.074***	−5.034***	−3.804***	−2.544***	−3.360***

Source: National Congregations Study 1998, 2006–2007, and 2012.

6.4 Congregational Networks and Political Activism

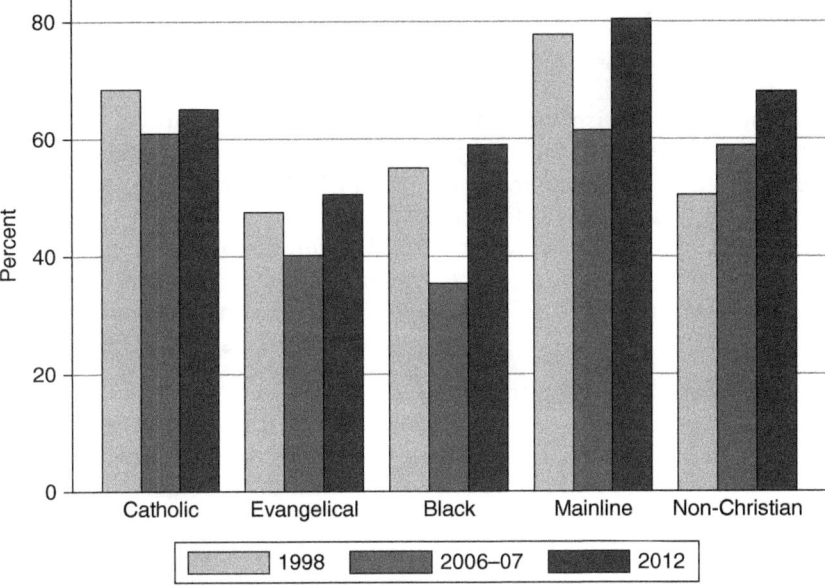

Figure 6.3 Percentage of congregations offering social services by religious tradition and year

with congregational political activity. All else being equal, it was positively associated with telling worshipers about opportunities for political activity; forming groups to demonstrate, march, lobby elected officials, discuss politics, or register people to vote; inviting political candidates or government officials to speak; and handing out voter guides.[12]

Summary

Although these results do not offer direct empirical support of the argument by Chaves, Giesel, and Tsitsos (2002) that providing social services helps congregations build ties with the wider society and create what Putnam calls bridging social capital, they are certainly consistent with it. But what about the contention of Chaves, Giesel, and Tsitsos (2002) that mainline Protestants outpaced other traditions in offering such activities? Figure 6.3, which plots the percentage of congregations offering social services by year and religious tradition, suggests that is indeed the case (see footnote 8).

---

[12] The direct effect of offering social service programs sometimes ceased to be statistically significant when the interaction effect of various religious traditions and the offering of social services were included in the models; in most cases, statistically significant effects were found for one or more of the interaction terms. Results are available on request.

6.5 Excursus: Church and State Separation and Civic Engagement

The political activism of people of faith and congregations inevitably gives rise to debates concerning the proper role that religion should play in public life – in particular, the degree to which, if at all, religious groups should and can be civically engaged (see, e.g., Neuhaus 1986; Rawls 1993; Hamburger 2002; Walker 2002; Lynn 2015). Some call for the complete relegation of religion to the private sphere, but others, such as (then) Senator Barack Obama, argue that it is neither possible nor desirable:

> What I am suggesting is this – secularists are wrong when they ask believers to leave their religion at the door before entering into the public square. Frederick Douglass, Abraham Lincoln, William Jennings Bryan, Dorothy Day, Martin Luther King – indeed, the majority of great reformers of American history – were not only motivated by faith but repeatedly used religious language to argue for their cause. To say that men and women should not inject their "personal morality" into public policy debates is a practical absurdity. Our law is by definition a codification of morality, much of it grounded in the Judeo-Christian tradition.[13]
> (Obama 2006)

The political scientist Jonathan Fox (2013, 2015) has helpfully sorted how people view church and state separation into four types or models. One, *laicism*, is the most hostile of the four toward religion. It "bans state support for any religion [and] ... restricts the presence of religion in the public square" (Fox 2015:29). The private expression of religion is permitted, but it assumes that the public expression of it can undermine democracy. That is why countries, such as France, which adopt laicism, place restrictions on religious institutions and public religious activities. "France's 2004 law banning any overt religious symbol in public schools, including the head coverings worn by Muslim women, is a classic example of this model" (Fox 2015:30). A second type, which Fox calls *absolute religion and state separation* (absolute SRAS), holds that the state must neither restrict nor support religion. The United States is generally considered an example of this type. "While there is a struggle between conservatives and liberals over the exact role that

---

[13] My own sense, which is very much influenced by the late Nat Hentoff (1992), is that most people support religious activism as long as it coheres with their political beliefs. However, if a group's religious activism runs afoul of their beliefs, they are quick to argue that it violates the separation of church and state. This is a testable proposition, of course, but it is one for another day.

6.5 Church and State Separation and Civic Engagement

religion should play in society and government, both sides support the expression of religion in public life. For example, the use of religious language by politicians is acceptable, but most state support for religion is not" (Fox 2013:33). A third type is what Fox calls *neutral political concern*. It embraces "equal treatment for all religions" (Fox 2015:30). Thus, countries following this model can support or restrict religion as long as they treat all religions the same. Closely related to this is a fourth and final type: *exclusion of ideals*. It differs from the third type in that it focuses on intent rather than outcome. "Thus, religions can in practice be treated differently as long as there is no specific intent to support or hinder a specific religion" (Fox 2015:31). These four types are summarized in Table 6.3.

These, of course, are not the only ways in which state and religion interact. Fox (2015) notes that some states officially support a specific religion; others are supportive of one religion over another; still others take a neutral stance toward religion; and finally, some states are hostile, in varying degrees, toward religion.[14] Nevertheless, when debates concerning church and state separation arise, it is usually over one or more of these models. What should we make of them? We believe that for at least two reasons, countries reap the greatest benefits when they adopt a neutral, rather than a hostile, stance toward religion.

One reason draws on Charles Tilly's (2004, 2005b) observation that states, particularly democratic ones, cannot survive without the partial integration of what he calls "trust networks" (e.g., trade diasporas, clandestine religious groups)[15] into civil society. Throughout history, however, these trust networks have often segregated themselves from what they perceive to be hostile or predatory regimes. It follows, then, that all else being equal, states that adopt policies that are often perceived by religious minorities as being hostile toward their beliefs and practices, will find it more difficult to integrate minority religious groups into civil society than will states that adopt more neutral policies. A second reason is that religious groups that are on the receiving end of government and/or social hostilities are more likely to respond violently than are groups that are not (Grim and Finke 2010). It is probably no coincidence that government repression of some religious groups has resulted in higher rates of violence in Algeria, Egypt, Kashmir, the Southern Philippines, and Chechnya (Hafez 2003). Thus, if a state's

---

[14] Currently, North Korea is the only country that falls into the category of states that oppose all forms of religion on ideological reasons; prior to 1990, however, almost all of the countries within the Soviet bloc would have fallen into this category (Fox 2015:56).
[15] Tilly defines trust networks as "ramified interpersonal connections, consisting mainly of strong ties, within which people set valued, consequential long-term resources and enterprises at risk to the malfeasance, mistakes, or failures of others" (Tilly 2005b:41).

Table 6.3 Types of church and state separation

	May the state support religion?	May the state restrict religion?	May the state restrict religion in political discourse?	May a specific tradition's ideals influence public policy?	Attitude toward religion
Laicism	No	Yes, in public square and if applied equally	Yes	No	Hostile
Absolute separation	No	No	No	Maybe, if there is no support or restrictions	Neutral
Neutral political concern	Yes, if applied equally	Yes, if applied equally	Yes, if applied equally	Yes, if there is no unequal treatment	Neutral
Exclusion of ideals	Yes, but no preference for any religion	Yes, but no preference for any religion	Yes, but no preference for any religion	No	Neutral

Source: Adapted from Fox 2015:29.

goal is to integrate all of its citizens (and potential citizens) into civil society, as well as to minimize religiously inspired violence, then it seems that adopting a neutral stance toward religion is the wisest course of action.

6.6 Summary and Conclusion

In this chapter, we have considered the effects that religious social networks have on the participation of people of faith in civic society. To this end, we began by considering the concept of social capital, which has been developed by various social theorists, most notably Robert Putnam. There we first noted the parallels between Putnam's bonding and bridging capital and Granovetter's strong and weak ties, which led to the observation that perhaps a blend of bonding and bridging capital is ideal. We then saw that social ties, and in particular religious ties, lead to higher rates of civic participation. Next, we explored the degree to which faith communities are civically engaged. Finally, we briefly considered the various types of church and state separation, which led us to suggest that adopting a neutral stance toward religion will lead to higher integration rates of minorities (including religious minorities) and lower rates of violence (including religious violence).

6.7 For Further Reading

Although Robert Putnam helped popularize the concept of social capital, he was not the first to explore and highlight its importance. Both Pierre Bourdieu and James Coleman were there before him. One could also argue that Robert Bellah, Richard Madsen, William Sullivan, Ann Swidler, and Steven Tipton covered much of the same ground in their classic work, *Habits of the Heart* (1985) as well as in their follow-up volume, *The Good Society* (1991). Here are some readings on the topic that might be quite helpful:

- Bourdieu, Pierre. 1986. "The Forms of Capital" in *Handbook of Theory and Research for the Sociology of Education*, edited by John G. Richardson. New York, NY: Greenwood Press, pp. 241–258; reprinted in *The Sociology of Economic Life*, 3rd. ed., edited by Mark Granovetter and Richard Swedberg, Boulder, CO: Westview Press, pp. 78–92.
- Coleman, James S. 1988. "Social Capital in the Creation of Human Capital." *American Journal of Sociology* 94 (Supplement):S95–S120.

- Edwards, Bob, and Michael W. Foley. 1998. "Civil Society and Social Capital beyond Putnam." *American Behavioral Scientist* 42(1):124–139.
- Field, John. 2008. *Social Capital*, 2nd ed. London: Routledge.
- Greeley, Andrew M. 1997. "Coleman Revisited: Religious Structures as a Source of Social Capital." *American Behavioral Scientist* 40(5):587–594.
- Lin, Nan. 2001. *Social Capital*. Cambridge: Cambridge University Press.
- Paxton, Pamela. 1999. "Is Social Capital Declining in the United States? A Multiple Indicator Assessment." *American Journal of Sociology* 105(1):88–127.
- Putnam, Robert D. 1995. "Bowling Alone: America's Declining Social Capital." *Journal of Democracy* 6:65–78.

Hypernetwork sampling has been around for some time, but it remains a largely untapped resource for social scientists. Miller McPherson (1982) provided the first exposition of the method in his analysis of voluntary organizations, a topic that we explored in some depth in Chapter 4. More recently, Kraig Beyerlein and several of his colleagues (2016) drew on the method in order to generate a random sample of protest events. A description of how the National Congregations Study used hypernetwork sampling can be found in three articles by Mark Chaves and his collaborators (Chaves et al. 1999; Chaves and Anderson 2008, 2014).

The rise of the Christian Right in the 1970s and 1980s not only led to a considerable amount of social scientific research (see, e.g., Liebman and Wuthnow 1983; Smidt 1989; Wilcox 1990; Green 1993; Guth et al. 1997; Manza and Brooks 1997; Regnerus, Sikkink, and Smith 1999; Wald and Calhoun-Brown 2005), but it also gave rise to a debate concerning the separation of church and state (see, e.g., Neuhaus 1986; Rawls 1993; Hamburger 2002; Walker 2002; Lynn 2015). A helpful place to start is Jonathan Fox's *Political Secularism, Religion, and the State* (2015) in which he lays out the four church and state separation models outlined in Table 6.3, but also explores the various ways in which church and state interact (establishment, support, neutral, hostile) around the world. As noted earlier, Brian Grim and Roger Finke's *The Price of Freedom Denied* (2010) provides empirical evidence that religious freedom and violence are inversely related. And they build, in part, on an earlier argument made by the economists Laurence Iannaccone and Eli Berman (Iannaccone 1999; Iannaccone and Berman 2006; Berman 2009), who contend that because unregulated religious markets tend to be pluralistic, the competition between churches and denominations will induce moderation not violence (Iannaccone and Berman 2006:122). Interestingly, they point out that Adam Smith (1965) was the first to make this argument in *The*

Wealth of Nations. Richard Neuhaus's *The Naked Public Square* (1986) is perhaps the most articulate argument by those who think that religion in the United States should have a greater presence in the public square than it already does, while the various materials available from the Baptist Joint Committee for Religious Liberty (formerly known as the *Baptist Joint Committee for Public Affairs*) offer the opposite perspective,[16] arguing (among other things), that the US's public square is anything but naked (Walker 2005, 2014).

---

[16] See http://bjconline.org.

Part IV

Ties That Build Up

7

Networks and Tradition

7.1 Introduction

Siddhārtha Gautama, the future Buddha, was the son of a wealthy landowner who served as the chief of a small state in the foothills of the Himalayas. According to legend, Siddhārtha's father suspected that if his son witnessed the suffering of the world, he would prefer to save humanity instead of rule it. Thus, he attempted to shield Siddhārtha by making his life so pleasurable that he would not want to abandon it. At the age of sixteen Siddhārtha married, and he and his wife had a son. However, one day he persuaded his charioteer to take him to a nearby city where he saw four sights that changed his life: an old man, a man suffering from a horrible disease, a dead man, and a wandering monk. The first three left him "dismayed by the impermanence of life and the existence of suffering," while the last "suggested the possibility of a life of renunciation" (Fisher 2003:105). Eventually, Siddhārtha concluded that he would never have peace of mind until he discovered the meaning of life, in particular, why there is so much suffering. Thus, at the age of twenty-nine he renounced his inheritance, shaved his head, and set off on a quest. He first spent time with a "famous Brahmin teacher who had many followers," and although he reportedly achieved a higher state of consciousness, he felt that a still higher one was attainable. He then studied under a teacher who helped him reach a higher state, but he was still unsatisfied that he had not attained total liberation from suffering. He then "sought out temple priests," but their animal sacrifices repelled him; after this he ran into "five pupils of his second teacher who were living as ascetics in the forest" (Fisher 2003:105, 106). Because he admired their efforts, he adopted their extreme asceticism for six years, but after his health began to fail, he adopted a more moderate approach. Although the five ascetics became disillusioned and deserted him, Siddhārtha sensed that enlightenment was near. So, he purchased a straw pallet, seated himself under a fig tree, and vowed that he would not move until he reached complete and final enlightenment, which he did. "After passing through four states of serene contemplation," Siddhārtha "recalled all of his previous lives," understood "the wheel of deaths and rebirths," and "realized the cause of suffering and the means for ending it" (Fisher 2003:106). The first people with whom he shared his insights were the five ascetics who had deserted him. They ridiculed him at first, but they eventually became his first disciples.

Much of this story could be apocryphal, but it is fairly well established that the Buddha came from a princely family. What is less well known is that most of his first converts came from the two upper classes of Indian society: the Brahmins and Kshatriyas (Collins 1998:205). According to Robert Lester (1987:27), fifty-five of the first sixty converts were from "prominent families." Moreover, the primary source of lay support was from landowning farmers (Collins 1998:205).

Buddhism's beginning was not unusual. Most new religious movements attract converts from among the privileged (Stark and Bainbridge 1985), something that often takes social scientists by surprise. For instance, many have assumed that Christianity began as a movement among the poor and dispossessed. Karl Marx's frequent collaborator, Friedrich Engels, is a case in point. He once remarked that "Christianity ... first appeared as the religion of slaves and emancipated slaves, of poor people deprived of all rights, of peoples subjugated or dispersed by Rome" (Engels 2008 [1894]:316), and sociologists such as Ernst Troeltsch (1960 [1911]), theologians such as H. Richard Niebuhr (1929), and historians such as Edwin Goodenough (1931) have shared Engels' assumption. However, the work of scholars such as Adolf von Harnack (1905), E. A. Judge (1960), Gerd Theissen (1982), Wayne Meeks (1983), Elizabeth Schüssler Fiorenza (1990, 1994), and others have challenged this assumption and essentially laid to rest "the romantic idea of a proletarian Christian community, a religious movement of the lower classes" (Theissen 1982:70). We are now fairly confident that the early Christian church recruited disproportionately from the middle and upper classes. For instance, "Abraham J. Malherbe (1977:29–59) analyzed the language and style of early church writers and concluded that they were addressing a literate, educated audience" (Stark 1996a:31). And in his first letter to the Corinthians (1 Cor. 1:26–29), the apostle Paul "mentions three categories of people: those who are wise, those who are powerful, and those of noble birth" (Theissen 1982:70), the first of which refers to those who were from the educated classes, the second to those who were influential, and the third to those who were well born. To be sure, because the majority of people living in the Roman Empire at the time were poor, it is likely that a number of the early Church's members did come from the lower class. However, it is also just as likely that a disproportionate share came from the middle and upper classes.

It is part of this chapter's task to examine why new religious movements attract converts from among the privileged; it also seeks to explain how this matters in terms of social networks. What we will see is that the networks of faith communities vary in terms of their social class and tradition. The chapter begins by reviewing the classic distinction between church and sect and how the networks of the former tend to be relatively sparse (i.e., cosmopolitan), while the networks of the latter tend to be quite dense (i.e., provincial). The chapter then turns to the dynamics of new religious movements; some refer to them as cults, but here they are referred to as independent religious movements or IRMs. As part of that discussion we will see *why* IRMs recruit disproportionately from the privileged and what this means for their network composition. The chapter concludes by exploring the ego networks of people of faith and how they vary in terms of religious tradition; in the process, it introduces readers to the mechanics of ego network analysis, an underused method that social scientists who study religion could find useful.

7.2 Church and Sect[1]

Karl Marx (2002) believed that one of religion's main functions was to blind the poor and oppressed to their own interests by claiming that God will compensate them for their suffering in this life with unspeakable joy in the next. He also argued that religion comforted the rich and powerful about their place in society by arguing that their position was God ordained because they were smarter, worked harder, or were simply more deserving. Taken together, these propositions suggest that in most societies we should find two types of religion: one for the rich and one for the poor. Marx did not pursue this line of thinking because he assumed, incorrectly, that the wealthy were relatively irreligious. Church-sect theorists have pursued this line of thinking, however. Max Weber (1963) was the first one to use the terms "church" and "sect." He argued that in most societies we should find two ideal types of religion: church and sect. "Church" types are inclusive and welcome those born into their midst, whereas "sect" types are exclusive and demand that prospective members undergo a religious conversion. Historically, church-type groups have included traditions such as Roman Catholicism, Lutheranism, and Anglicanism, which baptize infants under the assumption that they will be brought up and grow into their respective faiths. In these types of churches, children are members once they are baptized. By contrast, sect-type religious bodies include groups such as the Baptists, Pietists, and the Amish, which generally do not baptize individuals until they make a conscious decision to follow Jesus. In such communities, the children

---

[1] Portions of this section are adapted from Everton (2005, 2015b).

of adult members do not become members themselves until they undergo conversion experiences.

Although Weber introduced the typology, it was his friend, Ernst Troeltsch (1960 [1911]), who popularized it. Troeltsch was a theologian, and he drew upon the typology to help explore the ethics of the two dominant types of Christian faith communities found in nineteenth-century Europe. Troeltsch argued that a church is a conventional religious organization that "accepts the secular order," whereas a sect is not and "may be indifferent, tolerant or hostile" toward secular society because sects "have no desire to control and incorporate" their "forms of social life" (Troeltsch 1960 [1911]:331):

> The fully developed Church ... utilizes the State and the ruling classes, and weaves these elements into her own life; she then becomes an integral part of the existing social order; from this standpoint, then, the Church both stabilizes and determines the social order; in doing so, however, she becomes dependent upon the upper classes, and upon their development. The sects, on the other hand, are connected with the lower classes, or at least with those elements in Society which are opposed to the State and to Society; they work upwards from below, and not downwards from above.
>
> (Troeltsch 1960 [1911]:331)

Troeltsch identified a number of characteristics of each type, but when other social scientists attempted to apply the two sets of characteristics that he had identified to other times and places (e.g., twentieth-century America), they discovered the match was seldom a good one. That is because there are few pure churches and sects in any society.

> What about a group like the Hutterites ... separated from the general society and stressing austerity, yet gaining members through birth rather than conversion and having no great emphasis upon voluntary joining than any large denomination? Is it a sect or a church? Clearly, the church-sect typology cannot be applied to religious groups in our own society without letting most cases be exceptions to the rule.
>
> (Stark and Bainbridge 1985:22)

Moreover, what is a sect in one society could be a church in another. As Finke and Stark (2005) argue, toward the end of the nineteenth century, European Roman Catholicism could correctly have been seen as a church, while in the United States it was more of a sect.

To solve this problem, Benton Johnson (1957, 1963, 1971) recast Weber's typology as a continuum based upon the degree to which a religious group is in a state of tension with its social environment. He

7.2 Church and Sect

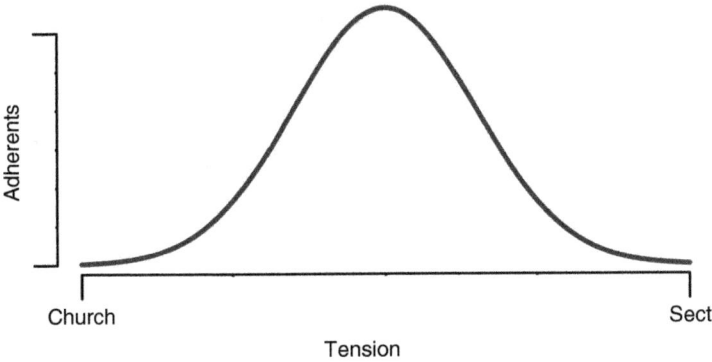

Figure 7.1 Church–sect continuum

defined the ideal church as a "religious group that accepts the social environment in which it exists" (low-tension) and the ideal sect as a "religious group that rejects the social environment in which it exists" (high-tension) (Johnson 1963:542). In Johnson's modified model, church and sect serve as poles on either end of a continuum, rather than as two distinct types into which all religious groups must fit. This is illustrated by Figure 7.1, where the ideal church sits at the far left of the continuum where the tension level is low, the ideal sect sits at the far right where the tension level is high, and most faith communities lie somewhere between the two extremes.

The continuum is given some empirical "meat" in Table 7.1, which plots selected results from Stark and Bainbridge's (1985) analysis of the *Survey of Northern California Church Bodies, 1963* (Glock and Stark 1966; Stark and Glock 1968).[2] The table illustrates how the tension level between faith communities and their surrounding society varies by tradition. For example, only 1 percent of members of low-tension Protestant denominations "disapproved of dancing," while 5 percent of medium-tension denominations and 55 percent of Southern Baptists (high tension) did. Low-tension denominations were also more likely to express skepticism about miracles.[3] Only 30 percent of low-tension Protestants agreed with the statement that it "is completely true that Jesus walked on water," while 57 percent of medium-tension Protestants and 99 percent of Southern Baptists agreed with the statement.

Figure 7.1 also captures Stark and Finke's (2000a:196, 197) normal curve argument that successful churches – those that attract the most

---
[2] The data can be downloaded from the *Association of Religion Data Archives* at www.TheARDA.com.
[3] Denominations grouped together as low tension include the United Church of Christ, United Methodists, Episcopalians, and Disciples of Christ; those grouped as medium tension are Presbyterians, American Lutherans, and American Baptists (Stark and Bainbridge 1985:53–55).

Table 7.1 Sociocultural tension by theological tradition

	Low Tension	Medium Tension	Protestants					Roman Catholics
			High Tension					
			Southern Baptist	Assemblies of God	Seventh-Day Adventist	All Protestants		
Disapproves of dancing	1%	5%	55%	86%	74%	13%		<1%
Darwin's theory of evolution could not possibly be true	11%	30%	75%	98%	94%	31%		31%
Drinking liquor would definitely prevent salvation	3%	4%	16%	30%	48%	7%		2%
It is completely true that the devil actually exists	15%	40%	94%	98%	97%	39%		70%
It is completely true that Jesus walked on water	30%	57%	99%	98%	100%	52%		74%
Definitely, Jesus will actually return to the earth some day	23%	50%	94%	100%	100%	46%		49%
In an average week, the respondent spends 2 or more nights at church	10%	16%	64%	76%	32%	22%		7%
Only those who believe in Jesus Christ can go to heaven	14%	40%	92%	89%	77%	37%		13%
Being of the Hindu religion would definitely prevent salvation	4%	18%	38%	46%	19%	16%		2%
Disapproves of religious mixed marriages	40%	54%	87%	90%	88%	52%		35%

Source: Survey of Northern California Church Bodies, 1963; Data downloaded from the *Association of Religion Data Archives*, www.TheARDA.com. Percentages recalculated by author.

adherents – are those that maintain a balance between strictness and leniency. Congregations that demand neither too much nor too little will typically enjoy more success than those at the extremes. This is because "some people always want the religious rewards available only from high-tension (strict) religion and are willing to pay high costs to obtain them, others want very low intensity and inexpensive faith, and some want no religion at all, while most people want religion that maintains some moral reservations vis-à-vis secular life, but not too many" (Stark and Finke 2000a:196). Put somewhat differently, they believe that in all societies "there exists a relatively stable set of demand or preference niches," the distribution of which resembles a normal curve (Stark 2017b:193).[4]

Church-Sect Theory: Sect to Church to Sect

H. Richard Niebuhr (1929), who wrote the introduction to the English translation of Troeltsch's book, was the first to apply the church-sect typology to the American religious scene. He tried to account for the vast number of Protestant denominations and in so doing identified some important dynamics.

For example, because church-type faith communities are typically composed of the wealthy and powerful, they tend to be "closely allied with national, economic, and cultural interests," and their ethics often "represent the morality of the respectable majority, not the heroic minority" (Niebuhr 1929:18). By contrast, because sectarian faith communities are generally composed of the poor and disinherited, they tend not to be "allied" with the majority's interests and, thus, often embrace an ethic that is at odds with the dominant culture. That is why they are more likely to not participate in the government (e.g., Jehovah Witnesses), refuse to fight in wars (e.g., Quakers), and separate themselves as much as possible from American society in order not to be tainted (e.g., Amish). Niebuhr also noted that most church-type groups began as sects. In their infancy, groups such as the Congregationalists, Methodists, Northern Baptists, and Presbyterians were sectarian protest movements that split from their parent churches, which in their opinion had become too worldly, too secular. However, over time they took on a worldliness of their own and became the very type of church they decried in the first place. This, in turn, set the stage for the birth of new sects, such as the Conservative Baptist Association, which left the Northern Baptist Convention because it believed the latter had become too liberal (i.e., worldly, secular).

---

[4] We will only find a normal curve distribution in societies where an open market for religion exists. If a single religious organization controls the market, it will be unable to satisfy everyone's religious preferences (Stark 2017b).

Although Niebuhr does not mention it, "sect-to-church" transformations are actually quite rare. Most sectarian groups stop growing or die out within a few years because they exist in such a high state of tension with society, that they are simply unable to recruit enough people to keep their movement alive (Stark and Bainbridge 1985; Stark and Finke 2000a). Those that do survive do so because they reduce the tension level between themselves and society, which enables them to attract enough new members to keep their movement alive and growing.

Undoubtedly, many factors are involved in the sect-to-church process, but upward, intergenerational social mobility is a commonly cited cause (Niebuhr 1929; Stark and Bainbridge 1985, 1987; Iannaccone 1988; Sherkat and Ellison 1999; Stark and Finke 2000a; Stark 2004). Many argue that this is a natural consequence of a sectarian lifestyle of diligence, frugality, and moral regeneration (see, e.g., Wilson 1966; Akers 1977), and this seems a reasonable hypothesis. However, as Stark and Bainbridge (1985) have pointed out, a substantial amount of it could simply be a matter of regression to the mean – that is, the tendency for a group whose traits lie far above or below the population mean to move (i.e., regress) toward the mean over time.[5] This suggests that if sectarian groups disproportionately recruit individuals who are relatively deprived in terms of secular rewards such as wealth, power, and prestige,[6] and if their status is due, at least in part, to nonascriptive, power-giving attributes (e.g., IQ), then all else being equal, we should observe more upward occupational mobility among sectarians than nonsectarians. In terms of the American scene, it suggests that we should expect to find that conservative Protestants have exhibited far more intergenerational upward mobility than American society as a whole. Unsurprisingly, that is exactly what has been found (Everton 2005). Using log-linear methods,[7] the occupational mobility of conservative Protestants when compared with members of other religious traditions, displays far more upward mobility than did others. Figure 7.2 graphically presents the results, plotting the odds that conservative Protestant males will have made a one-, two-, three-, or four-

---

[5] An example is how the IQs of children of extremely low or high IQ parents will, on average, cluster closer around the mean than those of their parents. Stark and Bainbridge (1985:154) note that two "assumptions must be met for regression to the mean to occur. First, the trait or traits of interest must tend to cluster around the population mean. Second, there must be variability in the trait or traits either over time or from one generation to the next."

[6] And as we saw in the first chapter, strict churches (Iannaccone 1994b) often do.

[7] Following traditional analyses of mobility tables (Hout 1984, 1986), analysis was limited to male respondents, cross-classifying son's and father's occupations into the five occupational groups typically used for this type of analysis (i.e., upper nonmanual, lower nonmanual, upper manual, lower manual, and farm and forestry) (see, e.g., Erikson and Goldthorpe 1985, 1992; Erikson, Goldthorpe and Portocarero 1979, 1983; Hout 1983, 1986).

7.2 Church and Sect

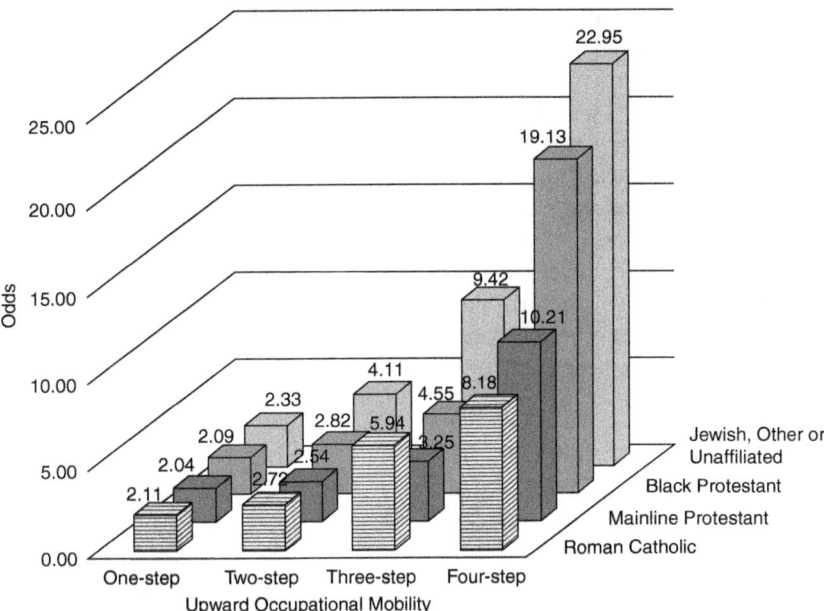

Figure 7.2 Conservative Protestant upward mobility odds compared to other religious traditions

step jump in occupational mobility,[8] as compared to males from four other broad religious categories (i.e., the higher the bar, the greater the odds). As it illustrates, conservative Protestant males have made more gains that all of the other four groups at all levels of occupational mobility. Their biggest gains have clearly come in terms of the jump from farming to upper-nonmanual occupations and primarily at the expense of black Protestant males and those who are unaffiliated with the four major religious traditions.

Church, Sect, and Network Density

Stark and Bainbridge (1979b, 1985) have noted that the networks of theologically conservative churches are typically denser than those of theologically liberal ones. Members of the former are more likely to say that more than half of the people they associate with were from their congregation than are members of theologically liberal churches (see

---

[8] An example of a one-step jump would be from lower manual to upper manual, an example of a two-step jump would be from farm to upper manual, an example of a three-step jump would be from lower manual to upper nonmanual, and an example of a four-step jump would be from farm to upper nonmanual.

Table 7.2). Why? Because, as noted earlier, theologically conservative churches tend to be stricter with regards to how often members are expected to attend and with whom they can associate (Iannaccone 1994b). Members are expected to attend worship services on a regular basis, and they are often discouraged from socializing outside of the congregation or the faith, associating with secular organizations, and participating in secular activities. With such prohibitions in place, almost by default, members of such congregations will form ties with people from their congregations at a greater rate than will members of more lenient organizations. This, in turn, causes stricter religious groups to be more interconnected than lenient ones because of the tendency for friends of friends to become friends.

Summary

The concepts of church and sect have been with us for some time. Some scholars still use "church" and "sect" more as ideal types than in terms of the continuum suggested by Benton Johnson. Others use "denomination" to designate an additional category, one that is distinct from church and sect. This, however, inevitably raises the question about what distinguishes denominations from churches and sects. Do they lie somewhere in between? If so, where does one draw the lines separating them? William Swatos (1975) has suggested that a "church" is something we find in a monopolistic religious market, whereas a "denomination" is something we find in a pluralistic one. He also differentiates between dynamic, established, and entrenched sects, again depending on the type of religious market. Although there is some merit in these distinctions, since most religious markets are neither pure monopolies nor absolutely free but instead lie on their own continuum, it is likely that we will experience difficulties drawing lines between the various categories identified by Swatos. Thus, it seems easier to simply adopt Johnson's model and then, in a manner similar to Stark and Bainbridge (1985), develop measures to assess the tension level between various religious groups and the social environment in which they are embedded. We can then use such measures to see whether various associations exist between tension level and other practices and behavior (e.g., tension level and social network density).

7.3 Church, Sect, and Cult: Independent Religious Movements

Stark and Bainbridge also noted that there is another type of religious group that is not captured by the church–sect continuum: cults or

Table 7.2 Network density by theological tradition

	Protestants						Roman Catholics
	Low Tension	Medium Tension	High Tension				
			Southern Baptist	Assemblies of God	Seventh-Day Adventist	All Protestants	
Half or more with whom the respondent associates are members of their congregation	30%	37%	51%	75%	69%	38%	48%
Three or more of the respondent's five closest friends are members of their congregation	22%	26%	51%	69%	83%	30%	36%

Source: Survey of Northern California Church Bodies, 1963; Data downloaded from the *Association of Religion Data Archives*, www.TheARDA.com. Percentages recalculated by author.

independent religious movements (IRMs).[9] Like sects, IRMs exist in a high state of tension with their sociocultural environments, but unlike sects, they do not have ties to an established religious tradition in their particular society. They "are *new faiths*, at least new in the society being examined" (Stark 1996a:33). Whereas sects leave a "parent body, not to form a new faith, but to reestablish the old one" (Stark and Bainbridge 1979b:125), IRMs arise either by being imported from another society (e.g., Zen Buddhism in the United States and Christianity in India) or through cultural innovation – that is, when new religious insights succeed in attracting followers (e.g., Mormonism in the United States) (Stark and Bainbridge 1979:125; Stark 1996a).[10]

IRMs differ from sects in another respect: sects tend to attract people of lower socioeconomic status while IRMs tend to attract people of higher socioeconomic status (Stark 1996a:39–44). This is because people who join new faiths generally find older, established faiths unsatisfying, and those who are most like to be dissatisfied with established religions are the highly educated. This may seem counterintuitive, but conversion to a new religion generally involves being interested in a new culture and new ideas, and better educated individuals are more capable of consuming and mastering new ideas (Stark 1996a:38). That is why in the United States, Zen Buddhism and Mormonism tend to appeal to people with higher levels of education (Stark 1996a), while in China it is evangelical Christianity that attracts individuals from the privileged classes (Stark and Wang 2014, 2015).

This dynamic is captured in Table 7.3, which presents the average education level of various religious traditions and essentially updates an earlier analysis by Stark (1996a:42). Using data from the 2008 American Religious Identification Survey (ARIS),[11] which surveyed more than 54,000 individuals and makes it possible to analyze groups with very few adherents, we calculated the percentage of Americans who attended college by churches, sects, IRMs, and the irreligious. As the table indicates, unsurprisingly, a higher percentage of members of church-type religious groups have attended college as compared to sect-type groups.

---

[9] The term "independent religious movement (IRM)" is preferable to the more common term "new religious movement" because not all IRMs are "new." Some may be new to a particular society (e.g., Zen Buddhism in the United States in the 1960s), but they are not new to other societies.

[10] Scholars debate whether Mormons should be considered a branch of Christianity or a separate religion. Mormons typically consider themselves to be Christians, but it is unclear whether other Christians feel the same way.

[11] The 2008 ARIS replicates the 1990 (and 2001) surveys that sought to identify the religious loyalties of the US adult population in the forty-eight contiguous states. The principal investigators were Barry A. Kosmin, Egon Mayer, and Ariela Keysar. The data are available at ARDA: www.thearda.com/Archive/Files/Descriptions/ARIS2008.asp.

7.3 Church, Sect, and Cult

Table 7.3 *Education of select American religious groups*

	Percent Who Attended College
Churches	
Congregational (UCC)	73.01
Disciples of Christ	81.19
Episcopal	83.14
Lutheran	60.59
Methodist	61.44
Presbyterian	73.21
Roman Catholic	59.91
Sects	
Assemblies of God	57.06
Baptist	45.90
Church of God	35.09
Jehovah's Witnesses	36.84
Nazarene	55.26
Pentecostal	39.29
Seventh-Day Adventist	60.98
IRMs (cults)	
Buddhist	76.86
Bahá'í	94.12
Deity	84.62
Eckankar	42.86
New Age	75.00
Spiritualist	83.50
Wiccan	64.81
Average IRMs	77.28
Mormon	67.95
Irreligious	
Agnostic	79.70
Atheist	65.65
None	62.61
Average Irreligious	63.68

Source: 2008 American Religious Identification Survey (ARIS)

However, this is also true of members of IRMs. The average percentage of IRM members who have attended college is quite high. The one exception is members of Eckankar, but only seven people gave their religious identification as Eckankar. In fact, only four people named New Age, and only thirteen named Deity. For this reason, we have summed and averaged the IRM cases, and one can see that 77.28 percent of IRM members have attended college. It is worth noting that this is higher than the average of those who identify as irreligious (63.68 percent).

All this has potentially interesting implications for the density of IRM networks. On the one hand, their high-tension should pressure their networks to be denser, more provincial; on the other, because they are disproportionately composed of people with higher levels of education, there should be countervailing pressure pushing them to be sparser, more cosmopolitan. It follows from this that the density of IRMs will be greater than churches but sparser than sects. This is confirmed in Table 7.4, which incorporates data from Table 7.2 but includes additional data on Mormon networks collected using an identical survey instrument at the same time and in the same location as the one used by Stark and Bainbridge. We can see that a higher percentage of Mormons (39 percent) than members of medium- and low-tension groups (i.e., churches) indicate that three or more of their closest friends are members of their congregations. This percentage, however, is lower than high-tension groups (i.e., sects), such as Southern Baptists, Assemblies of God, and Seventh-Day Adventists. Note, however, that a far higher percentage of Mormons living in Salt Lake City indicated that three or more of their closest friends were members of their congregation. This is not surprising given that congregational (i.e., ward) membership in the LDS Church is determined geographically, and in Salt Lake City most of one's neighbors are Mormon.[12]

On a final note, the tendency for IRMs to disproportionately attract from among the privileged is why Rodney Stark (1986, 1996a) believes that it makes complete sense that early Christianity was not a proletarian movement. He argues that in the early Roman Empire, Christianity is best seen as a cult movement – as an IRM. It had roots in Judaism, much like Mormonism has roots in Christianity, and initially Christianity could have been regarded as one of many competing Jewish sects, which, in fact, it was (Ehrman 2003). However, once it began proclaiming something new, Christianity ceased being a sect and became an IRM. This was especially true once it moved outside of Palestine:

> It is unnecessary to believe in the Resurrection to see that because the Apostles believed in it, they were no longer just another Jewish sect. Although it took time for the fact to be recognized fully (in part because of the immense diversity of Judaism in this

---

[12] In 1980, 86.5 percent of church adherents and 61.4 percent of the Salt Lake City metropolitan statistical area belonged to the LDS Church: www.thearda.com/rcms2010/r/m/41620/rcms2010_41620_metro_name_1980.asp.

Table 7.4 Network density by theological tradition including Mormons

	Protestants						Mormons		
			High Tension						
	Low Tension	Medium Tension	Southern Baptist	Assemblies of God	7th Day Adventist	All Protestants	San Francisco	Salt Lake City	Roman Catholics
Three or more of respondent's five closest friends are members of their congregation	22%	26%	51%	69%	83%	30%	39%	90%	36%

Source: From Table 7.2 and calculated from the *San Francisco Survey of Mormons, 1967–69*, which were originally collected by Armand Mauss, PI. The data were downloaded from the Association of Religion Data Archives, www.TheARDA.com.

era), beginning with the Resurrection Christians were participants in a new religion, one that added far too much new culture to Judaism to be any longer an internal sect movement ... Moreover, whatever the relationship between Christianity and Judaism, when historians speak of the *early* church, they do not mean the church in Jerusalem but the Pauline church – for this is the church that triumphed and changed history. And there can be no doubt that Christianity was not a sect movement within conventional paganism.

(Stark 1996a:44, 45)

Stark recognizes that this does not prove that the early Christian church disproportionately recruited from among the privileged. "Had Paul sent out not simply letters but questionnaires, such proof might be forthcoming" (Stark 1996a:45). However, as we have already seen, contemporary New Testament scholars now believe that the early Christian church was a movement among the middle and upper classes. In fact, when Stark first came across the discussion of New Testament scholar Robin Scroggs (1980) about how biblical scholars no longer viewed early Christianity as a proletarian movement, his initial response was, "Of course it wasn't; cult movements never are" (Stark 1996a:47).

7.4 Ego Networks and Religious Tradition

In the second chapter we discussed ego networks, which focus on a single actor (ego), the set of actors (i.e., alters) to which ego has ties, and the ties among ego's alters (Crossley et al. 2015). There are generally two ways of obtaining ego network data. One is to use whole network data and then extract the ego networks of an actor or set of actors. The other is to survey individuals from whom ego network data are then collected. Each respondent is generally asked for a set of contacts (Burt 1984, 1985), after which they are then asked about the ties (if any) between their contacts (e.g., whether they know one another, whether they attend the same church, if they are friends, and so on), as well as their various attributes (e.g., gender, race, education level, religious tradition, etc.). For instance, the 1985 and 2004 General Social Surveys (GSSs) (Smith, Marsden, and Hout 2016) included a social networks module. To generate a list of contacts, they asked respondents: "From time to time, most people discuss important matters with other people. Looking back over the last six months, who are the people with whom you discussed matters important to you?" If respondents listed less than five contacts, interviewers probed for more; if respondents listed more than five, interviewers only recorded

7.4 Ego Networks and Religious Tradition

the names of the first five. They then asked the respondents questions, such as how close they were to each of their contacts, whether their contacts were kith (co-worker, neighbor, friend, adviser) or kin (e.g., parent, sibling, spouse, child), and their contacts' basic demographic information (e.g., age, race, years of education, religion). Interviewers also asked whether their contacts knew one another, and if so, how close they were with one another.

More recently, the 2006 Portraits of American Life Survey (PALS) (Emerson and Sikkink 2006) asked a series of ego network questions. To generate a series of contacts, interviewers first asked respondents:

> Now think about the persons outside your home that you feel closest to. These may be friends, co-workers, neighbors, relatives, or anyone else who does not live here. Not including people living in your home, about how many people, if any, would you say you feel close to?

Next, they asked them to identify the four people to whom they felt the closest (if any). Then, they asked them to name two additional individuals with whom they feel closest who were members of their congregation (again, if any). After they identified these six potential contacts, they asked a series of questions similar to those asked by the GSS, including whether the contacts knew one another. What is nice about the PALS data is that we can explore the relationship between individuals' ego networks and their religious affiliation. More specifically, it allows us to compare the density of respondents' congregational networks with the religious tradition with which they identify (Steensland et al. 2000). To illustrate, first consider Figure 7.3. To calculate ego network density, we first remove "ego" from the graph ("E") and then calculate the density of ties among the remaining nodes. The top row presents two ego networks with "ego" still included, while the bottom row presents the same two networks, except that ego and his or her ties to their respective alters have been removed. It is with this second set of networks that we compute ego network density, and as we can see, the network at the left has an ego network density of 0.467, while the one on the right has an ego network density of 0.400.

This does not account for whether the respondents' contacts are members of their congregations. To estimate the density of ego's networks taking into account only his or her ties with fellow congregants (over total possible ties), we need to eliminate ties between alters if one or both are not members of the respondent's congregation. Figure 7.4 illustrates this approach. Here the two networks in the first row are identical to those in Figure 7.3, except node shade

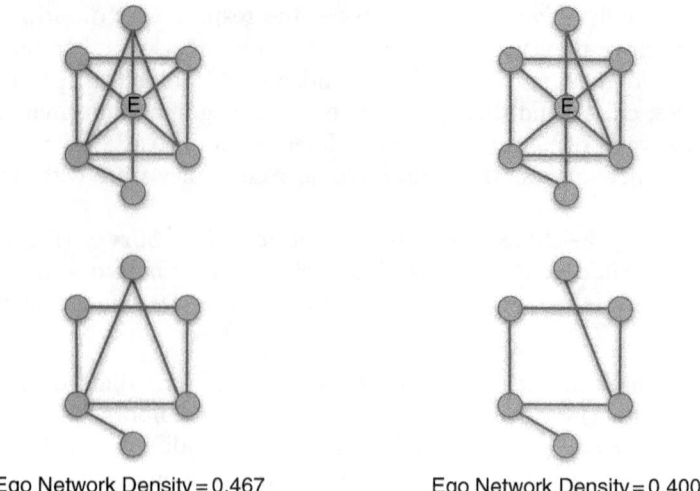

Ego Network Density = 0.467   Ego Network Density = 0.400

Figure 7.3 Hypothetical ego networks

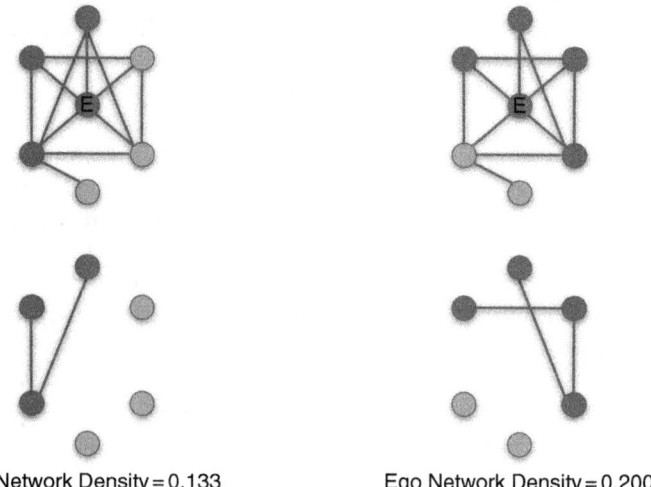

Ego Network Density = 0.133   Ego Network Density = 0.200

Figure 7.4 Hypothetical ego networks shaded by religious affiliation

indicates the religious tradition with which the respondents and their contacts identify. The networks in the second row not only differ from those in 7.3 in terms of node shade but also in terms of ties. Only ties between contacts who share the same religious affiliation

7.4 *Ego Networks and Religious Tradition* 215

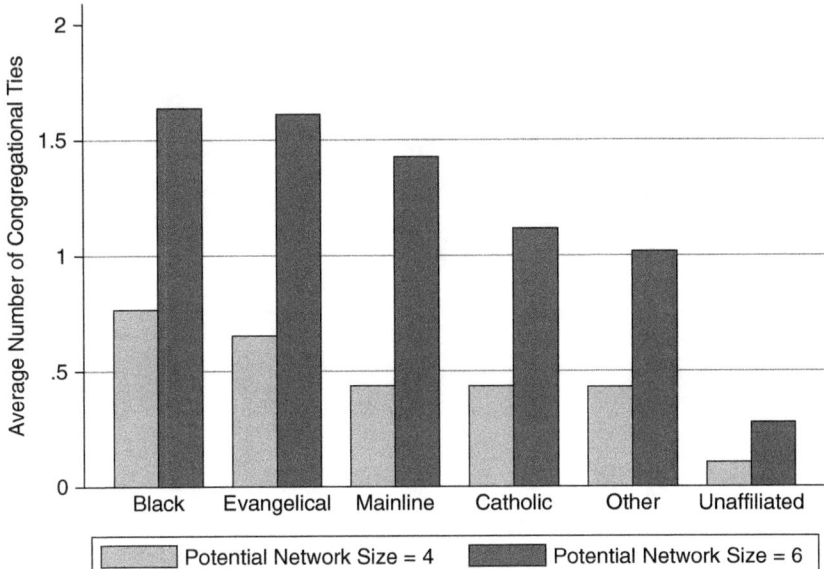

Figure 7.5 Average number of congregational ties by religious tradition, 2006 PALS

as the respondent have been retained, and as we can see, now the ego network on the right has a higher density (0.200) than the one on the left (0.133).

We use this approach to analyze the 2006 PALS data in order to determine how peoples' ego networks vary by tradition. The results are presented in Figures 7.5 through 7.7. Figure 7.5 presents the number of ties of respondents to other members of the congregations, broken down between whether we only consider the four contacts identified by respondents or all six. As the figure indicates, black Protestants have the most ties to other congregants, followed by evangelical Protestants, then mainline Protestants, Roman Catholics, members of other religious traditions,[13] and the unaffiliated. Unaffiliated are included in the figure because as we saw in the first chapter, some of those who identify as unaffiliated attend religious services. Figure 7.6 compares the reported network size by religious tradition. Here, we can see that when only taking into account the first four contacts identified by respondents, there is very little difference among the various faith traditions.[14] There is a greater difference, however, if we consider the six contacts identified by

---

[13] Included in the other category are Mormons, Hindus, Buddhists, etc., which makes the category essentially uninterpretable.
[14] A one-way ANOVA of mean differences found there were no statistically significant differences between any of the faith traditions.

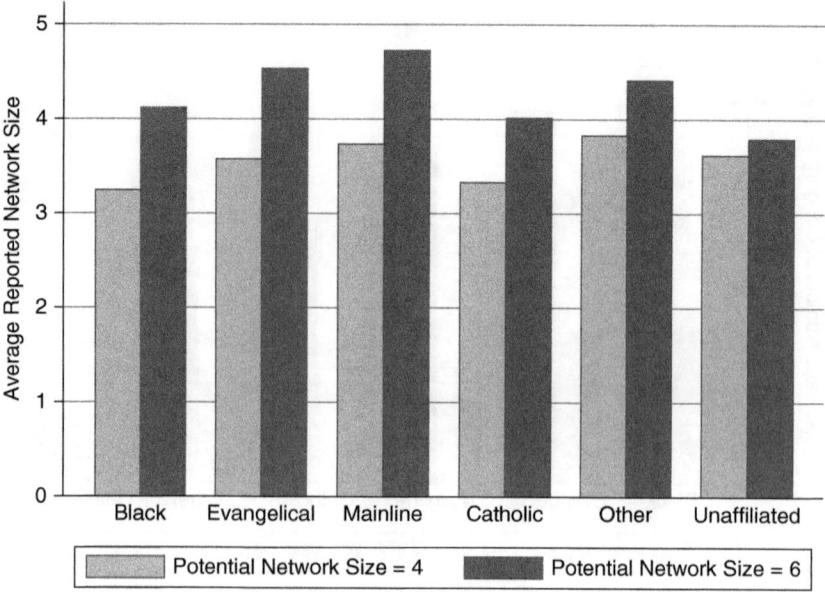

Figure 7.6 Reported network size by religious tradition, 2006 PALS

respondents. Mainline Protestants, with the most total contacts on average, differed significantly (statistically) from all other faith traditions except evangelical Protestants. Evangelicals, with the second most contacts, differed significantly (statistically) from Roman Catholics and the unaffiliated, and members of other faith traditions differed, on average, from the unaffiliated. Figure 7.7 presents the results in which we are most interested in the present context. It shows that, on average, black Protestants have the densest congregational ego networks, followed by evangelicals, mainline Protestants, Roman Catholics, members of other faith traditions, and the unaffiliated.[15] How do these results compare to our analysis in the previous two sections (Tables 7.2 and 7.4)? It is unsurprising that black and evangelical Protestants have on average the densest congregational ego networks since they are the most sectarian of the various faith traditions. It is interesting that the congregational ego networks of mainline Protestants and Roman Catholics are roughly the same. When Roman Catholics first arrived in the United States, they were quite sectarian and, in fact, held meetings that were remarkably similar to Baptist and Methodist revivals

---

[15] This is not to suggest that the unaffiliated are characterized by sparse networks. When all ties between contacts are taken into account, not just those between individuals who are members of a respondent's congregation, there is no statistically significant difference between members of the various faith traditions and those who belong to no faith tradition at all.

7.4 Ego Networks and Religious Tradition

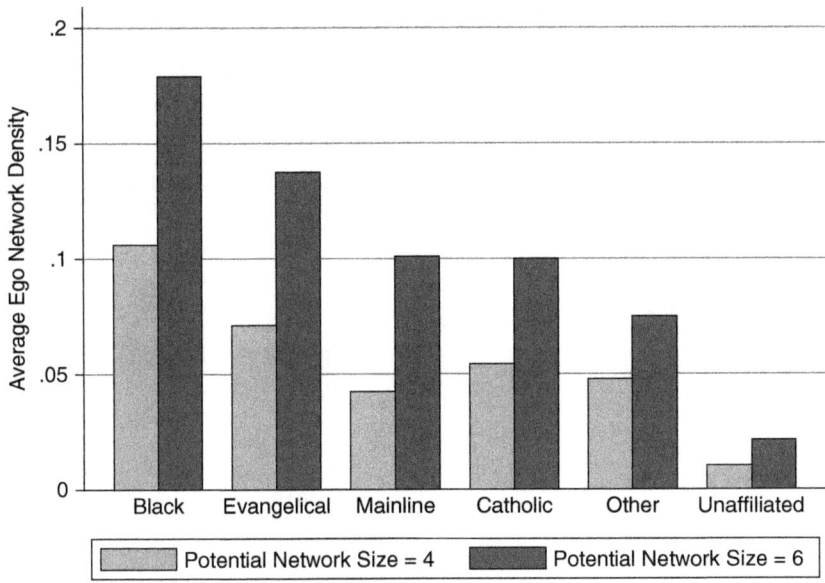

Figure 7.7 Average congregational ego network density by religious tradition, 2006 PALS

(Finke and Stark 2005). However, it has been nearly fifty years since Vatican II, so it is likely that the results reflect the fact that Roman Catholics are simply a part of the American mainstream. In other words, the results presented in Tables 7.2 and 7.4 capture Roman Catholicism prior to the reforms of Vatican II, while those in Figure 7.7 reflect a Roman Catholicism that has essentially become more "church-like" (in the Johnson sense) over time.

Table 7.5 presents the results of a generalized structural equation model that attempts to identify the mechanisms lying behind the variation in the ego network density of individuals' congregational networks.[16] The model regresses congregational ego network density on a series of predictors, including religious tradition, as well as service attendance on the same set of predictors. As the table indicates, congregational ego network density is driven in large part by how often a respondent attends church services and how long he or she has been involved in the

---
[16] The coefficients were estimated without sampling weights. As Winship and Radbill (1994) note, estimating OLS regression equations without sampling weights yield unbiased, consistent, and smaller standard errors and, as such, are preferred. That said, equations were estimated using sampling weights and yielded similar results, especially in terms of the variables of interest here.

Table 7.5 *Generalized structural equation model predicting ego network density*

	Reported Network Size			
	Four		Six	
	Congregational Ego Network Density			
Service attendance (days)	0.001***	0.001***	0.002***	0.001***
Black Protestant	0.014	0.004	0.047**	0.050*
Evangelical Protestant	−0.002	−0.014	0.010	0.004
Mainline Protestant	−0.026+	−0.035	−0.011	−0.014
Other faith tradition	0.025	0.053	0.010	0.027
Unaffiliated	−0.014	−0.030	−0.025+	−0.045
College degree	−0.007	−0.018	−0.012	−0.032+
Age	−0.001*	−0.001+	−0.001*	−0.001+
Female	0.009	0.007	0.006	−0.014
White	−0.016+	−0.035+	−0.023	−0.042*
Income	0.001	0.001	0.001	−0.002
County population	0.001	0.001	−0.000	0.000
South	0.001	0.013	0.003	0.018
Years at residence	−0.000		−0.001	
Years at residence (logged)		−0.007		−0.001
Years in congregation	0.003***		0.005***	
Years in congregation (logged)		0.027***		0.038***
Intercept	0.036	0.087	0.073	0.174
	Service Attendance (Days)			
Black Protestant	9.064***	9.492*	9.064***	9.492*
Evangelical Protestant	16.462***	19.098***	16.462***	19.098***
Mainline Protestant	−1.061	−4.222	−1.061	−4.222
Other faith	−9.253**	−12.381*	−9.253**	−12.381*
Unaffiliated	−11.182***	−21.679***	−11.182***	−21.679***
College degree	4.293*	5.680+	4.293*	5.680+
Age	0.066	0.276**	0.066	0.276**
Female	3.380*	0.648	3.380*	0.648
White	−2.995+	−1.441	−2.995+	−1.441
Income	0.422*	0.079	0.422*	0.079
County population	−0.054	0.162	−0.054	0.162
South	3.427*	6.807**	3.427*	6.807**
Duration of residence	−0.061		−0.061	
Duration of residence (logged)		2.344+		2.344+
Years in congregation	0.683***		0.683***	
Years in congregation (logged)		−1.873		−1.873
Intercept	4.596	15.653	4.596	15.653
Variance				
Network density	0.037	0.066	0.037	0.064
Church attendance	1,128.910	1,577.685	1,128.910	1,577.685
N	2,292	1,106	2,292	1,106
AIC	21,623	11,487	21,645	11,441
BIC	21,812	11,652	21,834	11,607

Note: + p <.10, * p <.05, ** p <.01, *** p <.001; reference faith tradition is Roman Catholic

congregation, while, except for black Protestants, religious tradition does not matter. Other factors – such as the age of the respondent, whether the respondent has a college degree, is female, or white – do not matter. Where religious tradition does matter is captured in the bottom half of the table, where we can see that religious tradition is a primary driver of service attendance. In particular, black and evangelical Protestants attend religious services at far higher rates than Roman Catholics (the comparison category), while members of other faith traditions and the unaffiliated attend at far lower rates. Mainline Protestants do not attend at statistically significantly lower rates than do Roman Catholics, although the former's estimated coefficient is negative. Again, factors come into play. Older individuals, people living in the South, those with a college degree, and (possibly) those who have lived at their current residence for a longer period of time attend worship services at higher rates. What is important to note here, however, is that, for the most part, religious tradition does not have a direct effect on congregational ego network density. Instead, its effect is indirect, either by increasing or decreasing the rate at which members attend religious services.

7.5 Summary and Conclusion

We have seen in this chapter that people from the privileged classes are more likely to be found in church-type faith communities and independent religious movement (IRMs) than they are in sect-type faith communities. This impacts the topological nature of the social networks that we find in different faith communities. Faith communities composed primarily of individuals from lower socioeconomic backgrounds tend to be more provincial (i.e., characterized by high levels of network density), whereas faith communities composed primarily of individuals from higher socioeconomic backgrounds tend to be more cosmopolitan (i.e., characterized by lower levels of network density). Other factors do come into play, however, such as the tension level between a faith community and its surrounding social environment. The higher the tension level, the more likely a group will seek to distance itself from mainstream society, which almost always increases the density of interactions among group members. As we will see in the next chapter, network density exerts, at least up to a point, a positive effect on the health and subjective well-being of network members because denser networks offer higher levels of material and social support. If networks become too dense, however, they increase the likelihood of conflict and radicalization. We take up the issue of conflict in Chapter 9 and the issue of radicalization in Chapter 10.

7.6 For Further Reading

There are numerous writings concerning religion and social class. Karl Marx's dictum about religion being the opium of the people is one of the best known, but Marx's remarks regarding religion are spread about. One of the best resources is John Raines's edited volume, *Marx on Religion* (2002), which collects several of Marx's writings on religion. There is, of course, Max Weber's *Protestant Ethic and the Spirit of Capitalism* (1996 [1905]), which has run into several empirical problems (see e.g., Tawney 1926; Delacroix 1992; Becker 1997; Sanderson, Abrutyn, and Proctor 2011;) but is still embraced as gospel by many. Weber's *Sociology of Religion*, which is embedded in his *Economy of Society* (1978 [1922]) but has been published separately (1963), contains some discussion of the distinction between church and sect. Classic treatments of church and sect are Ernst Troeltsch's, *The Social Teachings of the Christian Churches* (1960 [1922]), H. Richard Niebuhr's, *The Social Sources of Denominationalism* (1929), while the critiques of Benton Johnson (1957, 1963, 1971) and Rodney Stark and William Bainbridge (1979b, 1985) are helpful correctives. William Swatos provides an excellent overview in both an article (1976) and encyclopedia entry (1998). See also the discussion of church-sect theory in Kevin Christiano, William Swatos, and Peter Kivisto's, *Sociology of Religion: Contemporary Developments* (2016:86–98).

Ego network analysis has been around for some time. Peter Marsden's 1987 study, "Core Discussion Networks of Americans," which appeared in the *American Sociological Review*, is considered something of a classic, while the 2006 study by Miller McPherson, Lynn Smith-Lovin, and Matthew Brashears, "Social Isolation in America," which also was published in the *American Sociological Review*, has been met with more skepticism, not because of any methodological errors on their part, but because of flaws in the data collection itself. Subsequent analyses have demonstrated that the drop in the number of contacts reported by respondents was due to a sampling artifact (Fischer 2009; Paik and Sanchagrin 2013; Eagle and Proeschold-Bell 2015). Nevertheless, numerous strides have been made in terms of analyzing ego networks. An accessible resource is the 2015 book written by Nick Crossley and several of his associates, *Social Network Analysis for Ego-Nets*, and Steve Borgatti (2006a) has

7.6 For Further Reading

developed a helpful software package (E-Net) for analyzing ego network data (Halgin and Borgatti 2012). Moreover, Borgatti, along with Brea Perry and Bernice Pescosolido (2018), recently released *Egocentric Network Analysis*, which explores in detail how to conceptualize, collect, and analyze ego network data.

8

Health and Happiness

8.1 Introduction

Rabbi Dovid Refson, the founder and current Dean of Neve College for Women, once exclaimed about the generosity of Jews: "Jews know they have to support their fellow man ... [They] are like the Talmud says they are: 'Modest, merciful, and charitable.' Those are the traits, and they're endemic. They are in the genes. A Jew can lose contact with everything – except his altruism." According to Refson, Jews even contribute to "causes which they *know* will give them grief!" (quoted in Landau 1993:254). Among ultra-Orthodox Jews, who seek to separate themselves as much as possible from secular society, this charity manifests itself primarily in the form of mutual aid or assistance. In fact, Israeli sociologist Menahem Friedman, who devotes most of his time studying Orthodox Judaism, has argued that the degree of mutual aid currently practiced by ultra-Orthodox Jews "exceeds anything known in the long history of the Jews" (quoted in Landau 1993:255). For instance, the economist Eli Berman (2009:75–76) has observed that among the ultra-Orthodox, "[n]o sick member is without visitors; no child lacks food and clothing." And the journalist David Landau (1993:262–263) has noted how in one orthodox Jerusalem neighborhood, flyers were distributed (in both English and Hebrew) that advertised numerous free goods and services, from playpens, baby cribs, and prams to frozen meals for the sick, the elderly, and mothers after childbirth. He has also noted that the ultra-orthodox have a well-organized fundraising system to pay for medical expenses not covered by insurance.

Mutual assistance is not unique to ultra-orthodox Jews. It is quite common among many, if not most, religious traditions and, as we will see in this chapter, is probably a reason why a positive association exists between religion and health (McCullough and Smith 2003; Koenig 2008; Shor and Roelfs 2013).

That there is a positive association between religion and health is undeniable. We know, for instance, that the "death rates for several major diseases are much lower" for regular worshipers (Argyle

8.1 Introduction

2000:156), and life expectancy for frequent religious attendees is longer than for non-attendees (Hummer et al. 1999; Hummer et al. 2004). It is also well established that "clergy, monks, and nuns have a lower death rate, that is, they live longer, and are less likely to die from heart attacks, most cancers, suicide, and accidents" (Beit-Hallahmi and Argyle 1997:68). Moreover, people of "strong faith also tend to enjoy better mental health, higher levels of life satisfaction, greater personal happiness, and fewer negative psychological consequences from traumatic life events" (Ellison 1991:80).[1]

That said, there is little consensus as to why a positive association between religion and health exists. Moreover, as Christian Smith and Melinda Denton (2005:233–240) have noted, isolating the relationship between religious faith and health and happiness is complex. It is difficult to ascertain which way the causal arrow points. For example, a positive correlation could exist between religion and health because people with certain personality types may be both attracted to religion and risk-averse behaviors, so it is their personality type that leads to positive health outcomes, not their religious faith. Or, individuals who regularly attend religious services but for whatever reason begin to engage in risky behaviors may stop attending, which leads them to be polled in surveys as less religious, thus creating a positive correlation between positive behaviors and those people of faith who did not drop out. Another possible reason is that religion may indirectly affect behavior that leads to positive health outcomes. It may, for example, strengthen families, which in turn reduces delinquency among young adults. Indeed, there is evidence that all of these explanations account for some of the positive associations between religion and health, but they do not account for all of them. Even after controlling for self-selection and indirect effects, religious belief and practice exert a positive effect on health and subjective well-being (Smith and Denton 2005). What are some of the more common explanations?

One is that religious involvement may facilitate well-being by regulating individual lifestyles and health-related behaviors in ways that decrease the risk of disease, such as discouraging alcohol and substance use and abuse, and promoting an ethic of moderation (Ellison and Levin 1999). Moreover, most religious communities have teachings that discourage risk-taking and deviant behaviors, provide guidance about sexual behavior and family life (e.g., marriage and child rearing), and shape other lifestyle choices (e.g., business ethics) in ways that reduce exposure to

---

[1] J. D. Vance, in his instant classic, *Hillbilly Elegy*, refers to this phenomenon as well: "Religious folks are much happier. Regular church attendees commit fewer crimes, are in better health, live longer, make more money, drop out of high school less frequently, and finish college more frequently than those who don't attend church at all ... It's not just that people who happen to live successful lives also go to church; it's that church seems to promote good habits." (Vance 2016:92).

various stressful events and conditions (Ellison and Levin 1999). People of faith consistently eat better, exercise more, drink and smoke less (or not at all), and moderate their sexual behavior (Beit-Hallahmi and Argyle 1997).

Another is that religion can provide people with psychological resources that contribute to better health. Rituals such as prayer in moments of anger or distress may help diminish the potentially harmful effects of negative emotions (Pargament et al. 1998). For example, individuals may "gain a sense of self-worth and control by developing an ongoing personal relationship with a [God] who loves and cares for [them] unconditionally" and with whom they can interact regularly through prayer, meditation, and various rituals (Ellison and Levin 1998:707). Studies have shown that religion can provide individuals with resources for coping during periods of high stress, such as when a loved one dies, an unexpected calamity strikes, or a health problem arises (Beit-Hallahmi and Argyle 1997; Pargament et al. 1998). Religion may also play a significant role in helping individuals assign meaning to potentially problematic situations (Pargament and Park 1995). The hope and optimism that personal faith can inspire may also help promote mental (and by extension) physical health (McFadden and Levin 1996).

Finally, there is evidence that faith communities provide opportunities for regular interaction and friendship formation among like-minded people, which can enhance their health and subjective well-being. "Frequent churchgoers report larger social networks, more favorable perceptions of their social relationships, and more types of social support" received through their network ties (Ellison and George 1994:46),[2] and most researchers believe that social support plays a crucial (and generally positive) role in terms of peoples' mental and physical health. As with other factors, social networks and the social support they provide do not account for all the observed variation in peoples' well-being. In fact, a recent study by Patrick Steffen, Kevin Masters, and Scott Baldwin highlights the important role that intrinsic religiosity plays. They note that positive mental health "is at least partly the result of people trying to live their religion in their daily lives" (Steffen, Masters, and Baldwin 2017:166). Nevertheless, there is strong evidence that the social networks of the faithful positively contribute to people's mental and physical well-being.

In exploring why this is so, this chapter begins by examining a study of the religious lives of US teenagers conducted by Smith and Denton (2005). Although they explore a number of aspects of teenage religiosity in *Soul Searching*, they devote a chapter to examining the effects that religious

---

[2] Social support ranges from spiritual support (confirmation of religious beliefs) to emotional comfort (it is easier to bear an illness or a depressing event in the company of friends than alone), and to material aid (e.g., goods and services – taking meals to people when they are sick, ministry).

belief and practice have on adolescent health and well-being. Next, the chapter considers the effect of religion on adult life satisfaction by examining two studies: one by Matthew Brashears (2010), which tests whether plausibility structures offer protection from anomie, and one by Chaeyoon Lim and Robert Putnam (2010), which explores the relationship between religion, social networks, and subjective well-being. These two provide a segue into the next section, which examines the relationship between social networks and suicide. It begins with a brief recap of Durkheim's (1951) classic study before turning to a series of studies that more explicitly tie religious faith, social networks, and suicide together. Finally, the chapter examines a unique application of social network theory to the health and well-being of people of faith. More precisely, it considers Rodney Stark's (1996a:73–94) argument that social networks probably played a crucial role in helping Christianity better survive the epidemics that swept through the ancient Roman Empire in the second and third centuries of the Common Era.

8.2 Networks and Adolescent Health and Happiness

In their book, *Soul Searching*, the first of three volumes that examined the religious lives of teenagers and young adults, Christian Smith and Melissa Denton (2005) explored the effects that religious belief and practice have on various life outcomes, including health-related outcomes. In doing so, they sorted the teenagers in their sample into four distinct groups or ideal types: the devoted, the regulars, the sporadic, and the disengaged (see Table 8.1). These ideal types accounted for 63 percent of the teens studied, which meant that 37 percent were excluded from this portion of their analysis. Although focusing only on those who fit neatly into those categories is not without its weaknesses, Smith and Denton (2005:220–221) have argued that doing so offered three distinct advantages. First, it reflected the way ordinary Americans categorize people of faith – "extradevoted believers, regular churchgoers, sporadic participants, and so on" – more so than, say, a religiosity scale constructed from numerous questions. Second, it helped them to "more clearly identify" differences between the teens who fit these distinct categories without having them "clouded by more ambiguous cases." And finally, it allowed them to "keep the number of tables" to a reasonable amount.

Table 8.2 summarizes some of their findings. It presents a selection of adolescent behaviors and attitudes, broken down by the four ideal types summarized in Table 8.1, as well as for teens across the United States as a whole.[3] The results suggest that a deeper religious faith is positively

---

[3] The results presented are reflective of all the results reported by Smith and Denton.

Table 8.1 *Adolescent religious ideal types*

	Devoted (8%)	Regular (27%)	Sporadic (17%)	Disengaged (12%)
Worship attendance	Weekly or more	2–3 times a month, or weekly	Few times a year to monthly	Never, or identifies as nonreligious
Importance of faith in everyday life	Very, or extremely important	Very to not very important	Somewhat to not very important	Somewhat, not very, not important
Closeness to God	Feels very, or extremely close	Variable	Variable	Somewhat, or less close
Currently involved in religious youth group?	Yes	Variable	Variable	No
Prayer	Prays a few times a week, or more	Variable	Variable	1–2 times a month or less
Scripture reading	1–2 times a month or more	Variable	Variable	1–2 times a month or less

Source: Adapted from Smith and Denton, 2005:220

associated with less risky behaviors, higher levels of subjective well-being, less impulsive moral reasoning, and more extensive ties to other adults and the wider community. Smith and Denton identified nine factors that could contribute to the positive association between religion and health, which they sorted into three broad categories or dimensions: moral order, learned competencies, and social and organizational ties (Smith and Denton 2005:240–250). We consider all three in the following paragraphs, but it is the last of these that is of most interest to us here.

Religious Factors Affecting Adolescent Health

Moral Order Smith and Denton argue that American religion offers adolescents moral directives, spiritual experiences, and role models that help them engage in fewer behaviors that generally contribute to more healthy life outcomes. With regards to the first factor, they note that religious faith often provides adolescents a series of norms that encourage self-control and personal virtue, which in turn can often lead them to make wise choices. Religions, of course, are not the only source of normative behavior, but compared to some, religions are more likely to promote virtues conducive to positive health outcomes. For example, "the moral order of mass-consumer market capitalism … does little to promote self-control,

Table 8.2 *Select behaviors and attitudes of US adolescents, ages 13–17, by religious ideal type*

	US	Religious Ideal Types			
		Devoted	Regular	Sporadic	Disengaged
Risky behaviors:					
Smokes cigarettes at least once a day	7	1	6	9	14
Drinks alcohol weekly or more	5	—	4	7	11
Cut class in school last year six or more times	7	2	5	10	12
Subjective well-being:					
Very happy about body and physical appearance	42	54	43	36	29
Never feels sad or depressed	19	23	21	17	14
Never feels alone or misunderstood	39	52	40	37	32
Moral reasoning:					
Believes that morals are relative, no definite right or wrong	45	22	46	57	61
In an unsure situation, do what gets one ahead	1	1	12	13	16
In unsure situation, do what makes one feel happy	27	6	27	36	40

Source: Adapted from Smith and Denton, 2005:222–231; National Survey of Youth and Religion, 2002–2003

moderation, the common good, sacrifice, honor for others, and other traditional religious virtues" (Smith and Denton 2005:242).

Smith and Denton also contend that American religions create opportunities for youth to have spiritual experiences, which in turn can help to reinforce the moral commitments of their respected faith communities. "The point here is that moral directives are not simply imposed from the outside by traditions and organizations ... Rather, humans internalize moral directives and orders in their subjective mental worlds ... and these subjective commitments prove often to have a fair amount of stability and continuity ... for individuals over time" (Smith and Denton 2005:242). A third, and final, factor they identify is the importance of role models. They believe that faith communities are uniquely positioned to hold up positive and negative role models, which can help make the moral directives of a religious faith more tangible. Role models "show what a good (and perhaps a bad) human life looks like, furnishing an instructive example of right (and wrong) living" (Smith and Denton 2005:243). Such examples can help reinforce the norms that youth have learned through the teachings and spiritual experiences of their faith, by providing them with examples of the consequences of living by such directives.

Learned Competencies According to Smith and Denton, religion not only influences adolescents' normative commitments, but it also facilitates their development and acquisition of various competencies, such as community and leadership skills, coping skills, and cultural capital, which in turn contribute to their well-being and increase the likelihood they will live successful adult lives. They argue, for instance, that faith communities often provide their youth with "opportunities to observe, learn, and practice the skills of community life and leadership" (Smith and Denton 2005:243), which not only help them navigate their religious congregations but also are easily transferable to nonreligious settings, such as student government, sports teams, political activism, civic engagement, and so on. They also believe that coping skills are important because they can help individuals deal with stressful situations, "process difficult emotions," and "resolve interpersonal conflicts"; they note that individuals who are better equipped to handle life's problems tend to be more healthy and functional (Smith and Denton 2005:244–245). Finally, they point out that many religious traditions offer youth opportunities for increasing their cultural capital:

> Adolescents who have soaked up the various kinds of cultural capital available through involvement in their religion may have gained a relative edge over those who have not ... Other factors being equal, they will likely converse more comfortably with a broader array of social contacts, perform better in their humanities and social science classes, and be more impressive in the lunch and dinner conversations of the job interviews, and more.
> (Smith and Denton 2005:246)

As Bourdieu (1985, 1986) has documented, there is strong evidence that cultural capital is positively associated with life chances.

Social and Organizational Ties The last category or dimension that Smith and Denton highlight concerns the role of social networks. Here, they argue that religious congregations can help to increase the social capital of adolescents, provide them with a close-knit community, and connect them with ties beyond the local community. In terms of social capital, a concept that we explored in Chapter 6, they argue that because religious communities are one of the "few remaining major social institutions" that are "not rigidly stratified by age," they create conditions in which youth can form ties with participants of all ages (Smith and Denton 2005:247). This can provide them with better access to various types of resources, information, and opportunities:

> The more (strong and weak) adult ties youth have in their religious congregations, the more likely they are through them to land a good summer job, be recommended for acceptance into

8.2 Networks and Adolescent Health and Happiness

Table 8.3 *Social and organizational ties of adolescents, ages 13–17, by religious ideal type*

	US	Religious Ideal Types			
		Devoted	Regular	Sporadic	Disengaged
Social ties and network closure:					
Fairly or very comfortable talking to adults other than parents	52	67	53	49	49
Number of adults can turn to for advice, etc. (other than parents)	5.7	8.4	5.5	4.9	5.0
Community ties:					
Planned event, led meeting, gave presentation for organization	31	56	33	30	20
Average number of organized activities or clubs involved in	2.1	3.1	2.4	2.0	1.5
Average total number of times per month teen volunteered	.65	1.1	.52	.61	.53

Source: Adapted from Smith and Denton, 2005:226, 231; National Survey of Youth and Religion, 2002–2003

a competitive program, know someone who can and will help them fix their computer or car, and much more. All of this helps to foster and reinforce positive life choices, behaviors, and outcomes.

(Smith 2003d:247)

And as Table 8.3 indicates, the more devoted youth are, the more likely they will say that they feel comfortable talking with adults other than their parents and they name a larger number of adults they can turn to for advice, support, help, and so on.

Closely related to this is the notion of network closure – that is, where networks are characterized by numerous ties between members and somewhat insulated from the sociocultural environment. Drawing on the work of James Coleman (1988, 1990), Smith and Denton argue that relatively dense networks of youth, parents, and other adults are generally associated with the health and happiness of teens because they enable parents to more effectively monitor their children's activities (Smith and Denton 2005:248). As we saw earlier (and will see again), networks can become too dense and lead to coercion, conflict, and occasionally radicalization and violence. For now, though, it is sufficient to note that dense networks ease the task of monitoring behavior (Granovetter 2005, 2017), which in the case of religious organizations and youth, can lead to positive life outcomes.

Finally, Smith and Denton stress the importance of links beyond the local community. They note that religious congregations offer youth ties to regional, national, and international levels through events such as summer camps, weekend retreats, service projects and mission trips, national youth events, and so on. Although programs like these can "strengthen the faith and commitment of youth, ... they probably do [much] more ... by moving youth out of local contexts and presenting them with new experiences and challenges, these programs also open up youth's imaginable aspirations and horizons, encourage their developmental maturity, and increase their knowledge, confidence, and competencies," and these, in turn, increase healthy attitudes, choices, and behaviors (Smith and Denton 2005:249). Results consistent with this argument are presented in Table 8.3, which shows that the more devoted a youth's faith, the greater the number of organized activities and clubs in which he or she is involved, the more often the youth volunteers.

Summary

Smith and Denton (2005) concede that religion does not always positively affect the life outcomes of adolescents. They stress that the nine factors they identify increase the likelihood of positive outcomes but do not guarantee it. Other competing influences and disruptive events can negate the positive effects of religion. As we saw in Chapter 7 religious traditions can vary considerably, and Smith and Denton note that given the right (or wrong) circumstances, some faith communities can and have produced negative effects among their youth. Nevertheless, in most cases participation in faith communities increases the likelihood that youth will experience positive life outcomes, and the evidence suggests that this is in part associated with religious social networks.

8.3 Networks and Life Satisfaction

Social scientists have long considered the association between religion and life satisfaction. The classic statement is probably Durkheim's (1951) study of suicide, which we will consider in the following section. Another is Peter Berger's (1967) notion of a sacred canopy, which we explored briefly in the first chapter. Recall that Berger argued that the plausibility of our religious beliefs depends largely on the social support they receive. As long as there is social support for a particular way of looking at the heavens (i.e., the sacred canopy), then it remains plausible. If that support erodes, however, it can fall apart. According to Berger, in premodern societies, this was generally not an issue because most everyone belonged to the same religious tradition. Everybody adhered to the same beliefs, so few challenged the status quo. In modern societies, however, where particular religious traditions no longer receive the broad

8.3 Networks and Life Satisfaction

social support they once did, Berger believes that religious belief has experienced a plausibility crisis because believers no longer take their religious worldviews for granted. Instead, they see them, including their own faith traditions, as different options competing for their allegiance.

Drawing on Berger's notion of a sacred canopy, Matthew Brashears has explored whether plausibility structures offer protection from anomie – that is, when individuals are "unable to determine correct behavior or the purpose of their own life" (Brashears 2010:188). Using ego network data collected with the 1985 General Social Surveys (GSS), where respondents were asked the religious affiliation of their named alters,[4] Brashears (2010:189) tested three primary hypotheses: (1) whether "individuals whose networks contain a larger proportion of religiously homogenous alters will report lower levels of anomia" and be less likely to say they are unhappy, (2) whether "individuals who spend a greater proportion of their time with religiously homogenous alters will report lower levels of anomia" and be less likely to say they are unhappy and (3) whether individuals who are embedded in a denser network of "religiously homogenous alters will report lower levels of anomia" and be less likely to say they are unhappy. He found support for the first two hypotheses but not the third. In summarizing his results, he stresses that it is the interaction of one's religious convictions and the convictions of one's associates that affords individuals protection from anomia and unhappiness:

> Put concretely, the effects are only present in interaction, but not in the main effects of either proportion (of ties and time) or religious attendance. Thus it is not the holding of a particular worldview, nor spending time with those who hold a particular worldview, but rather spending time with those who reinforce your own view that shields an individual from angst. This is an important point and precisely matches what we expect from plausibility argument.
>
> (Brashears 2010:194)

Interestingly, Brashears (2010:194) argues that the lack of support for the third hypothesis "confirms the sacred canopy argument in its more restricted 'sacred umbrella' formulation."[5] Perhaps, but it is a bit of

---

[4] The nature of ego network data was discussed in Chapter 2 and explored in depth in Chapter 7. The 2004 GSS also collected ego network data, but given its split-form design, the respondents who were asked about their ego networks were not asked the question that Brashears used to construct his dependent variables (see Brashears 2010:190).

[5] Recall that Christian Smith has argued that in the modern world, individuals do not need sacred canopies in order to maintain their religious beliefs, but only "sacred umbrellas" – that is, "small, portable, accessible relational worlds ... 'under' which their beliefs can make complete sense" (Smith et al. 1998:106).

a stretch to even consider that respondents' ego networks adequately capture Berger's notion of a sacred canopy.[6]

Another interesting exploration of the relationship among religion, social networks, and subjective well-being was conducted by Chaeyoon Lim and Robert Putnam (2010). Using both cross-sectional and panel data from the Faith Matters Study (Putnam and Campbell 2010), Lim and Putnam found that the number of friends within an individual's congregation was an important and positive factor in determining the person's feelings of life satisfaction.[7] However, when they interacted the number of church friends with a dummy variable indicating if respondents considered religion to be very important to them, the interaction was statistically significant but the main effects of the two variables were not,[8] suggesting that those for whom religion was important *and* with numerous congregational friends were more likely to be extremely satisfied with their lives.[9]

In short, both Brashears (2010) and Lim and Putnam (2010) offer evidence that faith communities, by providing opportunities for regular interaction and friendship formation among like-minded people, help enhance the subjective well-being of their adherents. By highlighting the importance of close friends who shared their religious convictions, as well as the importance of a strong religious commitment to their religious tradition, they also uncovered support for the important role that religious umbrellas play in the lives of people of faith.[10] As hinted earlier, religion may also play a protective role in preventing individuals from committing suicide. The results of these two studies suggest that social networks may prove to be an important mechanism in this relationship.

8.4 Networks and Suicide

In one of the best-known sociological studies, Emile Durkheim (1951) sought to demonstrate that suicide was more than an individual matter but was also something subject to broad social forces. As such, rather than studying individual suicides, he examined how suicide rates vary across and within countries. In his analysis, he identified two causes and four types of suicide. One cause was the level at which group norms, beliefs,

---

[6] It is important to note that the 1985 GSS did not allow Brashears to determine whether a respondent's alters attended the same congregation.

[7] Respondents were asked, on a ten-point scale, how satisfied they were with their lives, from extremely dissatisfied on one end (0) to extremely satisfied on the other (10).

[8] When the interaction variable was not included in the models, both variables were statistically significant.

[9] They also found that the number of an individual's close friends exerted a positive and statistically significant effect on a respondent's level of life satisfaction.

[10] Lim and Putnam do not refer to Christian Smith's (1998) notion of sacred umbrellas; nevertheless, their results are consistent with his argument.

and values regulate behavior, and he called the two types of suicide associated with it *anomic* and *fatalistic*. The other cause was the degree to which people are integrated into social groups and society, and he referred to the two types associated with it *altruistic* and *egoistic*. In this section, we briefly explore these causes and types before considering a few of the critiques of Durkheim's study, as well as how some theorists have reframed Durkheim's insights in terms of social networks.

Durkheim's Types of Suicide

Regulatory According to Durkheim, *anomic suicide* occurs when the desires and passions of individuals become unregulated, which often happens during periods of rapid change when a society's moral code fails to maintain its hold over individuals. In such situations, people tend to desire more than they can achieve, which leads to increasing unhappiness among some and suicide to those predisposed to it. Durkheim believed that industrialization can lead to anomic forms of suicide because it uproots people from local communities and drops them into urban settings where their old moral values no longer apply or at least are not enforced. Durkheim only discussed *fatalistic suicide* in a short footnote. It is the opposite of anomic suicide in that it involves too much regulation. Durkheim argued that excessive regulation blocks peoples' desires and passions to such an extent that there is little or no reason to continue living. When people are regulated to such an extent that they are "violently choked by oppressive discipline" (Durkheim 1951:276), they are left with no sense of personal autonomy or freedom and thus become potential suicide victims. In an interesting test of the theory, Akbar Aliverdinia and William Pridemore (2009) examined the variation of female suicide rates across Iranian provinces and found that they were higher in areas characterized by greater levels of social control.

Integrative. *Altruistic suicide* occurs when individuals are so strongly attached to a group that they are willing to commit suicide for the good of the group. In such situations, individuals are of little importance, so they subordinate their interests to those of the group. An example could be certain forms of suicide bombings, such as the Kamikaze attacks used by Japan during World War II, or the bombers who flew planes into the Pentagon and the World Trade Center towers on 9/11. *Egoistic suicide* is when peoples' ties to society become or are excessively weak. Durkheim argued that people with weak social, community, and family ties are more likely to commit suicide because they lack a supportive network that offers solace in the face of personal difficulties. Although he believed that religion helped integrate individuals into a larger community, he found that the level of protection offered by religion varied across traditions. For example, he found that suicide rates were lower in Roman Catholic countries and regions than they were in Protestant ones. In part, Durkheim attributed this difference to the degree to which the two religious traditions encouraged freedom of inquiry. He argued that Protestantism, with its expectation that adherents would read and interpret the Bible for themselves, encouraged more freedom of inquiry. Thus, they are "more the authors of their faith" than Roman Catholics, who accept their faith unquestioningly (Durkheim 1951:158). He also believed that Protestantism responds to the advent of modernity "by loosening its hold on members' collective lives" (Pescosolido and Georgianna 1989:34), which renders it less able to constrain peoples' self-destructive impulses. Finally, he argued that Roman Catholicism has a tighter and more centralized clergy system than does Protestantism. Taken together, these factors led him to conclude that Catholics have lower suicide rates because they are more integrated into their respective communities than are Protestants.[11]

Critiques

Durkheim has attracted his share of critics. For instance, Robert Baller and Kelly Richardson (2002) have taken him to task for dismissing the role that imitation may have played in the variation of suicide rates across regions and countries. And Benton Johnson (1965) and Whitney Pope (1976) have argued that Durkheim's distinction between regulation and integration is problematic since one cannot have the former without the latter. Pope (1976) has also highlighted a number of mathematical problems in Durkheim's analysis, calling into question whether a Protestant-Catholic difference actually exists. Rodney Stark, Daniel Doyle, and Jesse Rushing (1983) have also challenged this difference, noting that Durkheim's attempt to account for why the suicide rate in Protestant England was lower than in many Catholic countries was ill informed. They also believe that Durkheim was mistaken to reduce religion's effect to social integration and to establish this point, they drew on data from 214 US standard metropolitan statistical areas (SMSAs) to show that church membership exerts a protective effect over and above the effects of social integration.

Their approach is illustrated by the maps presented in Figure 8.1.[12] The top map indicates church membership by state (church members per 1,000 individuals in 1980), while the bottom indicates suicide rates by

---

[11] Freedom of inquiry also implies that people with higher education rates should be more likely to commit suicide, and he did find evidence for that. He also noted that suicide rates tend to be higher among widowed, single, and divorced people than among married people, and higher among people without children than among parents.
[12] The maps were created using the MicroCase Analysis System (Wadsworth 2003) and its compiled dataset, "The Fifty States of the United States, 2006."

8.4 Networks and Suicide

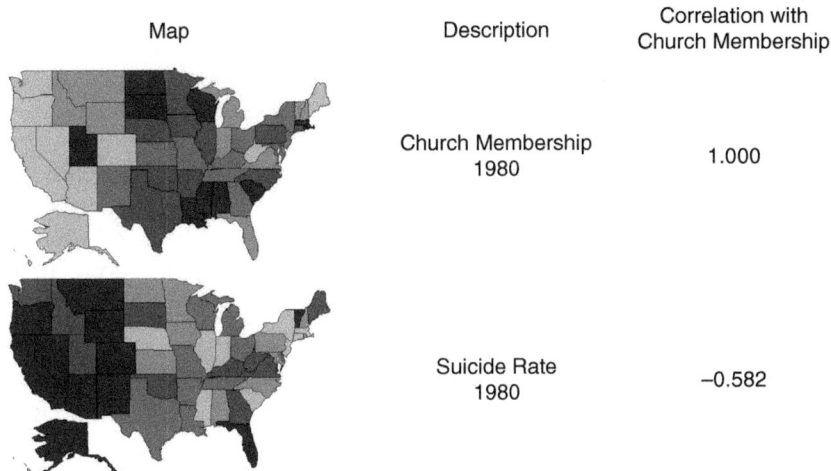

Figure 8.1 Church membership by suicide rates, 1980

state (suicides by 100,000 individuals in 1980). The negative correlation (−0.582) between the two variables can be clearly seen by comparing the two maps where the lighter states in the membership map (where church membership is lower) roughly correspond to the darker states in the suicide map (where suicides are higher). Because the maps are at the state level, they undoubtedly miss some of the nuances that Stark and his colleagues captured using SMSA data. Nevertheless, they nicely illustrate what they found.

Why do they believe religion exerts an independent effect on suicide? They identify several reasons, but one is that religious beliefs and practices affect peoples' level of social integration:

> First of all, religious organizations are easily accessible to people and are a generous source of affect and self-esteem. Pastors will listen to troubles. Other members do rally to the support of those overtaken by misfortune. The lonely do find sociability in church. Granted that these are all "this-worldly" aspects of religions and in that sense somewhat akin to Durkheim's reduction of religion to social relations. But it is noteworthy that it is the "other-worldly" concerns and doctrines of religions that make them so much more effective in this respect than other voluntary organizations. Lonely, impoverished widows can't get the same levels of response from country clubs, welfare offices, or the local Democratic caucus.
> (Stark, Doyle, and Rushing 1983:125)

They note, however, that historically many social scientists have been loath to grant any power of religion, probably because they believed it to be false and thus incapable of doing anything for individuals. Stark and his colleagues believe that this is a mistake. They note that one does not need "to believe in religion to suppose it has effects. W. I. Thomas' admonishment that things people define as real have real consequences might have sufficed to help social scientists to see that *for believers faith is real*. Put another way, it makes a difference if, on the one hand, one thinks one's problems are overwhelming and unsharable, or, on the other, if one thinks that Jesus knows and cares" (Stark, Doyle, and Rushing 1983:125). For their study, they used population turnover as their measure of social integration, but they note that social networks, and in particular social network density, would have been ideal:

> The most conceptually useful definition of social integration is in terms of social networks. The greater the density and intensity of interpersonal attachments among members of a group, the more the group can be said to be socially integrated. Defined in this way the concept is devoid of cultural content. That is, "intense collective life," as Durkheim put it, is defined as a network of relations without reference to any cultural elements that might support these relations and which might dominate the exchanges among network members. This conceptualization frees us from the grip of tautology. It becomes possible to see if religion, for example, does influence social integration as Durkheim claimed it did. Ideally, then, we would want to operationalize social integration in this study in terms of the density and intensity of network ties in these SMSAs.
>
> (Stark, Doyle, and Rushing 1983:125)

Interestingly, Bernice Pescosolido and Sharon Georgianna (1989), who were familiar with Stark, Doyle, and Rushing's study, did operationalize social integration (and regulation) in terms of social network density. It is to their study that we now turn.

Social Networks and Suicide

Bernice Pescosolido and Sharon Georgianna (1989) drew on data from 404 counties in the United States (Washington DC, Alaska, and Hawaii were excluded) to explore the causes of suicide. They began by regressing the 1970 suicide rate (number per 100,000) on several relevant variables, including the proportion of twenty-seven different religious groups (Roman Catholic, Jewish, and twenty-five Protestant denominations) in each county, and they found that the presence of Jewish, Roman Catholic and some evangelical Protestant groups exerts a protective effect against suicide, while the presence of mainline Protestant groups exerts an

8.4 Networks and Suicide

aggravating effect.[13] Next, they sought to identify the factors underlying the variation in religious tradition effects. Here, they began by considering a number of explanations, such as whether a denomination was theologically liberal, moderate, or conservative, whether it was "ecumenical" or not, the level of tension that existed between it and the wider society, and its type of governance (i.e., its polity – congregational, presbyterian, or episcopal). They ultimately rejected these in favor of a social network one, arguing that all of them tap into "an underlying dimension critical to contemporary American religion: the nature and strength of social bonds" (Pescosolido and Georgianna 1989:41). They also argued that both social regulation and integration are a function of social networks, so they reframed Durkheim's theory in terms of social networks. For this, they used two proxies for network density: the percentage of respondents in each religious tradition who report (1) attending church weekly and (2) having a spouse of the same religion. And after controlling for the same factors as in the first part of their analysis, they found that denominations with a higher rate of weekly attendance (–0.77) and those that exhibit greater religious homogamy (–0.90) exert a greater protective effect against suicide (Pescosolido and Georgianna 1989:42).

In the end, they concluded that the density of individuals' social networks has a curvilinear (or inverted ∪) relationship to suicide. Individuals whose social networks are very sparse or very dense are far more likely to commit suicide than are those whose networks lie somewhere between the two extremes. Why? On the one hand, people located in sparse social networks often lack the social and emotional ties that provide them with the support they need during times of crisis. They also typically lack ties to others who might otherwise prevent them from engaging in self-destructive behavior (Finke and Stark 2005; Granovetter 2005, 2017). On the other hand, individuals embedded in dense networks are often cut off from people outside of their immediate social group, which increases the likelihood that they will lack the ties to others who would otherwise prevent them from taking that final, fatal step.

As appealing as their findings are, we probably should not dismiss the possible impact of religious beliefs and practices. Pescosolido and Georgianna are probably correct in stating that the density of individuals' networks exert, up to a point, a protective effect against suicide. However, as we have seen, theological ideas affect the interconnectedness of peoples' networks. A primary reason why some faith communities have denser social networks than do others is because their theological beliefs demand

---

[13] To be clear, they do not argue that being Catholic or being evangelical Protestant keeps people from committing suicide, but that the presence of Catholics and evangelical Protestants exerts a protective effect against suicide.

238 Health and Happiness

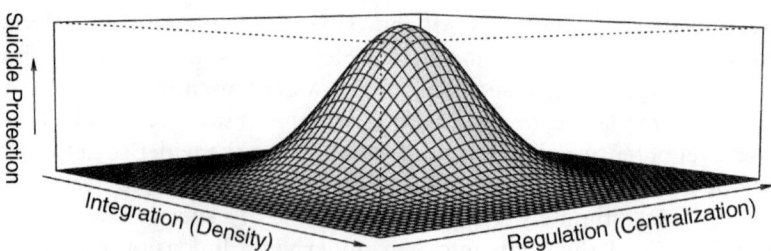

Figure 8.2 Hypothetical association between integration/regulation, and suicide protection

that their members spend more time at church and less time with non-members (Iannaccone 1994b).

Summary

There seems to be little doubt that a relationship exists between religion and suicide, whether it is tied to religious tradition, frequency of church attendance, social network density, or possibly all three. After all, as we saw in the previous chapter, religious tradition helps to drive church attendance rates, which in turn affect social network density. However, it is worth asking if density is the only network dimension that affects suicide rates. What about network centralization? Centralized networks are often associated with the degree of command and control that leaders have over a network, so it is not unreasonable to argue that centralization, more than density, affects the level of social regulation in a faith community. If this is correct, then we can imagine that suicide is a function of both a faith community's density and centralization (see Figure 8.2). Too much or too little of either (or both) lowers the protective effect that the faith community exerts against suicide, while a balance of the two increases the effect.

8.5 Epidemics, Networks, and the Rise of Christianity (with Robert Schroeder)

In one of the more innovative applications of social network theory, Rodney Stark (1996a:73–94) has made the case that social networks played a key role in helping early Christians better survive the epidemics that swept through the ancient Roman Empire in the second and third centuries of the Common Era. Social networks were not the only reason, but Stark believes they were one of three reasons why the early Christian church was better equipped to respond to the epidemics than were its

8.5 Epidemics, Networks, and the Rise of Christianity

pagan competitors.[14] In particular, he argues that (1) the church offered better explanations for and appeared more effective in combatting the epidemics; (2) its doctrines on love, charity, and social service led to higher survival rates among Christians; (3) and because pagans had lower survival rates, large numbers of them would have lost their social ties to other pagans, which would have otherwise prevented them from converting to Christianity. We will consider all three of these arguments, but our focus is primarily on the last two since they relate directly to social networks.

Explanations and Effectiveness

Stark begins by noting that natural and social disasters often produce crises of faith. "Typically this occurs because the disaster places demands upon the prevailing religion that it appears unable to meet" (Stark 1996a:77). According to Stark, this can happen in at least two ways. First, the prevailing religion (or religions) may be unable to offer adequate explanations of the disaster, and second, they may be, or at least appear to be, ineffective in the face of the disaster. When such crises occur, societies often adopt new faiths. Anthony Wallace (1956) probably overstated his case when he argued that all religions arise in response to some crisis, but evidence suggests that new religious movements often appear when societies experience rapid change (Wilson 1975).

Stark believes that a crisis of faith probably occurred in the Roman Empire when the epidemics struck. He argues that in the face of the epidemics, neither the pagan priests nor the philosophers could offer adequate explanations. The priests could not explain why the epidemics occurred, why some people died and others did not, why the gods had "sent such misery," whether the gods were involved, or whether they even cared (Stark 1996a:79), and the philosophers could not offer much more than appeals to luck or natural causes. "For a science that [knew] nothing of bacteria (let alone viruses) the phrase 'natural causes' in connection with these great epidemics is simply how philosophers say, 'Who knows?'" (Stark 1996a:80). Stark, of course, does not deny that survival involved an element of randomness, but he argues that individuals prefer explanations that help them make sense of life over those that do not, which is why he believes Christianity possessed an advantage over pagan religions. Christianity's teachings "made life meaningful even amid sudden and surprising death ... [it] was ... a system of thought and feeling thoroughly adapted to a time of troubles in which hardship, disease, and violent death commonly prevailed" (McNeill 1976:108, quoted in Stark

---

[14] Because Christianity was largely an urban phenomenon (Meeks 1983), "the term *paganus* or 'countryman' came to refer to non-Christians (pagans)" (Stark 1996a:10). Stark uses it as an umbrella term to refer to all non-Christians.

1996:80–81). As Stark notes, both Cyprian, the bishop of Carthage, and Dionysius, the bishop of Alexandria, greeted the epidemic of 250–260, not with dread, but as an opportunity for testing and joy (Stark 1996a: 81–82). They believed that only non-Christians had anything to fear from the epidemics because for Christians death was not the final word (1 Cor. 15:55). "Thus, at a time when all other faiths were called to question, Christianity offered explanation and comfort" (Stark 1996a:82).

However, not only did Christianity offer its adherents better explanations, Stark believes that it was probably more effective in combating the epidemics. Because of doctrines that insisted that Christians minister to the sick and dying, it is likely that Christians enjoyed higher survival rates, and this would have been seen by many non-Christians as nothing short of miraculous. Moreover, the higher survival rates would have produced a larger proportion of Christians who were immune to the disease because those who contracted it and recovered were protected from further infection. Thus, they could "pass among the afflicted with seeming invulnerability" (Stark 1996a:90), and this was almost certainly seen by some non-Christians as evidence of the superiority of God, or at least the Christian God.

Christian Charity and Differential Survival

Although at the time there were no cures for the epidemics, the historian William McNeill notes that "elementary nursing will greatly reduce mortality. [The s]imple provision of food and water, for instance, will allow persons who are temporarily too weak to cope for themselves to recover instead of perishing miserably" (McNeill 1976:108, quoted in Stark 1996a:88). Indeed, "modern medical experts believe that conscientious nursing without any medications could cut the mortality rate by two-thirds or even more" (Stark 1996a:89). Unfortunately, during the epidemics most people did not receive such nursing, which is why between "a quarter and a third of the population perished" (Stark 1996a:76). Stark argues that a primary reason why was because when the epidemics hit, most people, or at least those who could, fled.[15] Why? Because the pagan religions at the time had no notion that people had an obligation to nurse the sick and dying. Thus, they were free to flee without fear of any retribution from the gods. By contrast, Christians could not flee because they believed God commanded them to love others as themselves:

> There was nothing new in the idea that the supernatural makes behavioral demands upon humans – the gods have always wanted

---

[15] Even the renowned physician and philosopher Aelius Galenus (i.e., Galen), who lived during the first epidemic, left Rome for a country estate until the dangers of the epidemics subsided.

8.5 Epidemics, Networks, and the Rise of Christianity

sacrifices and worship. Nor was there anything new in the notion that the supernatural will respond to offerings – that the gods can be induced to exchange services for sacrifices. What was new was the notion that more than self-interested exchange relations were possible between humans and the supernatural. The Christian teaching that God loves those who love him was alien to pagan beliefs ... Equally alien ... was the notion that because God loves humanity, Christians cannot please God unless they *love one another*. Moreover, such responsibilities were to be extended beyond the bonds of family and tribe, indeed to "all those who in every place call on the name of our Lord Jesus Christ" (1 Cor. 1:2). These were revolutionary ideas.

(Stark 1996a:86)

And these ideas evidently translated into action, in particular, to ministering to those who had contracted the disease. For instance, the bishop Dionysius, contrasted the "heroic" nursing efforts of Christians with the lack of response by non-Christians (Stark 1996a:83), and a century later the Roman Emperor Julian complained to a pagan priest about the Christian commitment to social service. He argued that the Christian church was growing because of the moral character of Christians and urged pagans to equal the Christians in their virtue (Stark 1996a:83–84). According to Stark, however, the pagan priests were incapable of motivating followers to engage in charitable works because their doctrines had no notion that God (or the gods) loved those who love him, and that people cannot please God unless they extend their love to others.

This led Stark to argue that when the epidemics broke out, most pagans fled the cities while most Christians remained behind, and this in turn led to higher survival rates among Christians. He illustrates this effect by imagining a hypothetical city in 160 CE consisting of 10,000 individuals of which 40 were Christians.[16] Assuming a mortality rate of 30 percent for pagans and 10 percent for Christians, along with a conversion rate of 40 percent per decade (Stark 1996a:6, 89), Stark estimates the effect the epidemics would have had on the number of pagans relative to the number of Christians from 160 to 260 CE.[17] The results are presented in Table 8.4. As indicated, the ratio of pagans to Christians falls from 249 to 1 in 160 CE to 4 to 1 in 260 CE. Had the epidemics not occurred and Christian growth only occurred through conversions, the ratio of pagans to Christians would have been 8 to 1 in 260 CE – still a substantial shift but not as extensive as it was with the epidemics.

---

[16] In an earlier chapter, he estimates that Christians made up approximately 0.4 percent of the population at the time (see Stark 1996a:7, 89).
[17] To keep the analysis simple, Stark assumes no population growth between the two epidemics.

Table 8.4 Stark's hypothetical city: the effect of epidemics on counts of pagans and Christians

Year (CE)	Pagan Population				Christian Population				Pagan to Christian Ratio
	Beginning	Pagan Conversions	Epidemic Deaths	Ending	Beginning	Pagan Conversions	Epidemic Deaths	Ending	
160	9,960	0	0	9,960	40	0	0	40	249:1
170	9,960	(16)	(2,988)	6,956	40	16	(4)	52	134:1
180	6,956	(21)	0	6,935	52	21	0	73	95:1
190	6,935	(29)	0	6,906	73	29	0	102	68:1
200	6,906	(41)	0	6,865	102	41	0	143	48:1
210	6,865	(57)	0	6,808	143	57	0	200	34:1
220	6,808	(80)	0	6,728	200	80	0	280	24:1
230	6,728	(112)	0	6,616	280	112	0	392	17:1
240	6,616	(157)	0	6,460	392	157	0	548	12:1
250	6,460	(219)	0	6,241	548	219	0	767	8:1
260	6,241	(306)	(1,872)	4,062	767	306	(77)	997	4:1

8.5 Epidemics, Networks, and the Rise of Christianity

Differential Survival and Network Ties

Stark then considers the effect that the differential survival rate would have had on ties between pagans and Christians. He concludes that it would have led to an increase in the number of Christian-pagan ties relative to pagan-pagan ties, which would have increased the likelihood that pagans would convert to Christianity. To keep things simple, Stark focuses on three types of ties: (1) Christian-to-Christian, (2) Christian-to-pagan, and (3) pagan-to-pagan. Using the differential mortality rates noted earlier, he shows the survival rate for the different types of ties would have been 81 percent for Christian-Christian ties (0.9 × 0.9), 63 percent for Christian-pagan ties (0.9 × 0.7), and 49 percent for pagan ties (0.7 × 0.7). In other words, while approximately 63 percent of the ties that pagans had with Christians would have survived one of the epidemics, only half of their ties to other pagans would have survived. Since a substantial number of pagans fled the cities during the epidemics, Stark considers a second scenario in which 20 percent of pagans fled the cities and either did not return or did not reestablish previous ties. Here, the percentage of pagan-to-pagan ties that survived an epidemic could have been as low as 25 percent (0.5 × 0.5). Finally, he notes the first two scenarios assume that only disease-stricken Christians would have received nursing care, but historical sources suggest otherwise. Thus, he posits a third scenario where the survival rate of Christian-pagan ties was higher, perhaps as high as 81 percent. Stark's three scenarios are reflected in Table 8.5, which distinguishes between the two types of Christian-pagan ties identified by Stark: those where pagans received nursing from Christians and those where pagans did not.

In light of these rates, Stark argues that the epidemics probably left Christian social networks relatively untouched while leaving pagan social networks in disarray and fragmented. To illustrate, he draws on the third scenario and imagines a pagan who, prior to one of the epidemics, has five close friends, four who are pagans and one who is a Christian. Chances are that after the epidemic, if he survives, only 25 percent of his ties to other

Table 8.5 *Stark's hypothetical city: likelihood of tie survival*

	Scenario 1 (%)	Scenario 2 (%)	Scenario 3 (%)
Christian-Christian	81	81	81
Christian-pagan (received nursing)			81
Christian-pagan (no nursing)	63	63	63
Pagan-pagan	49	25	25

pagans remain, leaving him with only a single tie to another pagan. At the same time, it is likely that his tie to his Christian friend is still intact. Thus, while prior to the epidemic the pagan's ratio of pagan-to-Christian ties is 4:1, after it is 1:1. Moreover, because the social network of his Christian friend is more likely to be intact than that of his pagan friend, there is a good chance that most of his new friends will be Christians rather than pagans, at least if he seeks out new friends through his existing social network. And finally, since conversion to a religion becomes more likely as the balance of an individual's ties shifts to that religion, Stark argues that the epidemics' disruption of pagan networks probably increased the probability that his imaginary pagan would eventually convert to Christianity.

Simulating Stark's Hypothetical City

Of course, Stark's imaginary pagan may or may not be representative of the pagan population writ large during the second epidemic.[18] The number of ties that pagans had with other pagans and Christians would have varied widely. Moreover, some would have been embedded in provincial networks while others would have been embedded in more cosmopolitan ones. Thus, to gain a better understanding of the possible effect that the epidemics had on pagan and Christian networks, we simulated a network that mirrors Stark's imaginary city in 250 CE just prior to the epidemic (see Table 8.4) with a population of 700, where 600 are pagans and 100 are Christians. The average Christian has about 3.0 ties to other Christians and 4.0 ties to pagans, while pagans have 5.6 ties to other pagans and 0.7 ties to Christians. Christians have a slightly higher number of ties due to their ability to survive from the previous plague.[19]

To compare the effects that Stark's three scenarios would have had on pagan and Christian social networks, we generated 100 networks for each of the three scenarios using the R package, *EpiModel*, (Jenness et al. 2017), which is designed to model the spread of diseases through a network.[20] The assumptions of our models were chosen so that they would reflect the three possible scenarios laid out by Stark. In particular, we assumed that the plague spread through the network by randomly infecting 10 individuals and that there is a 0.04 probability that infected individuals will infect those to whom they have a tie. The model runs monthly for 10 years (i.e., from 250 to 260 CE), or 121 time periods (with

---

[18] Stark, of course, never suggested that his hypothetical pagan is in any way representative of the average pagan living in the Roman Empire in the third century CE.
[19] These beginning numbers reflect a separate analysis where we simulated networks for all 100 years of Stark's hypothetical city (Everton and Schroeder 2017).
[20] The randomly generated networks are from the exponential random graph model (ERGM) family, with the connections being normally distributed and the mean average degrees for all of the networks in 250 CE.

8.5 Epidemics, Networks, and the Rise of Christianity

Table 8.6 *Simulated hypothetical city: final status*

			Scenario 1 (%)	Scenario 2 (%)	Scenario 3 (%)
Christian	Survival rate	Total	89.59	89.54	91.75
		Susceptible	23.17	24.34	40.52
		Infected	0.08	0.07	0.17
		Recovered	66.34	65.13	51.06
	Mortality rate		10.41	10.46	8.25
Pagan	Survival rate	Total	72.49	58.46	64.24
		Susceptible	21.27	17.17	26.04
		Infected	0.39	0.35	0.50
		Recovered	50.83	40.94	37.70
	Migrated			14.47	16.30
	mortality rate		27.51	27.07	19.46

the initial network being time 1). Infected individuals can either die or recover, and those who recover are then immune from future infections.[21] The likelihood that infected individuals will die is 0.0285 for each of the time periods in which they are infected. In order to achieve a mortality rate similar to those suggested by Stark, the recovery rate for pagans who did not receive nursing was set at 0.05 for each time period, while the recovery rate for Christians and pagans who did receive nursing was set at 0.15.

The results from the three scenarios are presented in Table 8.6. In scenario 1, pagans neither flee (migrate) the city nor receive any nursing, while in the second scenario, 20 percent leave but none receive any nursing, and in the third, 20 percent leave and those who are connected to at least one Christian share the same recovery probability as Christians.[22] For each of the scenarios, the disease spread across 100 randomly generated networks. As the table indicates, in the first two scenarios the respective mortality rates for Christians and pagans are essentially unchanged.[23] The Christian mortality rate "increases" from 10.41 to 10.46 percent, while the pagan mortality rate drops slightly from 27.51 to 27.07 percent. What is interesting is that when some pagans receive nursing (third scenario), it not only benefits those pagans who do, but it also benefits Christians and pagans in general (including pagans who did not receive

---
[21] A SIR model is used in order to mimic a plague similar to smallpox, where once a person recovers from the disease the person will be immune to it.
[22] Migration was calculated by having 20 percent of pagans who were alive at the last time period leave the network, which results in having the final percentage of pagans who migrated be less than 20 percent of the initial population.
[23] Although the second scenario's average mortality rate is lower, it is not statistically different from the first scenario.

Table 8.7 *Stark's hypothetical city: likelihood of tie survival*

	Scenario 1 (%)	Scenario 2 (%)	Scenario 3 (%)
Christian-Christian	79.58	79.40	82.81
Christian-pagan (received nursing)			61.51
Christian-pagan (no nursing)	63.30	51.05	
Pagan-pagan	50.00	32.71	39.78

nursing) because fewer people in both groups become infected in the first place. As one can see, the Christian mortality rate falls to 8.25 percent while the pagan mortality rate falls to 19.46. Moreover, with fewer pagans dying, the results for percentage of ties that remain differs slightly from Stark's initial scenario (see Table 8.7).

Table 8.8 summarizes for all three of Stark's scenarios how the distribution of ties between and among Christians and pagans changes from before the onset of the plague to after. As it shows, prior to the epidemic, both pagans and Christians had more ties to pagans than to Christians. This might strike some as wrong or surprising, but it is a mathematical truism that members of minority groups (in this case, Christians) have, on average, more ties outside of their community than members of majority groups (in this case, pagans) have, on average, to members of minority groups (Blau 1977, 1994).[24] In all three scenarios, at the plague's end, the average pagan lost between 1.8 and 2.5 ties, most of which were to other pagans, whereas the average Christian lost somewhere between 1.5 and 2.1 ties, and these losses were primarily to pagans as well. To get a sense of change in the makeup of the two sets of networks, we can compare the ratio of ties that the average pagan and Christian have to group and nongroup members. As the decline in the ratios from all three scenarios indicates, the average pagan has relatively fewer ties to other pagans after the plague than before the epidemic. According to our simulations of the third scenario, from 250 to 260 CE, the average pagan would have lost approximately two ties, most likely to other pagans, thus reducing the ratio of pagan to Christian ties from approximately 8:1 to 5:1. The decline is not as dramatic as that of Stark's imaginary pagan, but it is substantial nonetheless. Thus, if Stark's assumptions concerning the differences in Christian and pagan mortality are accurate, he is probably correct in

---

[24] To illustrate, imagine a society of 100 individuals, consisting of two groups, where 80 belong to the majority and 20 belong to the minority. Now, assume that a total of 160 ties exist between members of the two groups. That means the average member of the majority has two ties (160/80 = 2) to members of the minority, while the average member of the minority has eight ties (160/20 = 8) to members of the majority.

Table 8.8 *Stark's hypothetical city, average number of ties between Christians and pagans*

		Average Number of Ties							
		Before the Epidemic, 250 CE				After the Epidemic, 260 CE			
		Total	Pagan	Christian	Ratio	Total	Pagan	Christian	Ratio
Scenario 1	Pagan	6.33	5.64	0.69	8.17	4.49	3.89	0.60	6.48
	Christian	7.09	4.16	2.93	1.42	5.54	2.94	2.60	1.13
Scenario 2	Pagan	6.31	5.63	0.68	8.27	3.75	3.15	0.60	5.25
	Christian	7.00	4.10	2.90	1.41	4.90	2.34	2.56	0.91
Scenario 3	Pagan	6.31	5.63	0.68	8.23	4.14	3.48	0.65	5.35
	Christian	6.98	4.10	2.88	1.42	5.34	2.74	2.60	1.05

concluding that the epidemics would have disrupted pagan social networks far more than they would have disrupted Christian social networks, which possibly may have enhanced the early Church's recruitment efforts.

Summary

Computer simulation offers analysts a method for testing theories when they do not have access to the three types of social network data mentioned in the second chapter: counts of ties, ego networks, and whole networks. It is especially appealing for those involved in historical investigations where the structure of networks can only be guessed at. In this section, we used it to test Rodney Stark's historically informed musings about how the epidemics early in the Common Era affected the social networks of pagans and Christians. In this case, the assumptions built into our models were chosen in order to replicate the broad outlines of Stark's argument, but it would be easy to recalibrate our models to reflect a different set of assumptions. That is the beauty of using computer simulation to test social network theories and why those of us who explore the interplay of religion and networks may draw on it more in the future.

8.6 Summary and Conclusion

This chapter began with the observation that a positive association exists between religion and health. On average, regular churchgoers not only live longer, but they also enjoy greater levels of life satisfaction and personal happiness, as well as experience fewer negative psychological effects from life's tragedies. It was also noted, however, that little consensus exists as to why religion has a positive effect on physical and mental health. With regards to religion's positive effect on physical health, many researchers believe that religious involvement regulates personal behavior in ways that decrease the risk of disease, such as discouraging alcohol and substance abuse, and promoting an ethic of moderation. Moreover, most faith communities discourage harmful behaviors, offer guidance about sexual behavior and family life, and help shape peoples' choices in ways that can reduce their exposure to stressful situations. As a consequence, people of faith tend to eat better, exercise more, drink and smoke less, and moderate their sexual behavior. With regards to mental health, there is considerable evidence that religious belief and practice provides individuals with resources such as rituals and beliefs that can help them attain a sense of dignity and control over their life. Rituals can also help them cope during periods of high stress, and beliefs can also help them assign meaning to challenging situations.

The mechanism that was the focus of this chapter, however, was the effect that religious social networks have on physical and mental health, noting that the social networks of faith communities provide members with various types of social support, such as offering emotional comfort during times of trouble and providing aid to the sick and dying. For instance, writing about the positive role that religion played in the life of his father and others growing up in Appalachia, J. D. Vance notes that his father's

> church offered something desperately needed by people like me. For alcoholics, it gave them a community of support and a sense that they weren't fighting addiction alone. For expectant mothers, it offered a free home with job training and parenting classes. When someone needed a job, church friends could either provide one or make introductions. When Dad faced financial troubles, his church banded together and purchased a used car for the family. In the broken world I saw around me—and for the people struggling in that world—religion offered tangible assistance to keep the faithful on track.
> (Vance 2016:93–94)

This chapter highlighted some of the ways that social networks promote the health and subjective well-being of people of faith. For example, we considered the positive role that social networks can play in terms of promoting the health of adolescents, contributing to the life satisfaction of adults, and the prevention of suicide, although in the case of the latter, we also saw that one can get too much of a good thing. Individuals embedded in very dense and isolated networks are more at risk for committing suicide than are those living in somewhat more open ones. We will return to this dynamic in Chapter 10, where we will see that dense networks that are isolated from the wider society are more likely to radicalize than those that are not. Finally, we considered Rodney Stark's three-fold argument as to why the early Christian church was better equipped than its pagan competitors to respond to the epidemics that swept through the Roman Empire in the second and third centuries. Using computer simulation, we saw that Stark was probably correct that the epidemics disrupted pagan social networks far more than they did Christian social networks, which in turn probably improved the early Church's efforts at bringing more people into the fold.

8.7 For Further Reading

The literature on religion and health is voluminous and cannot be done justice here, but one would not go wrong by attending to the research of scholars such as Christopher Ellison (a sociologist), Harold Koenig (a psychiatrist), Neal Krause (a sociologist), Jeffrey Levin (an epidemiologist), and Kenneth Pargament (a psychologist) (see, e.g., Ellison, Gay, and Glass 1989; Ellison and George 1994; Pargament et al. 1994; Ellison and Levin 1998; Krause, Ellison, and Wulff 1998; Pargament et al. 1998; Koenig, McCullough, and Larson 2001; Krause and Ellison 2003; Koenig 2008; Krause 2008; Levin 2009, 2015, 2016; Ellison and Hummer 2010; Ellison 2012; Koenig, King, and Carson 2012). Those looking for overviews of the field should find the following helpful:

- Christopher G. Ellison and Jeffrey S. Levin. 1998. "The Religion-Health Connection: Evidence, Theory, and Future Directions." *Health Education and Behavior* 25(700–720).
- Harold G. Koenig, 2008. *Medicine, Religion, and Health: Where Science and Spirituality Meet.* West Conshohocken, PA: Templeton Press.
- Harold G. Koenig, Dana E King, and Verna Benner Carson. 2012. *Handbook of Religion and Health*, vol. 2. New York: Oxford University Press.
- Harold G. Koenig, Michael E. McCullough, and David B. Larson. 2001. *Handbook of Religion and Health*, vol. 1. New York: Oxford University Press.
- Levin, Jeffrey S. 2009. "'And Let Us Make Us a Name': Reflections on the Future of the Religion and Health Field." *Journal of Religion and Health* 48:125–145.
- Levin, Jeffrey S. 2016. "'For They Knew Not What It Was': Rethinking the Tacit Narrative History of Religion and Health Research." *Journal of Religion and Health* 56(1):28–46.

These following two lectures by Christopher Ellison and Jeffrey Levin also provide nice overviews of the field:

- Ellison, Christopher G. 2012. *Does Faith Matter?* Waco, TX: Baylor University. [Video File]. Retrieved from www.youtube.com/watch?v=JVMDbKGR2gI.
- Levin, Jeffrey S. 2015. *Godless Lives? Does Religion Matter for Our Well-Being?* Waco, TX: Baylor University. [Video File]. Retrieved from www.youtube.com/watch?v=R34B-IgMeGg.

For a conceptual overview on religion and mortality, see Hummer et al. "Religious Involvement and Adult Mortality in the United States: Review and Perspective" in the December 2004 issues of the *Southern Medical Journal*. Neal Krause's work on congregational support systems, *Aging in the Church* (Templeton Foundation Press, 2008), is also quite well done.

Part V

Ties That Tear Down

9

Conflict and Cohesion

9.1 Introduction

The self-named "Crunchy Con," Rod Dreher (2006), who was raised Methodist but is now Eastern Orthodox, has proposed that Christians adopt "the Benedict Option" (Dreher 2009, 2015, 2017), which is a fledgling movement that calls on traditional Christians to create local institutions, communities, and networks in which they can live apart, at least to some degree, from a society that Dreher sees as hostile to Christian values. Dreher is also critical of most forms of mainstream Christianity, both in its conservative and liberal guises, arguing that it has uncritically embraced consumer capitalism, which he believes undermines traditional Christian values with its radical individualism. He believes that in order for the church to survive, it will have to return to its roots, in terms of both practice and belief. "We are going to have to learn habits of the heart forgotten by believers in the West. We are going to have to change our lives, our approach to life, in radical ways. In short, *we are going to have to be the church*, without compromise, no matter what it costs" (Dreher 2015:3, emphasis in original). A handful of such institutions and communities have sprung up across the United States, such as Clear Creek in Hulbert, Oklahoma, where several families have settled near a Benedictine monastery that celebrates the traditional Latin Mass (Lovett 2017), and the Alleluia Community, which is a lay community of charismatic (Pentecostal) Protestants and Catholics in Augusta, Georgia.[1] Others, including Dreher and his family, have moved to neighborhoods near their congregations so that they live close to others who share their beliefs and practices.

The term "Benedict Option" takes its name from St. Benedict, who around 500 CE left ancient Rome because he was horrified by Rome's moral decadence. He left, not out of any great desire to become a hermit, but so that he could live a more faithful life. Benedict ended up founding twelve monasteries, which Dreher credits with the later rebirth of Western

---

[1] See www.yeslord.com.

civilization. It was not Benedict who initially inspired Dreher, however. Rather, it was the philosopher Alasdair MacIntyre, who in the final paragraph of his book *After Virtue* argues that the only way to sustain a coherent moral culture in today's world is to form local communities that march to a different beat than modern culture:

> If my account of our moral condition is correct, we ought also to conclude that ... we ... have reached a turning point. What matters at this stage is the construction of local forms of community within which civility and the intellectual moral life can be sustained through the new dark ages which are already upon us ... This time however the barbarians are not waiting beyond the frontiers; they have already been governing us for quite some time. And it is our lack of consciousness of this that constitutes part of our predicament. We are waiting not for a Godot, but for another – doubtless very different – St. Benedict.
>
> (MacIntyre 1984:263)

According to Dreher, although the Benedict Option entails a partial withdrawal from the political sphere, it does not necessitate complete political quietism. Traditional Christians can still voice their opinion on public issues, but they should no longer seek to play key roles in presidential politics. Dreher sees the Benedict Option as "a radical shift in perspective among Christians, one in which we see ourselves as living in the ruins (though very comfortable ones!) of Christian civilization," with the coming task of keeping "orthodox Christianity alive in the hearts and minds of believers *living as exiles in an ever more hostile culture*" (Dreher 2015, emphasis added). It would place an emphasis on education and culture and be primarily "a theological and cultural project" based on radically rethinking "our place within this order."

The majority of conservative Christians, whether evangelical, Roman Catholic, or Eastern Orthodox, have not opted out of the modern world. In fact, Dreher believes that most have embraced it far too enthusiastically. Nevertheless, many do feel that they are under attack, either by secular culture or liberal Christians. Recall the lament of the Presbyterian woman we met in the first chapter who believes that "Christians are not treated too nicely ... [and] are mocked and made fun of by mainstream America" (quoted in Smith et al. 1998:141). As we noted there, Christian Smith (1998) believes this sense of embattlement has actually helped American evangelicalism because conflict, real or perceived, can strengthen a group's identity, solidarity, and internal cohesion. Georg Simmel (1955 [1908]) and Lewis Coser (1956) were among the first to note this dynamic, but others have as well, such as anthropologist Scott Atran (2010) and social psychologist Jonathan Haidt (2012). Even former US President Ronald Reagan recognized the benefits of conflict:

9.2 Cohesion and Conflict: Zablocki's Urban Communes

"I couldn't help but say to [Mr. Gorbachev], just think how easy his task and mine might be ... if suddenly there was a threat to this world from another planet. [We would] find out once and for all that we really are all human beings on this earth together" (cited in Atran 2010:66).

In this chapter, we will examine and extend a handful of studies that have explored the interplay between conflict and cohesion. We begin with Benjamin Zablocki's (1980) study of American communes; Zablocki found, among other things, that more cohesive groups experienced higher turnover and were more likely to disband than less cohesive ones. We then briefly consider Sampson's (1968) monks, which were first introduced in Chapter 2, and see how reforms introduced by the Roman Catholic Church in the 1960s produced conflict among the novices and how the conflict propelled them into three or four distinct and cohesive subgroups. This will also give us an opportunity to introduce readers to balance theory, which analysts use to partition social networks into various clusters. In the chapter's final section, we will again draw on balance theory in order to explore some of the intellectual networks mapped by Randall Collins (1998). In particular, we will examine the Islamic, Jewish, Christian, and secular philosophical networks active in Europe from 900 to 1600 CE. But first, Zablocki's urban communes.

9.2 Cohesion and Conflict: Zablocki's Urban Communes

In the 1970s Benjamin Zablocki (1980) led a group of researchers who collected data, including social network data, on sixty urban communes located in six geographical regions in the United States. The communes ranged in size from five to approximately forty members. The researchers collected data at both the group and individual level. Group-level data included the year the commune was founded, the size of the group at the time of its founding, the number of ex-members, the basis of its decision making (e.g., rational, irrational, mixed), if it was disbanded (and if so, when), its ideology (e.g., religious, political), and so on. At the individual level, the researchers obtained basic demographic information of commune members, but then also asked about their ties to other members in the commune. In a page-long questionnaire, researchers first asked members to describe their relationship with every other member (e.g., "how much time the two spent together," "which of the two had more power in the relationship," and whether the other member "ever acted like a mother, father, sister, brother, son, or daughter to them" (Martin, Yeung, and Zablocki 2002:57); members were also asked to rate their relationship with every other member on a number of different dimensions (e.g., loving, jealous, sexual, hateful, exciting, etc.). In general, researchers identified that a tie existed between two members when both

Table 9.1 *Emotional cathexis and commune turnover and disintegration rates*

	Emotional Cathexis				
	Cold	Cool	Warm	Hot	Smoldering
Turnover Rate (%)	28	50	55	63	65
Disintegration Rate (%)	0	0	8	33	60

Source: Zablocki, 1980:165

members indicated that there was a relationship on the same dimension.[2] For example, if two members indicated that their relationship was a jealous one, then the researchers considered that a jealous tie existed between the two. However, if only one indicated it as such, then the researchers did not draw a "jealous" tie between the two.

One of their most interesting findings concerned the effect of loving (but not necessarily sexual) ties on commune stability. The researchers classified the communes in terms of the density of loving ties (i.e., the proportion of the ties that were "loving"), what they called the level of "emotional cathexis." Classifications ranged from "cold" to "smoldering" (see Table 9.1), the former characterized by very few loving ties and the latter by numerous ones. A widely held assumption at the time was that communes where anyone and everyone could love whomever they wanted would be more stable than those that placed restrictions on peoples' behavior, but that is not what Zablocki found. As Table 9.1 indicates, the level of emotional cathexis and communal instability were inversely associated with one another. "Hot" and "smoldering" communes exhibited far higher turnover rates and were far more likely to disintegrate than were the more restrictive communes.

As interesting as these results are, because the communes vary in size, network density is not necessarily an ideal measure of emotional cathexis. As noted in Chapter 2, density is inversely related to network size, which is why social network analysts often use alternative measures for capturing a network's interconnectedness, such as average degree. This raises the important issue as to whether or not the effect that Zablocki and his team found was indeed a function of network density or network size.

To explore this possibility, we reexamined Zablocki's analysis of the urban commune data.[3] This was harder than one might think. For

---

[2] For more complete descriptions of the data, see Zablocki (1980) and Martin, Yeung, and Zablocki (2002). The data are available at John Levi Martin's website: http://home.uchicago.edu/~jlmartin/UCDS/UCDS.
[3] In particular, the analysis that follows seeks to replicate or approach Zablocki's fourth model (1980: 158).

9.2 Cohesion and Conflict: Zablocki's Urban Communes

instance, identifying the thirty-seven communes Zablocki included in his regression models proved difficult (1980:158). Zablocki dropped twenty because they lacked adequate relational data; in particular, he excluded those where the response rate on the relational questionnaires was less than 85 percent (Zablocki 1980:375). He excluded an additional three because he and his team considered them outliers and thus skewed the results. Identifying these twenty-three cases was next to impossible, however. For instance, although the three outlier communes were all led by a charismatic authority who lived in the commune itself (rather than somewhere else), a total of twelve communes had charismatic leaders who lived in residence, but there is no variable that identifies the three outliers. Similarly, although a variable indicates whether or not each individual completed a valid relationship questionnaire, if we eliminate communes where less than 85 percent of their members completed a questionnaire, only thirty-one remain. Interestingly, though, if we set the cut-off at 80 percent, thirty-seven communes remain – the same number as in Zablocki's final analysis. Whether these are the same thirty-seven that Zablocki analyzed is unclear, but given the similarity, we chose to use these thirty-seven communes in the analysis that follows.

Another difficulty encountered concerned the dependent variable. Zablocki used each commune's turnover rate, which he defined as the "proportion of the membership of a commune at time $t-1$ who [were] no longer members at time t (Zablocki 1980:154). Such data are unavailable in the 1974 urban communes dataset, however. Instead, it includes data on the number of individuals in each commune at the time of their founding and the number of ex-members at the time of the analysis (i.e., 1974). Although the latter can be treated as time t, the former cannot be treated as time $t-1$ because some of the communes were founded as early as eight years before. Consequently, we used a dichotomous variable that indicates whether or not a commune disbanded in the year of observation or in a subsequent year up to and including 1978.

Emotional cathexis, which is described earlier in this chapter, was estimated, except that in addition to calculating the density of each commune's "love" network, we also calculated the average number of ties (i.e., average degree) of each network. Another density measure included by Zablocki was "dyadic partiality," which he defined as two individuals both listing the others as significant *and* their knowing what the other person's father's job was – "informal discussions with a number of social psychologists indicated that this was a good way of identifying people who had spent some time talking with each other about themselves" (Martin, Yeung, and Zablocki 2002:57). We were able to estimate these, but again, both density and average degree are used in the models. Because the relationship between density and average degree is a function of network size, we included network size as a control variable in all of our models.

Zablocki also included the level of rational decision making in each commune. This was a five-point scale, ranging from "no collective decision making" on one end to "serious rationality" on the other. Zablocki also estimated a number of models that included the group's ideology, but he found that only those with a "political" ideology exerted a statistically significant effect, so he only presented those in his book. Unfortunately, of the thirty-seven communes included in our analysis, political ideology perfectly predicts whether a commune disbanded, so we included a "religious" dummy variable instead. It indicates whether a commune was classified as either Christian or Eastern religious, and since this is a book on networks and religion, this seemed like a reasonable alternative. Finally, Zablocki included a dummy variable indicating whether the community was led by a charismatic leader. However, it is unclear how Zablocki operationalized the presence of a charismatic authority in each commune. The variable ranges from zero ("no charismatic influence") to six ("fully routinized charisma"), but the highest level of charismatic authority ("definite charismatic influence") is assigned a score of three. Thus, to be safe, in our models we included a variable that indicates just the opposite – namely, one that identifies communes without a charismatic leader.

The results are presented in Table 9.2. Four models were estimated: two using average degree as a measure of emotional cathexis, and two using network density. The first model included all of the variables just discussed, while the second included only those variables that were statistically significant in the first model. Although in both sets of models the pseudo R2 scores decline from the first to the second model, the AIC and BIC scores improve (i.e., they are lower in the second than in the first),

Table 9.2 *Logistic regression Predicting commune disbanding*

	Average Degree		Network Density	
	Model 1	Model 2	Model 1	Model 2
Emotional cathexis	0.903+	1.036*	5.718	6.958*
Dyadic partiality	−0.998		−3.862	
Rational decision making	−1.476		−1.358	
Religious ideology	−0.933		−0.299	
No charismatic leader	3.740+	2.131+	3.994+	2.291+
Size	−0.506+	−0.486+	−0.158	0.006
Intercept	5.913	−1.599	2.403	−5.392
Pseudo R2	0.347	0.277	0.302	0.224
AIC	37.448	33.965	39.037	35.842
BIC	48.724	40.409	50.314	42.286

Note: Urban Communes Dataset, 1974; + $p < .10$, * $p < .05$; $N = 37$

9.2 Cohesion and Conflict: Zablocki's Urban Communes 259

suggesting that we focus on the second model for interpretation. As these results indicate, Zablocki's initial findings hold. Emotional cathexis is a predictor of a commune disbanding, whether we include average degree or network density as a measure. The results also suggest that the lack of a charismatic leader increases the likelihood that a commune will disband and that larger communes are more likely to survive than smaller ones.

Figure 9.1 graphically captures the results of this analysis. It plots the probability of a commune disbanding by its level of emotional cathexis. In the upper panel, average degree is used as a measure, while in the lower panel, network density is.[4] Both graphs indicate that as emotional cathexis increases, so too does the probability that a commune will disband. To be sure, the association between network density and disbanding appears to be greater than the association between average degree and disbanding. However, in both cases the association is positive, and as we saw in Table 9.2, statistically significant.

To further explore the relationship between these factors and the likelihood that a commune will disband, we estimated two sets of generalized structural equation models. Table 9.3 presents the results. Note that the results for predicting commune disbanding (upper part of table) are identical to those presented in Table 9.2, which is as they should be. This model, however, also includes factors predicting each commune's level of emotional cathexis and the likelihood that a commune would lack a charismatic leader. As before, the second model in each set eliminates variables found to be statistically insignificant in the first, and in both cases, AIC and BIC indicate that the reduced models are preferred over the full model.

In order to ease interpretation, Figure 9.2 offers a graphic representation of the results presented in Table 9.3 (model 2). As both the table and figure indicate, higher levels of emotional cathexis and the lack of a charismatic leader increase the likelihood that a commune will disband, while larger communes (i.e., network size) decreases the likelihood. Interestingly, although religious ideology does not exert a direct effect on commune disbanding, it appears to have an indirect effect through two different pathways: one positive, one negative. In particular, religious ideology appears to be positively associated with a commune's level of emotional cathexis, whether we estimate it using average degree or network density. At the same time, it is negatively associated with the lack of a charismatic leader; that is, it is positively associated with the presence of some kind of charismatic leader. On the one hand, then, these results suggest that by increasing the level of emotional cathexis in a commune, religious ideology indirectly increases the likelihood that a commune will

---

[4] In both cases, model 2 was used to estimate the predicted probability of a commune disbanding.

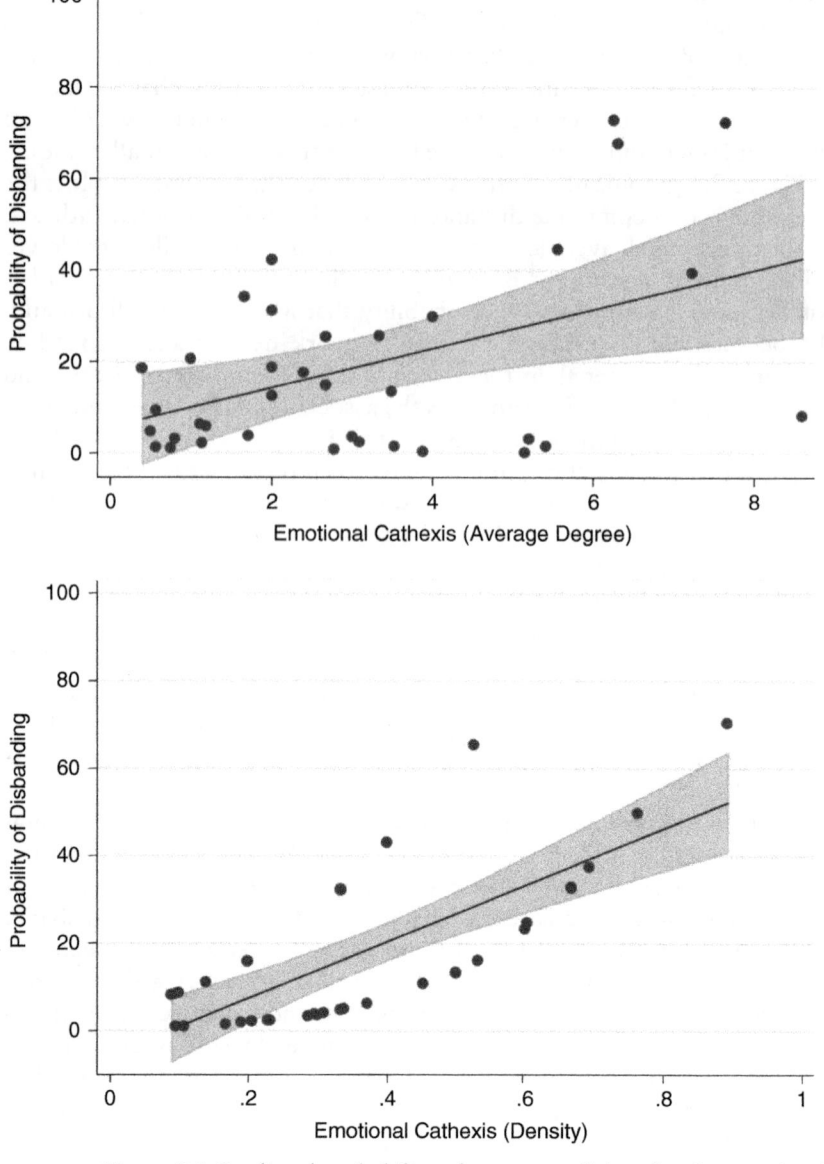

Figure 9.1 Predicted probability of commune disbanding by emotional cathexis

disband. On the other hand, the results suggest that by increasing the likelihood that a commune will have a charismatic presence, religious ideology indirectly decreases the likelihood that a commune will disband. The first of these results could possibly be at odds with the findings of

9.2 Cohesion and Conflict: Zablocki's Urban Communes

Table 9.3 *Generalized structural equation model predicting commune disbanding*

	Average Degree		Network Density	
	Model 1	Model 2	Model 1	Model 2
	Commune Disbanding			
Emotional cathexis	0.903+	1.036*	5.718	6.958*
Dyadic partiality	−0.998		−3.862	
Rational decision making	−1.476		−1.358	
Religious ideology	−0.933		−0.299	
No charismatic leader	3.740+	2.131+	3.994+	2.291+
Network size	−0.506+	−0.486+	−0.158	0.006
Intercept	5.913	−1.599	2.403	−5.392
	Emotional Cathexis			
Religious ideology	1.963***	1.963***	0.255***	0.255***
Network size	0.253***	0.253***	−0.009	−0.009
Intercept	−0.098	−0.098	0.354	0.354
	No Charismatic Leader			
Religious ideology	−0.359*	−0.388**	−0.359*	−0.388**
Network size	−0.016		−0.016	
Intercept	0.589	0.455	0.589	0.455
Variance				
Emotional cathexis	1.866	1.865	0.028	0.028
No charismatic leader	0.167	0.173	0.167	0.173
AIC	220.363	216.054	66.936	62.916
BIC	244.527	233.774	91.100	80.636

Note: Urban Communes Dataset, 1974; + $p < .10$, * $p < .05$, ** $p < .01$, *** $p < .001$

Rosabeth Kanter (1972) and others (Hall 1988; Sosis 2000; Sosis and Bressler 2003), who have found that religious communes tend to survive longer than secular ones. However, as Zablocki notes, his finding that political communes are negatively associated with turnover rate probably reflects "more of a sampling artifact than an enduring property of political communes" (Zablocki 1980:157). Thus, we should probably consider our finding that a religious ideology may indirectly increase the likelihood that a commune will disband with a grain of salt.

Summary

One of Zablocki's more interesting findings is that although high levels of emotional cathexis increase the probability of communal instability, people were more likely to remain in a commune if they were mentioned by other members as an object of love. That is, "the number of times that

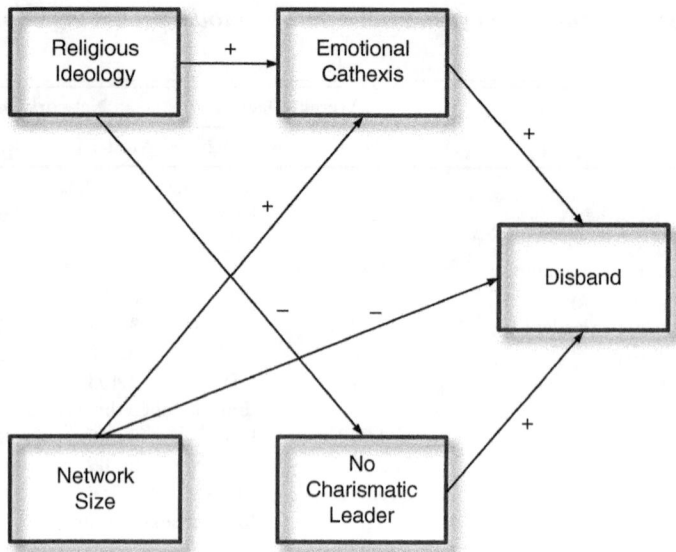

Figure 9.2 Simplified model predicting commune disbanding

a person is mentioned by fellow commune members as an object of love is strongly and *inversely* related to the probability of leaving" (Zablocki 1980:128). This paradox is difficult to reconcile. At the individual level, it makes complete sense that those who feel less loved by their fellow members are more likely to leave. But why does the effect change at the network level? Zablocki (1980:180) ultimately concluded that "too much relatedness can be as harmful for social structure as too little." Or as Rodney Stark later observed:

> Despite the ideology of "love one another," in practice there wasn't enough time, enough energy, or the inclination to actually love everyone equally. Thus, although communes were based on the ideal that everyone would be equal, and although members tried to share all material things in common, they overlooked the fact that love, too, is a valuable "good" and that it is far harder to parcel it out equally than it is to give everyone the same clothing allowance. Thus, many communes were so "full of love" that they burst, often in a spectacular fashion, leaving many bitter ex-members. In contrast, the groups that were the most durable tended to be those that minimized jealousy and emotional entanglements ... In regulating or prohibiting sex, of course, these modern communes followed the pattern of successful religious communes throughout history.
> (Stark 2007:106)

9.3 Conflict and Cohesion: Sampson's Monks

Although this paradox will not be explored any further here, it highlights how social forces sometimes exert different effects at the micro and macro levels. We now turn our attention to a method for identifying clusters (i.e., subgroups) in networks coded with positive and negative ties. We begin with a relatively simple network: the novices observed by Samuel Sampson (1968). In the following section, we attempt to apply the method to more complex networks: the philosophical networks mapped by Randall Collins (1998).

9.3 Conflict and Cohesion: Sampson's Monks

Earlier, in Chapter 2, we saw how the conflict among the novices observed by Samuel Sampson led them to sort themselves into three subgroups. We also noted how social network analysts use various clustering algorithms to identify subgroups within a network. Most of these only use positive ties in their calculations, but there are some that take into account both positive and negative ties. In this section, we introduce one such algorithm, the Doreian-Mrvar (1996) algorithm, which is based on balance theory, and apply it to the positive and negative interactions among Sampson's novices. We begin with a brief overview of balance theory.

Balance Theory

Balance theory has its roots in the work of Fritz Heider (1946, 1958), who noted that people often feel uncomfortable when they disagree with a friend about a particular topic. Figure 9.3, which analysts refer to as a P-O-X triple (de Nooy, Mrvar, and Batagelj 2011), illustrates Heider's understanding of such a situation. "P is a person, O is another person

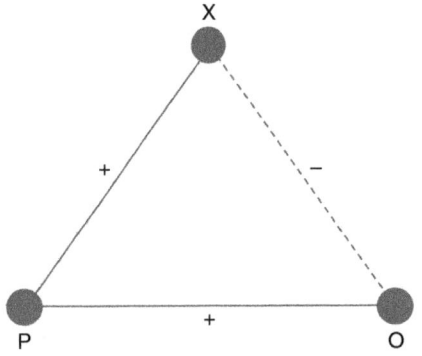

Figure 9.3 Heider's person-other-object (P-O-X) triple

(the Other), and X represents a topic or object" (de Nooy, Mrvar, and Batagelj 2011:98). The positive (+) line between P and O indicates that P likes O, while the positive line between P and X indicates that P holds a favorable opinion about X. However, P does not believe that O has a positive opinion about X, as the negative (−) line between O and X indicates, and as such the situation is "out of balance." It is important to note that Heider was only concerned with P's perception of the situation. O, in fact, may hold a positive opinion about X or think poorly of P, but in Heider's model that does not matter. What matters is what P perceives to be true.

Theodore Newcomb (1953) extended Heider's model to interpersonal relations so that O's opinion of X reflects O's opinion, not P's perception of it. In order to symbolize this change, Newcomb substituted A for P and B for O, and X can be an object, idea, or person. Nevertheless, the logic remains the same. In imbalanced situations, people will feel uncomfortable and attempt to bring the relationship "back into balance."[5] They can do this in numerous ways, such as adjusting their opinion of X, attempting to change their friend's opinion of X, altering their opinion of their friend, or convincing themselves that their friend actually holds a positive opinion of X. Unsurprisingly, small group research has found support for this theory, as many, if not most, of us have found ourselves in imbalanced situations, such as when we have disagreed with a friend over a hot button issue (e.g., abortion) or about a particular person (e.g., a political candidate). And such situations can create a level of tension that can prove difficult to overcome, even if the parties involved wish to do so (Ross 2016).

A social psychologist, Dorwin Cartwright, and a mathematician, Frank Harary (1956), extended Heider's and Newcomb's model in several ways. First, they translated Heider's and Newcomb's ideas into the language of graph theory and thus were the first to assign ties between individuals with either a positive or negative sign, as well as the first to draw positive ties as solid lines and negative ties as dashed lines (see Figure 9.3). Such graphs are generally referred to as signed graphs. Second, they expanded their models to networks of more than three nodes and where the nodes are individuals rather than a mix of individuals and objects. Finally, they developed the notion of structural balance, which holds that in a balanced network, there should only be positive ties within clusters and negative ties across clusters. An example of a balanced network is presented in Figure 9.4, where all of the ties within the clusters are positive and all the ties between them are negative.[6]

---

[5] In balanced graphs, there is always an even number of negative signs, either zero or two.
[6] This and all of the remaining figures in the chapter were created in Pajek (Batagelj and Mrvar 2017) because it draws negative ties as dashed lines.

9.3 Conflict and Cohesion: Sampson's Monks

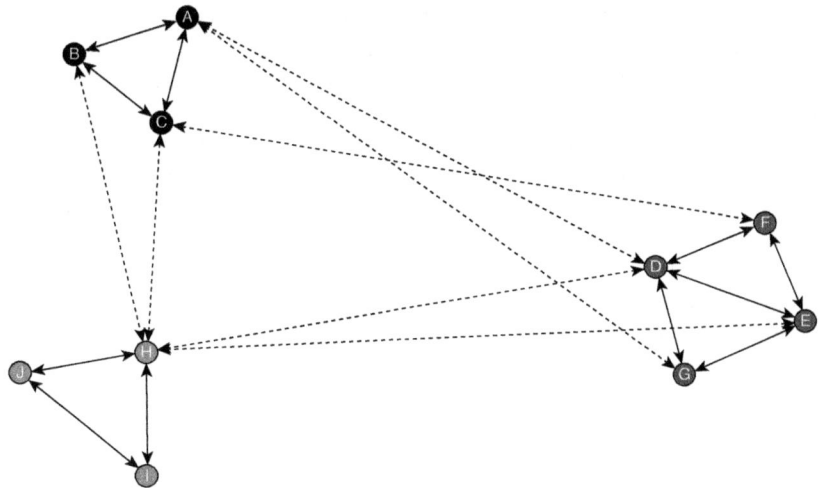

Figure 9.4 Balanced social network

Of course, seldom can networks be partitioned into clusters where there are only positive ties within clusters and negative ties between them. However, Patrick Doreian and Andrej Mrvar (1996) have developed a method for partitioning signed networks into clusters that seeks to minimize the number of such "forbidden" ties. To illustrate their approach we will examine the positive and negative interactions among the novices observed by Samuel Sampson (1968).

Structural Balance and Clusterability

Recall that Sampson recorded various types of "ties" among the novices: esteem and disesteem; like and dislike; positive influence and negative influence; and praise and blame. Each novice only ranked his top three choices for each type of tie, where a 3 indicates his first choice, a 2 his second, and a 1 his third (some subjects offered tied ranks for their top four choices). During Sampson's stay in the monastery, a "crisis in the cloister" occurred in response to some of the changes proposed by the Second Vatican Council (Vatican II). This led to four novices being expelled and several others leaving voluntarily. Based on his observations, Sampson partitioned (i.e., sorted) the novices into four groups: (1) the young Turks, (2) the loyal opposition, (3) the outcasts, and (4) the neutrals. The young Turks arrived later and questioned the practices of the monastery, which members of the loyal opposition defended. Not coincidentally, most of the members of the loyal opposition attended seminary together prior to their arrival. The outcasts were those not accepted at all into the larger group, and the neutrals were those who refused to take sides. Here we use the version of the Sampson data recoded by Wouter de Nooy, Andrej Mrvar, and Vladimir Batagelj (2011:101), which only take into account the novices' first choices in terms of like and dislike and coded 1 and –1 respectively.

Figures 9.5 and 9.6 present the results of the analysis. The first (Figure 9.5) partitions the novices into three clusters while the second (Figure 9.6) partitions them into four. The difference between the two is that the cluster in the lower right of Figure 9.5 is broken into two clusters in Figure 9.6. In both cases, there is one forbidden tie. In Figure 9.5 there is a negative tie between Mark and John Bosco, although they belong to the same cluster. In Figure 9.6 there is a positive tie between Gregory and John Bosco, and here they belong to separate clusters.

Which solution is correct? When multiple partitions share the same measure of fit (i.e., the number of forbidden ties or what are sometimes called "inconsistencies"), we generally need to inspect them visually. We are inclined to select the four-cluster partition (Figure 9.6) since the only tie that holds the group together in Figure 9.5 is the positive tie between Gregory and John Bosco. However, the correlation between the factions identified by Sampson is higher for the three-cluster solution (0.814) than the four-cluster solution (0.674). Thus, a case could be made for three rather than four clusters.[7] One could also argue, however, that Sampson erred in his partitioning of the novices into different groups and was in need of the Doreian-Mrvar algorithm. It was unavailable, of course.

Summary

De Nooy, Mrvar, and Batagelj (2011) extended their analysis of the Sampson network in order to test whether the network became more clustered over time. Table 9.4 reproduces their findings (de Nooy 2011:109). The numbers in the cells indicate the error score by the number of clusters into which the network has been partitioned by time period. In this case, all of the novices' choices were used, not just their top choices as we did. As the table indicates, in each time period, a three-cluster partition yields the lowest error score with the lowest error attained at the third time period. What these results suggest is that not only is a three-cluster partition the most optimal but that over time, as the conflict among the novices escalated, the network became increasingly divided into three cohesive subgroups.

---

[7] It is not unusual for there to be several solutions that fit equally well. That, in fact, is the case with the Sampson data analyzed here. Pajek identified 3 three-partition solutions and 2 four-partition solutions each with only one forbidden tie. The two presented here make the most "visual" sense in our opinion.

9.3 Conflict and Cohesion: Sampson's Monks

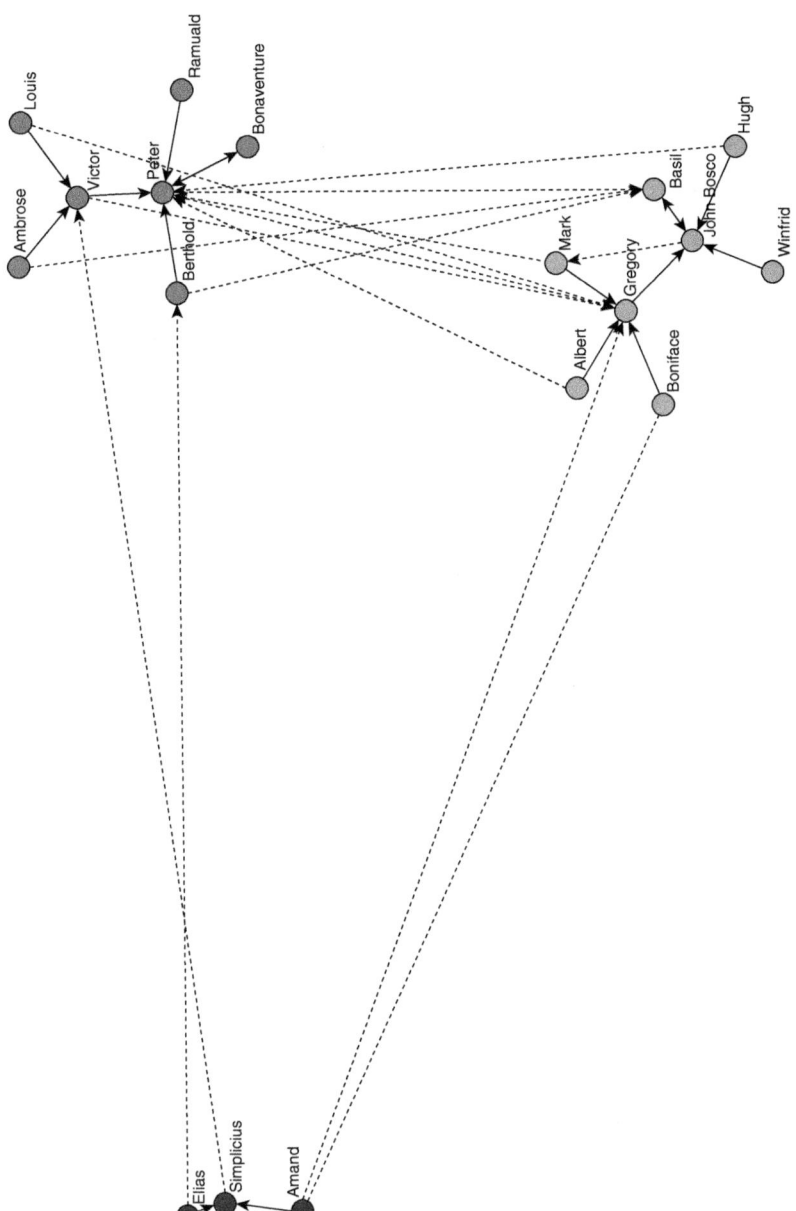

Figure 9.5 Sampson's novices, three clusters

268   Conflict and Cohesion

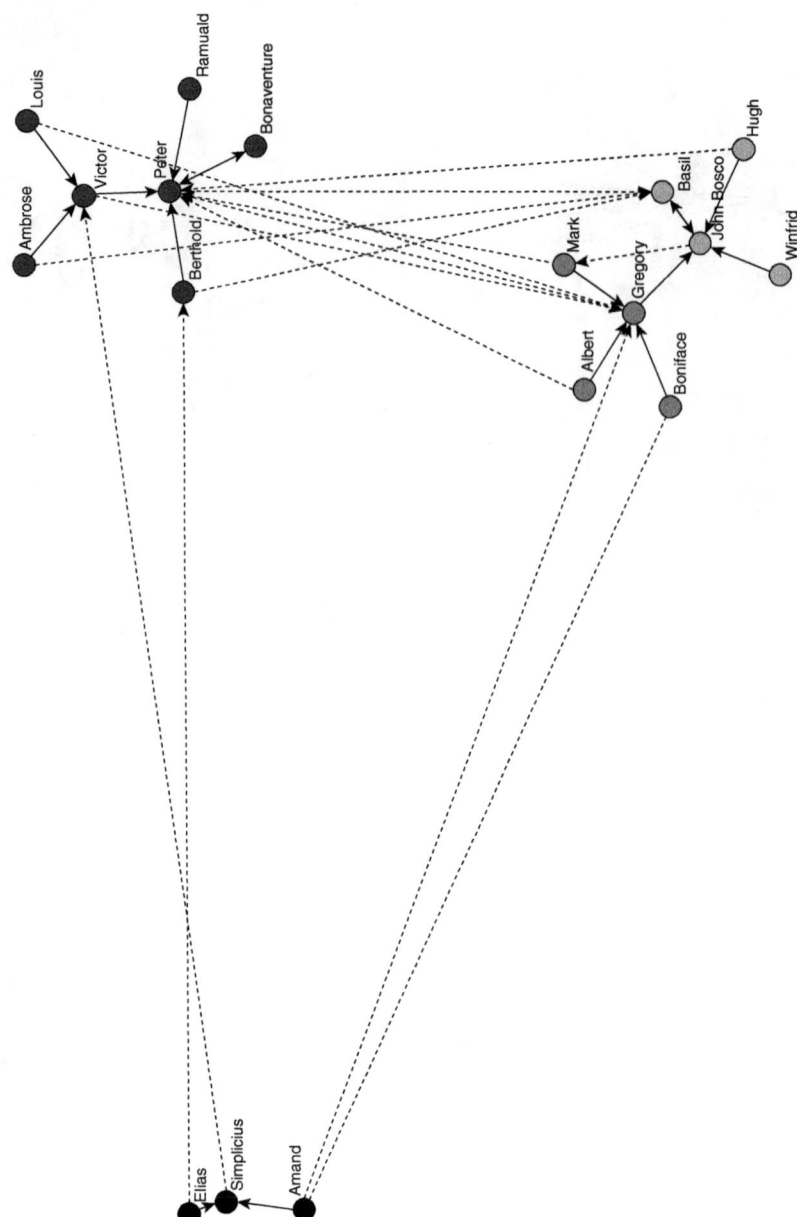

Figure 9.6 Sampson's novices, four clusters

9.4 Conflict and Creativity

Table 9.4 *Error score of the sampson network over time*

Number of clusters	Time Period		
	1	2	3
2	21.5	16.0	12.5
3	17.5	11.0	10.5
4	19.0	13.5	12.5
5	20.5	16.0	15.0

Source: From de Nooy, Mrvar, and Batagelj 2011:109

We now turn our attention to a more complex example: Randall Collins's (1998) philosophical networks. Collins mapped the positive and negative ties between philosophers in order to explore the dynamics of intellectual creativity and stagnation. It allows us to apply the Doreian-Mrvar approach to a more complex network. With larger networks it can be difficult to cleanly sort members into distinct subgroups. It is not unusual for intellectuals to have positive ties to two individuals who are at loggerheads with one another, or for three philosophers to consistently attack one another. In other words, in the philosophical world the intellectual enemy of one's friend is not necessarily an enemy, and the enemy of one's enemy is not necessarily a friend. Thus, we will employ two methods for partitioning the network into clusters: the Doreian-Mrvar method and a variation of the Louvain community detection algorithm (Blondel et al. 2008) designed for signed networks (Esmailian and Jalili 2015).

9.4 Conflict and Creativity: Collins's Philosophical Networks

In his magisterial *The Sociology of Philosophies*, Randall Collins (1998) delineates a theory as to why philosophical ideas emerge when and where they do. His basic argument is that ideas are not produced by lone intellectuals working in quiet isolation; rather they emerge through their interaction with numerous others, all of whom are competing for attention, recognition, and praise. Collins believes that we can trace all macro-level phenomena back to micro-situations,[8] in particular, to what he calls interaction rituals (Collins 2004). He argues that the "entire macro-social structure ... is anchored on ritual interactions. What we call structure is a shorthand way of describing repetitive patterns, encounters that people

---
[8] For Collins, the place to begin any analysis is at the micro level, what he calls the local situation. He is careful to note, however, that this is only the beginning, for the consequences of the local situation "extend outward through social networks to as macro a scale as one might wish" (Collins 1998:20).

keep coming back to, a recycling of rituals" (Collins 1998:28–29).[9] The term "interaction ritual" was first coined by Erving Goffman (1967), but Collins's use of it is heavily influenced by Emile Durkheim's (1965) analysis of religious rituals. In Collins's scheme, interaction rituals are constituted by a set of common "ingredients" (Collins 1998:22–23):

1. A group of at least two individuals must be physically co-present (i.e., face-to-face), and they must share a mutual focus of attention and a common emotion or mood.
2. This shared focus and mood "cumulatively intensifies," such that "bodily motions, speech acts, and vocal micro-frequencies become attuned into a shared rhythm" and participants become "temporarily united in a shared reality."
3. As a consequence, the individuals present begin to "feel that they are members of a group, with moral obligations to one another."
4. Participation in the ritual fills individuals with emotional energy, the level of which is positively associated with "the intensity of the interaction."

According to Collins, "lectures, discussions, conferences, and other real-time gatherings" (Collins 1998:25) function as philosophical interaction rituals. Such face-to-face rituals are important because they "focus members' attention on a common object and transient emotion, produce emotions of solidarity, [and] charge the participants with emotional energy" (Goodman 2001:94). Moreover, they give rise to distinct philosophical schools that inevitably come into conflict with one another. Consistent with Simmel and Coser, Collins sees such conflict in a positive light. He believes that not only does conflict lead to cohesion among philosophical schools, but it also begets creativity. "Intellectual life is first of all conflict and disagreement. Teaching may give the opposite impression, when initiates relate to novices what we claim to know; but the forefront where ideas are created has always been a discussion among oppositions" (Collins 1998:1).

Collins contends that during any period there will be upper and lower bounds to the number of philosophical schools that will be able to reproduce themselves across generations, a phenomenon that he calls the "law of small numbers":

> There is a strong lower limit; creativity can scarcely occur without rival positions, and almost always in any creative period there are at least three. There is also an upper limit; whenever there are

---

[9] In other words, Collins believes that "large and long-term social structures are built from interaction rituals that have been strung together over time" (Turner 2013:481).

9.4 Conflict and Creativity

more than about four to six distinct positions, most of them are not propagated across subsequent generations.

(Collins 1998:81)

When the number of philosophical schools becomes too large, the intellectual attention space becomes overcrowded, making it difficult for smaller schools to attract followers. In such situations, it is not uncommon for weaker schools to combine and synthesize their positions.[10] If they do not, they may disappear altogether. For example, although the number became quite large in Greece during the time of Plato, most disappeared "within a generation or two, leaving a structural limit of three to six" (Collins 1998:82).

All this interaction does not occur in a vacuum, however. Collins argues that intellectual creativity requires an organizational base, such as universities, publishers, churches, monasteries, patrons, and the like, which supply intellectuals with material resources. These organizations, in turn, are a function of the economic and political machinations of the day. That is why although intellectual creativity cannot be reduced to the surrounding social environment, political and economic changes can indirectly produce periods of intellectual creativity:

> Intellectual creativity is no mere reflex of economics and politics. There are three levels of causality: (1) economic-political structures, which in turn shape (2) the organizations which support intellectual life; and these in turn allow the buildup of (3) networks among participants in centers of attention on intellectual controversies, which constitute the idea-substance of intellectual life. Economic-political conditions determine ideas not directly but by way of shaping, and above all by changing, the intermediate level, the organizational base of intellectual production.
> (Collins 1998:324)

Nevertheless, Collins's primary focus is on micro-interactions between individuals, and in this book, he conceptualizes these in terms of social networks where the actors are individual philosophers and the ties between them indicate whether they were acquaintances, rivals, or master-pupil. Figure 9.7, for instance, presents the Islamic and Jewish

---

[10] "A person can pick a quarrel with someone else, contradicting what the other is saying. That will gain an audience of at least one; and if the argument is loud enough, it might attract a crowd. Now, suppose everyone is tempted to try it. Some arguments start first, or have a larger appeal because they contradict the positions held by several people; and if other persons happen to be on the same side of the argument, they gather around and provide support. There are first-mover advantages and bandwagon effects. The tribe of attention seekers, once scattered across the plain, is changed into a few knots of argument. The law of small numbers says that the number of these successful knots is always about three to six. The attention space is limited; once a few arguments have partitioned the crowds, attention is withdrawn from those who would start yet another knot of argument" (Collins 1998:38).

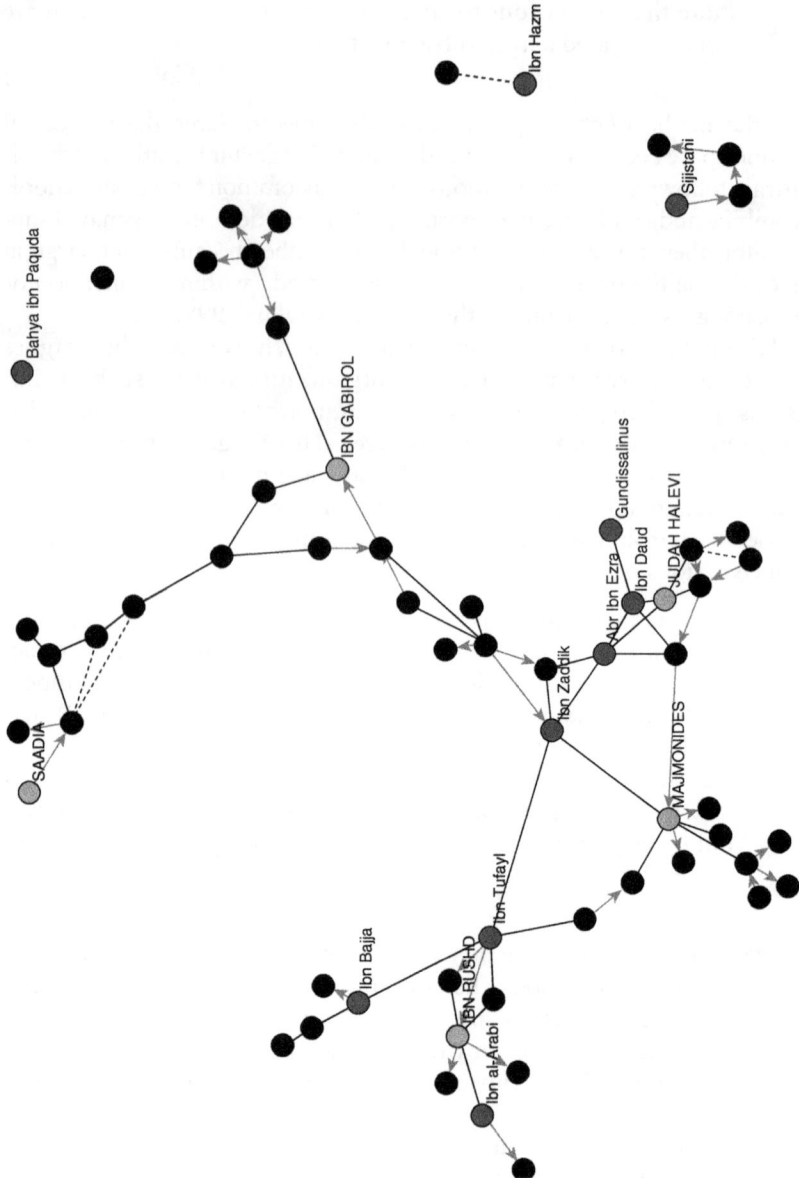

Figure 9.7 Islamic and Jewish philosophers, Spain, 900–1235 CE (redrawn from figures 8.4 and 8.5 in Collins 1998: 435, 438)

philosophical network in Spain from 900 to 1235 CE (adapted from figures 8.4 and 8.5 in Collins 1998:435, 438) where major philosophers (according to Collins) are colored black, secondary philosophers dark gray, and minor philosophers light gray, and master-pupil ties are indicated by arcs (i.e., arrows), acquaintances by edges (i.e., no arrows), and rivals by dashed lines. The names of the minor philosophers have been hidden. As one can see during this period of approximately 300 years, there were very few rivalries and most of the network is connected.

Collins argues that successful philosophers have more network ties to other philosophers than less successful philosophers do. They are also more likely to have ties to other successful philosophers, both "friends and foes" alike (Collins 2004:191). Not only do they tend to cluster into groups of like-minded thinkers, but they also are likely to engage in disputes with other philosophers. Successful philosophers also have ties across generations. They "have more pupils and grandpupils who are relatively successful than lesser philosophers do" (Collins 2004:190). Having students who become important thinkers helps secure a philosopher's reputation. "Greatness" is determined not just by an individual philosopher's ideas but by how those ideas are embraced by future generations, if at all. This leads to an interesting phenomenon: intellectual success not only "propagates forward but also backward" (Collins 2004:190):

> This last point seems counterintuitive; presumably the future cannot cause the past; what happens after one's death cannot determine what a thinker will do while he or she is alive. Here again we need to make a gestalt switch. The individual is not determining what the network does, but rather vice versa; it is the action of the network across generations that determines how much attention is paid to the ideas that are formulated at any particular point in it ... This is not an argument that canonical reputations are merely constructed, irrespective of what the merits of those ideas actually were; it is an argument that the merit of those ideas is not contained in themselves, in some platonic sphere outside of history, but is created by the entire network as it works with ideas that are constantly being decomposed and reintegrated in varying combinations.
> (Collins 2004:190–191)

If Collins is correct, then we should expect that successful philosophers will score higher in terms of various measures of centrality than less successful philosophers. This is indeed the case. As Table 9.5 indicates the average degree, closeness, betweenness, and eigenvector scores for the major philosophers are greater than those of the secondary and minor philosophers, and the average scores of the secondary philosophers are

Table 9.5 *Average normalized centrality scores by philosophical rank*

Philosophical Rank	Average Degree	Average Closeness	Average Betweenness	Average Eigenvector
Major	0.069	0.256	0.109	0.203
Secondary	0.046	0.195	0.100	0.196
Minor	0.034	0.195	0.040	0.081

greater than those of the minor philosophers.[11] In other words, Collins's thesis that major philosophers will, on average, be better connected than secondary and minor philosophers holds true.[12]

This chapter, of course, is more interested in the interplay of conflict and cohesion. Thus, for the remainder of this section we will explore how to identify clusters of philosophers active in medieval Europe. Here we will use the Doreian-Mrvar algorithm introduced in the previous section, along with the Louvain community detection algorithm designed for signed networks.

Medieval Christian Philosophers

In his book's ninth chapter, Collins traces the evolution of the philosophical networks of medieval Christendom, from 1000 CE to 1600 CE.[13] Collins analyzes the networks at time periods: 1000–1200, 1200–1335, 1335–1465, and 1465–1600. In the network graphs presented in this section, the three types of ties (master-pupil, acquaintance, and conflictual) were coded directly from Collins's figures (1998:464, 470, 489, 498) along with information on the minor philosophers included in one of Collins's appendices (Collins 1998:931–935, 936–940).[14] Known ties were assigned a value of "2," while probable ties were assigned a value of "1." A total of 280 philosophers appear in Collins's four figures.

---

[11] For the purposes of calculating centrality scores, all ties, including negative ties (i.e., rivalries), were assigned a value of "1." Ties were also symmetrized (e.g., master-pupil ties treated as reciprocal). Closeness centrality was estimated using average reciprocal distance (ARD), which better accounts for the infinite distances present in disconnected networks such as we have here (Borgatti 2006b; Cunningham, Everton, and Murphy 2016:151–152) and is now standard in UCINET (Borgatti, Everett, and Freeman 2002).

[12] Collins ranked the philosophers into major, secondary, and minor, based on how many pages they received in histories of philosophies, not in terms of their number of ties, so the centrality scores serve as independent confirmation of his initial rankings.

[13] Collins includes some non-philosophers as well, such as Dante, Fibonacci, Cosimo de Medici, and Chaucer. For simplicity purposes, we will simply refer to all actors in these networks as "philosophers."

[14] Thanks to Kevin McFeely for reviewing the coding and identifying errors. All remaining errors are mine.

9.4 Conflict and Creativity

Philosophers who were not in a cluster of size two or greater were then dropped,[15] leaving a total of 258: sixty-four from 1000–1200, eighty-seven from 1200–1335, fifty-seven from 1335–1465, and sixty-three from 1465–1600.[16] In Figures 9.8 through 9.11, two versions of each network are presented. In the top panel the philosophers are partitioned into clusters using the Doreian-Mrvar (1996) algorithm;[17] in the bottom panel, they are partitioned using the Louvain community detection algorithm,[18] both of which are implemented in Pajek (Batagelj and Mrvar 2017). Table 9.6 summarizes the results of these algorithms, and as it indicates, the number of clusters identified by the two algorithms differ substantially.

Collins begins by focusing on the networks from 1000 to 1200, which he considers the period when the "argumentative network" began to form (1998: 464). Figure 9.8 presents the network, where node color indicates cluster and the names of the minor philosophers have been hidden in order to make the network less cluttered and easier to read. In this network, the Doreian-Mrvar method identifies three, while the Louvain method identifies fourteen (see Table 9.6)![19] We can attribute some of the difference to how they partition philosophers who are located in different parts of the network graph. For instance, the Doreian-Mrvar algorithm assigns Roscelin and the two philosophers with whom he has a positive tie to the same cluster of Gilbert of Poitiers and Alan of Lille; by contrast, the Louvain algorithm assigns them to separate clusters. Another difference reflects how they handle pendants (i.e., actors who are connected by only one tie), especially those connected by negative ties. For example, the Doreian-Mrvar assigns St. Peter Damiani to the same cluster as Gilbert of Poitiers and Alan of Lille, although he does not share a tie with anyone in their cluster. In fact, Damiani's only tie to the group is a negative tie to

---

[15] The one exception was a cluster of size three where the ties among the three philosophers were all conflictual (negative) – this cluster was dropped as well. It consisted of three minor philosophers active around 1100 CE, one of which whose name is unknown.

[16] The total sums to more than 258 because some appear in two of Collins's network maps. For example, William of Ockham appears in both figure 9.4 and figure 9.6 of Collins's book because they overlap in dates (1335 CE).

[17] For each of the networks, partitions of numerous sizes were estimated in order to identify the one that yielded the best measure of fit – that is, the one that yielded the fewest "forbidden ties" or "inconsistencies." When two partitions of different size (i.e., they identified a different number of clusters) yielded the same measure of fit, the one that partitioned the network in the highest number of clusters was chosen because the Louvain algorithm consistently estimated a higher number of clusters than did the Doreian-Mrvar algorithm. When the latter produced multiple solutions for a single partition, then the solution with the highest modularity score was chosen.

[18] Community detection algorithms are probably the most popular method for identifying clusters within a network. See Appendix A.

[19] Most community detection algorithms assume that the partition (i.e., number of clusters) that yields the highest modularity score is the most optimal. See Appendix A for a discussion of modularity.

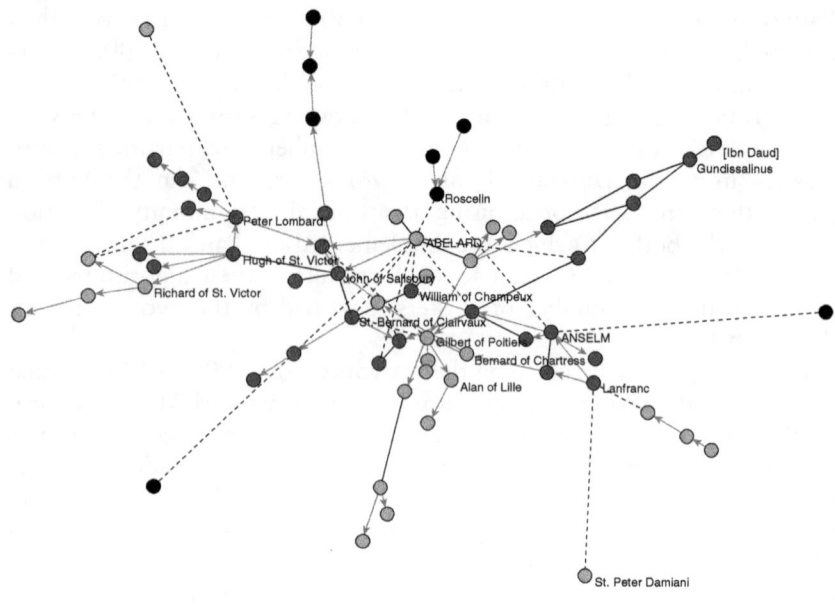

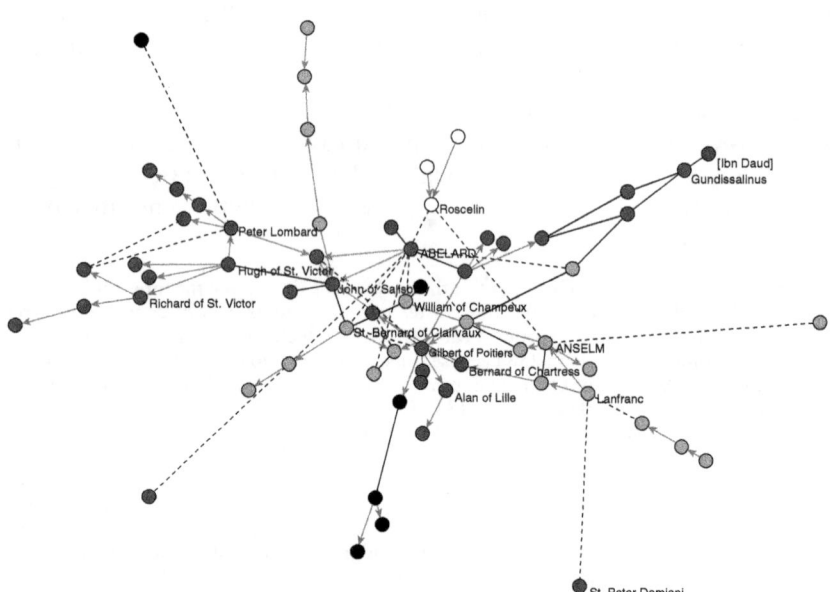

Figure 9.8 Medieval Christian philosophers, 1000–1200 (redrawn from figure 9.3 in Collins 1998:464)

9.4 Conflict and Creativity

Table 9.6 *Number of clusters identified by Doreian-Mrvar and Louvain algorithms*

	Time Period			
	1000–1200	1220–1335	1335–1465	1465–1600
Actors	64	87	57	68
Doreian-Mrvar				
Clusters	3	5	5	3
Inconsistencies	7.0	6.0	1.5	1.5
Modularity	0.387	0.380	0.496	0.481
Louvain				
Clusters	14	28	10	14
Inconsistencies	9.5	9.5	3.5	4.5
Modularity	0.403	0.394	0.480	0.423

Table 9.7 *Comparison of Louvain and Doreian-Mrvar clusters, 1000–1200*

	Doreian-Mrvar Clusters			
Louvain Clusters	Abelard	Anselm	Various	Total
Abelard	12			12
Anselm		13		13
John of Salisbury		11		11
Various	14	6	8	28
Total	26	30	8	64

Lanfranc, which is undoubtedly why the Louvain algorithm assigns him to his own individual cluster. In fact, it assigns five individuals to clusters of which they are the only member.

Of the nine remaining Louvain clusters, three are relatively large and of particular interest. One, which is located near the center of the network, consists of twelve individuals who are also assigned to the same cluster by the Doreian-Mrvar algorithm, including Abelard, Bernard of Chartres, Gilbert of Poitiers, and Alan of Lille (see Table 9.7). The other two consist of thirteen and eleven philosophers, who are sorted into the same cluster by Doreian-Mrvar (see Table 9.7). The first of these includes Anselm, Lanfranc, William of Champeux, and St. Bernard of Clairvaux, while the second includes Hugh of St. Victor, John of Salisbury, and Peter Lombard. The primary reason why Louvain separates these individuals and Doreian-Mrvar does not is due to when these philosophers were active. The first group was active early in this period, while the second was active later. The remaining six clusters identified by Louvain are relatively small (none containing more than five philosophers) and feature no major philosophers.

Collins emphasizes that during this time period, philosophers were primarily sorted into two camps: Abelard's and St. Bernard of Clairvaux's, and both algorithms capture this division (Clairvaux is clustered with Anselm). According to Collins, they "were rival organizers of the social structure taking place at the time" (Collins 1998:466). Collins does argue that a third camp formed around Bernard of Chartres, but both algorithms group him with Clairvaux and Anselm. Collins also suggests that late in this period two additional clusters formed that influenced later generations: one centered around John of Salisbury and another around Peter Lombard. Interestingly, both the Doreian-Mrvar and Louvain algorithms sort them into the same cluster. In short, we can tentatively conclude that there were three, maybe four, major philosophical clusters active during this time period, along with a handful of smaller clusters that struggled to attract the attention of their contemporaries.

Collins notes that during the late twelfth century, philosophical creativity began to fade and give way to method. "Abelard's most successful pupil was Peter Lombard, not an original thinker but the compiler of *Sentences*, a book of opinions on disputed questions," which became the most successful textbook of the time. In fact, the "predominant mode of composition came to be the practice of writing a commentary on Lombard's *Sentences*" (Collins 1998:467). It was also a time when Arab and ancient Greek texts were imported into Europe, and according to Collins, the "temporary downturn in indigenous creativity is typical of what happens during a generation of importers" (Collins 1998:468).

Collins argues that intellectual creativity took off again after 1200. That is certainly the sense one gets from Figure 9.9, which presents the network of philosophers from 1200 to 1335. One does not have to be a social network analyst in order to see that the intellectual attention space was quite crowded during this time period. Eighty-seven philosophers were active, compared to sixty-four in the previous period. Of these, the Doreian-Mrvar algorithm identifies five clusters, while the Louvain algorithm identifies twenty-eight (see Table 9.8). The high number identified by Louvain is a bit misleading, however, since seventeen of them consist of a single philosopher, and several include only two or three. In fact, only six clusters contain five or more, and only five contain nine or more. Of these, one is centered around Albert Magnus and includes other notable philosophers such as Meister Eckhart and St. Dominic. Another is dominated by Roger Bacon and includes the secondary philosophers Grosseteste, William of Auvergne, and Peter of Spain. A third features Bonaventure and includes a number of secondary philosophers such as Peckham, Matthew of Aquasparta, and Peter John Olivi. A fourth is centered around Thomas Aquinas and includes other notables such as Giles of

9.4 Conflict and Creativity 279

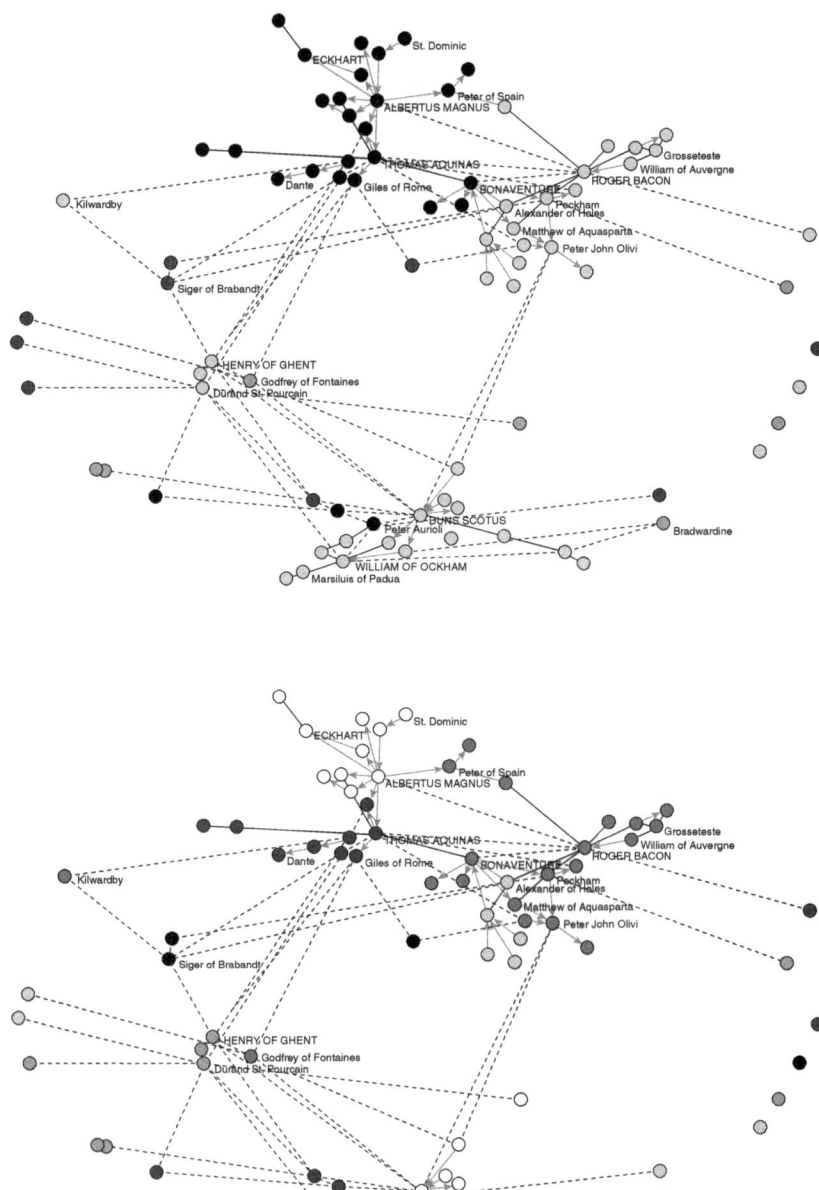

Figure 9.9 Medieval Christian philosophers, 1200–1335 (redrawn from figure 9.4 in Collins 1998:470)

Table 9.8 *Comparison of Louvain and Doreian-Mrvar clusters, 1200–1335*

Louvain Clusters	Doreian-Mrvar Clusters				Total
	Roger Bacon	Thomas Aquinas	Duns Scotus	Various	
Albert Magnus		10			10
Roger Bacon	7	2			9
Bonaventure	6	3			9
Thomas Aquinas		12			12
Duns Scotus			13		13
Various	10	5	5	16	36
Total	23	30	18	16	87

Rome and Dante. Finally, a fifth features Duns Scotus and William of Ockham; however, it includes no other major philosophers and only one secondary philosopher: Marsiluis of Padua.

The philosophers sorted into these five Louvain clusters are distributed across only three clusters according to the Doreian-Mrvar algorithm (see Table 9.8). In fact, Doreian-Mrvar partitions Albert Magnus, Meister Eckhart, Bonaventure, and Thomas Aquinas into the same cluster. The clustering together of Magnus, Eckhart, and Aquinas together is not too surprising since all were Dominicans, Magnus was one of Aquinas's teachers, and students of both Magnus and Aquinas were teachers of Eckhart. Collins (1998:485) does note, however, that Eckhart created a little separation from other Dominicans with his emphasis on mysticism, which was in part a reaction to the attacks of Duns Scotus. Grouping Bonaventure with these three is somewhat surprising since Bonaventure was a Franciscan, and the Franciscans and Dominicans were bitter rivals during this time.[20] However, Bonaventure and Aquinas were acquaintances, and both shared negative ties with Bacon, a classic case of the enemy of my enemy is my friend.

It seems reasonable to separate Bonaventure from Magnus and Aquinas. Bacon was a nominal Franciscan and apparently enjoyed attacking the positions of all of his contemporaries, which is undoubtedly why both algorithms sorted him into a cluster separate from Magnus, Bonaventure, and Aquinas. Finally, both algorithms cluster Duns Scotus and William of Ockham together into their separate cluster. Both were Franciscans, and the Franciscans groomed Scotus to lead the attack against the Dominicans, but he did so by not only attacking Aquinas but also Bonaventure (Collins 1998:481–482). Ockham, however, sought to

---

[20] For example, the Franciscans forbade the teaching of Aquinas.

9.4 Conflict and Creativity

distance himself from Scotus; he "lumped [him] with his predecessors and antagonists – Aquinas, Bonaventure, and all the rest – into what became known as the 'via antiqua.' Ockham, by contrast, exemplifies the 'via moderna'" (Collins 1998:485). Nevertheless, according to Collins's mapping of the network (1998:470), Ockham never directly attacked Scotus, and at least two of his teachers were students of Scotus. Thus, it is not surprising that the algorithms clustered them together. In sum, the period between 1200 and 1335 appears to have been an extremely creative one. Franciscans and Dominicans were rivals, the former led by Bonaventure, Scotus, and Ockham, while the latter was dominated by Aquinas and to a lesser extent, Eckhart. Thus, it appears that there were four to five schools of thought that dominated the intellectual marketplace during this time, along with numerous others who sought, unsuccessfully, to attract attention.

Figure 9.10 presents the network of medieval Christian philosophers from 1335 to 1465, and the comparison of the results of the clustering algorithms are presented in Table 9.9. During this time period, the number of active philosophers falls to fifty-seven, suggesting that this may have been a time when creativity declined. Collins, in fact, considers it a time of intellectual stagnation. The network map leaves one with the impression that it was a time of factional consolidation. There are five distinct factions of philosophers disconnected from one another (in terms of positive ties). Located at the top of the network is a cluster of philosophers who were active at Merton College in Oxford and centered around Bradwardine. The cluster on the left of the graph that features Meister Eckhart and Thomas à Kempis is a network of mystics that gained prominence during this time, while at the bottom is a cluster of philosophers that were active in Paris. On the far right is the network of some of the first humanists, funded in large part by Cosimo di Medici, who would help give birth to the Italian Renaissance. Finally, located in the center is the network of nominalists centered on William of Ockham. Both algorithms subdivide some of these factions into separate clusters, suggesting that during this time period somewhere between five and seven schools of thought were active.[21]

What leads to intellectual stagnation? Collins identifies three types or causes: loss of cultural capital, dominance of the classics, and technical refinement. The first occurs when ideas are simply forgotten by intellectuals.

> Aristotle's doctrine was lost for several centuries after his death; the achievements of Stoic logic were forgotten by late antiquity, Mergarian logic even sooner. In India after the 1600s, the acute

---

[21] The Louvain algorithm detected ten clusters with only six having more than five philosophers, while the Doreian-Mrvar algorithm detected five clusters.

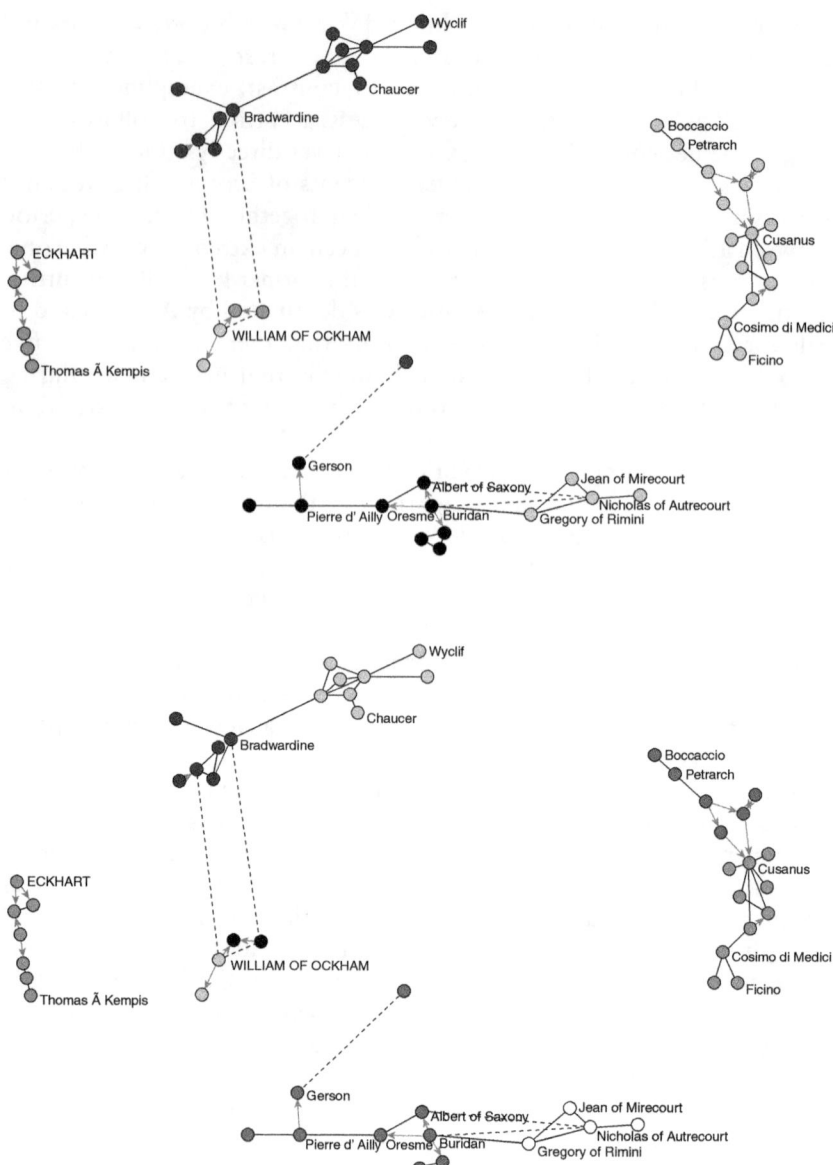

Figure 9.10 Medieval Christian philosophers, 1335–1465 (redrawn from figure 9.6 in Collins 1998:489)

metaphysics of the previous periods was swallowed up in a simplified Advaita Vedanta. In China the sophisticated positions of the late Warring States period ... were largely eclipsed by the religious Confucianism of the Han dynasty ... The loss of

Table 9.9 *Comparison of Louvain and Doreian-Mrvar clusters, 1335–1465*

Louvain Clusters	Doreian-Mrvar Clusters					Total
	Eckhart	Chaucer	Buridan	Petrarch	Various	
Eckhart	7					7
Chaucer		8				8
Buridan			9			9
Petrarch				8		8
Cusanus				10		10
Various	2	7			6	15
Total	9	15	9	18	6	57

ideas makes us think of a Dark Age, brought about by destruction of material conditions of civilization, such as the decline of Rome in the West. But these examples show that idea loss can also happen during prosperous periods of high civilizations; indeed, the loss of Greek culture had started in Rome long before the barbarian conquests.

(Collins 1998:502)

The second cause is the opposite of the first. It "occurs when the ideas of the greatest thinkers overshadow those of their successors." Although there is no new creativity, it is not a period of low culture; "one might say that it stays at the peak: the ideas that are taught and circulated are the best yet achieved" (Collins 1998:503). Collins notes that the third cause, technical refinement, may not be intellectual stagnation at all but only appears as such and is characterized by increasing levels of abstraction, when a field gets too technical, too refined. This was certainly a charge leveled by the humanists at Duns Scotus, who "were particularly put out by Duns's style, both his neologisms in metaphysics ... and the long tortuous sentences with clause after clause of careful qualifications" (Collins 1998:503). Collins notes that technical refinement often leads to alienation; thus, one might argue that indirectly Scotus and his followers helped give birth to the Renaissance as well. Collins ultimately concludes that the stagnation of the late fourteenth century was due primarily to the dominance of the classics. He argues that Aquinas and Scotus simply "towered over constructive philosophy, as did Ockham on the critical side" and "enshrined an extremely high level of creativity" (Collins 1998:503).

The period from 1465 to 1600 sees a slight increase in the number of philosophers to sixty-three. The Louvain algorithm identifies fourteen clusters (but only six containing more than five), while the Doreian-Mrvar

Table 9.10 *Comparison of Louvain and Doreian-Mrvar clusters, 1465–1600*

Louvain Clusters	Doreian-Mrvar Clusters			Total
	Erasmus	Luther	Calvin	
Erasmus	9			9
Luther		6		6
Bricot (minor)			8	8
Pomponazzi		7		7
Paracelsus	8			8
Calvin			9	9
Minor	6	6	4	16
Total	23	19	21	63

algorithm identifies only three (see Table 9.10). The network appears to have broken into numerous factions, some following in the footsteps of the humanists and mystics, others carrying on the traditions of the Aquinas, Scotus, and Ockham. This, of course, was the time of the Protestant Reformation, which explains the prominence of Luther and Calvin, as well as Erasmus, who called for reform of the Roman Catholic Church but disagreed with Luther on a number of counts and remained a Catholic his entire life. Collins (1998:501) considers this period unfocused and scattered:

> The scholastics were stalled in their factionalism; the mystics had largely abandoned abstract discourse; the Humanists were engrossed in reviving the classic texts of antiquity ... Universities, once centered in France and England, now proliferated, especially in Germany. The most sustained network of successful Humanists were the religious politicians who constituted the intellectual core of the Reformation ... But the Reformation was radically decentralizing and these networks, marginally philosophical at best, lead no further in abstract philosophy.
>
> (Collins 1998:500)

Figure 9.11 certainly seems to reflect this dynamic. There does not appear to be a coherent core to network. As unstable as intellectual life appears to have been, it was about to give birth to modern science.

Summary

If we ignore the various isolated individuals and small groups that failed to attract a following, then Collins's law of small numbers appears to hold.

9.4 *Conflict and Creativity* 285

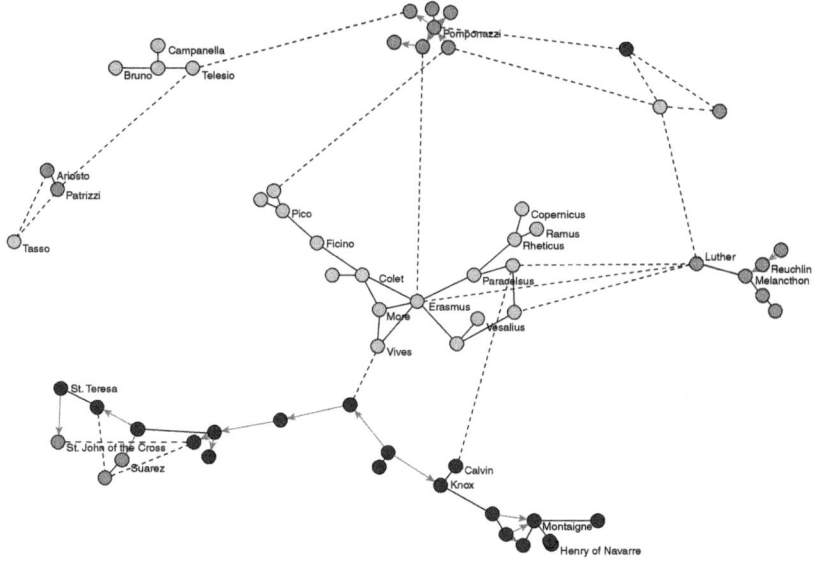

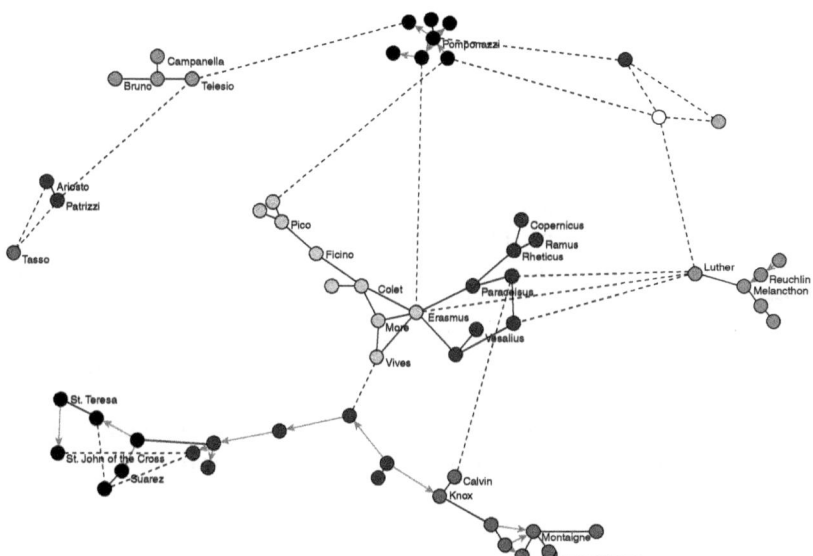

Figure 9.11 Medieval Christian philosophers, 1465–1600 (redrawn from figure 9.7 in Collins 1998:498)

In any single time period, the number of large clusters of philosophers never exceeds six. Perhaps more interesting, is that Collins's method for analyzing philosophical networks could be adapted by those who draw on the insights offered by the concept of religious economies. Recall from the first chapter that this approach argues that, when free to do so, religious groups will target unfilled niches in the religious market. As Collins's analysis suggests, however, such targeting will generally occur both in alignment with and opposition toward other competitors, including secular ones. This suggests that religious markets could be mapped as networks, which could offer insights into previously unexplained dynamics. In fact, one might be tempted to argue that religious markets emerge from religious networks, not the other way around (White 2001). It is unclear at this point whether such an analysis would focus on local congregations, denominational affiliation, broader classifications such as evangelical Protestant, Roman Catholic, black Protestant, etc. (see, e.g., Steensland et al. 2000), some hybrid of the three, or something else. Analyses could focus on local or national markets, although a comparison of local markets strikes me as probably more fruitful. Collins's analysis also suggests that there is probably a lower and upper limit to the number of clusters of congregations active in any religious market. When the number approaches the lower bound, new clusters will emerge in opposition to the currently dominant ones, and when the number exceeds the upper bound, the weaker clusters will either consolidate or fail, while the stronger ones will maintain their position.

9.5 Summary and Conclusion

Conflict is often viewed in a negative light, but it can have positive effects, such as promoting group cohesion and generating intellectual creativity. This was certainly the case with Sampson's novices and Collins's philosophers. Conflict sorted the novices and philosophers into distinct groups, although the saga of Sampson's novices did not end well. Cohesion can lead to conflict as well. As we saw with Zablocki's study of communes, too much cohesion, too much "love," increased the likelihood that the groups would disband. In the next chapter, we will see that too much cohesion may also increase the likelihood that a group will radicalize and possibly commit violence.

9.6 For Further Reading

A handful of papers have been published using Zablocki's Urban Communes data (see, e.g., Martin 2002; Martin 2005; Yeung 2005;

9.6 For Further Reading

Vaisey 2007; Martin, Gunten, and Zablocki 2012), but the primary source remains Zablocki's *Alienation and Charisma*, which was published in 1980. The dataset can be acquired from John Levi Martin's website at the University of Chicago,[22] and a helpful description of the data is presented in an article co-authored by Martin, King-To Yeung, and Zablocki (2002).

For learning how to use balance theory to identify clusters in signed networks, there is no better place to start than Wouter de Nooy, Andrej Mrvar, and Vladimir Batagelj's book *Exploratory Social Network with Pajek*. Chapter 4 ("Sentiments and Friendship") presents an accessible introduction to balance theory along with examples as to how to use Pajek to identify clusters with signed graphs. Patrick Doreian, Vladimir Batagelj, and Anuska Ferligoj (2005) also explore it in chapter 10 ("Balance Theory and Blockmodeling Signed Networks") in their book *Generalized Blockmodeling*. You can, of course, read the original article by Doreian and Mrvar (1996) and some of its extensions (see, e.g., Doreian and Mrvar 2009; Mrvar and Doreian 2009).

---

[22] http://home.uchicago.edu/~jlmartin/UCDS/UCDS/index.htm

10

Radicalization and Violence

10.1 Introduction

In August 1997, approximately 150 members of the Chen Tao movement arrived in Garland, Texas, announcing that a flying saucer would soon land in Garland and God would be aboard. This occurred not too long after the highly publicized murder/suicides of two other religious groups: the Order of the Solar Temple and Heaven's Gate (Balch 1980; Introvigne 1995; Hall, Schuyler, and Trinh 2000; Balch and Taylor 2002; Bogdan 2011; Zeller 2011). So the Garland Police Department was concerned and determined to prevent a similar event from happening on its turf. It first "mobilized its resources, tasked a group of officers with planning strategy and communicating with the members, and took the lead role in coordinating the various branches of local government that the group's presence might impact" (Szubin, Jensen, and Gregg 2000:21). It also assessed the threat the group potentially posed by researching the group's history and by consulting with experts on independent religious movements (also known as new religious movements), such as Lonnie Kliever from Southern Methodist University. Perhaps most important, the department created an ongoing dialogue with members of the group, as well as with the local community, which was unsettled by the group's presence, and the media (Szubin, Jensen, and Gregg 2000:22). Kliever (1999) credits these efforts for preventing the group from resorting to violence or suicide after God did not appear as expected. As Miriam Goldman later noted:

> Police and popular media in Garland, Texas, developed an ongoing dialogue with Chen Tao representatives that facilitated the group's calm departure after their prophecy failed. [They] avoided violence because they cultivated external social networks and diminished social isolation.
>
> (Goldman 2011:313)

10.1 Introduction

Goldman is probably correct that the ties the Garland Police Department formed with Chen Tao leaders may have prevented a violent reaction by the group after God failed to arrive. There is increasing evidence that relatively dense and isolated groups are more likely to embrace radical beliefs and engage in violent behavior than those that are not (della Porta 2013; Everton 2016). And in this chapter, drawing upon Cass Sunstein's (2002, 2003, 2009) "law of group polarization," we explore how certain types of interaction patterns can facilitate the rise of radical beliefs and, on occasion, violent behavior. The analysis shares commonalities with other works that approach radicalization from a relational perspective (see e.g., Tilly 2005a; Brym and Araj 2006; Alimi 2011; della Porta 2013). The chapter begins with a brief summary of Sunstein's law of group polarization, which it then reframes in terms of social networks. It begins with a relatively simple model that is then expanded to identify the relevant social network processes at work, as well as various factors, including religious ones, that affect these processes. The chapter then considers three qualitative case studies – Peoples Temple, the Armed Islamic Group of Algeria (GIA), and the Branch Davidians – that function as a preliminary test of the argument. It then turns to a formal statistical analysis of the model, using network data of sixteenth-century Anabaptist leaders, some of whom participated in the Münster Rebellion, which was one of the most violent episodes of the Protestant Reformation. It concludes with a few reflections on the possible policy implications of the theory outlined in this chapter.

Before proceeding, an important caveat is in order: although the study of religious violence has become popular among academics since the 9/11 terrorist attacks (Juergensmeyer 2001; Stern 2003), the threat is almost certainly exaggerated (Levitt and Dubner 2015; Sageman 2017). Most religious groups, even those who hold extreme beliefs, tend to avoid violence when possible (see, e.g., Kurzman 2011). The Amish are an obvious example, but there are others, such as the Hasidim, Sufis, Jains, and most Buddhists. In fact, violence is quite rare (Collins 2008) and, in spite of rhetoric to the contrary, appears to be in decline (see, e.g., Roth 2001, 2009; Eisner 2003; Lacina and Gleditsch 2005; Pinker 2011). Moreover, nonreligious groups can be just as violent as religious ones, with Sri Lanka's LTTE (Liberation Tigers of Tamil Elam), Colombia's FARC (*Fuerzas Armadas Revolucionarias de Colombia* – Revolutionary Armed Forces of Colombia), and Turkey's PKK (*Partiya Karkerên Kurdistan* – Kurdish Worker's Party) serving as examples. Nevertheless, it is true that some religious groups are violent, and this chapter explores religious violence from a social network perspective.

10.2 Group Polarization and Religious Radicalization[1]

Cass Sunstein's (2002, 2003, 2009) "law of group polarization" holds that when like-minded individuals deliberate as a group, the group's opinion will move toward the extreme versions of its collective belief. It is similar to the echo-chamber effect, except that rather than simply holding that ideas and beliefs can become amplified when a group meets regularly with little exposure to competing views, it contends that the beliefs of a group will gravitate to the views of its most extreme members.[2]

> In a product-liability trial, for instance, if nine jurors believe the manufacturer is somewhat guilty and three believe it is entirely guilty, the latter will draw the former toward a larger award than the nine would allow on their own. Or, if people who object in varying degrees to the war in Iraq convene to debate methods of protest, all will emerge from the discussion more resolved against the war.
>
> (Bauerlein 2004)

The term "group polarization" can be misleading. It does not mean that group members move to opposite poles on an issue, but rather that they collectively shift to a more polarizing view. "The effect of deliberation is both to decrease variance among group members, as individual differences diminish, and also to produce convergence on a relatively more extreme point among predeliberation judgments" (Sunstein 2002:178).

Social Networks and Group Polarization[3]

Sunstein's law implies that groups that distance themselves from the wider society and engage in intense social interaction are more likely to become polarized. Reframed in terms of social network analysis, this suggests that groups are more likely to radicalize if they become increasingly dense and more isolated, a process that social network scholars sometimes refer to as network closure, which we briefly considered in Chapter 8. Figure 10.1 presents a simple model of group polarization (i.e., radicalization). Although there are numerous factors that undoubtedly affect network closure, here two are highlighted: (1) coercion (social and political) and (2) sociocultural tension. The former refers to the degree that the political

---

[1] Earlier versions of the argument that appears in this section appeared in Cunningham, Everton, and Murphy (2016) and Everton (2016).
[2] It is also similar to the "risky-shift" effect, which is the tendency for people to make more daring decisions when they are in groups, than when they are alone (Stoner 1961), as well as Stark and Bainbridge's (1979a, 1987) notion of social implosion. Thanks to Larry Iannaccone, David Elliot, and an anonymous reviewer for pointing out these similarities.
[3] The theory presented in this chapter is adapted from Everton (2016).

10.2 Group Polarization and Religious Radicalization

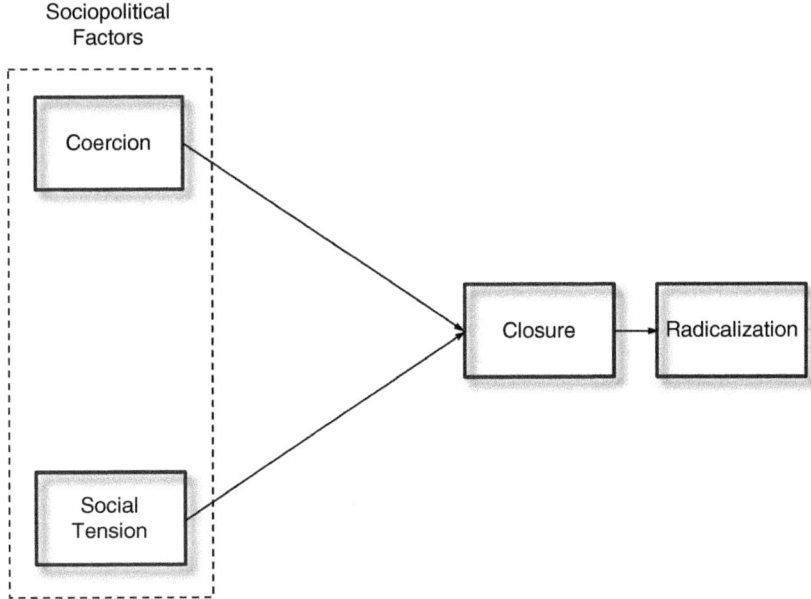

Figure 10.1 A simple model of group radicalization

or social environment restricts the ability of groups to meet and deliberate. This can occur through governmental regulations, such as how governments sometimes limit the ability of religious groups to meet, or social sanctions, such as when a society's citizens try to prevent some groups from meeting (Grim and Finke 2010). Sociocultural tension, which we explored in Chapter 7, refers to the extent that a group's beliefs and practices deviate from accepted cultural norms (Stark and Bainbridge 1985). Figure 10.1 posits that the higher the level of coercion and/or sociocultural tension there is, the greater the likelihood that groups will distance themselves from government authorities and society at large. To be sure, coercion and sociocultural tension can go hand-in-hand; high-tension groups often experience government and/or social coercion. They are not, however, the same. Coercion is a society-wide phenomenon, and sociocultural tension is the relation between specific groups and the larger society. That is why we would expect high-tension groups, such as the Amish, to exhibit more network closure in societies where coercion is high than in societies where it is low.

The model outlined in Figure 10.1 treats network closure as a black box and does not identify the specific social network mechanisms by which closure occurs. Figure 10.2 adds these mechanisms to the model: (1) recruitment through strong (i.e., trusted) ties, (2) limiting or severing ties to nonmembers, and (3) increased interaction among existing members.

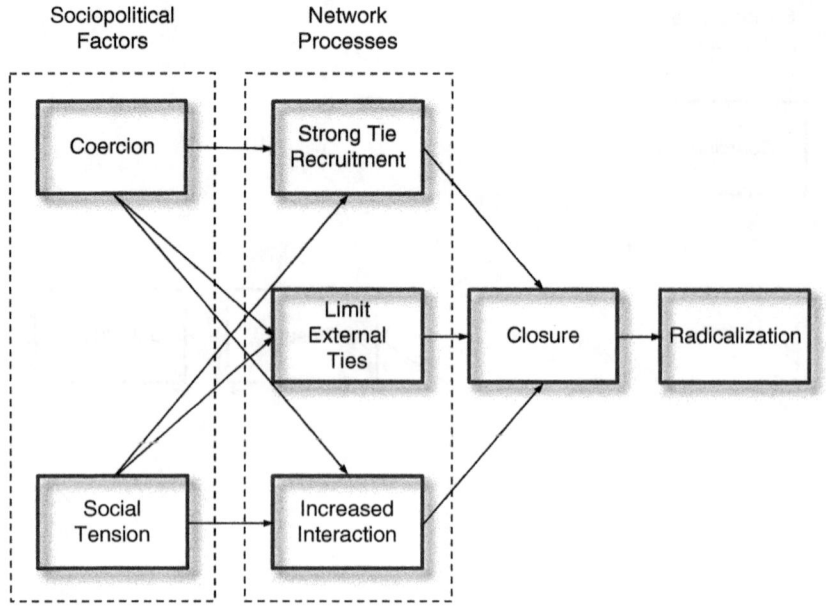

Figure 10.2 Social networks and group radicalization

The first builds on the tendency of groups to recruit new members through social ties (see Chapter 3) and argues that groups seeking to distance themselves from the larger society tend to recruit primarily through ties of trust (i.e., strong ties) (Passy 2003), especially when a group's survival is at stake. Indeed, careless recruitment can lead to one's undoing, as the case of Ramzi Yousef, one of the 1993 World Trade Center bombers, illustrates (see Sageman 2004:109–110). Yousef attempted to enlist Ishtiaque Parker, a South African student whom Yousef met through his brother-in-law. At first, Yousef told Parker little, but eventually he disclosed his involvement in the World Trade Center bombing. Yousef first convinced Parker to transport a bag overseas and later sent him to an airport with explosive-packed suitcases with instructions to place them on a US carrier. Parker chose not to go through with the plan and lied that airport security was too tight. In response, Yousef told Parker that Philippine authorities had confiscated Yousef's computer, which had Parker's name in it. This frightened Parker, so when Yousef asked him to take a small package to a Shiite mosque, Parker called the US Embassy. This led to Yousef's arrest and extradition to the United States, where he is now serving two life sentences.

Recruiting primarily through strong ties increases network closure because it becomes more likely that ties will form between previously unlinked actors, a process known as triadic closure, which is illustrated

10.2 Group Polarization and Religious Radicalization

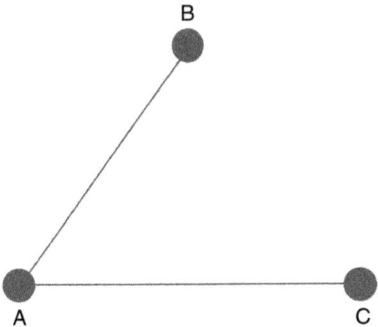

Figure 10.3 Granovetter's forbidden triad

by Mark Granovetter's "forbidden triad" (Figure 10.3). Granovetter (1973) argued that this triad would not exist for long because if actor A has strong ties to both actors B and C, eventually B and C will meet and a tie will form (Rapoport 1953a, 1953b; Rapoport and Horvath 1961; Holland and Leinhardt 1976). The tie could be weak or strong, but a tie will form nonetheless.

Groups seeking to put some distance between themselves and the wider society also tend to limit their ties with outsiders. Doing so limits the exposure of group members to competing views, which can benefit clandestine groups. As Donna della Porta (2013:258) notes: "Underground organizations in fact required total commitment, often including the renunciation of external ties. As clandestinity drastically reduced external contacts, isolation from external channels of information strengthened commitment."

Finally, independent of the first two factors, increased interaction contributes to network closure because it limits the opportunity for members to interact with outsiders.

Religion, Social Networks, and Group Polarization

Religion's role in the group polarization process is reflected in Figure 10.4, which indicates that certain types of beliefs can either indirectly or directly affect the degree of network closure or feed extremist beliefs about the surrounding world. As discussed previously, "social groups know who they are in large measure by knowing who is in and who is not. Ingroups establish what it means to be 'in' primarily by contrasting with outgroups whose members are 'out'" (Smith et al. 1998:91). And religious groups, especially those with theologically distinct beliefs, tend to excel at drawing boundaries between insiders and outsiders, which typically increases the tension between groups and their sociocultural environment (Stark and Bainbridge 1985). We have also seen that theologically distinct groups

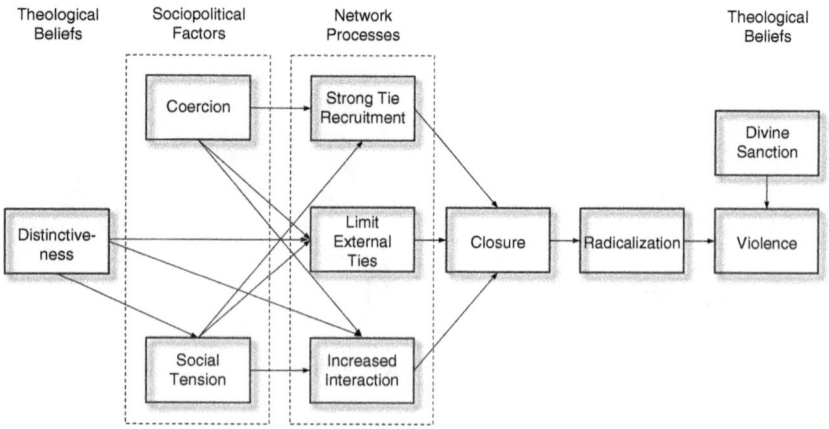

Figure 10.4 Religion, social networks, and group radicalization

place considerable demands on their adherents in terms of finances, time, what they can wear, where they can go, who they can marry, and what they can enjoy (Iannaccone 1994b). Such demands tend to reduce their ties with outsiders, not only because they are encouraged to socialize with other members, but also because these demands limit the time that members have to form and maintain ties with nonmembers.

Finally, it is far more likely for group radicalization to manifest itself violently if groups believe that the use of violence is divinely sanctioned. This often occurs in tandem with apocalyptic beliefs that hold that the final confrontation between good and evil, and that the end of the world will occur soon.[4] As Mark Juergensmeyer (2001) noted, religions resort to violence when they believe they are in the midst of a cosmic war between good and evil. It is also not uncommon for apocalyptic groups to believe in the redemptive power of violence – that is, the belief that destruction can hasten the arrival of a new divine age (Wink 1992). Such beliefs can feed what Mohammed Hafez (2003, 2004) calls anti-system frames, which see state and society (i.e., the system) as beyond redemption and therefore in need of annihilation. As Figure 10.5 indicates, apocalyptic beliefs play an independent role in the model. They increase the likelihood that radicalization will devolve into violence. This does not mean that most apocalyptic groups are violent. All it suggests is that the presence of apocalyptic beliefs increases the likelihood a group will embrace violence.

[4] The Islamic State of Iraq and Syria (ISIS), for example, believes that violence against infidels is justified because Islam is under attack; however, they also want to control the town of Dabiq, which according to some Islamic traditions is where the apocalypse will occur, where Muslim and Christian armies will face off with the former emerging victorious (Fraser 2014). Dabiq is also the name of ISIS's online magazine (Wikipedia 2016a).

10.3 Peoples Temple, the Armed Islamic Group, and the Branch Davidians

We now consider three case studies that explore how network closure affects the radicalization process. It begins with Jim Jones's Peoples Temple, and then turns its attention to the Armed Islamic Group of Algeria (GIA), and the Branch Davidians.

Peoples Temple

The Rev. Jim Jones founded Peoples Temple in the 1950s in Indianapolis, Indiana. Although Jones always considered himself a communist and later claimed to be an atheist, he saw the church as a vehicle through which he could implement his vision of an interracial, egalitarian community.[5] Indeed, he asked wealthier members to attend worship in casual clothes so poorer members would not feel out of place, and the church provided shelter for the needy, offered rent assistance, and opened a soup kitchen that at one time served thousands of meals per month (Hall 1987:52). Although he affiliated his church with the mainline Protestant denomination, the Christian Church (Disciples of Christ), Jones adopted the trappings of Pentecostalism, such as performing miracles, conducting faith healings, and prophesying. Interestingly, there is some evidence that Jones believed he possessed what Pentecostals refer to as "gifts of the spirit" (Hall 1987:19, 21), and members of his congregation believed he possessed the gift of healing (Hall 1987:20–22). Moreover, he appears to have considered himself a Christ-figure (Hall 1987:30), and his messianic outlook probably fueled his vision of creating a promised land, a place to where he and his people could escape and live free.

In the mid-1960s Jones moved the church to California because he claimed to have had a vision of a nuclear holocaust in which Indianapolis would be destroyed. In all likelihood, he was simply looking for a reason to move to a more welcoming climate. The group's interracial worship services attracted the hostility of a large part of the Indianapolis population that opposed racial mixing, and this fueled his desire to relocate the church in a friendlier sociocultural climate. The group initially settled in Ukiah, but as it grew it relocated its headquarters to San Francisco and opened congregations in Los Angeles, San Francisco, and several other California towns. It even maintained a branch and

---

[5] Although Jones claims to have been an atheist, many of the people who joined Peoples Temple were not. Moreover, Jones was sometimes ambivalent about whether he was or not an atheist. "Jones himself occasionally allowed that he was an atheist, but the self-proclaimed messiah also admitted ... that he acted ... under 'a sort of dual concept – a doubter and yet a believer'" (Hall 1987:38).

dormitory at Santa Rosa Junior College (Hall 1987:90). The Temple regularly used bus caravans to transport members throughout California to recruit and fund raise, and in the 1970s, it began sending members across the United States, including some to Washington, DC. It also raised money through direct-mail, selling photos of Jones, pieces of his robes, healing oil, lockets, key chains, and so on, and selling records of its youth choir and orchestra.

The Temple became more politically active after relocating to San Francisco. For instance, it helped mobilize volunteers and voters on behalf of George Moscone's successful 1975 mayoral campaign, and as a reward, Moscone appointed Jones as Chair of the San Francisco Housing Authority Commission, a position from which he led a fight against the eviction of tenants from San Francisco's I-Hotel. Jones's left-leaning political activism attracted the support of several political figures, including California Governor Jerry Brown, California Assemblyman Willie Brown, and San Francisco Supervisor Harvey Milk. Jones also met with vice presidential candidate Walter Mondale shortly before the 1976 election, and he later met and corresponded with First Lady Rosalynn Carter.

While still in Indianapolis, the Temple demanded high levels of commitment from its members, such as limiting their ties to nonmembers and asking them to spend Thanksgiving and Christmas with the church rather than with their families (Wikipedia 2014b). By the time they settled in California, meetings consumed much of their time, at least for the more committed members. They met several times a week in addition to their weekly worship services and recruitment trips up and down California (Moore 2011:101). The Temple also provided "corrective fellowship" to members who did not live up to Jones's standards (Hall 1987:54).

> These ranged from socially accepted types of coercion, such as discipline and behavior modification, to less acceptable types, including behavior control and terror. They also varied as to technique, encompassing both physical violence (spankings, boxing, beatings, rape, and torture) and emotional violence (verbal abuse, threatening language, public humiliation, fantasizing about violent acts, and obligatory self-criticism).
>
> (Moore 2011:99)

These measures reflected Jones's desire "to forge an intensely loyal, highly disciplined, and tightly controlled organization based on his own personal rulership, and guided by an ethic of total commitment to pursuit of certain ends regarded as moral absolutes, regardless of actions required for their fulfillment" (Hall 1987:27).

Jones's efforts intensified with the move to San Francisco. The Temple began vetting newcomers through an extensive indoctrination and screening process (Hall 1987:87–88), and Jones strongly encouraged members to live in community where members donated their material possessions to the Temple in exchange for the Temple meeting all of their needs. Jones founded Peoples Temple on the principle that it functioned as a substitute for the natural family. It "made family like demands for economic contribution to the general welfare, and in turn supported people who took on the communal commitment to the Temple as their family place of work" (Hall 1987:80). Those who chose to "go communal" not only gave their income to the Temple but also their real estate, insurance policies, and other valuable possessions (Hall 1987:92).

The Temple eventually attracted unfavorable attention for its support of the Symbionese Liberation Army (e.g., its leaders attended San Francisco Temple meetings), a critical 1972 exposé by journalist Lester Kinsolving, and the defection of eight members who wrote a letter complaining about the group's practices. Shortly after this defection, Jones called thirty members to his home and declared, "[W]e should all kill ourselves and leave a note saying that because of harassment, a socialist group cannot exist at this time" (quoted in Wikipedia 2014b). Although they did not go through with it, the group started conducting fake suicide rituals, and shortly thereafter, began renting land in Guyana. Jones also used the unfavorable attention the Temple attracted to increasingly isolate the group. "By projecting himself as a threat to the established order, Jones heightened the gulf between his followers and society at large, and this isolation left the group as the sole collective arbiter of reality" (Hall 1987:110).

As scrutiny of the group increased, the pressure for Jones to leave intensified, and an article by Marshall Kilduff and Phil Tracy (1977) proved to be the straw that broke the camel's back. Just before its publication, *New West* magazine's editor telephoned Jones to read it to him. She explained that she was only doing so because of "all the support letters we received on your behalf, from the Governor of California (Jerry Brown)" and others. While still on the phone listening to the article's allegations, Jones wrote a note to others in the room with him that said, "We leave tonight. Notify Georgetown (Guyana)" (quoted in Wikipedia 2014b). After Jones moved to Guyana, he encouraged members to follow, and the settlement's population grew to more than 900 people by late 1978. Those who moved were promised a tropical paradise, free from the wickedness of the outside world (Wikipedia 2014b). Indeed, that is how Jones envisioned it: a promised land that was both a socialist paradise and a sanctuary from a hostile world.

Unfortunately, it was not. Over the next year, the group became the target of various state and federal investigations, and there was increasing pressure from relatives of Temple members. All of this led Jones to sever ties between Jonestown and the outside world, and he "took on the task of resocializing his followers to a leftist perspective on world events" (Hall

1987:237). Through public humiliation, heavy work, and psychotherapeutic drugs, he exerted considerable control over members, and because external ties were all but nonexistent, there were few if any countervailing forces to challenge the sway he had over his followers. That said, Jones's efforts at social control were not completely effective, which is why when Leo Ryan, a congressman from the San Francisco Bay Area investigating claims of abuse within the Peoples Temple, visited Jonestown, a handful of Temple members expressed a desire to leave and accompanied him to the airstrip the next day. There, Temple security guards intercepted the group and opened fire, killing Congressman Ryan, three journalists, and one of the defectors. That evening, Jones ordered members to drink a cyanide-laced, grape-flavored powdered drink, and told parents to inject their children with the same drink if they were under a certain age. He claimed they were committing an act of "revolutionary suicide" as a protest against "the heartless and unjust system of capitalism that existed in the United States" (Moore 2011:95). All told, 918 people died, including more than 200 children and 100 seniors.

Armed Islamic Group (GIA)

The Armed Islamic Group (*Groupe Islamique Armé*, GIA) emerged in the early 1990s in response to Algerian state policies that repressed the political activity of Islamic groups. From 1979 to 1989 Islamists engaged in very little political activity but instead focused their efforts on preaching and proselytizing. In 1989, however, Islamic groups took advantage of Algeria's implementation of a more pluralistic political system. Numerous religious parties emerged, but the most dominant was the Islamic Salvation Front (*Front Islamique du Salut*, FIS). In 1990, the FIS enjoyed a high level of success in local elections and subsequently mobilized various resources for the national elections scheduled to take place in 1991. However, because of the FIS's increasing power and the appearance it would emerge from the national election victorious, the Algerian military carried out a bloodless coup in 1991, nullified the electoral process, and implemented several anti-FIS measures, such as banning the party in 1992, ordering the destruction of its mosques, closing its cultural and charitable organizations, and killing, prosecuting, and imprisoning thousands of its activists as terrorists. "By 1996, according to an Algerian human rights organization, there were 116 prisons with 43,737 prisoners, half of whom were accused of terrorism" (Hafez 2004:46). This harsh treatment of FIS and other Islamic activists led many to join groups that "rejected democracy, the electoral process, and the Algerian ruling regime" (Hafez 2004:46). Eventually, many of the groups banded together in order to found the GIA and quickly became the most prominent armed group.

10.3 Islamic Group, and the Branch Davidians

The GIA evolved into what Mohammed Hafez (2003; 2004) called an exclusive organization, one that recruited only trustworthy activists and limited external ties. Indeed, it required members to sever all ties with non-GIA groups and declare complete allegiance to the GIA. Those who sought to leave "were considered apostates, defectors, opportunists, or potential informers and corrupters [and] their punishment was death" (Hafez 2004:49). The GIA adopted increasingly extreme practices the longer it remained isolated from Algerian society. Because it viewed the social order as wholly corrupt and incapable of reform, it eventually directed violence against anyone it identified as an enemy of the movement, including the very people who once sympathized and supported it:

> Political violence in Algeria initially took the form of clashes with security forces and assassinations of policemen and military personnel. In 1993, violence expanded to include government officials. Violence eventually expanded to include representatives of opposition groups, foreigners, journalists, intellectuals, and ordinary citizens killed randomly through bombings or deliberately through executions and massacres ... of entire towns and villages.
> (Hafez 2004:50, 51)

Not surprisingly, "many stopped giving their support, while others turned against the movement. Some began to join the government-sponsored militias to counter the violence of the insurgents" (Hafez 2003:170). The GIA continues to operate, but it is no longer as effective as it once was.

Branch Davidians

The Branch Davidians, founded by Benjamin Roden in 1955, were (and are) a religious group that split from the Davidian Seventh-Day Adventists ("Davidians"), which, in turn, had split from the Seventh-Day Adventist Church (SDA). Until the events of 1993 (see the discussion that follows), group members lived at Mount Carmel Center, which was located just west of Waco, Texas. When Roden died in 1978, his wife, Lois, assumed leadership of the group. This enraged their son, George, who believed he was the rightful heir. Lois introduced a number of new teachings that caught the attention of the wider world, such as the claim that God was both male and female, the Holy Spirit was female, and with the second coming the Messiah would be female. In 1979, she began publishing *SHEkinah* magazine, which contained articles from people of many different religious backgrounds (Christian and otherwise) that explored the femininity of the Holy Spirit and women in ministry for which she won an award from *Religion in Media* in the 1980s.

Lois Roden eventually formed an alliance with a young David Koresh (when he still called himself Vernon Howell), who had accepted a job as a handyman at Mount Carmel in 1981, and in 1983 she announced that he would succeed her. This did not guarantee that Koresh would actually lead the group at some point, however. In fact, George Roden successfully wrested control from his mother in 1985 and promptly kicked Koresh out (by gunpoint, according to some). Koresh and his followers settled nearby in Palestine, Texas, where they eked out a living and plotted how they would regain control of Mount Carmel. Ironically, it was the younger Roden's missteps with the law that eventually landed him in jail, allowing Koresh to regain control of Mount Carmel (Pitts 1995:37).

Ever since they arrived at Mount Carmel in the 1930s, the Davidians attempted to keep the local community at arms. They forbade members from marrying nonbelievers, and many of those who converted to the movement divorced their spouses when they joined (Pitts 1995:28). They also printed their own currency, and like "other communal organizations (Kanter 1972), they regulated information coming into the community" (Pitts 1995:29). They also sought to be self-sufficient through farming. However, complete self-sufficiency was unattainable, so some had to take jobs in the nearby communities; the Davidians also owned and operated a gun and gun-accessory business, as well as an automobile repair and restoration shop known as the "Mag Bag."

The group's isolation increased under Koresh. Much of it resulted from Koresh's "New Light" doctrine. Koresh believed he was a second messiah who would help set in motion the events that would bring an end to this world. He also claimed he was the perfect mate for all female adherents, and part of his role was to create a new spiritual lineage of God's children, a "House of David."[6] In practical terms, this meant that all female Branch Davidians could become one of his spiritual wives, and he married a number of young girls as well as the female spouses of some of the married couples living at Mount Carmel. Koresh's doctrine provided his critics with ammunition. For example, Mark Breault, who defected from the group in 1989, teamed up with an Australian reporter, Mark King, to produce a television exposé on the group that alleged (among other things) the statutory rape of young females and child abuse (Ellison and Bartkowski 1995). He also served as a witness in the custody battle over the daughter of an estranged sect member's husband, hired a private investigator to gather damaging information on the group, and contacted a Michigan congressman for assistance in gaining help from the FBI (Wright 1995b:84). Things came to a head in early 1992, about a year

[6] "Koresh" is Hebrew for "Cyrus," the Persian king who defeated the Babylonians, and "David" of course refers to King David, from whom many believe the messiah will be descended. Thus, by taking this name, Koresh signaled that he was the spiritual descendant of King David (Bromley and Silver 1995:57).

before the raid: Breault and King's exposé appeared on television, the custody battle was being fought in the courts, Texas' Child Protection Services visited the Branch Davidians over the charges of statutory rape, and a SWAT team held practice exercises near the Mag Bag (Hall 1995: 219–220).

It was in response to allegations that the Branch Davidians possessed illegal firearms materials and were converting semiautomatic rifles into machine guns that the Bureau of Alcohol, Tobacco, and Firearms (BATF) began planning a raid on the compound (Tabor and Gallagher 1995). Breault was the BATF's primary source of information, and he convinced the agency that Koresh would not "surrender" peacefully, which is why it only planned an assault rather than less coercive approaches (Tabor and Gallagher 1995; Wright 1995b). Breault's characterization of Koresh appears to have been disingenuous, however. Local law enforcement officials enjoyed relatively good relations with the Branch Davidians and had visited Mount Carmel several times over the years without incident. In fact, Waco's former district attorney "criticized the siege as 'a vulgar display of power on the part of the feds' and stated that 'if they'd [the BATF] called and talked to them, the Davidians would've given them what they wanted'" (Wright 1995b:86). That, of course, is not what happened, and when the smoke finally cleared, six BATF agents and eighty Branch Davidians were dead, including twenty-one children.

Things probably could have turned out differently (Hall 1995; Tabor and Gallagher 1995; Wright 1995b). Although the Branch Davidians became more isolated under Koresh's leadership, they were not entirely cut off. They still had ties with the wider community, and while Koresh's New Light doctrine made them an easy target, much of what the media reported was based on unfounded charges leveled by disgruntled former members (Tabor and Gallagher 1995). There is no doubt that Koresh was taking young wives – at the time Texas law allowed girls as young as fourteen years old to marry as long as they had parental permission. Also, the evidence for child abuse was "more limited and more ambiguous than media accounts and government portrayals typically indicated" (Ellison and Bartkowski 1995:113), suggesting "that allegations were treated uncritically by the authorities" (Wright 1995c:xxi). Nevertheless, media attacks combined with the SWAT team's exercises at the Mag-Bag contributed to the Branch Davidians' increasing sense of isolation and the final outcome. Even after the siege began, there were still opportunities to resolve it peacefully. Biblical scholars Phillip Arnold and James Tabor offered their services and engaged in conversations with Koresh's theological spokesperson, Livingstone Fagan. Unfortunately, their efforts were too late. By the time their conversations began to produce results, the decision had already been made to resolve the standoff with force (Tabor and Gallagher 1995:5).

Summary

Although the three groups' stories differ in details, they illustrate how network closure can increase the likelihood that a group will become increasingly radicalized and engage in violent behavior. In all three cases, distinct beliefs combined with high demands increased the isolation of the groups from their surrounding societies. All three limited their members' ties to outsiders and became increasingly dense. Radicalization, by itself, does not beget violence, however. Belief in the divine sanctioning of violence is also needed, and the Peoples Temple, the GIA, and the Branch Davidians entertained such beliefs, albeit in different ways.

10.4 Violent Anabaptists

We now consider one final example: the Anabaptist movement that emerged during the Protestant Reformation. Although the Anabaptist movement was predominantly nonviolent (and is the forerunner of today's Amish and Mennonite groups), one Anabaptist group was violent and briefly established a theocracy in Münster, Westphalia, where torture and mass executions became commonplace. This section begins with a brief history of the Anabaptist movement with a focus on those involved in the Münster Rebellion. It then introduces readers to stochastic actor-oriented models, which are statistical models (SAOMs) designed for longitudinal social network data. Here, we consider two different types of SAOMs: (1) the standard model, which seeks to only model the dynamics of tie formation (i.e., social selection), and (2) the coevolution model, which also captures the mechanisms of social influence.

Sixteenth-Century Anabaptists and the Münster Rebellion

Anabaptists trace their roots to Zurich in 1524 – they were a small group known as the Zwingli Radicals, which later became known as the Swiss Brethren (Williams 1975). They originally followed the teachings of the Protestant Reformer Ulrich Zwingli, but after they began practicing adult baptism, magisterial and religious authorities quickly outlawed the practice and made it punishable by death (McDaniel 2007). Although in today's world adult baptism is seen as a legitimate practice, in the sixteenth century it was seen as a form of revolt. Infant baptism not only marked individuals as Christians, it also marked them as citizens of the state. Thus, authorities sought to prevent adult baptism because they saw religious groups that practiced it, including the Anabaptists, as outlaws.

Anabaptists are generally associated with pacifism. However, in 1534 a small group seized control of Münster, Westphalia (present-day Germany) and installed a theocracy that turned violent. The group was indirectly influenced by Melchior Hoffman, an Anabaptist leader with ties to the Netherlands and the Lower Rhine region (Williams 1975). Hoffman converted to Lutheranism in 1522, and in 1525 he traveled to Wittenberg in order to receive Luther's blessing for his preaching (Neff and Packull 1987). Hoffman traveled extensively through Europe and increasingly incorporated into his teachings apocalyptic beliefs about the end times and the imminent return of Jesus Christ (Neff and Packull 1987). He was not unique in this regard. Luther himself often speculated about the end times. After contact with a group of Anabaptists in Strasbourg in 1530, Hoffman became an Anabaptist and founded his own sect, which became known as the Melchiorites (Geortz 1996). He initially practiced adult baptism, but after authorities executed nine of his followers, he stopped and declared that in the final days true baptism would resume with the coming of the Holy Spirit (Stayer 1979). Hoffman believed that God had called him to reveal the secrets of Christ's second coming. He taught that Christ would return soon, the city of Strasbourg would become the "New Jerusalem," and he and his followers would meet Christ (Clasen 1972). Although Hoffman was not a pacifist – he believed that governments (including Christian rulers) could use violence to maintain order – he did not believe Christians could use violence to advance the faith or hasten cosmic events (Stayer 1979). Hoffman was arrested in 1533 for his heterodox beliefs and sentenced to ten years in prison. He continued to write during this time, but his influence waned because his predictions about the end times failed to come true. After Hoffman's arrest, Jan Matthys, a baker from Haarlem, assumed leadership of the Melchiorites (Stayer 1979). Matthys reinstated adult baptism (Klötzer 2007) and attracted a substantial following.

At about this time, hundreds of Anabaptists were moving to Münster, where Anabaptist beliefs and practices were increasingly being accepted, largely because of the influence of the local Lutheran pastor, Bernhard Rothmann, who embraced believer's baptism and condemned the private ownership of property (McDaniel 2007). As the Anabaptists grew in power, Münster's Lutherans and Catholics became increasingly uncomfortable and upwards of 2,000 left the city. Two of Matthys's followers – John van Leyden and Gerrit Boekbinder – visited Münster and reported back that Rothmann was teaching doctrines similar to their own (Wikipedia 2015b). Shortly thereafter Matthys identified Münster as the

"New Jerusalem" and sent several of his followers to Münster in January of 1534, where they baptized (or rebaptized) more than 1,000 adults, including several prominent leaders such as Rothmann (Wikipedia 2015b; Williams 1975). By early February the Anabaptists gained control of the city, and when a perihelion appeared in sky, they interpreted it as a sign of their imminent redemption and the destruction of the damned, so they began evicting those who were unwilling to be baptized (Williams 1975; Klötzer 2007). By this time Matthys had moved to Münster, and he and the other leaders sent out apostles to invite people to the New Jerusalem. As many as 2,500 people migrated to the city and replaced the Lutherans and Catholics who had left (McDaniel 2007).

After the Anabaptists gained control of Münster, the prince-bishop of the region,[7] Franz von Waldeck, amassed an army and laid siege to the city (Wikipedia 2015b). In April on Easter Sunday Matthys, who had previously prophesied that God's judgment would come to the wicked on that day, led a small band of followers and attacked the prince-bishop's army. Matthys was killed, and his head was cut off and placed on a pole outside the city gates (Krahn, van der Zijpp, and Stayer 1987; McDaniel 2007). John van Leyden then seized control and proclaimed himself king of Münster. He legalized polygamy, married Matthys's widow (plus sixteen other women), and renamed Münster the "New Israel" because he believed they were ushering in God's kingdom by punishing God's enemies (Klötzer 2007). He ruthlessly administered "justice" and participated in the public executions of those who offended the kingdom or were seen as a threat (Stayer 1979). This led to numerous defections, and with the help of a few Anabaptist guards, the prince-bishop regained control of the city in June of 1535, killing hundreds in the process (McDaniel 2007). In January 1536, van Leyden and several other leaders were tortured and then executed in Münster's marketplace. Their bodies were exhibited in cages, which were hung from the steeple of St. Lambert's Church. Their bones have since been removed, but the cages remain to this day (McDaniel 2007; Wikipedia 2015b).

Network Data and Statistical Methods

In what follows, we test for evidence of network closure and the influence of apocalyptic beliefs among Anabaptist leaders. As we saw in Chapter 3, traditional tests of statistical inference are inapplicable for social network data, so we will use the SAOMs developed by Tom Snijders and his colleagues (Van de Bunt, Van Duijin, and Snijders 1999; Snijders 2005; Snijders, Van de Bunt, and Steglich 2010). SAOMs are similar to exponential random graph models (ERGMs) in that they assume that the

---

[7] Prince-bishops were leaders in both the secular and religious realms.

10.4 Violent Anabaptists

observed network structure is, in part, a function of local patterns of ties that reflect endogenous social processes. Like ERGMs they test whether a particular pattern occurs more frequently than one would expect given the presence of other patterns in the network. They differ in that they are designed for longitudinal social network data and explicitly model the choices of actors, who "are assumed to control their outgoing ties and to make changes in these ties according to short-term goals and restrictions (Snijders and Koskinen 2013:138). Like ERGMs, they share similarities with general linear models and include important modifications to account for the dependencies of observations. Formally, the objective function of SAOMs is assumed to be a linear combination of effects (i.e., social processes, micro-configurations):

$$f_i(\beta, x) = \sum_k \beta_k S_{ki}(x) \tag{10.1}$$

where $f_i(\beta, x)$ equals the objective function for actor i depending on the state x of the network, the functions $S_{ki}(x)$ are the effects, and the weights, β_k are the statistical parameters (Snijders, Van de Bunt, and Steglich 2010:47). Because SAOMs use a panel data approach, each network has to include the same number and set of actors. Thus, we introduced structural zeroes so that each network includes the same number and same set of actors while at the same time indicating that it is no longer possible to form or maintain ties with actors who had been killed or arrested.

The approach for estimating a SAOM is similar to that of an ERGM: first, hypothesize as to what social processes gave rise to a particular network's global properties, and then build a model that takes these into account. Endogenous processes are operationalized in terms of the various micro-configurations found within a network, while exogenous factors are operationalized in terms of actor attributes. In the models discussed in the following paragraphs, we include two micro-configurations – closed triads and alternating triangles (see Table 3.3 in Chapter 3) – that specifically test for increased network closure. Alternating triangles are simply a series of closed triads in which two actors share ties with numerous other actors in the network, so it is possible that one will be statistically significant but not the other. The estimated models also control for four additional micro-configurations: degree (edges), balance, actor popularity, and isolates. In SAOMs the estimated degree coefficient is analogous to the intercept in standard regression models; the balance coefficient captures the tendency for actors to form ties with those who are structurally similar;[8] the actor

---

[8] Structural similarity refers to actors who share the same or similar patterns of ties to others; the term is often used to express similarities in tie patterns that result from similar job functions.

popularity coefficient measures the degree to which one or a handful of actors form numerous ties; and the isolates coefficient captures the effect of isolates in the network.

The network data consists of sixty-seven actors, fifty-five of whom were sixteenth-century Anabaptist leaders (McLaughlin 2015a). The remaining twelve were prominent Protestant Reformation leaders (e.g., Martin Luther, John Calvin, Ulrich Zwingli, Martin Bucer, Philip Melanchthon), who had contact with and influenced some of the Anabaptist leaders included in the dataset. The original data were collected by Matthews et al. (2013) and consisted of forty-nine actors. Because the original data did not include relational data on prominent Anabaptist leaders, such as Menno Simons (from whom the Anabaptist group, the Mennonites, takes its name), McLaughlin (2015a, 2015b) drew on numerous other sources (e.g., Clasen 1972; Williams 1975; Stayer 1979; Krahn, van der Zijpp, and Stayer 1987; Bender, Friedmann, and Klassen 1990; Klötzer 2007) to expand the dataset. The data were then time-coded in order to capture when actors entered and left the network, allowing us to examine the data longitudinally. The analysis begins by summarizing an earlier study of the Anabaptist leadership network by Cunningham et al. (2016), which employed descriptive statistics and SAOMs. This will be followed by a coevolution SAOM, which not only models social selection processes but social influence processes as well.

A Longitudinal Analysis of the Münster Rebellion

We begin the analysis with a graph of the entire network along with some descriptive network statistics. Figure 10.5 presents the entire Anabaptist leadership network. In the figure, black colored nodes indicate Anabaptists who were involved in the rebellion, gray colored nodes indicate those who were not, and white nodes indicate the non-Anabaptist Protestant Reformers included in the dataset.[9] Interestingly, without the non-Anabaptist Protestant Reformers, the Anabaptists leaders would be cut off from one another; that is, at least at the leadership level, Protestant Reformers functioned as brokers between different sets of Anabaptist leaders.

Now let us consider some basic SNA interconnectedness of the leadership network from 1530 to 1540 (in five-year intervals): size, density, average degree, cohesion, the global clustering coefficient, and the E-I index (Table 10.1).[10] In the table, the highest score has been bolded.

---

[9] Figure 10.5 was created in R.
[10] Size is the number of actors in the network. Density and average degree have been discussed previously. Cohesion equals the proportion of all pairs of actors that can either directly or indirectly reach one another (Borgatti, Everett, and Johnson 2013). The global clustering coefficient (Watts 1999b; Watts and Strogatz 1998), which is the same as average ego network density (Davis 1967; Marsden 1987), equals the average

10.4 Violent Anabaptists

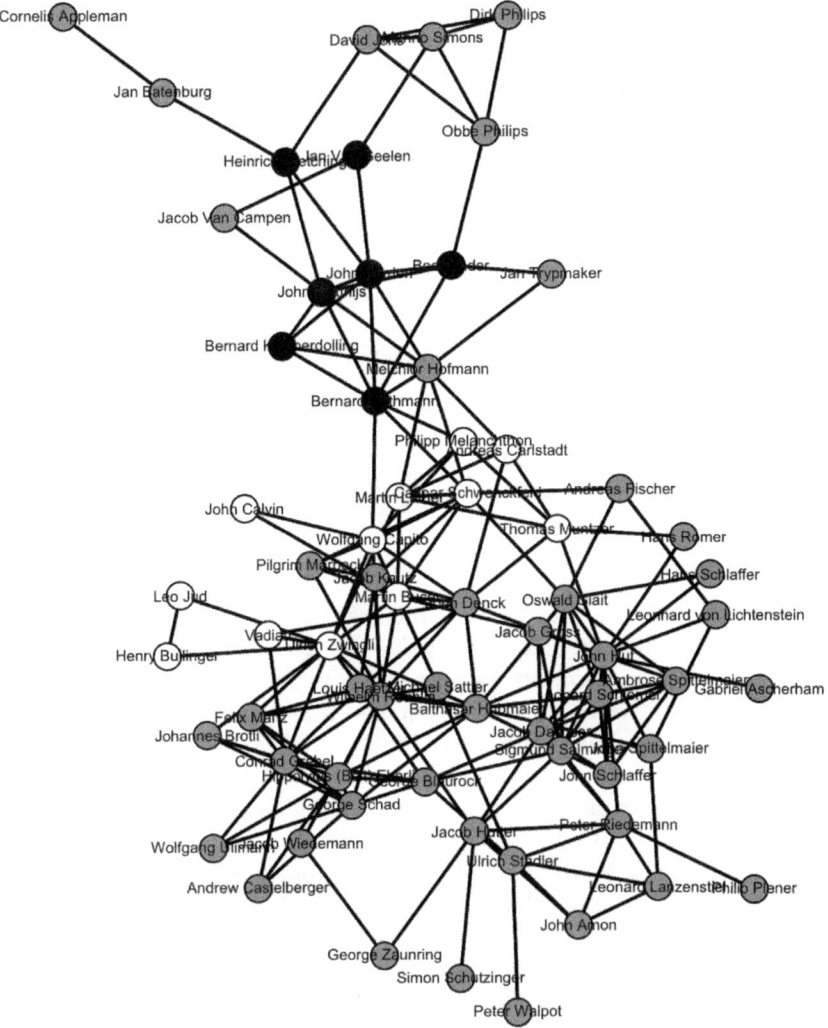

Figure 10.5 Anabaptist leadership network

The density, average degree, and cohesion scores suggest that the interconnectedness of the leadership network peaked in 1530, while the global clustering coefficient suggests that it peaked in 1540. What these scores

> level of density among each actor's neighbors. The E-I index measures the ratio of external to internal ties (Krackhardt and Stern 1988). Scores range from –1.00 to 1.00 where –1.00 indicates that group members only have ties to other members, a score of 1.00 indicates that group members only have ties to nonmembers, and a score of 0.00 indicates that in the aggregate members have an equal number of internal and external ties. See Appendix A.

Table 10.1 *Measures of Anabaptist leadership network interconnectedness, 1530–1540*

	1530	1535	1540
Size	36	37	28
Density	0.102	0.086	0.098
Average degree	3.556	3.081	2.643
Cohesion	0.890	0.794	0.251
Global clustering coefficient	0.374	0.381	0.534
E-I Index (Anabaptists)	–0.650	–0.671	–0.524
E-I Index (non-Melchiorite Anabaptists)	–0.758	–0.689	–0.481
E-I Index (Melchiorite Anabaptists)	–0.143	–0.647	–0.600
% apocalyptic (Melchiorites/non-Melchiorites)	100/4.76	72.73/0.00	33.33/0.00

Note: Adapted from Cunningham, Everton, and Murphy 2016: 283; source: McLaughlin (2015a)

suggest is that the network became increasingly fragmented as Anabaptist leaders were killed or executed. The decreasing cohesion score best captures this decline. However, as the network fragmented, it broke into small groups in which most everyone had ties to everyone else, which is why the clustering coefficient peaked in 1540. More telling is the three sets of E-I indices for all Anabaptists, non-Melchiorite Anabaptists, and Melchiorite Anabaptists. They indicate that the non-Melchiorites reached their highest level of internal interconnectedness (i.e., when its E-I index reached its lowest level) in 1530, while Melchiorites (and Anabaptists as a whole) reached their highest level in 1535, which coincides with the Münster Rebellion. Still, the E-I index of non-Melchiorites is lower than the E-I index of the Melchiorites. That is why the final statistic listed in the table is important: the percentage of members (Melchiorite and non-Melchiorite) who held apocalyptic beliefs. As one can see, in the lead up to the Münster Rebellion the percentage of Melchiorites who held apocalyptic beliefs was quite high, which is entirely consistent with the theory outlined earlier: namely, that apocalyptic beliefs combined with group radicalization increase the likelihood that groups will engage in violent behavior.

Table 10.2 presents the results from stochastic actor-oriented models estimated by Daniel Cunningham, Sean Everton, and Philip Murphy (2016: 285). Model 1 converged adequately (the maximum convergence is less than 0.25), but none of the estimated parameters are statistically significant. Thus, the second and third models dropped the balance, alternating triads, and isolate effects and added either the Melchiorite

10.4 Violent Anabaptists

Table 10.2 *Estimated coefficients of stochastic actor-oriented models*

	Model 1	Model 2	Model 3	Model 4
Structural variables				
Degree (intercept)	0.508	−1.146***	−1.259***	−1.278***
	(3.575)	(0.288)	(0.342)	(0.319)
Transitive triads	−3.755	0.622***	0.715***	0.704***
	(7.205)	(0.213)	(0.251)	(0.234)
Balance	0.751			
	(1.199)			
Alternating triangles	5.938			
	(11.216)			
Isolates	4.799			
	(6.998)			
Commonalities				
Melchiorite	2.616	0.892		
	(7.462)	(0.550)		
Münster Rebellion	−5.174		−1.807+	−1.958+
	(12.645)		(1.053)	(1.093)
Believer's baptism	−0.105	0.587	0.556	
	(1.243)	(0.428)	(0.518)	
Apocalyptic	1.653	−0.117	1.431	1.632+
	(4.658)	(0.539)	(0.870)	(0.907)
Rate parameters				
Rate period 1	0.447	0.995	0.822	0.810
	(0.105)	(0.252)	(0.195)	(0.193)
Rate period 2	0.120	0.200	0.187	0.190
	(0.060)	(0.099)	(0.092)	(0.092)
Overall maximum Cconvergence	0.085	0.076	0.041	0.039

Note: + = p < .10; *** = p < .001 (two-tailed)
Source: Cunningham, Everton, and Murphy 2016:285

(model 2) or Münster Rebellion (model 3) covariates because those involved in the Münster Rebellion were also Melchiorites. Although the transitive triads parameter was not statistically significant in the first model, once the other configurations were dropped, it was and thus was retained in models 2 and 3. The degree effect was kept in the model because it is analogous to the intercept in a multivariate regression model. It is notable, however, that like the transitive triads parameter, it became statistically significant once the balance, alternating triads, and isolate parameters were dropped from the models.

The overall convergence statistics for the second and third models indicate improvement. The negative degree coefficient indicates that there was an overall negative tendency to tie formation. This may strike one as counterintuitive, but it is true only after the effects of the other variables in the model are taken into account. More importantly, in both models the transitive triads parameter is positive and statistically significant, which indicates that over time the network did tend toward network closure. In model 2, the Melchiorite coefficient is positive but not statistically significant, so it does not appear that two individuals identifying as Melchiorites were any more likely to form a tie with one another. By contrast, the Münster Rebellion coefficient is statistically significant. The fact that it is negative probably indicates that the majority of those in the leadership network avoided forming ties with those who eventually participated in the Münster Rebellion. That may help to explain why their beliefs and practices were not embraced in the years after the rebellion. The two remaining coefficients in both models are not statistically significant. It is perhaps not surprising that the believer's baptism parameter is not since the majority of those in the network embraced believer's baptism. Thus, it probably had little or no effect on tie formation among network members. It is somewhat surprising that the estimated apocalyptic coefficient is not statistically significant since it seems to be a defining feature of some network members.

However, because the apocalyptic effect is "almost" statistically significant in the third model at the $p < 0.10$ level, the fourth and final model includes the Münster Rebellion and apocalyptic effects, but drops the effect for believer's baptism. This led to a slight improvement in the model's overall convergence, and the estimated degree, transitive triad, and Münster Rebellion coefficients remain statistically significant and relatively unchanged. More importantly, the apocalyptic coefficient is now statistically significant, which suggests that those who shared apocalyptic beliefs were more likely to form ties with one another. In other words, the result suggests that shared apocalyptic beliefs may have had a positive effect on tie formation among the Melchiorites. This dynamic is not captured in theory outlined in Figure 10.4, but it is suggestive nonetheless.

A Coevolution Model of the Münster Rebellion

A variation on the stochastic actor-oriented models is the SAOM coevolution models, which allow analysts to not only model tie formation but also behavioral dynamics (Steglich, Snijders, and Pearson 2010). That is, they allow researchers to model both social selection from social influence. They "are unique because they are designed specifically to model tie changes and simultaneously link these alterations to changes in behavioral variables so that socialization effects 'control' for selection, and vice versa" (Cheadle and Schwadel 2012: 1202–1203).

10.4 Violent Anabaptists

Formally, the behavioral objective function is similar to the network objection function noted earlier (equation 10.1). It is a linear combination of effects:

$$f_i^{beh}(x,z) = \sum_k \beta_k^{beh} S_{ik}^{beh}(x,z) \qquad (10.2)$$

where the behavioral dependent variable is denoted by z and the dependent network variable by x, $f_i^{beh}(x,z)$ equals the objective function for actor i depending on the state x of the network and z of the dependent variable, β_k^{beh} are the statistical parameters, and $S_{ik}^{beh}(x,z)$ are the effects (Ripley et al. 2017:135).

The results of a series of coevolution SAOMs, where the dependent behavioral variable was whether an actor engaged in actual violent behavior (rather than simply supported the use of violence), are presented in Table 10.3. Notice that the models retain only the microconfigurations and attributes (commonalities) included in model 4 of the standard SAOM estimated earlier (Table 10.2). Although the parameter estimates differ, they are all statistically significant and point in the same direction, lending additional support to the findings presented earlier. What is new is the behavioral portion of the models, which include the effects of the number of ego's ties, the number of dense triads in which ego was embedded, and whether holding apocalyptic beliefs increases the likelihood that ego will engage in violent behavior.

In the end only the main effect of apocalyptic beliefs had a direct effect on violent behavior. That is, the individuals who hold apocalyptic beliefs were more likely to engage in violent behavior than were those who did not. Interestingly, the number of dense triads in which ego was embedded did not have a statistically significant effect, and in fact ultimately was removed from the models because its presence made it difficult for the model to converge. This indicates that while over time the Anabaptist leadership network tended toward network closure, the presence of individual actors in dense triads did not lead to violent behavior. It suggests that network closure may only have an indirect effect on violence or that individual actors being embedded in dense triads is not enough; rather the actors need to be embedded in a dense network in which apocalyptic beliefs are widely held.[11]

---

[11] These conclusions should be taken with a grain of salt, however, because a number of the Anabaptist leaders were either arrested or killed after 1530, which meant that there was a lot of missing observations for the dependent behavioral variable (violence) in 1535 and 1540, and this caused the models to be very unstable and difficult to converge. A more robust test of these data would be to first expand the network to include all Protestant Reformation leaders and then test whether increased isolation among apocalyptic Anabaptists increased the likelihood of violent behavior.

Table 10.3 *Estimated coefficients of coevolution stochastic actor-oriented models*

	Estimate (SE)			
	Model 1	Model 2	Model 3	Model 4
Network dynamics				
Structural variables				
Degree (intercept)	−2.121*** (0.607)	−2.146*** (0.646)	−2.154*** (0.427)	−2.129*** (0.412)
Transitive triads	1.348*** (0.390)	1.355*** (0.470)	1.362*** (0.337)	1.367*** (0.334)
Commonalities				
Münster Rebellion	−2.307 (1.876)	−2.288 (1.959)	−2.323+ (1.314)	−2.308+ (1.230)
Apocalyptic	2.609** (1.018)	2.606 (1.952)	2.618** (1.014)	2.575** (0.991)
Behavior dynamics				
Structural variables				
Degree	−1.218 (9.669)		−1.755 (2.818)	
Dense triads	−2.599 (117.119)	−5.681 (101.721)		
Similarity				
Apocalyptic	4.526 (5.268)	5.430 (8.221)	4.500* (2.240)	4.035+ (2.279)
Rate parameters				
Network dynamics				
Rate period 1	0.708 (0.200)	0.708 (0.362)	0.711 (0.176)	0.706 (0.161)
Rate period 2	0.190 (0.098)	0.192 (0.125)	0.191 (0.098)	0.190 (0.100)
Behavior dynamics				
Rate period 1	0.644 (0.276)	0.590 (1.002)	0.659 (0.368)	0.337 (0.129)
Rate period 2	0.428 (0.209)	0.423 (0.237)	0.439 (0.196)	0.362 (0.170)
Overall maximum convergence	0.102	0.147	0.078	0.071

Note: + = $p < .10$; * = $p < .05$; ** = $p < .01$; *** = $p < .001$ (two-tailed)

10.5 Summary and Conclusion

This chapter introduced a model of social networks and religious violence, and then tested it with both qualitative case studies and statistical models. Its argument is relatively straightforward: various socioeconomic factors can increase the likelihood that groups will distance themselves from the

10.5 Summary and Conclusion

societies in which they are embedded. They will accomplish this by encouraging members to interact more with one another, limit their ties to outsiders, and only recruit new members through strong ties. This will help protect their integrity, but it also means that they are more likely to radicalize. Distinctive religious beliefs and practices can also contribute to this process. If such radicalization is combined with apocalyptic beliefs, the probability that groups will engage in violent behavior increases.

If this argument is correct, certain implications follow (Everton 2016). Perhaps the most important thing authorities can do is to maintain ties with groups that are in danger of radicalizing, such as how the state of Oregon interacted regularly with the Rajneeshpuram, an intentional community that settled in central Oregon in the 1980s, which according to Marion Goldman (2011) helped prevent the group from engaging in large-scale violence although it possessed the potential for doing so. Of course, some groups have already distanced themselves before authorities become aware of their presence, so in that case they need to take steps to reintegrate them back into society. As noted in Chapter 6, societies are more likely to thrive when minority religious groups are integrated into civil society (Tilly 2004, 2005b). Although this can be accomplished in multiple ways, access to the political system encourages groups to "become more like political parties and interest groups, and less like social protest movements or revolutionary groups" (Hafez 2003:208). Related to this is minimizing media scrutiny and public ridicule, which can drive groups into isolation. It is hard to do but it is possible. For instance, Oregon's attorney general sought to limit the interference, harassment, and ridicule of the Rajneeshpuram community while actively pressing for legal solutions "to accusations of criminal activities and violation of civil laws at Rajneeshpuram" (Goldman 2011:318).[12] Finally, policy makers should advocate policies that promote religious freedom. Brian Grim and Roger Finke (2010) have demonstrated that, net of other factors, a lack of religious freedom is positively associated with religious persecution and violence. For example, government repression has led to higher rates of violence in Algeria, Egypt, Kashmir, the Southern Philippines, and Chechnya (Hafez 2003). In short, we need to do all we can to keep religious groups from isolating themselves from the wider society in which they are embedded.

---

[12] This is not to suggest that individuals and groups should not be prosecuted for injurious behavior. However, it can be done while respecting religious freedoms. For example, when Aum Shinrikyo released sarin gas in the Tokyo subway, killing twelve people and injuring hundreds more, the Japanese government prosecuted those who were guilty, but it did not outlaw the group. "Rather than criminalizing the Aum religion, the government allowed it to continue and prosecuted only the individuals who engaged in criminal activities that hurt or aimed to hurt others. This defused the violent side of the religion without further radicalizing the group" (Grim and Finke 2010:213).

10.6 For Further Reading

Unfortunately, at present there is no book that provides an overview of stochastic actor-oriented models (SAOMs). There are, however, numerous articles that have applied the method to a variety of social network data. Some of these are listed as follows, but a more complete list can be found at the SIENA website:[13]

- Tom A. B. Snijders. 2005. "Models for Longitudinal Network Data." In *Models and Methods in Social Network Analysis*, edited by Peter J. Carrington, John Scott, and Stanley Wasserman. New York, NY: Cambridge University Press, pp. 215–247.
- Tom A. B. Snijders, Gerhard G. Van de Bunt, and Christian Steglich. 2010. "Introduction to Stochastic Actor-Based Models for Network Dynamics." *Social Networks* 32:44–60.
- Christian Steglich, Tom A. B. Snijders, and Michael Pearson. 2010. "Dynamic Networks and Behavior: Separating Selection from Influence." *Sociological Methodology* 40:329–393.

Two helpful introductions to SAOMs can be found on pages 145–147 in Stephen Borgatti, Martin Everett, and Jeffrey Johnson's, *Analyzing Social Networks* (2013) and on pages 238–248 in Christina Prell's, *Social Network Analysis* (2011). Tom Snijders offers a somewhat more in-depth introduction in his chapter on network dynamics in *The SAGE Handbook of Social Network Analysis*, edited by John Scott and Peter J. Carrington (2011). Finally, an invaluable guide to building a SAOM is the *Manual for RSiena*, which has been written and continually updated by Ruth Ripley, Tom Snijders, Zsófia Boda, András Vörös, and Paulina Preciado (2017).

---

[13] See www.stats.ox.ac.uk/~snijders/siena.

Part VI

Conclusion

11

Lessons Learned: The End of the Beginning

11.1 Introduction

We have almost reached the end. We began by observing that religion is remarkably resilient in the face of modernizing pressures and then considered three research programs that seek to explain its persistence. While these programs are not entirely compatible with one another, there is certainly some overlap. There has always been a close relationship between the religious economies and rational choice approaches, but as we have seen, subcultural identity theory borrows freely from the notion of religious markets and its assertion that congregations are more likely to thrive if distinct boundaries are drawn between themselves and the surrounding culture; this is quite similar to why rational choice theorists believe that strict churches are strong. Just as important, all three traditions draw on notions of network ties and structures, and the remainder of the book has focused on how social network dynamics are integrally related to religious belief and practice. For instance, we have seen that network structure varies by faith tradition, largely reflecting the tradition's underlying demographics and beliefs, and this impacts the health and well-being of congregational members, the cohesiveness of faith communities, and the likelihood that groups will experience conflict, become radicalized, or engage in destructive violence. We have also observed evidence that congregational social networks are key for attracting new members as well as retaining old ones, that they play an essential role in connecting followers to opportunities for volunteering and civic engagement, and that they are instrumental in the spread of religious beliefs and practices.

Along the way, we have been introduced to a number of social network analysis concepts and methods. For instance, network topography (e.g., density and centralization) was central to discussions of social capital, civic engagement, faith traditions, the health and well-being of people of faith, the cohesiveness of congregations, and the likelihood that a religious group will radicalize and/or become violent. This is important to note because it is tempting to just focus on the ties of actors and their related effects rather than on how the networks in which actors are embedded impact behavior and belief. We have also explored some of the ways that social network analysts identify subgroups within networks, from community detection algorithms to methods designed for networks with positive and negative ties (i.e., signed networks). Although we often do not need such algorithms when examining smaller networks, they can prove quite valuable for exploring larger ones. We have also considered centrality and brokerage metrics, but these were kept to a minimum, primarily because they are relatively intuitive and widely used. In fact, one could argue that they are overused; analyses that use whole network data (religious and otherwise) almost always seek to identify a network's central actors (Roberts and Everton 2016). Not that such information cannot be important, but too often centrality becomes the default metric for analysts when so many others are available and often more informative. Nevertheless, we have drawn on the four most popular measures of centrality – degree, closeness, betweenness, and eigenvector – to explore the Islamic philosophical networks active from the tenth through the thirteenth centuries. Finally, aside from providing a brief overview of positional approaches in Chapter 2, we have only indirectly illustrated blockmodeling as a method for identifying structural equivalent actors with the Doreian-Mrvar (2009) algorithm used in Chapter 9. It is quite similar to the blockmodeling approach advocated by Patrick Doreian, Vladimir Batagelj, and Anuska Ferligoj (2005) in *Generalized Blockmodeling*. In fact, they include a chapter on balance theory and the blockmodeling of signed networks.

It is important to keep in mind that the metrics and algorithms used for measuring network topography, detecting subgroups, and identifying central actors are exploratory in nature. However, if we want to draw statistical inferences about a network or its underlying patterns, we need to turn to explanatory methods. One approach is to calculate a network measure and then include it in a standard statistical model as either an independent or dependent variable. We have adopted this approach when exploring the likelihood that a denomination will begin ordaining women, whether network interconnectedness (density) is positively associated with communal disbanding, and whether faith tradition helps to explain the density of peoples' ego networks. An alternative approach is to use a statistical model designed specifically for social network data. Two of these were introduced in Chapter 3. One, known as the quadratic assignment procedure (QAP), is similar to bootstrapping in that it involves the random rearrangement of a network's rows and columns thousands of times in order to calculate a distribution of statistics that we can then compare to the statistics generated by the observed network. If they differ significantly, we can conclude that the observed statistics could not have occurred by random chance and are thus "statistically significant."

11.2 Ethics and Social Network Research

Exponential random graph models (ERGMs), the second type introduced in the chapter, are designed to examine the endogenous and exogenous social processes that have given rise to observed network patterns. They are similar to the general linear models (in particular, logistic regression models), except that they include certain modifications to account for observational dependence. A third type, which was introduced in Chapter 10, are stochastic actor-oriented models (SAOMs), which share similarities to ERGMs but which are designed for longitudinal data and assume that actors control and make changes to their ties according to various constraints and goals.

Finally, in most of the chapters we examined and conducted studies that have drawn on either whole or ego network data. However, we also encountered three additional "types" of network data that were not discussed in Chapter 2: archeological networks, simulated networks, and hypernetworks. Archeological networks technically constitute whole network data because, at least in theory, they include all relevant nodes and ties. However, it is the various methods archeologists use for determining what is and is not a tie that makes this approach to network data collection unique. This approach also indirectly highlights the importance of being explicit when defining what we mean by a tie, a concern that applies to all network data, not just archeological network data. Simulated networks also constitute whole network data. As we have seen, they are useful for testing network hypotheses when network data are unavailable. Finally, we have briefly considered hypernetwork sampling, which is a method that allows researchers to select a representative sample of organizations through the random sampling individuals affiliated with such organizations. We have focused primarily on how it has been used to select a random sample of religious congregations, but it has also been used to examine voluntary organizations in general (see Chapter 4) and social movement events. Table 11.1 summarizes the various social network analysis topics covered in this book by chapter (with the first and last chapters excluded).

11.2 Ethics and Social Network Research

One area which we have not considered is the ethics of social network analysis. Like other social sciences, discussions of ethics and SNA tend to focus on three areas – professional ethics, marketplace or consumption ethics, and human subjects research – although it is the last of these that receives the most attention. *Professional ethics* focuses on the responsibilities that social scientists have to their colleagues and the wider public when conducting research (see, e.g., Abbott 1983; Babbie 1986; Neuman 1997). It is concerned with the importance of carrying out research as

Table 11.1 *Summary of SNA topics and methods by chapter*

			Social Network Analysis Topics & Methods											
			Exploratory Social Network Analysis				Explanatory Social Network Analysis			Network Data				
Part	Chapter	Short Title	Topography	Subgroups	Centrality, Brokerage	Roles and Positions	QAP	ERGM	SAOM	Ego Networks	Whole Networks	Hyper-networks	Archeological Networks	Simulated Networks
Introduction	1	Religion's Surprising Persistence												
Ties That Bind	2	What Is SNA?	X	X	X		X	X	X	X	X			
	3	Recruitment & Conversion					X	X			X			
	4	Commitment & Conformity										X		
Ties That Loose	5	Diffusion & Innovation									X		X	
	6	Politics & Community	X									X		
Ties That Build Up	7	Networks & Tradition	X							X				
	8	Health & Happiness	X							X				X
Ties That Tear Down	9	Conflict & Cohesion	X	X	X	X					X			
	10	Radicalization & Violence	X		X				X		X			
Conclusion	11	Lessons Learned												

objectively as possible and duly sharing the results of research in a timely manner. Although social network analysts disagree about whether research can or should be value-free, most affirm the importance of interpreting data as objectively as possible, while acknowledging that our values and interests may influence the topics we study and may lead us to recuse ourselves from researching some topics because of our inability to distance ourselves from them.

Marketplace ethics is concerned with how the tools, techniques, theories, and what we disseminate in classrooms, at professional meetings, online, in various publications, and through consulting engagements are consumed and used by others – in particular whether they are used in ways that are harmful to individuals not even involved in our studies (Everton 2012a). The often unspoken answer is that since we cannot control our research after we produce and publish it, we can only hope it will be used for good rather than ill (Cordoba 2006). Nevertheless, most social network researchers consciously or unconsciously try, when possible, to set limits as to who has access to their research and how it can be used (Kadushin 2005).

Finally, *human subjects research* concerns itself with the need to protect the privacy and rights of the individuals being studied (i.e., the subjects). Although there is widespread agreement about what constitutes the ethical and unethical treatment of individuals, SNA raises its own unique set of issues because asking questions such as, "Who do you consider a friend?" and "To whom do you go for advice?" makes it impossible to offer anonymity to respondents. All we can really offer is confidentiality (Borgatti, Everett, and Johnson 2013; Robins 2015). Closely related to this issue is the fact that anonymity is not always possible, even when someone chooses to not participate in a study, because "other respondents may still list that person as a friend, enemy, etc." For example, a "person who does not wish to be embarrassed by their poor standing in [a] group will still be found to be the person most often named as difficult to work with" (Borgatti, Everett, and Johnson 2013:40). Researchers could eliminate all nonparticipants from the final dataset, but doing so would harm the quality of the data and possibly skew the results and conclusions. This is especially true if the missing participants are central players in the network. In short, in terms of human subjects research, social network research "generally requires more attention to ethical issues than ordinary studies" (Borgatti, Everett, and Johnson 2013:42). Thus, those of us who engage in it need to pay extra attention to what research we carry out and how.

11.3 Summary and Conclusion

We have now reached the end, but hopefully it is just the beginning. This book has merely scratched the surface of what social network analysis can potentially offer to those engaged in the social scientific study of religion. There is so much more that can be done, and the network data needed are out there, just waiting to be collected and analyzed. Moreover, the statistical models specifically designed for such data continue to evolve and expand their reach. And they are becoming increasingly user-friendly, which will help make them more accessible to those who do not, and have no intention to, specialize in social network methods. To be sure, social network analysis is not a magic bullet that can answer all of our questions. It is, however, a powerful tool for teasing out the dynamics of religious belief and practice.

Appendix A: Glossary of Terms

actor: An actor can be a person, subgroup, organization, collectivity, community, nation-state, etc. An actor is sometimes referred to as a node or vertex.

affiliation network: See *two-mode network*.

arc: An arc is a directed tie that connects one actor to another actor. See *edge*.

attribute: Attributes are nonrelational characteristics of the individual actors in the network. Examples of attributes of individuals include gender, race, ethnicity, years of education, income level, age, and region/country of birth. Examples of organizational attributes include total sales, net income, age of the corporation, and the number of employees/members. Examples of country attributes include GDP per capita, population size, and continent.

auto-logistic actor attribute models (ALAAMs): Auto-logistic actor attribute models, commonly known as social influence models, are a variation on the exponential random graph models (ERGMs) except that the dependent variable is an attribute (i.e., behavior). See *exponential random graph models (ERGMs)*.

average degree: Average degree equals the average number of ties among all actors in a network. It is sometimes used as an alternative measure to network density because unlike density, it is not sensitive to network size.

average distance: Average distance refers to the average length of all the shortest paths (i.e., geodesics) between all connected actors in a network and could indicate the speed that information (and other resources) diffuses through a network.

betweenness centrality: Betweenness centrality measures the extent to which each actor lies on the shortest path between all other actors in a network.

blocks, blockmodels, and blockmodeling: A set of structurally equivalent actors is referred to as a "block"; the process by which blocks are identified is referred to as blockmodeling; the resulting partition of actors into blocks is a blockmodel. See *positional analysis*.

bridge: Formally, a tie is said to be a bridge if deleting it would cause a network to disconnect into different components. Less formally, it refers to a tie that bridges a gap (i.e., structural hole) in a network. Edge betweenness centrality is sometimes used to identify bridges in a network. See *edge betweenness centrality* and *structural hole*.

broker: An actor that is in a position to broker the flow of material and nonmaterial goods through a network. Analysts have developed numerous algorithms to capture brokerage, including betweenness centrality, structural holes, cut points, cut sets, and Gould and Fernandez's brokerage roles.

brokerage role: The brokerage role of an actor (e.g., consultant, coordinator, gatekeeper, itinerant broker, liaison, representative) is a function of the combination of a pattern of ties and group affiliation.

centrality: Centrality measures give a rough indication of the social power of an actor based on his or her position within the network. A central actor can be someone who has numerous ties to other actors (*degree centrality*), who is closer (in terms of path distance) to other actors in a network (*closeness centrality*), who lies on the shortest path (geodesic) between any two actors in a network (*betweenness centrality*), and/or who has ties to actors who are highly central (*eigenvector centrality*).

centralization: Centralization uses the variation in actor centrality within the network to measure the level of centralization. More variation yields higher network centralization scores; less variation yields lower scores. The larger a centralization index, the more likely it is that a single actor is very central while the other actors are not, so centralization measures can be seen as measuring how unequal the distribution of individual actor values are.

church: Informally, the term is used to refer to a Christian congregation. In terms of church-sect theory, a church is a conventional religious organization that exists in a relatively low state of tension with its environment. Also see *sect, independent religious movement (IRM)*, and *church-sect theory*.

church-sect theory: This theory holds that over time sects will transform into churches (i.e., they will lower the tension level between themselves and their environment), which in turn will give birth to new sects which believe that their parent body has become too worldly.

closeness centrality: Closeness centrality captures how close (in terms of shortest path distance – i.e., geodesic distance) each actor is to all other actors in a network.

coevolution stochastic actor-oriented model: A variation on the stochastic actor-oriented models that allow analysts to not only model tie formation but also behavioral dynamics. Put differently, they model both social selection and social influence.

cohesion: The proportion of all pairs of actors that are connected, either directly or indirectly, with one another. The software package UCINET (see Appendix C) calculates both this measure of cohesion and a distance-weighted version that takes into account the shortest path distance between pairs of actors. It equals the additive inverse of fragmentation. See *fragmentation*.

community detection algorithm: Community detection algorithms are a series of clustering algorithms that detect subgroups such that there are more ties within than across the subgroups than one would expect. The optimal number of subgroups generally uses modularity as a measure of fit. See *modularity*.

complete network: Also known as a whole or full network. See *whole network*.

component: A component is a subnetwork in which members have ties to one another but do not have ties with members of other subnetworks. In directed networks, you can identify two types: strong and weak. Strong components take into consideration the direction of ties, whereas weak components do not. In a strong component, each pair of actors is connected by a (directed) path, and no other actor can be added without destroying its connectedness. By contrast, in a weak component, each pair of actors is connected by an undirected path, and no other actor can be added without destroying its connectedness.

cult: Also known as an "independent religious movement" or a "new religious movement." See *independent religious movement*.

degree centrality: Degree centrality equals the count of the number of an actor's ties.

density: Density refers to the degree to which a network is connected. Formally, it is the number of ties in a simple network, expressed as a proportion of the maximum possible number of ties. It is inversely related to network size (i.e., the larger the network, the lower the density) because the number of possible lines increases exponentially as actors are added to the network, while the number of ties that each actor can maintain tends to be limited. Consequently, analysts use other measures, such as average degree, to compare networks of different size. See *average degree*.

diameter: The diameter of a network refers to a network's longest geodesic and could be interpreted as how spread out a network is. See *geodesic*.

directed network (graph): Also known as a diagraph (from directed graph), a directed network where one or more ties (arcs) are directed from one actor to another.

directed tie: See *arc*.

dyad: Two actors connected by a tie.

edge: An undirected tie that connects one actor to another actor. See *arc*.

edge betweenness centrality: Edge betweenness is similar to (node) betweenness centrality, except that it estimates the betweenness centrality of edges (i.e., ties) rather than nodes (i.e., actors). Like node betweenness, edge betweenness measures the extent to which each edge in a network lies on the shortest path linking all pairs of actors in the network.

ego network: An ego network is an actor's (i.e., ego's) immediate social environment: the set of actors to which the actor has ties (i.e., alters, contacts, neighbors) and the ties among those actors.

ego network density: Ego network density is the ratio of the actual number of ties between ego's alters and the total possible number of ties between ego's alters. Same as the local clustering coefficient.

eigenvector centrality: Eigenvector centrality assumes that ties to central actors are more important than ties to peripheral actors and thus weights each actor's summed connections to others by their centrality. With an undirected network, eigenvector centrality scores are the same as hubs and authorities scores.

E-I index: An E-I index measures the ratio of external to internal ties. Scores range from –1.00 to 1.00, where –1.00 indicates that group members only have ties to other members; a score of 1.00 indicates that group members only have ties to nonmembers; and a score of 0.00 indicates that in the aggregate, members have an equal number of internal and external ties.

exponential random graph models (ERGMs): Exponential random graph models assume that observed social networks are built upon local patterns of ties, sometimes called micro-configurations (e.g., reciprocal ties, closed triads), that are a function of local social processes (e.g., homophily, closure). They are designed to predict the probability of tie formation in an observed network, while taking into account the network's properties as well as any covariates that pertain to the network's actors and the ties among them. In particular, they test whether a particular configuration occurs more frequently than one would expect given the other configurations included in the model. They are similar to the general linear models except that they include important modifications in order to account for the dependencies between observations. See *stochastic actor-oriented models (SAOMs)*.

faction: A faction is a subnetwork where each actor is tied to all other actors within his or her own subnetwork but has no ties to actors in other subnetworks.

fragmentation: The standard measure of fragmentation equals the proportion of all pairs of actors that are not connected, either directly or indirectly, with one another. UCINET calculates both this measure of fragmentation and a distance-weighted one that takes into account the shortest path distance between pairs of actors. It equals the additive inverse of cohesion. See *cohesion*.

full network: Also known as a complete or whole network. See *whole network*.

geodesic: A geodesic is the shortest path between two actors. The longest geodesic in a network is the network's diameter.

global clustering coefficient: In some software packages (e.g., ORA), the global clustering coefficient equals the sum of each actor's local clustering coefficient divided by the number of actors in the network. In other packages, it equals the sum of each actor's local clustering coefficient divided by the number of actors with two or more alters (actors with less than two alters have a local clustering coefficient of zero). See *local clustering coefficient*.

independent religious movement (IRM): Also referred to as a "cult" or a "new religious movement." Like sects, IRMs exist in a high state of tension with their sociocultural environment, but unlike sects, they do not have ties to an established religious tradition in their particular society. They arise either by being imported from another society (e.g., Buddhism in the United States and Christianity in India) or through innovation (e.g., Islam in Mecca or Mormonism in the United States).

k-core: Formally, a k-core is a maximal group of actors, all of whom are connected to some number (k) of other group members.

local clustering coefficient: The local clustering coefficient is the ratio of actual number of ties between ego's alters and the total possible number of ties between ego's alters. Same as ego network density. See *global clustering coefficient*.

longitudinal network: A longitudinal network is network data recorded over time. See *stochastic actor-oriented models (SAOMs)*.

modularity: Modularity is a measure of fit that compares the ties within and across groups to what one would expect in a random graph of the same size and having the same number of ties. See *community detection algorithms*.

network closure: Where a social network is characterized by numerous ties between members and somewhat insulated from the sociocultural environment.

network size: The number of actors in the network.

new religious movement: Also known as a "cult" or "independent religious movement." See *independent religious movement (IRM)*.

one-mode network: A one-mode network is a network that consists of a single set of actors. See also *two-mode network*.

partition: A network partition is a discrete classification or clustering of actors that assigns each actor to exactly one class or cluster.

path: A path is a walk (i.e., a sequence of actors and ties) in which no actor and no tie in between the first and last actor of the walk occurs more than once. The one exception is that the first and last actor in a path can be the same actor.

path distance: The distance between pairs of actors in a network. The shortest path between a pair of actors is known as the geodesic.

pendant: An actor that is connected to a network by only one tie.

positional analysis: Positional analysis seeks to identify actors who hold similar positions in the social structure. A position (e.g., student) is typically connected to a particular role or set of roles and located within a larger system of positions, which is why some social network analysts believe that actors occupying a particular position/role will exhibit similar types of behavior. See *blocks, blockmodels,* and *blockmodeling*.

QAP (quadratic assignment procedure): QAP is similar to bootstrapping in that it involves the random rearrangement of a network's rows and columns thousands of times in order to calculate a null distribution of statistics that can then be compared to the statistics generated using the actual network. If the actual statistics differ from a substantial proportion of those in the null distribution, then an analyst may conclude that the observed statistics could not have occurred by random chance and are "statistically significant."

rational choice: Formally, rational choice theory assumes that people are rational actors who evaluate the costs and benefits of a given action and then act in order to maximize their net benefits (i.e., their utility).

Less formally, it argues that in the arena of religion people respond to incentives just as they do in other aspects of their lives.

religious economy: The set of religious institutions competing for adherents within a particular society or geographical area. The religious economy approach to the social scientific study of religion assumes that just as there are markets for commercial goods, there are markets for religious goods where various firms (i.e., religious institutions such as churches, synagogues, and mosques) seek to attract and retain customers. Its central assumption is that, all else being equal, church participation is inversely associated with the level of state regulation.

roles and positions: See *blocks, blockmodels, blockmodeling,* and *positional analysis.*

sacred canopy: Widespread social support for religious beliefs and practices. The term is associated with Peter Berger, who argued that religion can only survive when there is widespread social support for a particular way of looking at the heavens. See *sacred umbrella.*

sacred umbrella: A religious reference group. The term was coined by Christian Smith, who argued that people do not need all-encompassing sacred cosmos to maintain their religious beliefs. Instead, they only need a religious reference group (i.e., a sacred umbrella) in order for their beliefs to seem plausible. See *sacred canopy.*

sect: A religious organization that exists in a high state of tension with its sociocultural environment. Sects typically form when they split off from a conventional religious organization (i.e., church) that they believe has become too worldly (i.e., secularized). Also see *church* and *independent religious movement (IRM).*

secularization: Historically, secularization theory has held that religious belief and practice is inversely related to societal modernization. It argues that pluralism and the spread of scientific knowledge will lead to a decline in religious belief and practice. Some have argued that religion will completely disappear; others have held that it will only be found in societal "backwaters." The term "secularization" can also refer to the process by which sects are transformed into churches. See *church-sect theory.*

social capital: The quantity and quality of resources (i.e., individual, group, or community) that individuals access through the various social networks in which they are embedded.

social network: A finite set or sets of actors that share ties with one another.

social structure: Social structure is the enduring patterns of behavior and relationships within social systems (e.g., roles) or the social institutions and norms that have become embedded in social systems in such a way that they shape behavior. Within social network analysis, social structures are seen in terms of social networks.

stochastic actor-oriented models (SAOMs): Stochastic actor-oriented models attempt to model network dynamics on the basis of observed longitudinal network data and evaluate these according to the paradigm of statistical inference. They are similar to exponential random graph models (ERGMs) in that they assume that the observed network structure is, in part, a function of local patterns of ties (e.g., closed triads) that reflect endogenous social processes (e.g., network closure). Like ERGMs, they test whether a particular configuration occurs more frequently than one would expect given the other configurations included in the model. They differ in that they are designed for longitudinal social network data and assume that actors control and change their ties according to short-term goals and constraints. They are similar to the general linear models except that they include important modifications in order to account for the dependencies between observations. See *exponential random graph models (ERGMs)*.

strictness: Associated with Dean Kelley and Laurence Iannaccone, the theory of strictness holds that strictness increases the average levels of commitment in a faith community because it eliminates free-riding, and this, in turn, leads to an increase in the net benefits of membership.

structural determinism, instrumentalism, and constructionism: The three social network paradigms to which most social network analysts adhere. *Structural determinism* ignores (or dismisses) the possible causal role that actors' beliefs, values, and commitments play in terms of social processes and historical change. *Structural instrumentalism* allows room for human agency but frames it solely in terms of rational choice, instrumental action, and utility maximization. *Structural constructionism* also allows room for human agency and, like structural instrumentalism, believes that actors respond to incentives; however, it also assumes that actors are motivated by additional concerns, such as norms, values, cultural commitments, and collective and individual identities. See *social structure* and *rational choice*.

structural hole: A concept (and measure) developed by Ron Burt; a structural hole is a gap in the social structure.

subcultural identity theory: Associated with Christian Smith, this theory holds that religion continues to survive in the modern world because it has created subcultures with collective identities that provide followers with a sense of meaning and belonging. It also argues that religious groups that engage with and maintain clear boundaries between themselves and others are more likely to thrive in pluralistic societies than those that do not.

tie: A tie is a relation between two actors. A tie can be either directed (arc) or undirected (edge). They can also vary in terms of strength.

topography: Network topography refers to the overall structure of the network. Commonly used measures include density, cohesion, fragmentation, network size, and centralization.

triad: A triad is a set of three actors that may or may not have ties between them. See *dyad*.

two-mode network: A network that consists of two sets of actors (i.e., dyadic network), or one set of actors and one set of events (i.e., affiliation network). See *one-mode network*.

undirected tie: An undirected tie is a line that connects two actors but does not point from one actor to another.

walk: A walk is a sequence of actors and ties that begins and ends with actors that can involve the same actor and the same tie more than once. See *path* and *path distance*.

whole network: A whole network not only includes all relevant actors but also all relevant ties between actors. Also known as a full or complete network.

Appendix B: Defining Religion

Much ink has been spilled defining religion, and here I only intend to offer a brief summary of how social scientists have thought about religion and my position on the matter.[1] Definitions generally fall under two broad categories: *functional* and *substantive*. The former focus on what religions do, while the latter focus on what they believe. Another way to think of it is that functional definitions see religion as performing certain functions for individuals, society, or both; for example, some believe that a primary function of religion is to help integrate people into wider society, while others argue that religion provides people with answers to questions about life's meaning. By contrast, substantive definitions generally concern themselves with religion's substance, its content, and how this affects what people do.

Undoubtedly, the best known functional definition is Emile Durkheim's. He argued that "a religion is a unified system of beliefs and practices relative to sacred things, that is to say, things set apart and forbidden – beliefs and practices which unite into one single moral community called a Church, all those who adhere to them" (Durkheim 1995 [1912]:44). There are two things worth emphasizing about Durkheim's definition. First, it argues that a religion consists of "a unified system of beliefs and practices" that are, in some way, "related to sacred things." Durkheim draws a distinction between the sacred and profane, rather than emphasize a belief in a God, gods, or some sort of supernatural force, because he argued (incorrectly) that belief in the supernatural is an "idea that appears very late in the history of religions" and can only be found in a handful of "advanced religions"; as such, it should not "be made a defining aspect of religion" (Durkheim 1995 [1912]: 24, 25). Consequently, functional definitions tend to be quite inclusive about what

---

[1] For fuller treatments, I commend to readers the thoughtful discussions by Peter Berger (1974); Kevin Christiano, William Swatos, and Peter Kivisto (2016:4–18); Michael Emerson, William Mirola, and Susanne Monahan (2011:4–12); Christian Smith (2017); and Rodney Stark (2017b).

social scientists consider to be a religion. Second, it emphasizes the importance on the communal aspects of religion. As Durkheim notes, by "showing that the idea of religion is inseparable from the idea of a Church, it conveys the notion that religion must be an eminently collective thing" (Durkheim 1995 [1912]:44).

Like all definitions, functional ones have attracted their share of criticism. A common critique is their insistence that not all religions believe in the supernatural. Durkheim, for instance, held up Buddhism as an example of a "godless" religion, and it is true that the Buddha and his early followers were agnostic with regards to the existence of the gods or God. Nevertheless, like most Indian religions, Buddhism advocates a belief in the supernatural force of samsara, that is, the endless cycle of birth and rebirth, from which Buddhists seek liberation. Moreover, as many scholars have noted, more popular forms of Buddhism, such as Pure Land Buddhism, are chock full of supernatural deities. A related concern is the vagueness of functional definitions. Rodney Stark, for instance, argues that Durkheim was quite vague in defining the sacred, "except to say that it is the opposite of 'profane'" (which he also left undefined) and that sacred things are "set apart and forbidden" (Stark 2001a:102 – also see Stark 2017b:3). And Christian Smith (2017:40, foonote 43) observes that "purely functional definitions ... are doomed to vagueness and failure." Nevertheless, most of us have an intuitive understanding of what is sacred and what is profane. For example, if on a Sunday morning we walked into the sanctuary of an evangelical Protestant church (and probably a mainline Protestant church) and knocked over a cross or threw a Bible displayed on a lectern on the floor, the reaction from worshippers would probably be unpleasant. Why? Because the cross and the Bible are sacred objects for Christians. Similarly, if we burned an American flag in the middle of a busy street in a US city, our action would be greeted by many patriotic onlookers with hostility.

This last example points to another common critique of functionalist definitions: they are simply too inclusive. They include as religions what most people do not consider to be a religion. For example, I once had a student who drew on a functional definition of religion in order to examine the "Raider Nation" as a religious phenomenon.[2] He identified the Oakland Coliseum as its place of worship, the "Black Hole" as its sanctuary, and the various costumes many fans wear to games as religious garb. He also noted that several of the "rituals" performed by fans have a sacred quality to them. This is not to suggest that religions do not contain sacred objects. Most do. It is just that identifying any phenomena that delineates between sacred from profane objects as a religion may be a bit of a stretch. Nor is it to suggest that notions of the sacred and profane

---

[2] See https://en.wikipedia.org/wiki/Raider_Nation.

are not useful concepts for analyzing social phenomena. They are. For instance, Christian Smith (2014) recently drew on them to analyze the discipline of sociology.

It is because of these objections, in particular the last, that I gravitate to substantive definitions of religion. As noted earlier, they focus on the content of a religion, what it believes. Moreover, they almost always contain some notion of the supernatural, such as a belief in a God or gods (Stark 2001a, 2017b), the supramundane (Christiano, Swatos, and Kivisto 2016), or superhuman powers (Smith 2017). Not all emphasize the collective aspect of religion, but most assume that belief in the supernatural brings with it a set of practices in which adherents participate collectively. Moreover, belief in the supernatural almost always leads to the generation of sacred texts and the development of doctrines that explore the meaning of life and the state and future of the world. Given these observations, I offer the following religion "checklist" in lieu of a formal definition:

1. Belief in a god, gods, or supernatural force (personal or impersonal).
2. A moral community composed of recognized leaders and lay adherents that collectively and individually engage in a set of practices, such as worship, rituals, ethical expectations, distinctive styles of dress, and dietary restrictions.
3. Sacred texts that capture revelations from the supernatural realm. Examples include
   - Judaism – Hebrew Bible, Talmud
   - Buddhism – Tripitaka, Mahayana Sutras, Tibetan Book of the Dead
   - Hinduism – Vedas, Upanishads
   - Christianity – Old Testament, New Testament
   - Islam – Qur'an
   - Mormons (LDS) – Old Testament, New Testament, Book of Mormon
4. Doctrines and explanations that address issues such as the meaning of life, the origins and destiny of the world, the problem of evil, and the destiny of human beings.

One could also argue that most religions also have a founder, a charismatic authority, who helped give birth to the movement, such as Moses for Judaism, Siddhārtha Gautama for Buddhism, Jesus of Nazareth for Christianity, Mohammad for Islam, and Joseph Smith for Mormonism. However, since some religions do not have an identified founder (e.g., Hinduism), I exclude it from the checklist.

Appendix C: SNA Software

Gephi (https://gephi.org) is a free, open-source, Java-based software written for Mac, PC, and Linux. It is an interactive visualization and exploration program for a range of networks, small and large. It was developed in 2008 by a French research team at the University of Technology of Compiegne (UTC), and the Gephi Consortium, which is a French nonprofit corporation, supports and manages its development. Its interface is available in several languages, including English, Spanish, French, and Japanese, and it has an online forum in which users can request updates and contribute to the open-source spirit of the program. Much of Gephi's functionality relies on "plugins," which are essentially add-ons that allow researchers to develop additional tools and techniques and subsequently share them with a larger community. Gephi provides users with a range of visualization options, including a customizable "Preview" tool in which users can make "finishing touches" on their network maps before dissemination. It reads several network file formats (e.g., .net files), and it is great for visualizing large networks, such as social media networks.

NetDraw (https://sites.google.com/site/netdrawsoftware/home) is a free social network visualization package that runs on Windows-compatible computers and can be downloaded from the Analytic Technologies website. It was developed by Steve Borgatti, who is also one of the developers of the social network analysis package, UCINET. Network maps created by NetDraw can be rotated, flipped, resized, and stored in several different formats. In addition, it also includes a handful of algorithms for calculating centrality, detecting subgroups, identifying sets of key players, and so on. Although it is technically a stand-alone program, it essentially functions as an extension of UCINET: it is distributed with UCINET, it can be opened from within UCINET, and it reads UCINET files without the need for using any importing and/or exporting functions. Whereas NetDraw's initial iterations did not handle large networks very well, more recent versions seem to do just fine. Moreover, if you save network data in

NetDraw's native ***.vna format, it can handle very large network files. Like UCINET, NetDraw is continually updated with new procedures, routines, and bug fixes.

Organizational Risk Analyzer (ORA) (http://netanomics.com) was developed by Kathleen Carley, who teaches at Carnegie Mellon University and is a former student of Harrison White. It is user-friendly and designed to find those actors, types of skills or knowledge, and tasks that are critical to a network's performance. Unlike most social network analysis programs, ORA is report-based. Instead of providing a single metric, ORA produces a report containing a series of related metrics. ORA includes both a main screen, where you can analyze networks using a variety of algorithms, and a draw screen, where you can visualize networks using different mapping algorithms in either two or three dimensions. A nice feature of the draw screen is that it implements several algorithms and metrics. It also includes features for simulating various scenarios, geospatially analyzing and mapping social networks that can then be plotted in various geospatial programs, creating different types of charts (e.g., histograms, bar charts, and scatter plots), and analyzing changes over time. Like the other programs, ORA has its weaknesses. For example, its reports sometimes include metrics that are inappropriate for a particular network, such as estimating closeness centrality when analyzing a disconnected network, or calculating Krackhardt's (1994) measure of hierarchy when examining an undirected (i.e., symmetric) network. And while its visualization capabilities are adequate and offer some useful options, the network maps it produces tend not to be as robust as other packages. Nevertheless, ORA is a powerful tool. It can be purchased from Netanomics, and there is an "ORA-LITE" version available for free at the Carnegie Mellon CASOS website (www.casos.cs.cmu.edu/projects/ora/software.php).

Pajek (http://mrvar.fdv.uni-lj.si/pajek) – "Pajek" means "spider" in Slovenian – was created by Vladimir Batagelj and Andrej Mrvar in 1996 and is designed to handle very large datasets. In particular, it includes routines that lend themselves to the visualization and simplification of large networks, and it allows users to visualize networks in two or three dimensions. It runs on Windows-compatible computers, can be downloaded for free, and is routinely updated by its developers. It also allows users to load and keep multiple networks and other data objects (e.g., partitions) in memory at the same time, which can then be stored in what Pajek calls a "project file." Being able to save all of one's work in a single file reduced the likelihood that you will have to later "recreate the wheel" of one of your analyses. Pajek's primary drawback is that it contains fewer algorithms than UCINET, and its network manipulation features are somewhat limited. Thus, many analysts sometimes use UCINET for data manipulation and then turn to Pajek for visualization. To Pajek's credit, however, it allows users to call up the statistical packages "R" and "SPSS" to perform procedures unavailable in Pajek. Recently, Pajek has introduced two additional versions of Pajek that can handle even larger networks and are much faster than standard Pajek: PajekXXL and Pajek3XL. According to the website, these additional versions can handle "huge" networks, which seems a fitting description given the current political climate. However, neither includes visualization options.

PNet (MPNet) (www.melnet.org.au/pnet) is a suite of programs developed for the simulation and estimation of exponential random graph models (ERGMs) and auto-logistic actor attribute models (ALAAMs) for social networks. There are three variations of PNet: (1) PNet, which is for one-mode networks, (2) MPNet, which is for multilevel networks, and (3) XPNet, which is for bivariate analysis. All of these programs are available free for noncommercial use. In terms of available micro-configurations, PNet does not currently offer as many options as the statnet library, ergm. Nevertheless, it is a powerful program that offers analysts a somewhat gentle entry into the world of ERGMs. It is the package that is used in Lusher et al.'s (2013) monograph on ERGMs. It is also what we used to estimate the ERGMs and ALAAMs in Chapter 3.

R is a programming language and software environment for statistical computing and graphics that is widely used among statisticians for developing statistical software and data analysis, including social network analysis. There are two primary suites of social network analysis software available in R: *statnet* (Handcock et al. 2003) and *igraph* (Csárdi and Nepusz 2006). The *statnet* library includes a number of interrelated programs, such as (1) *ergm*, which unsurprisingly is designed to estimate exponential random graph models; (2) *network*, which is designed to create, store, modify, and plot network data; (3) *sna*, which is a set of tools for traditional social network analysis; and (4) *EpiModel*, which is designed for modeling infectious diseases (and what we used in Chapter 8). Also available is *RSiena* (Ripley et al. 2017), which we used for estimating the coevolution stochastic actor-oriented models presented in Chapter 10, as well as *tnet* (Opsahl 2009), which is designed for two-mode, weighted, and longitudinal networks.

UCINET (https://sites.google.com/site/ucinetsoftware/home) was initially developed by Linton Freeman at the University of California, Irvine (which is where the "UCI" in "UCINET" comes from) and later refined by others, in particular, Steve Borgatti and Martin Everett. It is the best known and most widely used social network analysis software package. Not only does it contain most of the routines needed for estimating measures of network topography, identifying subgroups, calculating actor centrality, detecting brokers and bridges, identifying structurally equivalent actors, and correlations and multivariate regression, it also includes tools for selecting subsets of files, merging and stacking data sets, transposing and/or recoding data, and the importing and exporting of data in a variety of formats. UCINET is menu-driven. Its commands open dialog boxes that specify the inputs needed for it to run its various routines; results are displayed using Window's *Notepad* program and saved in log files. UCINET's comprehensiveness is what makes it so valuable. In UCINET, social network data are recorded in matrix format. Users can enter data using either UCINET's internal spreadsheet functions or with a Microsoft Excel wrapper that calls up an Excel spreadsheet within UCINET. UCINET also reads edge and node lists, which is quite useful when working with large datasets. For storing data, UCINET uses a dual file system: one containing the actual data (***.##d) and one containing information about the data (***.##h). Both files are needed in order to analyze social network data in UCINET, and this can occasionally lead to problems, such as when one of the files ends up in one folder and the other in a different folder. Because UCINET's creators regularly provide updates to the program in order to fix bugs and glitches, problems such as this are generally corrected relatively quickly. UCINET can be purchased from Analytic Technologies.

All of these packages possess a tremendous amount of power and include most of the SNA metrics and algorithms that we cover in this book. That said, there is a steep learning curve with R. We suspect that most researchers will gravitate to the stand-alone SNA packages, such as UCINET, ORA, Pajek, and PNet.

References

Abbott, Andrew. 1983. "Professional Ethics." *American of Sociology* 88(5):855–885.
Adamczyk, Amy, and Jacob Felson. 2006. "Friends' Religiosity and First Sex." *Social Science Research* 35(4):924–947.
adams, jimi, and Jenny Trinitapoli. 2009. "The Malawi Religion Project: Data Collection and Selected Analysis." *Demographic Research* 21(10):255–288.
Akers, Ronald L. 1977. *Deviant Behavior: A Social Learning Approach*. Belmont, CA: Wadsworth.
Alimi, Eitan Y. 2011. "Relational Dynamics in Factional Adoption of Terrorist Attacks: A Comparative Perspective." *Theory and Society* 40(1):95–118.
Aliverdinia, Akbar, and William Alex Pridemore. 2009. "Women's Fatalistic Suicide in Iran: A Partial Test of Durkheim in an Islamic Republic." *Violence Against Women* 15(3):307–320.
Alwin, Duane F. 1990. "Cohort Replacement and Changes in Parental Socialization Values." *Journal of Marriage and Family* 52:347–360.
Ammerman, Nancy Tatom. 1987. *Bible Believers: Fundamentalists in the Modern World*. New Brunswick, NJ: Rutgers University Press.
　1997. "Religious Choice and Religious Vitality: The Market and Beyond." In *Rational Choice Theory and Religion: Summary and Assessment*, edited by Lawrence A. Young. New York: Routledge, pp. 119–132.
Argyle, Michael. 2000. *Psychology and Religion: An Introduction*. London: Routledge.
Aristotle. 1998. *The Nichomachean Ethics*, translated by David Ross, J. L. Ackrill, and J. O. Urmson. Oxford: Oxford University Press.
Asch, Solomon E. 1951. "Effects of Group Pressure upon the Modification and Distortion of Judgment." In *Groups, Leadership and Men*, edited by Harold S. Guetzkow. Pittsburgh, PA: Carnegie Press, pp. 222–236.
　1955. "Opinions and Social Pressure." *Scientific American* 193:31–35.
Atran, Scott. 2002. *In Gods We Trust: The Evolutionary Landscape of Religion*. Oxford: Oxford University Press.
　2010. *Talking to the Enemy: Faith, Brotherhood, and the (Un)making of Terrorists*. New York: HarperCollins.

Averill, Lloyd J. 1989. *Religious Right, Religious Wrong*. New York: The Pilgrim Press.
Azarian, G. Reza. 2005. *The General Sociology of Harrison C. White: Chaos and Order in Networks*. New York: Palgrave Macmillan.
Babbie, Earl. 1986. *The Practice of Social Research*, 4th ed. Belmont, CA: Wadsworth Publishing Co.
Bader, Christopher D., Joseph O. Baker, and F. Carson Mencken. 2017. *Paranormal America*. New York: New York University Press.
Baker, Joseph O., and Buster G. Smith. 2015. *American Secularism: Cultural Contours of Nonreligious Belief Systems*. New York: New York University Press.
Balch, Robert W. 1980. "Looking Behind the Scenes in a Religious Cult: Implications for the Study of Conversion." *Sociological Analysis* 41:137–143.
Balch, Robert W., and David Taylor. 2002. "Making Sense of the Heaven's Gate Suicides." In *Cults, Religion, and Violence*, edited by D. G. Bromley and G. J. Melton. Cambridge: Cambridge University Press, pp. 209–229.
Baller, Robert D., and Kelly K. Richardson. 2002. "Social Integration, Imitation, and the Geographic Patterning of Suicide." *American Sociological Review* 67(6):873–888.
Banerjee, Abhijit, Arun G. Chandrasekhar, Esther Duflo, and Matthew O. Jackson. 2013. "The Diffusion of Microfinance." *Science* 341(26):363–370.
Barabási, Albert-László. 2002. *Linked: The New Science of Networks*. Cambridge, MA: Perseus Publishing.
Barabási, Albert-László, and Reka Albert. 1999. "Emergence of Scaling in Random Networks." *Science* 286:509–512.
Barnes, John A. 1954. "Class and Committee in a Norwegian Island Parish." *Human Relations* 7:39–58.
Barrett, Justin L. 2004. *Why Would Anyone Believe in God?* Walnut Creek, CA: AltaMira Press.
  2011. *Cognitive Science, Religion, and Theology*. West Conshohocken, PA: Templeton Press.
Barro, Robert J. 2005. "Which Countries Have State Religions?" *Quarterly Journal of Economics* 120(4):1331–1370.
Barro, Robert J., and Rachel M. McCleary. 2003. "Religion and Economic Growth across Countries." *American Sociological Review* 68(5):760–781.
  2005. "Which Countries Have State Religions?" *Quarterly Journal of Economics* 120(4):1331–1370.
Batagelj, Vladimir, and Andrej Mrvar. 2017. *Pajek 5.01*. Lubljijana, Slovenia: University of Ljubljana.
Bauerlein, Mark 2004. "Liberal Groupthink Is Anti-Intellectual." *Chronicle of Higher Education*, November 12, pp. B6–B10.
Bavelas, Alex. 1950. "Communication Patterns in Task-Oriented Groups." *Journal of the Acoustical Society of America* 22:725–730.
Becker, Gary S. 1976. *The Economic Approach to Human Behavior*. Chicago: University of Chicago Press.

Becker, George. 1997. "Replication and Reanalysis of Offenbacher's School Enrollment Study: Implications for the Weber and Merton Theses." *Journal for the Scientific Study of Religion* 36(4):483–495.
  2009. "The Continuing Path of Distortion: The Protestant Ethic and Max Weber's School Enrollment Statistics." *Acta Sociological* 52(3):195–212.
Becker, Penny E., and Pawan H. Dhingra. 2001. "Religious Involvement and Volunteering: Implications for Civil Society." *Sociology of Religion* 62(3):315–335.
Becker, Sascha, Steven Pfaff, and Jared Rubin. 2016. "Causes and Consequences of the Protestant Reformation." *Explorations in Economic History* 62:1–25.
Beit-Hallahmi, Benjamin, and Michael Argyle. 1997. *The Psychology of Religious Behavior, Belief and Experience*. London: Routledge.
Bellah, Robert N. 1967. "Civil Religion in America." *Daedalus* 96(1):1–21.
  2011. *Religion in Human Evolution: From the Paleolithic to the Axial Age*. Cambridge, MA: Belknap Press.
Bellah, Robert N., Richard Madsen, William M. Sullivan, Ann Swidler, and Steven M. Tipton. 1985. *Habits of the Heart: Individualism and Commitment in American Life*. New York: Harper & Row.
  1991. *The Good Society*. New York: Alfred A. Knopf.
Bender, Harold S., Robert Friedmann, and Walter Klassen. 1990. "Anabaptism." *Global Anabaptist Mennonite Encyclopedia Online*. Retrieved from http://gameo.org/index.php?title=Anabaptism&oldid=128087 (last accessed September 21, 2015).
Bergen, Peter. 2015. "'Jihadi John': The Bourgeois Terrorist." *CNN*. Retrieved from www.cnn.com/2015/02/19/opinion/bergen-terrorism-root-causes/index.html (last accessed July 13, 2015).
Berger, Peter L. 1967. *The Sacred Canopy: Elements of a Sociological Theory of Religion*. Garden City, NY: Doubleday.
  1969. *A Rumor of Angels: Modern Society and the Rediscovery of the Sacred*. Garden City, NY: Doubleday.
  1974. "Some Second Thoughts on Substantive versus Functional Definitions of Religion." *Journal for the Scientific Study of Religion* 13(2):124–133.
  1999. "The Desecularization of the World: A Global Overview." In *The Desecularization of the World: Resurgent Religion and World Politics*, edited by Peter L. Berger. Grand Rapids, MI: Wm. B. Eerdmans Publishing Co., pp. 1–18.
Bering, Jesse. 2011. *The Belief Instinct: The Psychology of Souls, Destiny, and the Meaning of Life*. New York: W. W. Norton & Co.
Berman, Eli. 2009. *Radical, Religious, and Violent: The New Economics of Terrorism*. Cambridge, MA: MIT Press.
Beyerlein, Kraig, Peter Barwis, Bryant Crubaugh, and Cole Carnesecca. 2016. "A New Picture of Protest: The National Study of Protest Events." *Sociological Methods & Research* 46:1–46.
Beyerlein, Kraig, and Mark Chaves. 2003. "The Political Activities of Religious Congregations in the United States." *Journal for the Scientific Study of Religion* 42(2):229–246.

Beyerlein, Kraig, and David Sikkink. 2008. "Sorrow and Solidarity: Why Americans Volunteered for 9/11 Relief Efforts." *Social Problems* 55(2):190–215.

Beyerlein, Kraig, and Stephen Vaisey. 2013. "Individualism Revisited: Moral Worldviews and Civic Engagement." *Poetics* 41:384–406.

Black, Donald. 2002. "The Geometry of Law: An Interview with Donald Black." *International Journal of the Sociology of Law* 30:101–129.

Blau, Peter M. 1977. *Inequality and Heterogeneity: A Primitive Theory of Social Structure.* New York, NY: Free Press.

—— 1994. *Structural Contexts of Opportunities.* Chicago, IL: The University of Chicago Press.

Blondel, Vincent D., Jean-Loup Guillaume, Renaud Lambiotte, and Etienne Lefebvre. 2008. "Fast Unfolding of Communities in Large Networks." *Journal of Statistical Mechanics* P10008.

Bogdan, Henrik. 2011. "Explaining the Murder-Suicides of the Order of the Solar Temple." In *Violence and New Religious Movements*, edited by James R. Lewis. New York: Oxford University Press, pp. 133–145.

Boorman, Scott A., and Harrison C. White. 1976. "Social Structure for Multiple Networks II: Role Structures." *American Journal of Sociology* 81(6):1384–1446.

Borg, Marcus J. 1987. *Jesus: A New Vision.* San Francisco, CA: Harper & Row, Publishers.

Borgatti, Stephen P. 2006a. *E-Network Software for Ego-Network Analysis.* Lexington, KY: Analytical Technologies.

—— 2006b. "Identifying Sets of Key Players in a Social Network." *Computational, Mathematical and Organizational Theory* 12:21–34.

—— 2011. *NetDraw 2.0.* Lexington, KY: Analytical Technologies.

Borgatti, Stephen P., Martin G. Everett, and Linton C. Freeman. 2002. *UCINET for Windows: Software for Social Network Analysis.* Harvard, MA: Analytical Technologies.

Borgatti, Stephen P., Martin G. Everett, and Jeffrey C. Johnson. 2013. *Analyzing Social Networks.* Thousand Oaks, CA: SAGE Publications.

Bott, Elizabeth. 1957. *Family and Social Network.* London: Tavistock.

Bourdieu, Pierre. 1985. *Distinction: A Social Critique of the Judgement of Taste.* New York: Taylor & Francis Books, Ltd.

—— 1986. "The Forms of Capital." In *Handbook of Theory and Research for the Sociology of Education*, edited by John G. Richardson. New York: Greenwood Press, pp. 241–258; reprinted in *The Sociology of Economic Life*, 3rd ed., edited by Mark Granovetter and Richard Swedberg, Boulder, CO: Westview Press, pp. 78–92.

Boyer, Pascal. 2001. *Religion Explained.* New York: Basic Books.

Bramoullé, Yann, and Rachel Kranton. 2006. "Public Goods in Networks." *Journal of Economic Theory* 135:478–494.

Branch, Taylor. 1988. *Parting the Waters: America in the King Years, 1954–1963.* New York: Simon and Schuster.

Brashears, Matthew E. 2008. "Gender and Homophily: Differences in Male and Female Association in Blau Space." *Social Science Research* 37:400–415.

2010. "Anomia and the Sacred Canopy: Testing a Network Theory." *Social Networks* 32(3):187–196.
Breiger, Ron, Kathleen M. Carley, and Philippa Pattison (eds.). 2003. *Dynamic Social Network Modeling and Analysis: Workshop Summary and Papers*. Washington, DC: National Academy of Sciences / National Research Council: National Academies Press.
Brinton, Mary C. 2000. "Social Capital in the Japanese Youth Labor Market: Labor Market Policy, Schools, and Norms." *Policy Sciences* 33(3–4):289–306.
Brockman, James R. 2005. *Romero: A Life*. Maryknoll, NY: Orbis Books.
Bromley, David G., and Edward D. Silver. 1995. "The Davidian Tradition: From Patronal Clan to Prophetic Movement." In *Armageddon in Waco: Critical Perspectives on the Branch Davidian Conflict*, edited by Stuart A. Wright. Chicago: University of Chicago Press, pp. 43–72.
Broodbank, Cyprian. 1993. "Ulysses without Sails: Trade, Distance, Knowledge and Power in the Early Cyclades." *World Archaeology* 24(3):315–331.
Brooks, Arthur C. 2006. *Who Really Cares?* New York: Basic Books.
Brown, John Seely, and Paul Duguid. 1991. "Organization Learning and Communities-of-Practice: Toward a Unified View of Working, Learning, and Innovation." *Organization Science* 2(1):40–57.
Brughmans, Tom. 2010. "Connecting the Dots: Toward Archaeological Network Analysis." *Oxford Journal of Archaeology* 29(3):277–303.
  2013. "Thinking through Networks: A Review of Formal Network Methods in Archaeology." *Journal of Archaeological Method and Theory* 20:623–662.
Brughmans, Tom, Anna Collar, and Fiona Coward (eds.). 2016. *The Connected Past: Challenges to Network Studies in Archaeology and History*. Oxford: Oxford University Press.
Brughmans, Tom, Simon Keay, and Graeme Earl. 2014. "Introducing Exponential Random Graph Models for Visibility Networks." *Journal of Archaeological Science* 49:442–454.
Brusco, Elizabeth. 1995. *The Reformation of Machismo*. Austin: University of Texas Press.
Brym, Robert J., and Bader Araj. 2006. "Suicide Bombing as Strategy and Interaction." *Social Forces* 84(4):1969–1986.
Buber, Martin. 1937. *I and Thou*, translated by Ronald Gregor Smith. New York: Charles Scribner's Sons.
Buchanan, Mark. 2001. *Ubiquity*. New York: Crown Publishers.
  2002. *Nexus: Small Worlds and the Groundbreaking Science of Networks*. New York: W. W. Norton & Company.
Burns, Tom, and G. M. Stalker. 1961. *The Management of Innovation*. London: Tavistock.
Burt, Ronald S. 1984. "Network Items and the General Social Survey." *Social Networks* 6(4):293–340.
  1985. "General Social Survey Network Items." *Connections* 8:119–122.
  1987. "Social Contagion and Innovation: Cohesion Versus Structural Equivalence." *American Journal of Sociology* 92(6):1287–1335.

1992a. "The Social Structure of Competition." In *Networks and Organizations: Structure, Form and Action*, edited by Nitin Nohria and Robert G. Eccles. Boston: Harvard University Press, pp. 57–91.

1992b. *Structural Holes: The Social Structure of Competition*. Cambridge, MA: Harvard University Press.

Burt, Ronald S., and Marc Knez. 1995. "Kinds of Third-Party Effects on Trust." *Rationality and Society* 7(3):255–292.

Butler, Jon. 2010. "Disquieted History in A Secular Age." In *Varieties of Secularization*, edited by Michael Warner, Jonathan VanAnterwerpen, and Craig Calhoun. Cambridge, MA: Harvard University Press, pp. 193–216.

Butts, Carter T. 2014. "sna: Tools for Social Network Analysis." R package version 2.3-2. http://cran.r-project.org/package=sna (last accessed March 22, 2018).

Cadge, Wendy. 2004. *Heartwood: The First Generation of Theravada Buddhism in America*. Chicago: University of Chicago Press.

Caldwell, Cleopatra Howard, Angela Dungee Green, and Andrew Billingsley. 1992. "The Black Church as a Family Support System: Instrumental and Expressive Functions." *National Journal of Sociology* 6:21–40.

Campolo, Tony. 1995. *Can Mainline Denominations Make a Comeback?* Valley Forge, PA: Judson Press.

Cantoni, Davide. 2012. "Adopting a New Religion: The Case of Protestantism in the 16th Century Germany." *Economic Journal* 122(560):502–531.

Caplow, Theodore. 1982. "Religion in Middletown." *Public Interest* 68:78–87.

Caplow, Theodore, Howard M. Bahr, and Bruce A. Chadwick. 1983. *All Faithful People: Change and Continuity in Middletown's Religion*. Minneapolis: University of Minnesota Press.

Carley, Kathleen M. 2016. *ORA-PRO*. Pittsburgh, PA: Netanomics.

Carnes, Tony. 2015. *A Journey through NYC Religions*. New York: Tony Carnes. www.nycreligion.info (last accessed April 11, 2015).

Carpenter, James, and Michael G. Kenward. 2013. *Multiple Imputation and Its Application*. Chichester: Wiley.

Cartwright, Dorwin, and Frank Harary. 1956. "Structural Balance: A Generalization of Heider's Theory." *Psychological Review* 63:277–292.

Cerna, Lucia, and Mary Jo Ignoffo. 2014. *Le Verdad: A Witness to the Salvadoran Martyrs*. Maryknoll, NY: Orbis Books.

Chaney, David. 1994. *The Cultural Turn: Scene Setting Essays on Contemporary Cultural History*. London: Routledge.

Chaves, Mark. 1994. "Secularization as Declining Religious Authority." *Social Forces* 72(3):749–774.

1996. "Ordaining Women: The Diffusion of an Organizational Innovation." *American Journal of Sociology* 101(4):840–873.

1997. *Ordaining Women: Culture and Conflict in Religious Organizations*. Cambridge, MA: Harvard University Press.

2004. *Congregations in America*. Cambridge, MA: Harvard University Press.

2006. "All Creatures Great and Small: Megachurches in Context." *Review of Religious Research* 47(4):329–346.

Chaves, Mark, and Shawna L. Anderson. 2008. "Continuity and Change in American Congregations: Introducing the Second Wave of the National Congregations Study." *Sociology of Religion* 69(4):415–440.
2014. "Changing American Congregations: Findings from the Third Wave of the National Congregations Study." *Journal for the Scientific of Religion* 53(4):676–686.
Chaves, Mark, and David E. Cann. 1992. "Regulation, Pluralism, and Religious Market Structure: Explaining Religion's Vitality." *Rationality and Society* 4(3):272–290.
Chaves, Mark, Helen M. Giesel, and William Tsitsos. 2002. "Religious Variations in Public Presence." In *The Quiet Hand of God*, edited by Robert Wuthnow and John H. Evans. Berkeley: University of California Press, pp. 108–128.
Chaves, Mark, and Philip S. Gorski. 2001. "Religious Pluralism and Religious Participation." *Annual Review of Sociology* 27:261–281.
Chaves, Mark, Mary Ellen Konieczny, Kraig Beyerlein, and Emily Barman. 1999. "The National Congregations Study: Background, Methods, and Selected Results." *Journal for the Scientific Study of Religion* 38:458–476.
Chaves, Mark, Peter J. Schraeder, and Mario Sprindys. 1994. "State Regulation of Religion and Muslim Religious Vitality in the Industrialized West." *Journal of Politics* 56(4):1087–1097.
Cheadle, Jacob E., and Philip Schwadel. 2012. "The 'Friendship Dynamics of Religion,' or the 'Religious Dynamics of Friendship'? A Social Network Analysis of Adolescents Who Attend Small School." *Social Science Research* 41:1198–1212.
Chen, Lu, Ingmar Weber, and Adam Okulicz-Kozaryn. 2014. "U.S. Religious Landscape on Twitter." Proceedings of the Sixth International Conference on Social Informatics (SocInfo'14):544–560.
Christakis, Nicholas. 2010. *The Hidden Influence of Networks*. [Video File]. Retrieved from: www.ted.com/talks/nicholas_christakis_the_hidden_influen ce_of_social_networks?language=en (last accessed September 30, 2017).
Christakis, Nicholas, and James Fowler. 2009. *Connected: The Surprising Power of Our Social Networks and How They Shape Our Lives*. London: Little, Brown and Company.
Christiano, Kevin J., William H. Swatos, Jr., and Peter Kivisto. 2016. *Sociology of Religion: Contemporary Developments*, 3rd ed. Lanham, MD: Rowman & Littlefield Publishers, Inc.
Clasen, Claus-Peter. 1972. *Anabaptism: A Social History, 1525–1618*. Ithaca, NY: Cornell University Press.
Clayton, Philip, and Paul Davies (eds.). 2006. *The Re-Emergence of Emergence: The Emergentist Hypothesis from Science to Religion*. New York: Oxford University Press.
Cleves, Mario A., William W. Gould, Roberto G. Gutierrez, and Yulia V. Marchenko. 2010. *An Introduction to Survival Analysis Using Stata*, 3rd ed. College Station, TX: Stata Press.
Coleman, James S. 1988. "Social Capital in the Creation of Human Capital." *American Journal of Sociology* 94(Supplement):S95–S120.

1990. *Foundations of Social Theory.* Cambridge, MA: Belknap Press.

Coleman, James S., Elihu Katz, and Herbert Menzel. 1957. "The Diffusion of an Innovation among Physicians." *Sociometry* 20:253–269.

1966. *Medical Innovation: A Diffusion Study*, vol. 20. New York: Bobbs Merrill.

Collar, Anna. 2013a. "Re-thinking Jewish Ethnicity through Social Network Analysis." In *Network Analysis in Archeology: New Approaches to Regional Interaction*, edited by Carl Knappett. Oxford: Oxford University Press, pp. 223–245.

2013b. *Religious Networks in the Roman Empire.* Cambridge: Cambridge University Press.

Collar, Anna, Fiona Coward, Tom Brughmans, and Barbara J. Mills. 2015. "Networks in Archeology: Phenomena, Abstraction, Representation." *Journal of Archaeological Method and Theory* 22(1):1–32.

Collins, Randall. 1993. "Emotional Energy as the Common Denominator of Rational Action." *Rationality and Society* 5(2):203–230.

1998. *The Sociology of Philosophies: A Global Theory of Intellectual Change.* Cambridge, MA: Belknap Press.

2004. *Interaction Ritual Chains.* Princeton, NJ: Princeton University Press.

2008. *Violence: A Micro-Sociological Theory.* Princeton, NJ: Princeton University Press.

Cook, Karen S., and J. M. Whitmeyer. 1992. "Two Approaches to Social Structure: Exchange Theory and Network Analysis." *Annual Review of Sociology* 18:109–127.

Cordoba, J-R. 2006. "Using Foucault to Analyse Ethics in the Practice or Problem Structuring Methods." *Journal of the Operational Research Society* 57(9):1027–1034.

Coser, Lewis A. 1956. *The Functions of Social Conflict.* Glencoe, IL: The Free Press.

Cox, Harvey. 1966. *The Secular City: Secularization and Urbanization in Theological Perspective*, rev. ed. New York: Macmillan.

Cress, Daniel M., J. Miller McPherson, and Thomas Rotolo. 1997. "Competition and Commitment in Voluntary Memberships: The Paradox of Persistence and Participation." *Sociological Perspectives* 40(1):61–79.

Crossley, Nick, Elisa Bellotti, Gemma Edwards, Martin G. Everett, Johan Koskinen, and Mark Tranmer. 2015. *Social Network Analysis for Ego-Nets.* London: SAGE Publications.

Csárdi, Gábor, and Tamás Nepusz. 2006. "The igraph Software Package for Complex Network Research." *InterJournal, Complex Systems* 1695(5):1–9.

Cunningham, Daniel, Sean F. Everton, and Philip J. Murphy. 2016. *Understanding Dark Networks: A Strategic Framework for the Use of Social Network Analysis.* Lanham, MD: Rowman and Littlefield.

Daraganova, Galina, and Philippa Pattison. 2013. "Autologistic Actor Attribute Model Analysis of Unemployment: Dual Importance of Who You Know and Where You Live." In *Exponential Random Graph Models for Social Networks*, edited by Dean Lusher, Johan Koskinen, and Garry Robins. New York: Cambridge University Press, pp. 237–247.

Daraganova, Galina, and Garry Robins. 2013. "Autologistic Actor Attribute Models." In *Exponential Random Graph Models for Social Networks*, edited by Dean Lusher, Johan Koskinen, and Garry Robins. New York: Cambridge University Press, pp. 102–114.

Davie, Grace. 2013. *The Sociology of Religion: A Critical Agenda*. London: SAGE Publications.

Davis, James A. 1967. "Clustering and Structural Balance in Graphs." *Human Relations* 20(2):181–187.

1979. "The Davis/Holland/Leinhardt Studies: An Overview." In *Perspectives on Social Network Research*, edited by Paul W. Holland and Samuel Leinhardt. New York: Academic Press, pp. 51–62.

Davis, Nancy J., and Robert V. Robinson. 1996. "Religious Orthodoxy in American Society: The Myth of a Monolithic Camp." *Journal for the Scientific Study of Religion* 35(2):229–245.

1999. "Their Brothers' Keepers? Orthodox Religionists, Modernists, and Economic Justice in Europe." *American Journal of Sociology* 104(6):1631–1665.

De Nooy, Wouter. 2011. "Networks of Action and Events over Time: A Multilevel Discrete-Time Event History Model for Longitudinal Network Data." *Social Networks* 33(1):31–40.

De Nooy, Wouter, Andrej Mrvar, and Vladimir Batagelj. 2005. *Exploratory Social Network Analysis with Pajek*. Cambridge: Cambridge University Press.

2011. *Exploratory Social Network Analysis with Pajek*, rev. and expanded ed. Cambridge: Cambridge University Press.

Delacroix, Jacques. 1992. "A Critical Empirical Test of the 'Common Interpretation' of The Protestant Ethic and the Spirit of Capitalism." Paper presented at the *International Association for Business and Society*. Leuven, Belgium.

Delacroix, Jacques, and Francios Nielsen. 2001. "The Beloved Myth: Protestantism and the Rise of Industrial Capitalism in Nineteenth-Century Europe." *Social Forces* 80(2):509–553.

Della Porta, Donatella. 2013. *Clandestine Political Violence*. New York: Cambridge University Press.

Diani, Mario. 2002. "Network Analysis." In *Methods of Social Movement Research*, edited by Bert Klandermans and Suzanne Staggenborg. Minneapolis: University of Minnesota Press, pp. 173–230.

Diani, Mario, and Doug McAdam (eds.). 2003. *Social Movements and Networks: Relational Approaches to Collective Action*. Oxford: Oxford University Press.

DiMaggio, Paul J., and Walter W. Powell. 1983. "The Iron Cage Revisited: Institutional Isomorphism and Collective Rationality in Organizational Fields." *American Sociological Review* 48(2):147–160.

Dobbelaere, Karel. 1999. "Towards an Integrated Perspective of the Processes Related to the Descriptive Concept of Secularization." *Sociology of Religion* 60(3):229–247.

Dodds, Peter Sheridan, Roby Muhamad, and Duncan J. Watts. 2003. "An Experimental Study of Search in Global Social Networks." *Science* 301:827–829.

Domke, David S., and Kevin Coe. 2008. *The God Strategy: How Religion Became a Political Weapon in America.* New York: Oxford University Press.

Doreian, Patrick, Vladimir Batagelj, and Anuska Ferligoj. 2005. *Generalized Blockmodeling.* Cambridge: Cambridge University Press.

Doreian, Patrick, and Andrej Mrvar. 1996. "A Partitioning Approach to Structural Balance." *Social Networks* 18:149–168.

2009. "Partitioning Signed Social Networks." *Social Networks* 31:1–11.

Doreian, Patrick, and F. N. Stockman (eds.). 1997. *Evolution of Social Networks.* Amsterdam: Gordon and Breach Publishers.

Dreher, Rod. 2006. *Crunchy Cons: How Birkenstocked Burkeans, Gun-loving Organic Gardeners, Evangelical Free-Range Farmers, Hip Homeschooling Mamas, Right-wing Nature Lovers and their Diverse Tribe of Countercultural Conservatives Plan to Save America (or at least the Republican Party).* New York: Crown Forum.

2009. "Becoming Barbarians." *The American Conservative.* www.theamericanconservative.com/articles/becoming-barbarians (last accessed June 8, 2015).

2015. "Christian and Countercultural: A Response to Michael Hanby." *First Things.* www.firstthings.com/article/2015/02/christian-and-countercultural (last accessed June 8, 2015).

2017. *The Benedict Option: A Strategy for Christians in a Post-Christian Nation.* New York: Sentinel.

DuBois, W. E. B. 1969. *The Souls of Black Folk.* New York: New American Library.

Durkheim, Emile. 1951. *Suicide: A Study in Sociology,* translated by John A. Spaulding and George Simpson. New York: The Free Press.

1965. *The Elementary Forms of the Religious Life,* translated by Joseph Ward Swain. New York: The Free Press.

1984. *The Division of Labor in Society,* translated by W. D. Halls. New York: The Free Press.

1995 [1912]. *The Elementary Forms of the Religious Life,* translated by Karen E. Fields. New York: The Free Press.

Eagle, David E. 2015. "Historicizing the Megachurch." *Journal of Social History* 48(3):589–604.

Eagle, David E., and Rae Jean Proeschold-Bell. 2015. "Methodological Considerations in the Use of Name Generators and Interpreters." *Social Networks* 40(1):75–83.

Easley, David, and Jon Kleinberg. 2010. *Networks, Crowds and Markets: Reasoning about a Highly Connected World.* New York: Cambridge University Press.

Ecklund, Elaine, and Christopher Scheitle. 2007. "Religion among Academic Scientists: Distinctions, Disciplines, and Demographics." *Social Problems* 54:289–307.

Edgell, Penny. 2012. "A Cultural Sociology of Religion: New Directions." *Annual Review of Sociology* 38:247–265.

Edgell, Penny, Joseph Gerteis, and Douglas Hartmann. 2006. "Atheists as 'Other': Moral Boundaries and Cultural Membership in American Society." *American Sociological Review* 71(2):211–234.

Edwards, Bob, and Michael W. Foley. 1997. "Social Capital and the Political Economy of Our Discontent." *American Behavioral Scientist* 40(5):669–678.
　1998. "Civil Society and Social Capital beyond Putnam." *American Behavioral Scientist* 42(1):124–139.
Ehrman, Bart D. 1999. *Jesus: Apocalyptic Prophet of the New Millennium.* New York: Oxford University Press.
　2000. *The New Testament: A Historical Introduction to the Early Christian Writings,* 3rd ed. New York: Oxford University Press.
　2003. *Lost Christianities: The Battles for Scripture and the Faiths We Never Knew.* New York: Oxford University Press.
Eisner, Manuel. 2003. "Long-term Historical Trends in Violent Crime." *Crime and Justice* 30:83–142.
Ekelund, Robert B., Jr., Robert F. Hébert, and Robert D. Tollison. 2002. "An Economic Analysis of the Protestant Reformation." *Journal of Political Economy* 110(3):646–671.
Ellison, Christopher G. 1991. "Religious Involvement and Subjective Well-Being." *Journal of Health and Social Behavior* 32:80–99.
　1995. "Rational Choice Explanations of Individual Religious Behavior: Notes on the Problem of Social Embeddedness." *Journal for the Scientific Study of Religion* 34(1):89–97.
　2012. *Does Faith Matter?* Waco, TX: Baylor University. [Video File]. Retrieved from: www.youtube.com/watch?v=JVMDbKGR2gI (last accessed October 18, 2017).
Ellison, Christopher G., and John P. Bartkowski. 1995. "Babies Were Being Beaten." In *Armageddon in Waco: Critical Perspectives on the Branch Davidian Conflict,* edited by Stuart A. Wright. Chicago: Chicago University Press, pp. 111–149.
Ellison, Christopher G., David A. Gay, and T. Glass. 1989. "Does Religious Commitment Contribute to Individual Life Satisfaction." *Social Forces* 68(1):100–123.
Ellison, Christopher G., and Linda K. George. 1994. "Religious Involvement, Social Ties, and Social Support in a Southeastern Community." *Journal for the Scientific Study of Religion* 33(1):46–61.
Ellison, Christopher G., and Robert A. Hummer (eds.). 2010. *Religion, Families, and Health: Population-based Research in the United States.* New Brunswick, NJ: Rutgers University Press.
Ellison, Christopher G., and Jeffrey S. Levin. 1998. "The Religion-Health Connection: Evidence, Theory, and Future Directions." *Health Education and Behavior* 25:700–720.
Ellison, Christopher G., and Darren E. Sherkat. 1990. "Patterns of Religious Mobility among Black Americans." *Sociological Quarterly* 31:551–568.
　1995. "The 'Semi-involuntary Institution' Revisited: Regional Variations in Church Participation Among Black Americans." *Social Forces* 73(4):1415–1437.
　1999. "Identifying the Semi-involuntary Institution: A Clarification." *Social Forces* 78(2):793–802.

Ellwood, Robert S., and Barbara A. McGraw. 2005. *Many Peoples, Many Faiths: Women and Men in the World Religions*, 8th ed. Upper Saddle River, NJ: Pearson Education.

Emerson, Michael O., William A. Mirola, and Susanne C. Monahan. 2011. *Religion Matters: What Sociology Teaches Us about Religion in Our World*. Boston: Allyn & Bacon.

Emerson, Michael O., and David H. Sikkink. 2006. *Portraits of American Life Study, 1st Wave*.

Emerson, Michael O., and Christian S. Smith. 2000. *Divided by Faith: Evangelical Religion and the Problem of Race in America*. Oxford: Oxford University Press.

Emerson, Richard M. 1962. "Power-Dependence Relations." *American Sociological Review* 27(1):31–41.

   1972a. "Exchange Theory, Part I: A Psychological Basis for Social Exchange." In *Sociological Theories in Progress*, vol. 2, edited by Joseph Berger, Morris Zelditch, and B. Anderson. Boston: Houghton-Mifflin, pp. 38–57.

   1972b. "Exchange Theory, Part II: Exchange Relations and Network Structures." In *Sociological Theories in Progress*, vol. 2, edited by Joseph Berger, Morris Zelditch, and B. Anderson. Boston: Houghton-Mifflin, pp. 58–87.

   1976. "Social Exchange Theory." In *Annual Review of Sociology*. Palo Alto, CA: Annual Reviews Inc, pp. 335–362.

Emirbayer, Mustafa, and Jeff Goodwin. 1994. "Network Analysis, Culture, and the Problem of Agency." *American Journal of Sociology* 99(6):1411–1454.

Engels, Friedrich. 2008 [1894]. "On the History of Early Christianity." In *On Religion*, edited by Karl Mark and Friedrich Engels. Mineloa, NY: Dover Publications, Inc, pp. 316–347.

Erickson, Bonnie H. 2001. "Social Networks." In *Blackwell Companion to Sociology*, vol. 102. Oxford, UK: Blackwell Publishing, Ltd, pp. 314–326.

Erikson, Robert, and John H. Goldthorpe. 1985. "Are American Rates of Social Mobility Exceptionally High? New Evidence on an Old Issue." *European Sociological Review* 1(1):1–22.

   1992. "The CASMIN Project and the American Dream." *European Sociological Review* 8(3):283–305.

Erikson, Robert, John H. Goldthorpe, and Lucienne Portocarero. 1979. "Intergenerational Class Mobility in Three Western European Societies: England, France and Sweden." *British Journal of Sociology* 30(4):415–441.

   1983. "Intergenerational Class Mobility and the Convergence Thesis: England, France and Sweden." *British Journal of Sociology* 34(3):303–343.

Esmailian, Pouya, and Mahdi Jalili. 2015. "Community Detection in Signed Networks: The Role of Negative Ties in Different Scales." *Scientific Reports* 5:14339.

Evans, John H. 2003. "The Creation of a Distinct Subcultural Identity and Denominational Growth." *Journal for the Scientific Study of Religion* 42(3):467–477.

Evans, Tim. 2017. "Which Network Model Should I Use? Toward a Quantitative Comparison of Spatial Network Models in Archaeology." In *The Connected*

Past: Challenges to Network Studies in Archaeology and History, edited by Tom Brughmans, Anna Collar, and Fiona Coward. Oxford: Oxford University Press, pp. 149–173.

Evans, Tim, Carl Knappett, and Ray Rivers. 2009. "Using Statistical Physics to Understand Relational Space: A Case Study from Mediterranean Prehistory." In *Complexity Perspectives on Innovation and Social Change*, edited by David Lane, Denise Pumain, Sander Van der Leeuw, and Geoffrey West. Berlin: Springer, pp. 451–479.

Everton, Sean F. 2004. *A Guide for the Visually Perplexed: Visually Representing Social Networks*. Stanford, CA: Stanford University.

  2005. "Social Mobility and Sect Transformation: Testing the Regression-to-the-Mean Hypothesis." *Interdisciplinary Journal of Research on Religion* 1 (article 9)(1), available at www.religjournal.com (last accessed September 18, 2017.

  2007. "Whose Faith-Based Initiative? How Kerry and Edwards Wooed African American Churchgoers." *Books and Culture: A Christian Review* (January/February):42–43.

  2012a. *Disrupting Dark Networks*. New York: Cambridge University Press.

  2012b. "Network Topography, Key Players and Terrorist Networks." *Connections* 31(1):12–19.

  2015a. "Church Activism." In *The SAGE Encyclopedia of Economics and Society*, vol. 1, edited by Frederick F. Wherry and Juliet Schor. Thousand Oaks, CA: SAGE Publications, pp. 368–371.

  2015b. "Networks and Religion: Ties that Bind, Loose, Build Up, and Tear Down." *Journal of Social Structure* 16(10): 1–34, available at www.cmu.edu/joss/content/articles/volume16/Everton.pdf (last accessed March 22, 2018).

  2016. "Social Networks and Religious Violence." *Review of Religious Research* 58(2):191–217 (published online in 2015: http://link.springer.com/article/10.1007%2Fs13644-015-0240-3).

Everton, Sean F., and Robert Schroeder. 2017. "Networks, Epidemics, and the Rise of Christianity." Paper presented at the annual meeting of the *1st North American Social Networks Conference*, Washington, DC, July 29, 2017.

Farley, Edward. 1990. *Good & Evil: Interpreting the Human Condition*. Minneapolis, MN: Fortress Press.

Field, John. 2008. *Social Capital*, 2nd ed. London: Routledge.

Finke, Roger, Avery M. Guest, and Rodney Stark. 1996. "Mobilizing Local Religious Markets: Religious Pluralism in the Empire State, 1855 to 1865." *American Sociological Review* 61(2):203–218.

Finke, Roger, and Rodney Stark. 1988. "Religious Economies and Sacred Canopies: Religious Mobilization in American Cities, 1906." *American Sociological Review* 53(1):41–49.

  1992. *The Churching of America, 1776–1990: Winners and Losers in Our Religious Economy*. New Brunswick, NJ: Rutgers University Press.

  2005. *The Churching of America, 1776–2005: Winners and Losers in Our Religious Economy*, 2nd ed. New Brunswick, NJ: Rutgers University Press.

Fiorenza, Elizabeth Schüssler. 1990. "Missionaries, Apostles, and Co-workers: Romans 16 and the Reconstruction of Women's Early Christian History."

In *Feminist Theology: A Reader*, edited by Ann Loads. Louisville, KY: Westminster John Knox Press, pp. 57–71.
  1994. *In Memory of Her: A Feminist Reconstruction of Christian Origins*. New York: Crossroad Publishing Company.
Fischer, Claude S. 2009. "The 2004 GSS Finding of Shrunken Social Networks: An Artifact?" *American Sociological Review* 74:657–669.
Fisher, Mary Pat. 2003. *Living Religions: Eastern Traditions*. Upper Saddle River, NJ: Prentice-Hall.
Flannelly, Kevin J., Andrew J. Weaver, David B. Larson, and Harold G. Koenig. 2002. "A Review of Mortality Research on Clergy and Other Religious Professionals." *Journal of Religion and Health* 41(1):57–68.
Fox, Jonathan. 2013. *An Introduction to Religion and Politics*. London: Routledge.
  2015. *Political Secularism, Religion, and the State: A Time Series Analysis of Worldwide Data*. New York: Cambridge University Press.
Fox, Jonathan, and Ephraim Tabory. 2008. "Contemporary Evidence Regarding the Impact of State Regulation of Religion on Religious Participation and Belief." *Sociology of Religion* 69(3):245–271.
Franck, Raphaël, and Laurence R. Iannaccone. 2014. "Religious Decline in the 20th Century West: Testing Alternative Explanations." *Public Choice* 159:385–414.
Frank, David John, Ann Hironaka, and Evan Schofer. 2000. "The Nation-State and the Natural Environment over the Twentieth Century." *American Sociological Review* 65(1):96–116.
Fraser, Giles. 2014. "To Islamic State, Dabiq Is Important – But It's Not the End of the World." *The Guardian*, available at www.theguardian.com/commentis free/belief/2014/oct/10/islamic-state-dabiq-important-not-end-of-the-world (last accessed March 22, 2018).
Frazier, E. Franklin. 1974 [1963]. *The Black Church in America*. New York: Knopf.
Freeman, Linton C. 2004. *The Development of Social Network Analysis: A Study in the Sociology of Science*. Vancouver: Empirical Press.
  2006. "Editing a Normal Science Journal in Social Science." *Bullitin de Methodologie Sociologique* 9:9–19.
  2011. "The Development of Social Network Analysis – with an Emphasis on Recent Events." In *The SAGE Handbook of Social Network Analysis*, edited by John Scott and Peter J. Carrington. London: SAGE Publications, pp. 26–39.
Froese, Paul. 2008. *The Plot to Kill God: Findings from the Soviet Experiment in Secularization*. Berkeley: University of California Press.
Fuchs, Stephan. 2001. *Against Essentialism: A Theory of Culture and Society*. Cambridge, MA: Harvard University Press.
Geortz, Hans-Jürgen. 1996. *The Anabaptists*. London: Routledge.
Gill, Anthony J. 1994. "Rendering unto Caesar? Religious Competition and Catholic Political Strategy in Latin America, 1962–79." *American Journal of Political Science* 38(2):403–425.
  1998. *Rendering unto Caesar: The Catholic Church and the State in Latin America*. Chicago: University of Chicago Press.

2005. "The Political Origins of Religious Liberty: A Theoretical Outline." *Interdisciplinary Journal of Research on Religion* 1(article 1).
2008. *The Political Origins of Religious Liberty*. New York: Cambridge University Press.
Gill, Anthony J., and Erik Lundsgaarde. 2004. "State Welfare Spending and Religiosity: A Cross-National Analysis." *Rationality and Society* 16(4):399–406.
Girvan, Michelle, and Mark E. J. Newman. 2002. "Community Structure in Social and Biological Networks." *Proceedings of the National Academy of Sciences USA* 99(12):7821–7826.
Glock, Charles Y., and Robert N. Bellah. 1976. *The New Religious Consciousness*. Berkeley: University of California Press.
Glock, Charles Y., and Rodney Stark. 1966. *Christian Beliefs and Anti-Semitism*. New York: Harper and Row.
Goffman, Erving. 1967. *Interaction Ritual: Essays on Face-to-Face Behavior*. Garden City, NY: Anchor Books.
Goldman, Marion S. 2011. "Cultural Capital, Social Networks, and Collective Violence." In *Violence and New Religious Movements*, edited by James R. Lewis. New York: Oxford University Press, pp. 307–323.
Goldstone, Jack A., and Charles Tilly. 2001. "Threat (and Opportunity): Popular Action and State Response in the Dynamics of Contentious Action." In *Silence and Voice in the Study of Contentious Politics*, edited by Ronald R. Aminzade, Jack A. Goldstone, Doug McAdam, Elizabeth J. Perry, William H. Sewell Jr., Sidnew Tarrow, and Charles Tilly. New York and Cambridge: Cambridge University Press, pp. 179–194.
Gondal, Neha, and Paul D. McLean. 2013. "What Makes a Network Go Round? Exploring the Structure of a Strong Component with Exponential Random Graph Models." *Social Networks* 35(4):499–513.
Goodenough, Edwin R. 1931. *The Church in the Roman Empire*. New York: Henry Holt and Co.
Goodman, Douglas. 2001. "What Collins's The Sociology of Philosophies Says about Sociological Theory." *Sociological Theory* 19(1):92–101.
Goodreau, Steven M., James A. Kitts, and Martina Morris. 2009. "Birds of a Feather, or Friend of a Friend? Using Exponential Random Graph Models to Investigate Adolescent Social Networks." *Demography* 46(1):103–125.
Gorski, Philip S., and Ates Altinordu. 2008. "After Secularization?" *Annual Review of Sociology* 34:55–85.
Gould, Roger V. 1991. "Multiple Networks and Mobilization in the Paris Commune, 1871." *American Sociological Review* 56:716–729.
1993a. "Collective Action and Network Structure." *American Sociological Review* 58(1):182–196.
1993b. "Trade Cohesion, Class Unity, and Urban Insurrection: Artisanal Activism in the Paris Commune." *American Journal of Sociology* 98(4):721–754.
2003. "Why Do Networks Matter? Rationalist and Structuralist Interpretations." In *Social Movement Networks: Relational Approaches to*

Collective Action, edited by Mario Diani and Doug McAdam. Oxford: Oxford University Press, pp. 233–257.

Gould, Stephen Jay. 1992. "Impeaching a Self-Appointed Judge." *Scientific American* 267(July):118–21.

Granovetter, Mark. 1973. "The Strength of Weak Ties." *American Journal of Sociology* 73(6):1360–1380.

    1974. *Getting a Job*. Cambridge, MA: Harvard University Press.

    1983. "The Strength of Weak Ties: A Network Theory Revisited." *Sociological Theory* 1:201–233.

    1985. "Economic Action and Social Structure: The Problem of Embeddedness." *American Journal of Sociology* 91:481–510.

    1992. "Problems of Explanation of Economic Sociology." In *Networks and Organizations: Structure, Form and Action*, edited by Nitin Nohria and Robert G. Eccles. Boston: Harvard University Press, pp. 29–56.

    2005. "The Impact of Social Structure on Economic Outcomes." *Journal of Economic Perspectives* 19(1):33–50.

    2017. *Society and Economy: Framework and Principles*. Cambridge, MA: Bellknap Press.

Greeley, Andrew M. 1993. "The Faith We Have Lost." *America* 169(9):14–16, 24–27.

    1994. "A Religious Revival in Russia?" *Journal for the Scientific Study of Religion* 33(3):253–272.

    1997a. "Coleman Revisited: Religious Structures as a Source of Social Capital." *American Behavioral Scientist* 40(5):587–594.

    1997b. "The Other Civic America." *The American Prospect* 32:68–73.

    1997c. "The Tocqueville Files: The Other Civic America." *The American Prospect* 8(32):68–73.

Green, John C. 1993. "Pat Robertson and the Latest Crusade: Religious Resources and the 1988 Presidential Campaign." *Social Science Quarterly* 74(1):157–168.

Green, Nile. 2014. *Terrains of Exchange: Religious Economies of Global Islam*. New York: Oxford University Press.

Greenberg, Jay. 1991. *Oedipus and Beyond: A Clinical Theory*. Cambridge, MA: Harvard University Press.

Grim, Brian J., and Roger Finke. 2006. "International Religion Indexes: Government Regulation, Government Favoritism, and Social Regulation of Religion." *Interdisciplinary Journal of Research on Religion* 2(1).

    2010. *The Price of Freedom Denied: Religious Persecution and Conflict in the Twenty-First Century*, 2nd ed. New York: Cambridge University Press.

Gross, Neil, and Solon Simmons. 2009. "The Religiosity of American College and University Professors." *Sociology of Religion* 70(2):101–129.

Gruber, Jonathan, and Daniel Hungerman. 2007. "Faith-based Charity and Crowd Out during the Great Depression." *Journal of Public Economics* 91(5–6):1043–1069.

    2008. "The Church vs. the Mall: What Happens When Religion Faces Increased Secular Competition?" *Quarterly Journal of Economics* 123:831–862.

Guth, James L., John C. Green, Lyman A. Kellstedt, Corwin E. Smidt, and Margaret M. Poloma. 1997. *The Bully Pulpit: The Politics of Protestant Clergy*. Lawrence: University of Kansas Press.
Guttierez, Gustavo. 1973. *A Theology of Liberation*. Maryknoll, NY: Orbis Books.
Hadden, Jeffrey K. 1987. "Toward Desacralizing Secularization Theory." *Social Forces* 65(3):587–611.
Hafez, Mohammed M. 2003. *Why Muslims Rebel: Repression and Resistance in the Islamic World*. Boulder, CO: Lynne Rienner Publishers.
  2004. "From Marginalization to Massacres: A Political Process Explanation of Violence in Algeria." In *Islamic Activism: A Social Movement Theory Approach*, edited by Quintan Wiktorowicz. Bloomington: Indiana University Press, pp. 37–60.
Hafez, Mohammed M., and Quintan Wiktorowicz. 2004. "Violence as Contention in the Egyptian Islamic Movement." In *Islamic Activism: A Social Movement Theory Approach*, edited by Quintan Wiktorowicz. Bloomington: Indiana University Press, pp. 61–88.
Haidt, Jonathan. 2012. *The Righteous Mind: Why Good People Are Divided by Politics and Religion*. New York: Pantheon Books.
Halgin, Daniel S., and Stephen P. Borgatti. 2012. "An Introduction to Personal Network Analysis and Tie Churn Statistics Using E-NET." *Connections* 32(1):37–48.
Hall, John R. 1987. *Gone from the Promised Land: Jonestown in American Cultural History*. Piscataway, NJ: Transaction Publishers.
  1988. "Social Organization and Pathways of Commitment: Types of Communal Groups, Rational Choice Theory, and the Kanter Thesis." *American Sociological Review* 53(5):679–692.
  1995. "Public Narratives and the Apocalyptic Sect: From Jonestown to Mt. Carmel." In *Armageddon in Waco: Critical Perspectives on the Branch Davidian Conflict*, edited by Stuart A. Wright. Chicago: University of Chicago Press, pp. 205–235.
Hall, John R., with Philip D. Schuyler, and Sylvaine Trinh. 2000. *Apocalypse Observed: Religious Movements, Social Order and Violence in North America, Europe, and Japan*. New York: Routledge.
Hamburger, Philip. 2002. *Separation of Church and State*. Cambridge, MA: Harvard University Press.
Handcock, Mark S., David R. Hunter, Carter T. Butts, Steven M. Goodreau, and Martina Morris. 2003. *statnet: Software tools for the Statistical Modeling of Network Data*. http://statnetproject.org (last accessed March 22, 2018).
Harary, Frank. 1953. "On the Notion of Balance in a Signed Graph." *Michigan Mathematical Journal* 2:143–146.
  1969. *Graph Theory*. Reading: Addison-Wesley.
Harary, Frank, and Robert Zane Norman. 1953. *Graph Theory as a Mathematical Model in Social Science*. Ann Arbor: University of Michigan Press.
Harnack, Adolf von. 1905. *The Expansion of Christianity in the First Three Centuries*, vol. 2. New York: Putnam and Sons.

Harris, Fredrick C. 1999. *Something Within: Religion in African-American Political Activism*. New York: Oxford University Press.

Harris, Jenine K. 2014. *An Introduction to Exponential Random Graph Modeling*. Los Angeles: SAGE Publications.

Heider, Fritz. 1946. "Attitudes and Cognitive Organization." *Journal of Psychology* 21:107–112.

——— 1958. *The Psychology of Interpersonal Relations*. New York: Wiley.

Hentoff, Nat. 1992. *Free Speech for Me But Not for Thee: How the American Left and Right Relentlessly Censor Each Other*. New York: HarperCollins.

Holland, Paul W., and Samuel Leinhardt. 1976. "Local Structure in Social Networks." *Sociological Methodology* 7:1–45.

Homans, George C. 1950. *The Human Group*. New York: Harcourt, Brace & World.

——— 1958. "Social Behavior as Exchange." *American Journal of Sociology* 62:597–606.

——— 1961. *Social Behavior: Its Elementary Forms*. New York: Harcourt Brace Jovanovich.

Hotelling, Harold. 1929. "Stability in Competition." *Economic Journal* 39(March):41–57.

Hout, Michael. 1983. *Mobility Tables*. Newbury Park, CA: SAGE Publications.

——— 1984. "Occupational Mobility of Black Men: 1962 to 1973." *American Sociological Review* 49:308–322.

——— 1986. "Opportunity and the Minority Middle Class: A Comparison of Blacks in the United States and Catholics in Northern Ireland." *American Sociological Review* 51(2):214–223.

Hout, Michael, and Claude S. Fischer. 2014. "Explaining Why More Americans Have No Religious Preference: Political Backlash and Generational Succession, 1987–2012." *Sociological Science* 1:423–447.

Hummer, Robert A., Christopher G. Ellison, Richard G. Rogers, Benjamin E. Moulton, and Ron R. Romero. 2004. "Religious Involvement and Adult Mortality in the United States: Review and Perspective." *Southern Medical Journal* 97(12).

Hummer, Robert A., Richard G. Rogers, Charles B. Nam, and Christopher G. Ellison. 1999. "Religious Involvement and U.S. Adult Mortality." *Demography* 36(2):273–285.

Hummon, Norman P., and Kathleen Carley. 1993. "Social Networks as Normal Science." *Social Networks* 15:71–106.

Hundeide, Karsten. 2003. "Becoming a Committed Insider." *Culture and Psychology* 9(2):107–127.

Hunt, Larry L., and Matthew O. Hunt. 1999. "Regional Patterns of African American Church Attendance: Revisiting the Semi-Involuntary Thesis." *Social Forces* 78(2):779–791.

Husserl, Edmund. 1960. *Cartesian Meditations: An Introduction to Phenomenology*, translated by Dorion Cairns. Netherlands: Nijhoff.

Hybels, Lynne, and Bill Hybels. 1995. *Rediscovering Church: The Story and Vision of Willow Creek Community Church*. Grand Rapids, MI: Zondervan Publishing House.

Iannaccone, Laurence R. 1982. "Let the Women be Silent?" *Sunstone* 7(3):38–45.
   1988. "A Formal Model of Church and Sect." *American Journal of Sociology* 94:S241–S68.
   1991. "The Consequences of Religious Market Regulation: Adam Smith and the Economics of Religion." *Rationality and Society* 3(2):156–177.
   1994a. "Progress in the Economics of Religion." *Journal of Institutional and Theoretical Economics* 150(4):737–744.
   1994b. "Why Strict Churches are Strong." *American Journal of Sociology* 99(5):1180–1211.
   1995. "Risk, Rationality, and Religious Portfolios." *Economic Inquiry* 38(2):285–295.
   1997. "Rational Choice: Framework for the Social Scientific Study of Religion." In *Rational Choice Theory and Religion: Summary and Assessment*, edited by Lawrence Young. New York: Routledge, pp. 25–45.
   1999. "Religious Extremism: Origins and Consequences." *Contemporary Jewry* 20(1):8–29.
Iannaccone, Laurence R., and Eli Berman. 2006. "Religious Extremism: The Good, the Bad, and the Deadly." *Public Choice* 128(1/2):109–129.
Iannaccone, Laurence R., Roger Finke, and Rodney Stark. 1997. "Deregulating Religion: The Economics of Church and State." *Economic Inquiry* 35(2):350–364.
Iannaccone, Laurence R., and D. Michael Makowsky. 2007. "Accidental Atheists? Agent-Based Explanations for the Persistence of Religious Regionalism." *Journal for the Scientific Study of Religion* 46(1):1–16.
Iannaccone, Laurence R., Rodney Stark, and Roger Finke. 1998. "Rationality and the Religious Mind." *Economic Inquiry* 36:373–389.
Ifill, Gwen. 1992. "Clinton Rallies Supporters for Final 'Long Walk'," *The New York Times*, pp. 1, 14.
Introvigne, Massimo. 1995. "Ordeal by Fire: The Tragedy of the Solar Temple." *Religion* 25:267–283.
Iyigun, Murat F. 2015. *War, Peace, and Prosperity in the Name of God: The Ottoman Role in Europe's Socioeconomic Evolution*. Chicago: University of Chicago Press.
Jackson, Matthew O. 2008. *Social and Economic Networks*. Princeton, NJ: Princeton University Press.
   2014. "Networks in the Understanding of Economic Behaviors." *Journal of Economic Perspectives* 28(4):3–22.
Jenkins, Philip. 2006. *The New Faces of Christianity: Believing the Bible in the Global South*. New York: Oxford University Press.
Jenness, Samuel, Steven M. Goodreau, Martina Morris, Emily Beylerian, Skye Bender-deMoll, and Kevin Weiss. 2017. "EpiModel: Mathematical Modeling of Infectious Disease." *R package version 1.3.0.* www.epimodel.org (last accessed March 22, 2018).
Johnson, Benton. 1957. "A Critical Appraisal of Church-Sect Typology." *American Sociological Review* 22 88–92.
   1963. "On Church and Sect." *American Sociological Review* 28(4):539–549.

1965. "Durkheim's One Cause of Suicide." *American Sociological Review* 30:875–876.

1971. "Church and Sect Revisited." *Journal for the Scientific Study of Religion* 10(2):124–137.

Johnson, Byron R. 2011. "The Good News about Evangelicalism: Evangelicalism Isn't Shrinking and the Young are Not Becoming Liberals." *First Things* (February):12–14.

Jones, James W. 2016. *Can Science Explain Religion? The Cognitive Science Debate*. New York: Oxford University Press.

Judge, E. A. 1960. *The Social Pattern of Christian Groups in the First Century*. London: Tyndale.

Juergensmeyer, Mark. 2001. *Terror in the Mind of God*. Berkeley: University of California Press.

Kadushin, Charles. 2005. "Who Benefits From Social Network Analysis: Ethics of Social Network Research." *Social Networks* 27:139–153.

2012. *Understanding Social Networks: Theories, Concepts, and Findings*. Oxford: Oxford University Press.

Kahneman, Daniel. 2011. *Thinking, Fast and Slow*. New York: Farrar, Straus and Giroux.

Kahneman, Daniel, and Amos Tversky. 1979. "Prospect Theory: An Analysis of Decision Under Risk." *Econometrica* 47:263–291.

Kalleberg, Arne L., David Knoke, Peter V. Marsden, and Joe L. Spaeth. 1996. *Organizations in America: Analyzing Their Structures and Human Resource Practices*. Thousand Oaks, CA: SAGE.

Kanter, Rosabeth Moss. 1972. *Commitment and Community: Communes and Utopias in Sociological Perspective*. Cambridge, MA: Harvard University Press.

Kelley, Dean M. 1972. *Why Conservative Churches Are Growing*. New York: Harper and Row.

1986. *Why Conservative Churches Are Growing: A Study in the Sociology of Religion with a New Preface for the ROSE Edition*: Macon, GA: Mercer University Press.

Kilduff, Marshall, and Phil Tracy. 1977. "Inside Peoples Temple." *New West*, pp. 30–38.

Kim, Hyojoung, and Steven Pfaff. 2012. "Structure and Dynamics of Religious Insurgency: Students and the Spread of the Reformation." *American Sociological Review* 77(2):188–215.

King, Martin Luther, Jr. 1958. *Strive toward Freedom: The Montgomery Story*. New York: Harper & Row.

Klein, Melanie. 1948. *Contributions to Psychoanalysis*. London: Horgarth Press.

Kleinberg, Jon. 1999. "Authoritative Sources in a Hyperlinked Environment." *Journal of the ACM* 46(5):604–632.

2000. "The Small World Phenomenon: An Algorithmic Perspective." *Proceedings of the 32nd ACM Symposium on Theory of Computing*, pp. 163–170.

Kleinfeld, Judith S. 2002. "The Small-World Problem." *Society* 39(2):61–66.

Kliever, Lonnie D. 1999. "Meeting God in Garland: A Model of Religious Tolerance." *Nova Religio* 3:45–53.

Klötzer, Ralf. 2007. "The Melchiorites and Münster." In *A Companion to Anabaptism and Spirtualism*, edited by John D. Roth and James M. Stayer. Leiden: Brill, pp. 217–256.
Knappett, Carl. 2011. *An Archaeology of Interaction: Network Perspectives on Material Culture & Society*. Oxford: Oxford University Press.
Knoke, David. 1990. *Political Networks: The Structural Perspective*. Cambridge: Cambridge University Press.
   2012. *Economic Networks*. Cambridge: Polity Press.
Knoke, David, and Arne L. Kalleberg. 1994. "Job Training in U.S. Organizations." *American Sociological Review* 59(4):537–546.
Knoke, David, and Song Yang. 2007. *Social Network Analysis*, 2nd ed. Thousand Oaks, CA: SAGE Publications.
Knott, Kim. 1998. *Hinduism: A Very Short Introduction*. Oxford: Oxford University Press.
Koch, James L., Ross Miller, Kim Walesh, and Elizabeth Brown. 2001. "Building Community: Social Connections and Civic Involvement in Silicon Valley." Santa Clara, CA: Santa Clara University: Center for Science, Technology and Society.
Koenig, Harold G. 2008. *Medicine, Religion, and Health: Where Science and Spirituality Meet*. West Conshohocken, PA: Templeton Press.
Koenig, Harold G., Dana E. King, and Verna Benner Carson. 2012. *Handbook of Religion and Health*, vol. 2. New York: Oxford University Press.
Koenig, Harold G., Michael E. McCullough, and David B. Larson. 2001. *Handbook of Religion and Health*, vol. 1. New York: Oxford University Press.
Kohut, Heinz. 1971. *The Analysis of the Self*. New York: International Universities Press.
Korte, Charles, and Stanley Milgram. 1970. "Acquaintance Linking between White and Negro Populations: Application of the Small World Problem." *Journal of Personality and Social Psychology* 15(2):101–118.
Koskinen, Johan H., Garry L. Robins, Peng Wang, and Philippa E. Pattison. 2013. "Bayesian Analysis for Partially Observed Network Data, Missing Ties, Attributes and Actors." *Social Networks* 35(4):514–527.
Kox, Willem, Wim Meeus, and Harm 't Hart. 1991. "Religious Conversion of Adolescents: Testing the Lofland and Stark Model of Religious Conversion." *Sociological Analysis* 52: 227–240.
Krackhardt, David. 1987a. "Cognitive Social Structures." *Social Networks* 9:109–134.
   1987b. "QAP Partialling as a Test of Spuriousness." *Social Networks* 9:171–186.
   1992. "The Strength of Strong Ties: The Importance of Philos in Organizations." In *Networks and Organizations: Structure, Form and Action*, edited by Nitin Nohria and Robert G. Eccles. Boston: Harvard University Press, pp. 216–239.
   1994. "Graph Theoretical Dimensions of Informal Organizations." In *Computational Organization Theory*, edited by Kathleen M. Carley and Michael J. Prietula. Hillsdale, NJ: L. Erlbaum Associates, pp. 89–111.

Krackhardt, David, and Robert N. Stern. 1988. "Informal Networks and Organizational Crises: An Experimental Simulation." *Social Psychology Quarterly* 51(2):123–140.

Krahn, Cornelius, Nanne van der Zijpp, and James M. Stayer. 1987. "Münster Anabaptists." *Global Anabaptist Mennonite Encyclopedia Online*. Available at http://gameo.org/index.php?title=Münster_Anabaptists (last accessed September 21, 2015).

Krause, Neal. 2008. *Aging in the Church: How Social Relationships affect Health*. West Conshohocken, PA: Templeton Foundation Press.

Krause, Neal, and Christopher G. Ellison. 2003. "Forgiveness by God, Forgiveness of Others, and Psychological Well-Being in Late Life." *Journal for the Scientific Study of Religion* 42(1):77–93.

Krause, Neal, Christopher G. Ellison, and Keith M. Wulff. 1998. "Church-based Emotional Support, Negative Interaction, and Psychological Well-Being: Findings from a National Sample of Presbyterians." *Journal for the Scientific Study of Religion* 37(4):725–741.

Kreuger, Alan. 2008. *What Makes a Terrorist: Economics and the Roots of Terrorism*. Princeton, NJ: Princeton University Press.

Krivitsky, Pavel N., and Martina Morris. 2017. "Inference for Social Network Models From Egocentrically-Sampled Data, with Application to Understanding Persistent Racial Disparities in HIV Prevalence in the US." *Annals of Applied Statistics* 11(1):427–455.

Kuhn, Thomas S. 1970. *The Structure of Scientific Revolutions*, 2nd ed. Chicago: University of Chicago Press.

Kurzman, Charles. 2011. *The Missing Martyrs: Why There Are So Few Muslim Terrorists*. New York: Oxford University Press.

Lacina, Bethany, and Nils Petter Gleditsch. 2005. "Monitoring Trends in Global Combat: A New Dataset of Battle Deaths." *European Journal of Population* 21:145–166.

Landau, David. 1993. *Piety and Power: The World of Jewish Fundamentalism*. New York: Hill and Wang.

Larson, Everett, and Larry Witham. 1998. "Leading Scientists Still Reject God." *Nature* 394:313.

Laumann, Edward O., Peter V. Marsden, and David Prensky. 1983. "The Boundary-Specification Problem in Network Analysis." In *Applied Network Analysis*, edited by Ronald S. Burt and Michael Minor. Beverly Hills, CA: SAGE, pp. 18–34.

  1989. "The Boundary-Specification Problem in Network Analysis." In *Research Methods in Social Network Analysis*, edited by Linton C. Freeman, Douglas R. White, and A. K. Romney. Beverly Hills, CA: SAGE, pp. 61–87.

Lave, Jean, and Etienne Wenger. 1991. *Situated Learning: Legitimate Peripheral Participation*. Cambridge: Cambridge University Press.

Lazarfeld, Paul F., and Robert K. Merton. 1954. "Friendship as Social Process: A Substantive and Methodological Analysis." In *Freedom and Control in Modern Society*, edited by Morroe Berger, Theodore Abel, and Charles H. Page. London: Octagon Books, pp. 18–66.

Leskovec, Jure, and Eric Horvitz. 2007. "Planetary-Scale Views on an Instant-Messaging Network." *arXiv:0803.0939 [physics.soc-ph]*.

Lester, Robert C. 1987. *Buddhism: The Path to Nirvana*. Prospect Heights, IL: Waveland Press, Inc.

Leuba, James H. 1916. *The Belief in God and Immorality: A Psychological, Anthropological, and Statistical Study*. Boston: Sherman, French.

Levin, Jeffrey S. 2009. "'And Let Us Make Us a Name': Reflections on the Future of the Religion and Health Field." *Journal of Religion and Health* 48:125–145.

 2015. *Godless Lives?: Does Religion Matter for Our Well-Being?* Waco, TX: Baylor University. [Video File]. Retrieved from: www.youtube.com/watch?v=R34B-IgMeGg (last accessed October 18, 2017).

 2016. "'For They Knew Not What It Was": Rethinking the Tacit Narrative History of Religion and Health Research." *Journal of Religion and Health* 56(1):28–46.

Levinas, Emmanuel. 1969. *Totality and Infinity: An Essay on Exteriority*. Pittsburgh, PA: Duquesne University Press.

Levine, Amy-Jill. 2006. *The Misunderstood Jew: The Church and the Scandal of the Jewish Jesus*. New York: HarperCollins.

Levitt, Steven D., and Stephen J. Dubner. 2005. *Freakanomics: A Rogue Economist Explores the Hidden Side of Everything*. New York: HarperCollins.

 2015. *When to Rob a Bank*. New York: William Morrow.

Levy-Storms, Lené, and Steven P. Wallace. 2003. "Use of Mammography Screening among Older Samoan Women in Los Angeles County: A Diffusion Network Approach." *Social Science and Medicine* 57:987–1000.

Lewin, Kurt. 1951. *Field Theory in the Social Sciences*. New York: Harper.

Lewis, C. S. 1940. *The Problem of Pain*. New York: HarperCollins.

 1942a. *Mere Christianity*. New York: HarperCollins.

 1942b. *The Screwtape Letters*. New York: HarperCollins.

 1950–1956. *The Chronicles of Narnia*. New York: Harper.

 1966 [1955]. *Surprised by Joy: The Shape of My Early Life*. London: Harvest Books.

Lewis, Hylan. 1955. *Blackways of Kent*. Chapel Hill: University of North Carolina Press.

Lewis, Ted G. 2009. *Network Science: Theory and Applications*. Hoboken, NJ: John Wiley & Sons, Inc.

Lewis, Valerie, Carol Ann MacGregor, and Robert D. Putnam. 2013. "Religion, Networks, and Neighborliness: The Impact of Religious Social Networks on Civic Engagement." *Social Science Research* 42: 331–346.

Lieberman, Matthew D. 2013. *Social: Why Our Brains Are Wired to Connect*. New York: Random House.

Liebman, Robert C., and Robert Wuthnow (eds.). 1983. *The New Christian Right: Mobilization and Legitimation*. New York: Aldine Publishing Company.

Lim, Chaeyoon, and Robert D. Putnam. 2010. "Religion, Social Networks, and Life Satisfaction." *American Sociological Review* 75(6):914–933.

Lin, Nan. 1999. "Social Networks and Status Attainment." In *Annual Review of Sociology*, vol. 25, edited by Karen S. Cook and John Hagan. Palo Alto, CA: Annual Reviews, pp. 467–487.
  2001. *Social Capital*. Cambridge: Cambridge University Press.
Lin, Nan, Karen S. Cook, and Ronald S. Burt (eds.). 2001. *Social Capital: Theory and Research*. New York: Aldine de Gruyter.
Lincoln, C. Eric, and Lawrence H. Mamiya. 1990. *The Black Church in the African American Experience*. Durham, NC: Duke University Press.
Lofland, John. 1977. "'Becoming A World-Saver' Revisited." *American Behavioral Scientist* 20:805–818.
Lofland, John, and Rodney Stark. 1965. "Becoming a World-Saver: A Theory of Conversion to a Deviant Perspective." *American Sociological Review* 30:862–875.
Lovett, Ian. 2017. "Wary of Modern Society, Some Christians Choose a Life Apart." *Wall Street Journal*, available at www.wsj.com/articles/communities-built-on-faith-1487349471 (last accessed February 20, 2017).
Lusher, Dean, Johan H. Koskinen, and Garry L. Robins (eds.). 2013. *Exponential Random Graph Models for Social Networks*. New York: Cambridge University Press.
Lynd, Robert S., and Helen M. Lynd. 1929. *Middleton*. New York: Harcourt, Brace. 1937. *Middletown in Transition*. New York: Harcourt, Brace.
Lynn, Barry W. 2015. *God and Government: Twenty-Five Years of Fighting for Equality, Secularism, and Freedom of Conscience*. Amherst, NY: Prometheus Books.
MacIntyre, Alasdair. 1984. *After Virtue: A Study in Moral Theory*, 2nd ed. Notre Dame, IN: University of Notre Dame Press.
Makowsky, Michael D. 2011a. "Religion, Clubs, and Emergent Social Divides." *Journal of Economic Behavior & Organization* 80(1):74–87.
  2011b. "A Theory of Liberal Churches." *Mathematical Social Sciences* 61(1):41–51.
  2012. "Emergent Extremism in a Multi-Agent Model of Religious Clubs." *Economic Inquiry* 50(2):327–347.
Malherbe, Abraham J. 1977. *Social Aspects of Early Christianity*. Baton Rouge: Louisiana State University Press.
Manza, Jeff, and Clem Brooks. 1997. "The Religious Factor in US Presidential Elections, 1960–1992." *American Journal of Sociology* 103(1):38–81.
Maoz, Zeev. 2011. *Networks of Nations: The Evolution, Structure, and Impact of International Networks, 1816–2001*. New York: Cambridge University Press.
Maoz, Zeev, and Errol Henderson. 2013. "The World Religion Dataset, 1945–2010: Logic, Estimates, and Trends." *International Interactions: Empirical and Theoretical Research in International Relations* 39(3):265–291.
Marcel, Gabriel. 1951. *The Mystery of Being*. London: The Harvill Press, Ltd.
Mark, Noah. 1998. "Birds of a Feather Sing Together." *Social Forces* 77(2):453–485.
Marsden, Peter V. 1987. "Core Discussion Networks of Americans." *American Sociological Review* 52(1):122–131.

Marsden, Peter V., and Joel M. Podolny. 1990. "Dynamic Analyses of Network Diffusion Processes." In *Social Networks Through Time*, edited by Jeroene Weesie and Henk Flap. Utrecht, Netherlands: ISOR, pp. 197–214.

Marti, Gerardo, and Gladys Ganiel. 2014. *The Deconstructed Church: Understanding Emerging Christianity*. New York: Oxford University Press.

Martin, John Levi. 2002. "Power, Authority, and the Constraint of Belief Systems." *American Journal of Sociology* 107:861–904.

2005. "Is Power Sexy?" *American Journal of Sociology* 111:408–446.

Martin, John Levi, Tod van Gunten, and Benjamin D. Zablocki. 2012. "Charisma, Status and Gender in Groups with and without Gurus." *Journal for the Scientific Study of Religion* 51:20–41.

Martin, John Levi, King-To Yeung, and Benjamin D. Zablocki. 2002. "The Urban Communes Data Set: A Gold Mine for Secondary Analysis." *Connections* 24(2):54–58.

Martin, William. 1996. *With God on Our Side: The Rise of the Religious Right*. New York: Broadway Books.

Marwell, Gerald, Pamela E. Oliver, and Ralph Prahl. 1988. "Social Networks and Collective Action: A Theory of the Critical Mass. III." *American Journal of Sociology* 94:502–534.

Marx, Karl. 2002. *Marx on Religion*, edited by John Raines. Philadelphia, PA: Temple University Press.

Matthews, Luke J., Jeffrey Edmonds, Wesley Wildman, and Charles Nunn. 2013. "Cultural Inheritance or Cultural Diffusion of Religious Violence? A Quantitative Case Study of the Radical Reformation." *Religion, Brain & Behavior* 3(1):3–15.

Mayhew, Bruce H. 1980. "Structuralism versus Individualism: Part I, Shadowboxing in the Dark." *Social Forces* 59(2):335–374.

1981. "Structuralism versus Individualism: Part II, Ideological and Other Obfuscations." *Social Forces* 59(3):627–648.

Mayo, Elton. 1933. *The Human Problems of an Industrial Civilization*. Cambridge, MA: Macmillan.

1945. *The Social Problems of an Industrial Civilization*. London: Routledge and Kegan Paul.

McAdam, Doug. 1982. *Political Process and the Development of Black Insurgency, 1930–1970*. Chicago: University of Chicago Press.

1986. "Recruitment to High Risk Activism: The Case of Freedom Summer." *American Journal of Sociology* 92:64–90.

1988a. *Freedom Summer*. New York: Oxford University Press.

1988b. "Micromobilization Contexts and Recruitment to Activism." *International Social Movement Research* 1:125–154.

1999 [1982]. *Political Process and the Development of Black Insurgency, 1930–1970*, 2nd ed. Chicago: University of Chicago Press.

McAdam, Doug, and Ronnelle Paulsen. 1993. "Specifying the Relationship between Social Ties and Activism." *American Journal of Sociology* 99:640–667.

McAdam, Doug, Sidney Tarrow, and Charles Tilly. 2001. *Dynamics of Contention*. Cambridge: Cambridge University Press.

McBride, Michael. 2008. "Religious Pluralism and Religious Participation: A Game Theoretic Analysis." *American Journal of Sociology* 114(1):77–106.
    2010. "Religious Market Competition in a Richer World." *Economica* 77(305):148–171.
McCauley, Robert. 2011. *Why Religion Is Natural and Science Is Not*. New York: Oxford University Press.
McCleary, Rachel M., and Robert J. Barro. 2006a. "Religion and Economy." *Journal of Economic Perspectives* 20(2):49–72.
    2006b. "Religion and Political Economy in an International Panel." *Journal for the Scientific Study of Religion* 45(2):149–175.
McCloskey, Deirdre. 1995. "The Insignificance of Statistical Significance." *Scientific American* (April):32–33.
McCloskey, Donald N. 1985. *The Rhetoric of Economics*. Madison: University of Wisconsin Press.
McClure, Jennifer M. 2015. "The Cost of Being Lost in the Crowd: How Congregational Size and Social Networks Shape Attenders' Involvement in Community Organizations." *Review of Religious Research* 57:269–286.
McCulloh, Ian, Helen Armstrong, and Anthony Johnson. 2013. *Social Network Analysis with Applications*. New York: Wiley.
McCulloh, Ian, and Kathleen M. Carley. 2011. "Detecting Change in Longitudinal Social Networks." *Journal of Social Structure*, 12(3), available at www.cmu.edu/joss/content/articles/volume12//McCullohCarley.pdf (last accessed March 22, 2018).
McCullough, Michael E., and Timothy B. Smith. 2003. "Religion and Health." In *Handbook of the Sociology of Religion*, edited by Michele Dillon. New York: Cambridge University Press, pp. 190–204.
McDaniel, Charles A., Jr. 2007. "Violent Yearnings for the Kingdom of God: Münster's Militant Anabaptism." In *Belief and Bloodshed: Religion and Violence across Time and Tradition*, edited by James K. Wellman. Lanham, MD: Rowman and Littlefield, pp. 63–80.
McFadden, S. H., and Jeffrey S. Levin. 1996. "Religion, Emotions, and Health." In *Handbook of Emotion, Adult Development, and Aging*, edited by C. Magai and S. H. McFadden. San Diego, CA: Academic Press, pp. 349–365.
McFarland, Daniel A. 2004. "Resistance as Social Drama: A Study of Change-Oriented Behaviors." *American Journal of Sociology* 109(6):1249–1318.
McGuire, Meredith B. 2002. *Religion: The Social Context*, 5th ed. Belmont, CA: Wadsworth Publishing Company.
McLaughlin, John M. 2015a. *Anabaptist Leadership Network* [Machine Readable Datafile].
    2015b. "Factors of Religious Violence and a Path to Peace." Master's thesis, Naval Postgraduate School, Department of Defense Analysis, Monterey, CA.
McNeill, William H. 1976. *Plagues and People*. Garden City, NY: Doubleday.
McPherson, J. Miller. 1982. "Hypernetwork Sampling: Duality and Differentiation among Voluntary Organizations." *Social Networks* 3:225–249.
    1983. "The Size of Voluntary Associations." *Social Forces* 64:1044–1064.

2004. "A Blau Space Primer: Prolegomenon to an Ecology of Affiliation." *Industrial and Corporate Change* 13:263–280.

McPherson, J. Miller, Pamela A. Popielarz, and Sonja Drobnic. 1992. "Social Networks and Organizational Dynamics." *American Sociological Review* 57(2):153–170.

McPherson, J. Miller, and James R. Ranger-Moore. 1991. "Evolution On a Dancing Landscape: Organizations and Networks in Dynamic Blau Space." *Social Forces* 70(1):19–42.

McPherson, J. Miller, and Thomas Rotolo. 1996. "Testing a Dynamic Model of Social Composition: Diversity and Change in Voluntary Groups." *American Sociological Review* 61(2):179–202.

McPherson, J. Miller, and Lynn Smith-Lovin. 1986. "Sex Segregation in Voluntary-Associations." *American Sociological Review* 51(1):61–79.

1987. "Homophily in Voluntary Organizations: Status Distance and the Composition of Face-to-Face Groups." *American Sociological Review* 52(3):370–379.

McPherson, J. Miller, Lynn Smith-Lovin, and Matthew E. Brashears. 2006. "Social Isolation in America: Changes in Core Discussion Networks over Two Decades." *American Sociological Review* 71(3):353–375.

McPherson, J. Miller, Lynn Smith-Lovin, and James M. Cook. 2001. "Birds of a Feather: Homophily in Social Networks." *Annual Review of Sociology* 27:415–444.

Mears, Daniel P., and Christopher G. Ellison. 2000. "Who Buys New Age Materials? Exploring Sociodemographic, Religious, Network, and Contextual Correlates of New Age Consumption." *Sociology of Religion* 61(3):289–313.

Meeks, Wayne A. 1983. *The First Urban Christians*. New Haven, CT: Yale University Press.

Melton, Gordon J. 1987. "How New is New? The Flowering of the 'New' Religious Consciousness since 2965." In *The Future of New Religious Movements*, edited by David G. Bromley and Philip E. Hammond. Macon, GA: Mercer University Press, pp. 45–46.

Merino, Stephen M. 2013. "Religious Social Networks and Volunteering: Examining Recruitment via Close Ties." *Review of Religious Research* 55:509–527.

Merleau-Ponty, Maurice. 1974. *The Phenomenology of Perception*, translated by Colin Smith. New York: Humanities Press.

Merton, Robert K. 1938. "Social Structure and Anomie." *American Sociological Review* 3(5):672–682.

Meyer, John W., John Boli, George M. Thomas, and Francisco O. Ramirez. 1997. "World Society and the Nation-State." *American Journal of Sociology* 103(1):144–181.

Meyer, John W., and Brian Rowan. 1977. "Institutionalized Organizations: Formal Structure as Myth and Ceremony." *American Journal of Sociology* 83(2):340–363.

Micklethwait, John, and Adrian Wooldridge. 2009. *God Is Back: How the Global Revival of Faith Is Changing the World*. New York: Penguin Press.

Milgram, Stanley. 1967. "The Small-World Problem." *Psychology Today* 1 (May):61–67.

———. 1974. *Obedience to Authority*. Princeton, NJ: Princeton University Press.

Mills, Barbara J., Jeffery J. Clark, Matthew A. Peeples, W. Randall Haas, Jr., John M. Roberts, Jr., J. Brett Hill, Deborah L. Huntley, Lewis Borck, Ronald L. Breiger, Aaron Clauset, and M. Steven Shackley. 2013a. "Transformation of Social Networks in the Late Pre-Hispanic Southwest." *Proceedings of the National Academy of Sciences of the United States of America* 110:5785–5790.

Mills, Barbara J., John M. Roberts, Jr., Jeffery J. Clark, W. Randall Haas, Jr., Deborah L. Huntley, Matthew A. Peeples, Lewis Borck, Susan C. Ryan, Meaghan Trowbridge, and Ronald L. Breiger. 2013b. "The Dynamics of Social Networks in the Late Prehispanic US Southwest." In *Network Analysis in Archeology: New Approaches to Regional Interaction*, edited by Carl Knappett. Oxford: Oxford University Press, pp. 185–206.

Mills, Barbara J., Matthew A. Peeples, W. Randall Haas, Jr., Lewis Borck, Jeffery J. Clark, and John M. Roberts, Jr. 2015. "Multiscalar Perspectives on Networks in the Late Prehispanic Southwest." *American Antiquity* 80:3–24.

Mitchell, J. Clyde (ed.). 1969. *Social Networks in Urban Situations: Analyses of Personal Relationships in Central African Towns*. Manchester, UK: Manchester University Press.

Moore, Rebecca. 2011. "Narratives of Persecution, Suffering, and Martyrdom: Violence in Peoples Temple and Jonestown." In *Violence and New Religious Movements*, edited by James R. Lewis. New York: Oxford University Press, pp. 95–111.

Moreno, Jacob L. 1953. *Who Shall Survive? Foundations of Sociometry, Group Psychotherapy and Sociodrama*. Beacon, NY: Beacon House.

Mrvar, Andrej, and Patrick Doreian. 2009. "Partitioning Signed Two-Mode Networks." *Journal of Mathematical Sociology* 33:196–221.

Nadel, Siegfried F. 1957. *The Theory of Social Structure*. London: Cohen and West.

Nash, Kate. 2001. "The 'Cultural Turn' in Social Theory: Towards a Theory of Cultural Politics." *Sociology* 35(1):77–92.

Neff, Christian, and Werner O. Packull. 1987. "Melchior Hoffman." *Global Anabaptist Mennonite Encyclopedia Online*, available at http://gameo.org/index.php?title=Hoffman,_Melchior_(ca._1495-1544%3F)&oldid=128083 (last accessed September 23, 2015).

Neitz, Mary Jo. 1987. *Charisma and Community*. New Brunswick, NJ: Transaction Publishers.

Nelsen, Hart M. 1988. "Unchurched Black-Americans: Patterns of Religiosity and Affiliation." *Review of Religious Research* 29(4):398–412.

Nelsen, Hart M., and Anne K. Nelsen. 1975. *Black Church in the Sixties*. Lexington: University Press of Kentucky.

Nelson, Hart, Raytha L. Yokley, and Anne K. Nelsen (eds.). 1971. *The Black Church in America*. New York: Basic Books.

Nepstad, Sharon Erickson. 2004. "Persistent Resistance: Commitment and Community in the Plowshares Movement." *Social Problems* 51(1):43–60.

2008. *Religion and War Resistance in the Plowshares Movement*. New York: Cambridge University Press.
Neuhaus, Richard John. 1986. *The Naked Public Square*, 2nd ed. Grand Rapids, MI: Wm. B. Eerdmans Publishing Co.
Neuman, W. Lawrence. 1997. *Social Research Methods: Qualitative and Quantitative Approaches*, 3rd ed. Boston: Allyn and Bacon.
Newcomb, Theodore M. 1953. "An Approach to the Study of Communicative Acts." *Psychological Review* 60:393–404.
Niebuhr, H. Richard. 1929. *The Social Sources of Religious Denominationalism*. New York: Henry Holt.
Nohria, Nitin. 1992. "Is the Network Perspective a Useful Way of Studying Organizations?" In *Networks and Organizations: Structure, Form, and Action*, edited by Nitin Nohria and Robert G. Eccles. Boston: Harvard Business School Press, pp. 1–22.
North, Charles M. 2014. "Regulation of Religious Markets." In *The Oxford Handbook of Christianity and Economics*, edited by Paul Oslington. New York: Oxford University Press, pp. 489–511.
North, Charles M., and Carl R. Gwin. 2004. "Religious Freedom and the Unintended Consequences of State Religion." *Southern Economic Journal* 71(1):103–117.
　2014. "Religious Freedom and the Unintended Consequences of State Religion." Paper presented at the annual meeting of the Association for the Study of Economics, Religion, and Culture, Orange, CA, March 22, 2014.
Obama, Barack. 2006. "Call to Renewal Keynote Address." *Call to Renewal Conference on Building a Covenant for a New America*. June 28, 2006, available at http://obamaspeeches.com/081-Call-to-Renewal-Keynote-Address-Obama-Speech.htm (last accessed March 22, 2018).
Olson, Daniel V. A. 1998. "Religious Pluralism in Contemporary U.S. Counties." *American Sociological Review* 63(5):759–761.
　1999. "Religious Pluralism and US Church Membership: A Reassessment." *Sociology of Religion* 60(2):149–173.
Onnela, Jukka-Pekka, Jari Saramaki, Jari Hyvönen, Gábor Szabó., David Lazer, Kimmo Kaski, János Kertész, and Albert-László Barabasi. 2007. "Structure and Tie Strengths in Mobile Communication Networks." *Proceedings of the National Academy of Sciences of the USA* 104(18):7332–7336.
Opsahl, Tore 2009. "Structure and Evolution of Weighted Networks." PhD thesis, London: University of London. Available at https://toreopsahl.com (last accessed March 22, 2018).
Ozment, Steven E. 1975. *The Reformation in the Cities: The Appeal of Protestantism to Sixteenth Century Germany and Switzerland*. New Haven, CT: Yale University Press.
Paik, Anthony, and Kenneth Sanchagrin. 2013. "Social Isolation in America: An Artifact." *American Sociological Review* 78(3):339–360.
Papachristos, Andrew V., David M. Hureau, and Anthony A. Braga. 2013. "The Corner and the Crew: The Influence of Geography and Social Networks on Gang Violence." *American Sociological Review* 78(3):417–447.

Pargament, Kenneth I., K. Ishler, E. F. Dubow, P. Stanik, R. Rouiller, P. Crowe, E. P. Cullman, M. Albert, and B. J. Royster. 1994. "Methods of Religious Coping With the Gulf-War: Cross-Sectional and Longitudinal Analyses." *Journal for the Scientific Study of Religion* 33(4):347–361.

Pargament, Kenneth I., and C. L. Park. 1995. "Merely a Defense? The Variety of Religious Means and Ends." *Journal of Social Issues* 51:13–52.

Pargament, Kenneth I., Bruce W. Smith, Harold G. Koenig, and Lisa Perez. 1998. "Patterns of Positive and Negative Religious Coping with Major Life Stressors." *Journal for the Scientific Study of Religion* 37(4):710–724.

Parker, Geoffrey. 1992. "Success and Failure during the First Century of the Reformation." *Past & Present* (136):43–82.

Passy, Florence. 2003. "Social Networks Matter. But How?" In *Social Movements and Networks: Relational Approaches to Collective Action*, edited by Mario Diani and Doug McAdam. Oxford: Oxford University Press, pp. 21–48.

Paxton, Pamela. 1999. "Is Social Capital Declining in the United States? A Multiple Indicator Assessment." *American Journal of Sociology* 105(1):88–127.

Peeples, Matthew A., Barbara J. Mills, W. Randall Haas, Jr., Jeffery J. Clark, and John M. Roberts, Jr. 2016. "Analytical Challenges for the Application of Social Network Analysis in Archaeology." In *The Connected Past: Challenges to Network Studies in Archaeology and History*, edited by Tom Brughmans, Anna Collar, and Fiona Coward. Oxford: Oxford University Press, pp. 59–84.

Perry, Brea L., Stephen P. Borgatti, and Bernice A. Pescosolido. 2018. *Egocentric Network Analysis*. New York: Cambridge University Press.

Pescosolido, Bernice A., and Sharon Georgianna. 1989. "Durkheim, Suicide, and Religion: Toward a Network Theory of Suicide." *American Sociological Review* 54(1):33–48.

Pfaff, Steven. 2013. "The True Citizens of the City of God: The Cult of Saints, the Catholic Social Order, and the Urban Reformation in Germany." *Theory and Society* 42(2):189–218.

Pfaff, Steven, and Katie E. Corcoran. 2012. "Piety, Power, and the Purse: Religious Economies Theory and Urban Reform in the Holy Roman Empire." *Journal for the Scientific Study of Religion* 51(4):757–776.

Pinker, Steven. 2011. *The Better Angels of Our Nature: Why Violence Has Declined*. New York: Viking.

Pitts, William L., Jr. 1995. "Davidians and Branch Davidians." In *Armageddon in Waco: Critical Perspectives on the Branch Davidian Conflict*, edited by Stuart A. Wright. Chicago: Chicago University Press, pp. 20–42.

Podolny, Joel M., and Karen L. Page. 1998. "Network Forms of Organization." In *Annual Review of Sociology 1998*, vol. 24. Palo Alto, CA: Annual Reviews, pp. 57–76.

Polkinghorne, John C. 1983. *The Way the World Is: The Christian Perspective of a Scientist*. London: Society for Promoting Christian Knowledge.

　1986a. *One World: The Interaction of Science and Religion*. London: Society for Promoting Christian Knowledge.

　1986b. *Quarks, Chaos, and Christianity: Questions to Science and Religion*. London: Society for Promoting Christian Knowledge.

1998. *Science and Theology: An Introduction*. Minneapolis, MN: Fortress Press.
2002. *Quantum Theory: A Very Short Introduction*. Oxford: Oxford University Press.
2003. *Belief in God in an Age of Science*. New Haven, CT: Yale University Press.
2011. *Science and Religion in Quest for Truth*. New Haven, CT: Yale University Press.
Pope, Whitney. 1976. *Durkheim's Suicide: A Classic Analyzed*. Chicago: University of Chicago Press.
Popielarz, Pamela A., and J. Miller McPherson. 1995. "On the Edge or in Between: Niche Position, Niche Overlap, and the Duration of Voluntary Association Memberships." *American Journal of Sociology* 101(3):698–720.
Portes, Alejandro. 1998. "Social Capital: Its Origins and Applications in Modern Sociology." In *Annual Review of Sociology*, vol. 24, edited by John Hagan and Karen S. Cook. Palo Alto, CA: Annual Reviews, pp. 1–24.
Powell, Walter W. 1990. "Neither Market Nor Hierarchy: Network Forms of Organization." In *Research in Organizational Behavior: An Annual Series of Analytical Essays and Critical Reviews*, vol. 12, edited by Barry M. Staw and Larry L. Cummings. Greenwich, CT: JAI Press, pp. 295–336.
Powell, Walter W., and Paul J. DiMaggio (eds.). 1991. *The New Institutionalism in Organizational Analysis*. Chicago: University of Chicago Press.
Powell, Walter W., and Laurel Smith-Doerr. 1994. "Networks and Economic Life." In *The Handbook of Economic Sociology*, edited by Neil J. Smelser and Richard Swedberg. Princeton, NJ: Princeton University Press, pp. 368–402.
Prell, Christina. 2011. *Social Network Analysis: History, Theory and Methodology*. London: SAGE Publications.
Putnam, Robert D. 1995a. "Bowling Alone: America's Declining Social Capital." *Journal of Democracy* 6:65–78.
1995b. "Tuning In, Tuning Out: The Strange Disappearance of Social Capital in America." *PS: Political Science and Politics* 28(4):664–683.
1996. "The Strange Disappearance of Civic America." *American Prospect* 24:34–48.
2000. *Bowling Alone: The Collapse and Revival of American Community*. New York: Simon & Schuster.
Putnam, Robert D., and David E. Campbell. 2010. *American Grace: How Religion Divides and Unites Us*. New York: Simon & Schuster.
Putnam, Robert D., and Lewis M. Feldstein. 2003. *Better Together: Restoring the American Community*. New York: Simon & Schuster.
Raab, Jörg, and H. Brinton Milward. 2003. "Dark Networks as Problems." *Journal of Public Administration Research and Theory* 13(4):413–439.
Radcliffe-Brown, Alfred R. 1940. "On Social Structure." *Journal of the Royal Anthropological Society of Great Britain and Ireland* LXX:1–12.
Rapoport, Anatole. 1953a. "Spread of Information Through a Population with Socio-Structural Bias I: Assumption of Transitivity." *Bulletin of Mathematical Biophysics* 15(4):523–533.

1953b. "Spread of Information Through a Population with Socio-Structural Bias II: Various Models with Partial Transitivity." *Bulletin of Mathematical Biophysics* 15(4):535–546.

Rapoport, Anatole, and William J. Horvath. 1961. "A Study of a Large Sociogram." *Behavioral Science* 6:279–291.

Rawls, John. 1993. *Political Liberalism*. New York: Columbia University Press.

Regnerus, Mark D., David Sikkink, and Christian S. Smith. 1999. "Voting with the Christian Right: Contextual and Individual Patterns of Electoral Influence." *Social Forces* 77(4):1375–1401.

Regnerus, Mark D., Christian S. Smith, and David Sikkink. 1998. "Who Gives to the Poor? The Influence of Religious Tradition and Political Location on the Personal Generosity of Americans Toward the Poor." *Journal for the Scientific Study of Religion* 37(3):481–493.

Ripley, Ruth M., Tom A. B. Snijders, Zsófia Boda, András Vörös, and Paulina Preciado. 2017. *Manual for RSiena*. Oxford: University of Oxford, Department of Statistics, Nuffield College.

Rivers, Ray. 2017. "Can Archeological Models Always Fulfil our Prejudices?" In *The Connected Past: Challenges to Network Studies in Archaeology and History*, edited by Tom Brughmans, Anna Collar, and Fiona Coward. Oxford: Oxford University Press, pp. 123–147.

Robbins, Thomas. 1995. "The Religious Right: The Assault on Tolerance and Pluralism in America." *Journal for the Scientific Study of Religion* 34(2):286–286.

Roberts, Keith A., and David Yamane. 2012. *Religion in Sociological Perspective*, 2nd ed. Thousand Oaks, CA: SAGE.

Roberts, Nancy, and Sean F. Everton. 2016. "Monitoring and Disrupting Dark Networks: A Bias Toward the Center and What It Costs Us." In *Eradicating Terrorism from the Middle East: Policy and Administrative Approaches*, edited by Alexander R. Dawoody. New York: Springer, pp. 29–42.

Robins, Garry L. 2011. "Exponential Random Graph Models for Social Networks." In *The SAGE Handbook of Social Network Analysis*, edited by John Scott and Peter J. Carrington. London: SAGE Publications, pp. 484–500.

2015. *Doing Social Network Research: Network-based Research Design for Social Scientists*. London: SAGE.

Robins, Garry L., Philippa E. Pattison, Yuval Kalish, and Dean Lusher. 2007. "An Introduction to Exponential Random Graph (p*) Models for Social Networks." *Social Networks* 29:173–191.

Robins, Garry, Philippa Pattison, and Peter Elliott. 2001. "Network Models for Social Influence Processes." *Psychometrika* 66(2):161–189.

Rodgers, Everett. 2003. *Diffusion of Innovations*. New York: The Free Press.

Roethlisberger, Fritz J., and William J. Dickson. 1939. *Management and the Worker*. Cambridge, MA: Harvard University Press.

Ronfeldt, David, and John Arquilla. 2001. "What Next for Networks and Netwars?" In *Networks and Netwars*, edited by John Arquilla and David Ronfeldt. Santa Monica, CA: RAND, pp. 311–361.

Ross, Martha. 2016. "Emotional Thanksgiving? Families Dread Holiday After Trump's Election Win." *San Jose Mercury News*, available at www.mercurynews.com/2016/11/16/for-thanksgiving-families-struggle-to-put-aside-election-politics (last accessed January 26, 2017).

Roth, Randolph. 2001. "Homicide in Early Modern England, 1549–1800: The Need for the Quantitative Synthesis." *Crime, History & Societies* 5:33–67.

2009. *American Homicide*. Cambridge, MA: Harvard University Press.

Rotolo, Thomas, and J. Miller McPherson. 2001. "The System of Occupations: Modeling Occupations in Sociodemographic Space." *Social Forces* 79(3):1095–1130.

Rubin, Donald B. 1987. *Multiple Imputation for Nonresponse in Surveys*. New York: Wiley.

1996. "Multiple Imputation after 18+ Years." *Journal of the American Statistical Association* 91:473–489.

Rubin, Jared. 2014. "Printing and Protestants: An Empirical Test of the Role of Printing in the Reformation." *Review of Economics and Statistics* 96:270–286.

Sageman, Marc. 2004. *Understanding Terror Networks*. Philadelphia: University of Pennsylvania Press.

2017. *Misunderstanding Terrorism*. Philadelphia: University of Pennsylvania Press.

Sampson, Samuel F. 1968. *A Novitiate in a Period of Change: An Experimental and Case Study of Relationships*. Unpublished Ph.D. Thesis, Cornell University.

Sanderson, Stephen K., Seth A. Abrutyn, and Kristopher R. Proctor. 2011. "Testing the Protestant Ethic Thesis with Quantitative Historical Data: A Research Note." *Social Forces* 89(3):905–12.

Sartre, Jean-Paul. 1956. *Being and Nothingness: An Essay on Phenomenological Ontology*, translated by Hazel E. Barnes. New York: Philosophical Library.

Sawyer, Mary R. 1982. *Black Politics, Black Faith*.

Schafer, Joseph L. 1997. *Analysis of Incomplete Multivariate Data*. New York: Chapman and Hall.

Schelling, Thomas C. 1971. "Dynamic Models of Segregation." *Journal of Mathematical Sociology* 1(2):143–186.

Schottroff, Luise. 1993. "Women as Followers of Jesus in New Testament Times." In *The Bible and Liberation: Political and Social Hermeneutics*, rev. ed., edited by Norman K. Gottwald and Richard A. Horsley. Maryknoll, NY: Orbis Books, pp. 453–461.

Schwadel, Philip, Jacob E. Cheadle, Sarah E. Malone, and Michael S. Stout. 2015. "Social Networks and Civic Participation and Efficacy in Two Evangelical Protestant Churches." *Review of Religious Research* 58(2):305–317.

Scott, John. 2013. Social Network Analysis, 3rd ed. London: SAGE Publications.

2017. *Social Network Analysis*, 4th ed. London: SAGE.

Scott, John, and Peter J. Carrington (eds.). 2011. *The SAGE Handbook of Social Network Analysis*. London: SAGE Publications.

Scroggs, Robin. 1980. "The Sociological Interpretation of the New Testament: The Present State of Research." *New Testament Studies* 26:164–179.

Sherkat, Darren E. 1997. "Embedding Religious Choices: Integrating Preferences and Social Constraints into Rational Choice Theories of Religious Behavior." In *Rational Choice Theory and Religion: Summary and Assessment*, edited by Lawrence A. Young. New York: Routledge, pp. 66–86.

Sherkat, Darren E., and Chris G. Ellison. 1999. "Recent Developments and Current Controversies in the Sociology of Religion." In *Annual Review of Sociology*, vol. 25, edited by Karen S. Cook and John Hagan. Palo Alto, CA: Annual Reviews, pp. 363–394.

Sherkat, Darren E., and John Wilson. 1995. "Preferences, Constraints, and Choices in Religious Markets: An Examination of Religious Switching and Apostasy." *Social Forces* 73(3):993–1026.

Shor, Eran, and David Roelfs. 2013. "The Longevity Effects of Religious and Non-Religious Participation: A Meta-Analysis and Meta-Regression." *Journal for the Scientific of Religion* 52(1):120–145.

Shulevitz, Judith. 2005. "The Power of the Mustard Seed: Why Strict Churches Are Strong." *Slate*: http://www.slate.com/id/2118313/ (last accessed July 15, 2017).

Simmel, Georg. 1950a. "The Isolated Individual and the Dyad." In *The Sociology of Georg Simmel*, edited by Kurt H. Wolf. New York: The Free Press, pp. 118–144.

1950b. "The Secret Society." In *The Sociology of Georg Simmel*, edited by Kurt H. Wolf. New York: The Free Press, pp. 345–376.

1950c. "The Triad." In *The Sociology of Georg Simmel*, edited by Kurt H. Wolf. New York: The Free Press, pp. 145–169.

1955 [1908]. *Conflict & The Web of Group-Affiliations*, translated by Kurt H. Wolff and Reinhard Bendix. New York: The Free Press.

1971 [1908]. *On Individuality and Social Forms*, translated by Donald Levine. Chicago: University of Chicago Press.

Smelser, Neil J. 1962. *A Theory of Collective Behavior*. New York: Free Press.

Smidt, Corwin E. (ed.). 1989. *Contemporary Evangelical Political Involvement: An Analysis and Assessment*. Lanham, MD: University Press of America.

Smilde, David A. 1997. "The Fundamental Unity of the Conservative and Revolutionary Tendencies in Venezuelan Evangelicalism: The Case of Conjugal Relations." *Religion* 27(4):343–59.

2005. "A Qualitative Comparative Analysis of Conversion to Venezuelan Evangelicalism: How Networks Matter." *American Journal of Sociology* 111(3):757–796.

Smith, Adam. 1965. *An Inquiry into the Nature and Causes of The Wealth of Nations*. New York: Modern Library.

Smith, Christian S. 1996. *Resisting Reagan: The U.S. Central America Peace Movement*. Chicago: University of Chicago Press.

2000. *Christian America? What Evangelicals Really Want*. Berkeley: University of California Press.

2003a. *Moral, Believing Animals: Human Personhood and Culture*. New York: Oxford University Press.

2003b. "Religious Participation and Network Closure among American Adolescents." *Journal for the Scientific Study of Religion* 42(2):259–267.

(ed.). 2003c. *The Secular Revolution: Power, Interests, and Conflict in the Secularization of American Public Life*. Berkeley: University of California Press.

2003d. "Theorizing Religious Effects Among American Adolescents." *Journal for the Scientific Study of Religion* 42(1):17–30.

2010. *What Is a Person? Rethinking Humanity, Social Life, and the Moral Good from the Person Up*. Chicago: University of Chicago Press.

2014. *The Sacred Project of American Sociology*. New York: Oxford University Press.

2017. *Religion: What It Is, How It Works, and Why It Matters*. Princeton, NJ: Princeton University Press.

Smith, Christian S., and Melinda Lundquist Denton. 2005. *Soul Searching: The Religious and Spiritual Lives of American Teenagers*. New York: Oxford University Press.

Smith, Christian S., Michael O. Emerson, Sally Gallagher, Paul Kennedy, and David Sikkink. 1998. *American Evangelicalism: Embattled and Thriving*. Chicago: University of Chicago Press.

Smith, Christian S., and David Sikkink 1999. "Is Private Schooling Privatizing?" *First Things* (April): 16–20.

Smith, Christian S., David Sikkink, and Jason Bailey. 1998. "Devotion in Dixie and Beyond: A Test of the 'Shibley Thesis' on the Effects of Regional Origin and Migration on Individual Religiosity." *Journal for the Scientific Study of Religion* 37(3):494–506.

Smith, Tom W., Peter V. Marsden, and Michael Hout. 2016. *General Social Surveys, 1972–2014: Cumulative Codebook*. Chicago: National Opinion Research Center.

Smith, Tom W., Peter V. Marsden, Michael Hout, and Jibum Kim. 2013. *General Social Surveys, 1972–2012: Cumulative Codebook*. Chicago: National Opinion Research Center.

Snijders, Tom A. B. 2005. "Models for Longitudinal Network Data." In *Models and Methods in Social Network Analysis*, edited by Peter J. Carrington, John Scott, and Stanley Wasserman. New York: Cambridge University Press, pp. 215–247.

2011. "Network Dynamics." Pp. 501–13 in *The SAGE Handbook of Social Network Analysis*, edited by John Scott and Peter J. Carrington. London: SAGE Publications.

Snijders, Tom A. B., Gerhard G. Van de Bunt, and Christian Steglich. 2010. "Introduction to Stochastic Actor-based Models for Network Dynamics." *Social Networks* 32(1):44–60.

Snijders, Tom, and Johan H. Koskinen. 2013. "Longitudinal Models." In *Exponential Random Graph Models for Social Networks*, edited by Dean Lusher, Johan Koskinen, and Gary Robins. New York: Cambridge University Press, pp. 130–140.

Snow, David A., and Cynthia L. Phillips. 1980. "The Lofland-Stark Conversion Model: A Critical Assessment." *Social Problems* 27:430–447.

Snow, David A., Louis A. Zurcher, and Sheldon Ekland-Olson. 1980. "Social Networks and Social Movements: A Microstructural Approach to Differential Recruitment." *American Sociological Review* 45:787–801.

Sosis, Richard. 2000. "Religion and Intragroup Cooperation: Preliminary Results of a Comparative Analysis of Utopian Communities." *Cross-Cultural Research* 34:70–87.

Sosis, Richard, and Eric R. Bressler. 2003. "Cooperation and Commune Longevity: A Test of the Costly Signaling Theory of Religion." *Cross-Cultural Research* 37:211–239.

Stark, Rodney. 1986. "The Class Basis of Early Christianity: Inferences From a Sociological Model." *Sociological Analysis* 47:216–225.

———. 1991. "Epidemics, Networks, and the Rise of Christianity." *Semeia* 56:159–175.

———. 1996a. *The Rise of Christianity: A Sociologist Reconsiders History*. Princeton, NJ: Princeton University Press.

———. 1996b. "Why Religious Movements Succeed or Fail: A Revised General Model." *Journal of Contemporary Religion* 11:133–146.

———. 1999. "Secularization, R.I.P." *Sociology of Religion* 60(3):249–273.

———. 2001a. "Reconceptualizing Religion, Magic and Science." *Review of Religious Research* 43(2):101–120.

———. 2001b. *Sociology: Internet Edition, 8th ed*. Belmont, CA: Wadsworth/ Thomson Learning.

———. 2004. *Sociology: Internet Edition, 9th ed*. Belmont, CA: Wadsworth Publishing Company.

———. 2005. *The Rise of Mormonism*, edited by Reid L. Nielson. New York: Columbia University Press.

———. 2006. *Cities of God: The Real Story of How Christianity became an Urban Movement and Conquered Rome*. San Francisco: HarperSanFrancisco.

———. 2007. *Sociology, 10th ed*. Belmont, CA: Wadsworth Publishing Company.

———. 2012. *America's Blessings: How Religion Benefits Everyone, Even Atheists*. West Conshohocken, PA: Templeton Press.

———. 2015. *The Triumph of Faith: Why the World Is More Religious Than Ever*. Wilmington, DE: Intercollegiate Studies Institute.

———. 2017a. *Reformation Myths: Five Centuries of Misconceptions and Some Misfortunes*. London: SPCK.

———. 2017b. *Why God? Explaining Religious Phenomena*. West Conshohocken, PA: Templeton Press.

Stark, Rodney, and William Sims Bainbridge. 1979a. "Cult Formation: The Compatible Models." *Sociological Analysis* 40(4):283–295.

———. 1979b. "Of Churches, Sects and Cults: Preliminary Concepts for a Theory of Religious Movements." *Journal for the Scientific Study of Religion* 18(2):117–133.

———. 1980a. "Networks of Faith: Interpersonal Bonds and Recruitment to Cults and Sects." *American Journal of Sociology* 85(6):1376–1395.

———. 1980b. "Towards a Theory of Religion: Religious Commitment." *Journal for the Scientific Study of Religion* 19(2 June):114–128.

———. 1985. *The Future of Religion*. Berkeley: University of California Press.

———. 1987. *A Theory of Religion*. Bern: Peter Lang.

Stark, Rodney, Daniel P. Doyle, and Jesse Lynn Rushing. 1983. "Beyond Durkheim: Religion and Suicide." *Journal for the Scientific Study of Religion* 22(2):120–131.
Stark, Rodney, and Roger Finke. 2000a. *Acts of Faith: Explaining the Human Side of Religion*. Berkeley: University of California Press.
  2000b. "Catholic Religious Vocations: Decline and Revival." *Review of Religious Research* 42(2):125–145.
Stark, Rodney, Roger Finke, and Laurence R. Iannaccone. 1995. "Pluralism and Piety: England and Wales, 1851." *Journal for the Scientific Study of Religion* 34(4): 431–444.
Stark, Rodney, and Charles Y. Glock. 1968. *American Piety*. Berkeley: University of California Press.
Stark, Rodney, and Laurence R. Iannaccone. 1994. "A Supply-Side Reinterpretation of the 'Secularization' of Europe." *Journal for the Scientific Study of Religion* 33(3):230–252.
Stark, Rodney, Laurence R. Iannaccone, and Roger Finke. 1996. "Religion, Science, and Rationality." *American Economic Review* 86(2):433–437.
  1998. "Rationality and the Religious Mind." *Economic Inquiry* 36:373–389.
Stark, Rodney, and Xiuhua Wang. 2014. "Christian Conversion and Cultural Incongruity in Asia." *Interdisciplinary Journal of Research on Religion* 10(article 2).
  2015. *A Star in the East: The Rise of Christianity in China*. West Conshohocken, PA: Templeton Press.
StataCorp. 2015a. *Stata 14 Multiple Imputation Reference Manual*. College Station, TX: StataCorp LP.
  2015b. *Stata Statistical Software: Release 14*. College Station, TX: StataCorp LP.
Stayer, James M. 1979. *Anabaptists and the Sword*. Lawrence, KS: Coronado Press.
Steensland, Brian, Jerry Z. Park, Mark D. Regnerus, Lynn R. Robinson, W. Bradford Wilcox, and Robert D. Woodberry. 2000. "The Measure of American Religion: Toward Improving the State-of-the-Art." *Social Forces* 79(1):291–318.
Steffen, Patrick R., Kevin S. Masters, and Scott Baldwin. 2017. "What Mediates the Relationship between Service Attendance and Aspects of Well-Being?" *Journal of Religion and Health* 56(1):158–170.
Steglich, Christian, Tom A. B. Snijders, and Michael Pearson. 2010. "Dynamic Networks and Behavior: Separating Selection From Influence." *Sociological Methodology* 40:329–393.
Stern, Jessica. 2003. *Terror in the Name of God: Why Religious Militants Kill*. New York: HarperCollins.
Stoner, James 1961. *A Comparison of Individual and Group Decisions Involving Risk*. Unpublished Master's Thesis, Massachusetts Institute of Technology, Boston, MA.
Strang, David, and Nancy Brandon Tuma. 1993. "Spatial and Temporal Heterogeneity in Diffusion." *American Journal of Sociology* 99(3):614–639.

Strauss, Gerald. 1975. "Success and Failure in the German Reformation." *Past & Present* 67(May 1975):30–63.

Sunstein, Cass R. 2002. "The Law of Group Polarization." *Journal of Political Philosophy* 10:175–195.

  2003. *Why Societies Need Dissent*. Cambridge, MA: Harvard University Press.

  2009. *Going to Extremes: How Like Minds Unite and Divide*. New York: Oxford University Press.

Swatos, William H. 1975. "Monopolism, Pluralism, Acceptance, and Rejection: An Integrated Model for Church-Sect Theory." *Review of Religious Research* 16(3):174–185.

  1976. "Weber or Troeltsch?: Methodology, Syndrome, and the Development of Church-Sect Theory." *Journal for the Scientific Study of Religion* 15(2):129–144.

  1998. "Church-Sect Theory." In *Encyclopedia of Religion and Society*, edited by William H. Swatos. Walnut Creek, CA: AltaMira Press, pp. 90–93.

Swidler, Ann. 1986. "Culture in Action: Symbols and Strategies." *American Sociological Review* 51(2):273–286.

Swift, Matthew 2012. "*Reexamining the Effects of State Religion on Religious Service Attendance.*" Thesis, Baylor University, Waco, TX.

Szubin, Adam, Carl J. Jensen, and Rod Gregg. 2000. "Interacting with Cults: Police." *FBI Law Enforcement Bulletin*, 69(9):16–24, available at www.scribd.com/document/30301290/FBI-Law-Enforcement-Bulletin-Sep00leb (last accessed March 22, 2018).

Tabor, James D., and Eugene V. Gallagher. 1995. *Why Waco? Cults and the Battle for Religious Freedom in America*. Berkeley: University of California Press.

Tawney, Richard H. 1926. *Religion and the Rise of Capitalism*. New York: Harper and Row.

Taylor, Charles. 2007. *A Secular Age*. Cambridge, MA: Belknap Press of Harvard University Press.

Taylor, Robert Joseph. 1988a. "Correlates of Religious Non-Involvement Among Black-Americans." *Review of Religious Research* 30(2):126–139.

  1988b. "Structural Determinants of Religious Participation Among Black-Americans." *Review of Religious Research* 30(2):114–125.

Terrell, John Edward. 1997. "Geographic Systems and Human Diversity in the North Solomons." *World Archaeology* 9(1):62–81.

  2010. "Language and Material Culture on the Sepik Coast of Papua New Guinea: Using Social Network Analysis to Simulate, Graph, Identify, and Analyze Social and Cultural Boundaries between Communities." *Journal of Island and Coastal Archaeology* 5:3–32.

Thalheimer, Fred. 1973. "Religiosity and Secularization in the Academic Professions." *Sociology of Education* 46:183–202.

The Economist. 2014. "Religion in China: Cracks in the Atheist Edifice." *The Economist*, (November 1, 2014), www.economist.com/news/briefing/21629218-rapid-spread-christianity-forcing-official-rethink-religion-cracks?frsc=dg%7Ca (last accessed March 22, 2018).

2017. "A Majority of Britons Now Follow no Religion." *The Economist*, (September 9, 2017). www.economist.com/news/britain/21728600-only-15-call-themselves-anglicans-dont-bet-church-losing-its-official-role-any-time (last accessed March 22, 2018).

The Pew Forum on Religion and Public Life. 2012. *"Nones" on the Rise: One-in-Five Adults Have No Religious Affiliation*. Washington, DC: Pew Research Center.

Theissen, Gerd. 1982. *The Social Setting of Pauline Christianity*. Philadelphia: Fortress Press.

Theunissen, Michael. 1984. *The Other: Studies in the Social Ontology of Husserl, Heidegger, Sarte, and Buber*. Cambridge, MA: MIT Press.

Thomas, Keith. 1991 [1973]. *Religion and the Decline of Magic: Studies in Popular Beliefs in Sixteenth- and Seventeenth-Century England*. London: Penguin.

Thrasher, Frederic M. 1927. *The Gang: A Study of 1313 Gangs in Chicago*. Chicago: University of Chicago Press.

Thumma, Scott, and Warren Bird. 2015. *Recent Shifts in America's Largest Protestant Churches: Megachurches 2015 Report*. Hartford, CT: Hartford Institute for Religious Research and Leadership Network.

Thumma, Scott, and Dave Travis. 2007. *Beyond Megachurch Myths: What We Can Learn from America's Largest Churches*. San Francisco: Jossey-Bass.

Tilly, Charles. 2004. "Trust and Rule." *Theory and Society* 33:1–30.

2005a. "Terror as Strategy and Relational Process." *International Journal of Comparative Sociology* 46:11–32.

2005b. *Trust and Rule*. New York: Cambridge University Press.

Toft, Monica Duffy, Daniel Philpott, and Timothy Samuel Shah. 2011. *God's Century: Resurgent Religion and Global Politics*. New York: W.W. Norton & Company.

Tönnies, Ferdinand. 1957 [1855]. *Community and Society*, translated by Charles P. Loomis. East Lansing: Michigan State University.

Travers, Jeffrey, and Stanley Milgram. 1969. "An Experimental Study of the Small World Problem." *Sociometry* 32(4):425–443.

Troeltsch, Ernst. 1960 [1911]. *The Social Teachings of the Christian Churches*, translated by Olive Wyon. Chicago: University of Chicago Press.

Tuma, Nancy Brandon, and Michael T. Hannan. 1984. *Social Dynamics: Models and Methods*. Orlando, FL: Academic Press.

Turner, Janice. 2017. "Politics and Religion are a Dangerous Mix." *The Times* (September 9, London, UK):25.

Turner, Jonathan H. 1998. *The Structure of Sociological Theory*, 6th ed. Belmont, CA: Wadsworth Publishing Company.

2006. *Sociology*. Upper Saddle River, NJ: Pearson Prentice Hall.

2013. *Theoretical Sociology: 1830 to the Present*. Los Angeles: SAGE Publishing.

Tversky, Amos, and Daniel Kahneman. 1974. "Judgment under Uncertainty: Heuristics and Biases." *Science* 185:1124–1131.

1981. "The Framing of Decisions and the Psychology of Choice." *Science* 211:453–458.

Uzzi, Brian. 1996. "The Sources and Consequences of Embeddedness for the Economic Performance of Organizations: The Network Effect." *American Sociological Review* 61(4):674–698.

Uzzi, Brian, and Jarrett Spiro. 2005. "Collaboration and Creativity: The Small World Problem." *American Journal of Sociology* 111(2):447–504.

Vaisey, Stephen. 2007. "Structure, Culture, and Community: The Search for Belonging in 50 Urban Communes." *American Sociological Review* 72:851–873.

Vala, Carsten T., and Kevin J. O'Brien. 2007. "Attraction without Networks: Recruiting Strangers to Unregistered Protestantism in China." *Mobilization: An International Journal* 12(1):79–94.

Valente, Thomas W. 1995. *Network Models of the Diffusion of Innovations*. Creskill, NJ: Hampton Press.

2005. "Network Models and Methods for Studying the Diffusion of Innovations." In *Models and Methods in Social Network Analysis*, edited by Peter J. Carrington, John Scott, and Stanley Wasserman. New York: Cambridge University Press, pp. 98–116.

Van de Bunt, G. G., M. A. J. Van Duijin, and Tom A. B. Snijders. 1999. "Friendship Networks through Time: An Actor-Oriented Statistical Network Model." *Computational and Mathematical Organization Theory* 5: 167–192.

Van Leeuwen, Mary S. 1990. "Life after Eden." *Christianity Today* (July 16):19–21.

Vance, J. D. 2016. *Hillbilly Elegy: A Memoir of a Family and Culture in Crisis*. New York: HarperCollins.

Verba, Sidney, Kay Lehman Schlozman, and Henry E. Brady. 1995. *Voice and Equality: Civic Volunteerism in American Politics*. Cambridge, MA: Harvard University Press.

Voas, David, and Mark Chaves. 2016. "Is the United States a Counterexample to the Secularization Thesis?" *American Journal of Sociology* 121(5):1517–1556.

Voas, David, Alasdair Crockett, and Daniel V. A. Olson. 2002. "Religious Pluralism and Participation: Why Previous Research Is Wrong." *American Sociological Review* 67(2):212–230.

Wadsworth. 2003. *MicroCase*. Boston: Cengage Learning.

Wald, Kenneth D., and Allison Calhoun-Brown. 2005. *Religion and Politics in the United States*, 5th ed. Lanham, MD: Rowman and Littlefield Publishers.

Walker, J. Brent. 2002. "Hamburger Wrong about Founders' and Early Baptists' View of Separation." *Baptist Joint Committee for Religious Liberty*, available at http://bjconline.org/hamburger-wrong-about-founders-early-baptists-view-of-separation (last accessed March 22, 2018).

2005. "Answering the Top 10 Lies about Church and State." *Baptist Joint Committee for Religious Liberty*, available at http://bjconline.org/wp-content/uploads/2014/03/Answering-the-Top-10-lies-About-Church-and-State.pdf (last accessed March 22, 2018).

2014. *What a Touchy Subject! Religious Liberty and Church-State Separation*. Macon, GA: Nurturing Faith, Inc.

Wallace, Anthony F. C. 1956. "Revitalization Movements." *American Anthropologist* 58:264–281.
  1966. *Religion: An Anthropological View*. New York: Random House.
Wang, Cheng, Michael Genkin, George Berry, Liuyuan Chen, and Matthew E. Brashears. 2015. "Blaunet: Calculate and Analyze Blau Statuses for Measuring Social Distance." *R package version 2.0.4*. https://cran.r-project.org/package=Blaunet (last accessed March 22, 2018).
Wang, Peng, Garry L. Robins, and Philippa E. Pattison. 2009a. "Exponential Random Graph (p*) Models for Affiliation Networks." *Social Networks* 31(1):12–25.
  2009b. *PNet: Program for the Simulation and Estimation of (p*) Exponential Random Graph Models*. Melbourne: Melbourne School of Psychological Sciences, The University of Melbourne, available at http://sna.unimelb.edu.au/PNet (last accessed March 22, 2018).
  2014. *MPNet: Program for the Simulation and Estimation of (p*) Exponential Random Graph Models for Multilevel Networks*. Melbourne: Melbourne School of Psychological Sciences, The University of Melbourne, available at http://sna.unimelb.edu.au/PNet (last accessed March 22, 2018).
Wang, Peng, Garry L. Robins, Philippa E. Pattison, and Johan H. Koskinen. 2014. *MPNET User Manual (June)*. Melbourne: Melbourne School of Psychological Sciences, The University of Melbourne, available at http://sna.unimelb.edu.au/__data/assets/pdf_file/0004/1185745/MPNetManual.pdf (last accessed March 22, 2018).
Warner, R. Stephen. 1993. "Work in Progress toward a New Paradigm for the Sociological Study of Religion in the United States." *American Journal of Sociology* 98(5):1044–1093.
Warner, W. Lloyd, and Paul S. Lunt. 1941. *The Social Life of a Modern Community*. New Haven, CT: Yale University Press.
Wasserman, Stanley, and Katherine Faust. 1994. *Social Network Analysis: Methods and Applications*. Cambridge: Cambridge University Press.
Watts, Duncan J. 1999a. "Networks, Dynamics, and the Small-World Phenomenon." *American Journal of Sociology* 105(2):493–527.
  1999b. *Small Worlds: The Dynamics of Networks between Order and Randomness*. Princeton, NJ: Princeton University Press.
  2003. *Six Degrees: The Science of a Connected Age*. New York: W. W. Norton & Company.
Watts, Duncan J., Peter Sheridan Dodds, and M. E. Newman. 2003. "Identity and Search in Social Networks." *Science* 296:1302–1304.
Watts, Duncan J., and Steven H. Strogatz. 1998. "Collective Dynamics of 'Small World' Networks." *Nature* 393:409–410.
Weber, Max. 1963. *The Sociology of Religion*, Edited by translated by Ephraim Fischoff. Boston: Beacon Press.
  1996 [1905]. *The Protestant Ethic and the Spirit of Capitalism*. Translated by Talcott Parsons. Los Angeles: Roxbury Publishing Company.
  1978 [1922]. *Economy and Society: An Outline of Interpretive Sociology*. Berkeley: University of California Press.

Welch, Michael R., and John Baltzell. 1984. "Geographic Mobility, Social Integration, and Church Attendance." *Journal for the Scientific Study of Religion* 23(1):75–91.
Wenger, Etienne. 1998. *Communities of Practice: Learning, Meaning, and Identity.* Cambridge: Cambridge University Press.
White, Harrison C. 1970. "Search Parameters for the Small World Problem." *Social Forces* 49(2):259–264.
  1992. *Identity and Control: A Structural Theory of Social Action.* Princeton, NJ: Princeton University Press.
  2001. *Markets from Networks: Socioeconomic Models of Production.* Princeton, NJ: Princeton University Press.
  2008. *Identity and Control: How Social Formations Emerge*, 2nd ed. Princeton, NJ: Princeton University Press.
White, Harrison C., Scott A. Boorman, and Ronald L. Breiger. 1976. "Social Structure from Multiple Networks I: Blockmodels of Roles and Positions." *American Journal of Sociology* 81:730–780.
Wikipedia. 2014a. "C. S. Lewis." https://en.wikipedia.org/wiki/C._S._Lewis (last accessed November 30, 2014).
  2014b. "Peoples Temple." http://en.wikipedia.org/wiki/Peoples_Temple (last accessed March 19, 2014).
  2015a. "Abu Ghraib Torture and Prisoner Abuse." (April 21, 2015). http://en.wikipedia.org/wiki/Abu_Ghraib_torture_and_prisoner_abuse (last accessed April 21, 2015).
  2015b. "Münster Rebellion." (September 23, 2015). https://en.wikipedia.org/wiki/Münster_Rebellion (last accessed September 23, 2015).
  2016a. "Dabiq (Magazine)." https://en.wikipediaorg/wiki/Dabiq_(magazine) (last accessed June 23, 2016).
  2016b. "John Polkinghorne." (September 23, 2015). https://en.wikipedia.org/wiki/John_Polkinghorne (last accessed June 17, 2016).
  2017a. "Aimee Semple McPherson." https://en.wikipedia.org/wiki/Aimee_Semple_McPherson (last accessed July 2, 2017).
  2017b. "Bhagavata Purana." https://en.wikipedia.org/wiki/Bhagavata_Purana (last accessed March 9, 2017).
  2017c. "A. C. Bhaktivedanta Swami Prabhupada." https://en.wikipedia.org/wiki/A._C._Bhaktivedanta_Swami_Prabhupada – CITEREFGoswami2002 (last accessed March 9, 2017).
  2017d. "Johann Tetzel." https://en.wikipedia.org/wiki/Johann_Tetzel (last accessed August 25, 2017).
  2017e. "Martin Luther." https://en.wikipedia.org/wiki/Martin_Luther (last accessed March 31, 2017).
  2017f. "Nanda Baba." https://en.wikipedia.org/wiki/Nanda_Baba (last accessed March 9, 2017).
Wilcox, Clyde. 1990. "Religion and Politics among White Evangelicals: The Impact of Religious Variables on Political-Attitudes." *Review of Religious Research* 32(1):27–42.
Wilde, Melissa J., Kristin Geraty, Shelley L. Nelson, and Emily A. Bowman. 2010. "Religious Economy or Organizational Field? Predicting Bishops'

Votes at the Second Vatican Council." *American Sociological Review* 75(4):586–606.
Williams, George Huntston. 1975. *The Radical Reformation*. Philadelphia: Westminster Press.
Wilson, Bryan. 1966. *Religion in Secular Society*. London: C. A. Watts.
  1975. *Magic and the Millennium*. Frogmore, UK: Paladin.
Wink, Walter. 1992. *Engaging the Powers*. Minneapolis, MN: Augsburg Fortress.
Winship, Christopher, and Larry Radbill. 1994. "Sampling Weights and Regression Analysis." *Sociological Methods and Research* 23(2):230–257.
Witherington, Ben III. 1995. *The Jesus Quest: The Third Search for the Jew of Nazareth*. Downer's Grove, IL: InterVarsity Press.
Witter, Robert A., William A. Stock, Morris A. Okun, and Marilyn J. Haring. 1985. "Religion and Subjective Well-Being in Adulthood: A Quantitative Synthesis." *Review of Religious Research* 26(4):332–342.
Woodberry, Robert D., and Christian S. Smith. 1998. "Fundamentalism et al.: Conservative Protestants in America." In *Annual Review of Sociology*, vol. 24, edited by John Hagan and Karen S. Cook. Palo Alto, CA: Annual Reviews, pp. 25–56.
Wright, Stuart A. (ed.). 1995a. *Armageddon in Waco: Critical Perspectives on the Branch Davidian Conflict*. Chicago: University of Chicago Press.
  1995b. "Construction and Escalation of a Cult Threat." In *Armageddon in Waco: Critical Perspectives on the Branch Davidian Conflict*, edited by Stuart A. Wright. Chicago: Chicago University Press, pp. 75–94.
  1995c. "Introduction: Another View of the Mt. Carmel Standoff." In *Armageddon in Waco: Critical Perspectives on the Branch Davidian Conflict*, edited by Stuart A. Wright. Chicago and London: Chicago University Press, pp. xiii–xxvi.
Wuthnow, Robert. 1976. *The Consciousness Reformation*. Berkeley: University of California Press.
  1989. *Meaning and Moral Order: Explorations in Cultural Analysis*. Berkeley: University of California Press.
  1993. "Small Groups Forge New Notions of Community and the Sacred." *The Christian Century* (December 8):1236–1240.
  1994a. "How Small Groups Are Transforming Our Lives." *Christianity Today* (February 7):20–24.
  1994b. *Sharing the Journey: Support Groups and America's New Quest for Community*. New York: The Free Press.
  2007. *After the Baby Boomers: How Twenty- and Thirty-Somethings Are Shaping the Future of American Religion*. Princeton, NJ: Princeton University Press.
Wuthnow, Robert, and Kevin J. Christiano. 1979. "The Effects of Residential Migration on Church Attendance in the United States." In *The Religious Dimension*, edited by Robert Wuthnow. New York: Academic Press, pp. 257–276.
Wuthnow, Robert, and John E. Evans (eds.). 2002. *The Quiet Hand of God: Faith-Based Activism and the Public Role of Mainline Protestantism*. Berkeley: University of California Press.

Yamane, D. 1997. "Secularization on Trial: In Defense of a Neosecularization Paradigm." *Journal for the Scientific Study of Religion* 36(1):109–122.

Yeung, King-To. 2005. "What Does Love Mean? Exploring Network Culture in Two Network Settings." *Social Forces* 84:391–420.

Yon, Vega George, Stephanie Dyal, Timothy Hayes, and Thomas W. Valente. 2017. "netdiffuseR: Analysis of Diffusion and Contagion Process on Networks." *R package version 1.18.1.* https://cran.r-project.org/package=netdiffuseR (last accessed March 22, 2018).

Young, Lawrence A. (ed.). 1997. *Rational Choice Theory and Religion: Summary and Assessment.* New York: Routledge.

Zablocki, Benjamin D. 1980. *Alienation and Charisma: A Study of Contemporary American Communes.* New York: Free Press.

Zeller, Benjamin E. 2011. "The Euphemization of Violence." In *Violence and New Religious Movements*, edited by James R. Lewis. New York: Oxford University Press, pp. 173–189.

Zhou, Xueguang, Nancy Brandon Tuma, and Phyllis Moen. 1996. "Stratification Dynamics under State Socialism: The Case of Urban China, 1949–1993." *Social Forces* 74(3):759–796.

Ziliak, Stephen T., and Deirdre N. McCloskey. 2008. *The Cult of Statistical Significance.* Ann Arbor: University of Michigan Press.

Zimbardo, Philip G. 1972. "Pathology of Imprisonment." *Society* 9:4–6.

  2007. *The Lucifer Effect: Understanding How Good People Turn Evil.* New York: Random House.

Zimbardo, Philip G., Christina Maslasch, and Craig Haney. 2000. "Reflections on the Stanford Prison Experiment: Genesis, Transformations, Consequences." In *Obedience to Authority: Current Perspectives on the Milgram Paradigm*, edited by Thomas Blass. Mahwah, NJ: Lawrence Erlbaum Associates, pp. 193–237.

Zuckerman, Phil. 2014. *Living the Secular Life: New Answers to Old Questions.* New York: Penguin Press.

Index

actor, 59
   definition, 323
adolescent health
   religious factors, 226
affiliation network. *See* two-mode network
ALAAMs (auto-logistic actor attribute models), 109, 323
arc, 60
   definition, 323
archeological networks, 139, 319
   maximum distance network (MDN), 141
   proximal point analysis (PPA), 139
   similarity network, 142
   suggested readings, 167
Aristotle, 173
Armstrong, H., 84
Arnold, P., 301
Asch, S., 53
Atran, S., 42, 254
attribute, 74
   definition, 323
average degree, 67, 256–57, 306, 307
   definition, 323
average distance, 66
   definition, 323

Bainbridge, W., 13, 44, 90, 123, 201, 206, 220
balance theory, 263
   Doreian-Mrvar algorithm, 265, 269, 274
   Louvain algorithm, 269, 274
   structural balance and clusterability, 265
   suggested readings, 287
Baldwin, S., 224
Baller, R., 234
Baltzell, J., 123
Baptist Joint Committee for Religious Liberty, 161, 193
Barnes, J., 48

Barrett, J., 42
Barro, R., 30
Batagelj, V., 83, 266, 287
   Pajek, 287, 336
Becker, G., 13
Becker, S., 167
Bellah, R., 4, 35, 171
Benedict Option, 253
Berger, P., 4, 44
   sacred canopy, 34, 35, 230, 329
Bering, J., 42
Berman, E., 222
   religious freedom and violence, 192
Berrigan brothers, 126
betweenness centrality. *See* centrality
   definition, 324
Beyerlein, K., 173, 175, 179
   hypernetwork sampling, 192
Blau, P., 116
   Blau Space, 117, 131
   suggested readings, 131
blockmodels. *See* roles and positions
   definition, 324
Boli, J., 150
Borgatti, S., 83, 314
   E-Net, 220
   NetDraw, 335
   UCINET, 337
Bott, E., 48
boundary specification, 79–80
Bourdieu, P., 170, 191
Boyer, P., 42
Branch Davidians, 299–302
Brashears, M., 220, 231
Breault, M., 300
Breiger, R., xxii, 48, 142
brokers and bridges, 71, 306, 318
   bridge
      definition, 324

brokers and bridges (cont.)
  broker
    definition, 324
  brokerage roles
    definition, 324
Brown, J., 296
Brown, W., 296
Brughmans, T., 167
Buber, M., 43
Buddhism, 198, 327, 333, 334
  Pure Land, 333
  Zen, 208
Burt, R., 43, 71, 167, 330
Butler, J., 7

Cann, D., 27, 29
Carley, K., 48
  ORA, 336
Carnes, T., 38
Carrington, P., 83
Carter, J., 178
Carter, R., 296
Cartwright, D., 264
centrality, 68–71, 274, 318
  betweenness centrality, 69
  closeness centrality, 69
  definition, 324
  degree centrality, 69
  eigenvector centrality, 69
centralization, 67, *See* network topography
  definition, 324
Chase, I., 48
Chaves, M., 82, 132, 175, 179, 181, 187
  hypernetwork sampling, 174, 192
  religious economies, 27, 29, 30
  secularization, 12
  women's ordination, 149
Christakis, N., 47
Christianity, xviii, 327, 334
  Black Protestantism, 129, 205, 215, 216, 219
    political activism, 176, 178
  early church
    benefits of strictness, 21
    surviving epidemics, 239–242
  evangelical Protestantism, 4, 23, 35, 36, 38, 61, 204, 216, 216, 219, 236, 333
    political activism, 177–178
  mainline Protestantism, 4, 19, 35, 36, 61, 172, 187, 215, 216, 219, 236, 295, 333
    political activism, 177, 178–179
  Pentecostal and Holiness traditions, 152
  Protestantism (Europe), 234
  Roman Catholicism, 5, 20, 23, 24, 60, 116, 126, 146, 147, 149, 199, 200, 215, 216, 219, 234, 236, 265
    political activism, 175, 177
  secularization, 5

Christiano, K., 14, 44, 123
church, 199
  and socioeconomic class, 203
  definition, 324
church and state
  suggested readings, 192
church-sect theory, 199, 203–205
  continuum, 201
  definition, 324
  denominations, 206
  network density, 205
  normal distribution of denominations, 201
  suggested readings, 220
clique, 68
closeness centrality. *See* centrality
  definition, 325
clustering coefficient
  global, 105, 306
    definition, 327
  local
    definition, 327
cohesion, 67, 306, 307
  definition, 325
Coleman, J., 166, 170, 191, 229
Collar, A., 141, 143, 167
Collins, R., 29, 269
  medieval Christian philosophers, 274–284
  secularization, 12
community detection algorithms, 68, 275, 318
  definition, 325
complete network. *See* whole network
component, 63, 68
  definition, 325
congregational political activism, 175–187
  congregational networks, 180–187
Consciousness Reformation, 25, 138
conversion and recruitment
  China, 94–95
  Freedom Summer, 91, 95
  global Salafi jihad, 93
  Hare Krishnas (ISKCON), 91
  Moonies (Unification Church), xxii, 89
  Mormons (LDS), 90
  Venezuelan evangelicalism, 93, 95, 96–97
Coser, L., 254, 270
counts of ties, 75
Coward, F., 167
Cox, H., 4, 138
Crossley, N., 220
Crunchy Con. *See* Dreher, R.
cult. *See* independent religious movement

data collection methods
  big data, 82

Index

cognitive social structure, 82
diaries, 82
direct observation, 81
experiments, 82
interviews, 81
questionnaires, 80–81
small world studies, 82
social media, 82
written records, 82
Davie, G., 44
Day, D., 126
de Nooy, W., 83, 266, 287
  Pajek, 287
degree centrality. *See* centrality
  definition, 325
della Porta, D., 293
density, 67, 257, 306, 307
  definition, 325
Denton, M., 223
  adolescent health, 225–230
diameter, 63, 66
  definition, 326
diffusion
  Protestant Reformation, 147
  Rabbinic Judaism, 142
  women's ordination, 149
DiMaggio, P., 54, 149
directed network (graph)
  definition, 326
disconnected network, 63
Dobbelaere, K.
  secularization, 12
Doreian, P., 265, 287
Doyle, D., 234
Dreher, R.
  Benedict Option, 253
DuBois, W. E. B., 132
Durkheim, E., 44, 232, 332
dyad, 48
  definition, 326
dynamic social networks, 57–58
Dyson, H., 87

Earl, G., 167
Easely, D., 84
Ecklund, E., 18
edge, 60
  definition, 326
edge betweenness, 71, 72
  definition, 326
ego network density, 215, *See* clustering coefficient
  definition, 326
ego networks, 76–77
  definition, 326
  density by religious tradition, 217
  hypothetical, 219
  suggested readings, 220–221

Ehrman, B., 148
E-I index, 308
  definition, 326
eigenvector centrality. *See* centrality
  definition, 326
Ellison, C., 129, 250
emergence, 56–57
Emerson, M., 44
  congregational racial homogeneity, 120–122
Emirbayer, M., 58
Engels, F., 198
ERGMs (exponential random graph models), 74, 103, 167, 319
  definition, 326
  suggested readings, 112
Erickson, B., 48
Evans, J., 46, 179
Everett, M., 83, 314
  UCINET, 337

faction, 68
  definition, 327
Faust, K., 58, 83
Federal Council of Churches, 152
Fernandez, R.
  brokerage roles, 324
Finke, R., 13, 24, 26, 31, 192, 313
  Churching of America, 8, 24, 44
Fiorenza, E. S., 148, 198
Fischer, C., 9
Fox, J., 30, 188, 192
fragmentation, 67
  definition, 327
Freedom Summer, 59, 91, 95, 125
Freeman, L., 49, 83
  UCINET, 337
Froese, P., 44
full network. *See* whole network

Gautama, S. (the Buddah), 197–198
geodesic, 63, 66, 326
  definition, 327
Georgianna, S., 236–238
Gephi
  description, 335
GIA (*Groupe Islamique Armé* – Armed Islamic Group), 298–299
Giesel, H., 181, 187
Gill, A., 13, 23, 33, 44
global Salafi jihad (GSJ), 92–93
Goffman, E., 270
Goldman, M., 288
Goodenough, E., 198
Goodwin, J., 58
Gorski, P.
  religious economies, 27

Gould, R., 15, 59, 96
  brokerage roles, 324
Gould, S. J., 3
Granovetter, M., xxii, 48, 49, 172
  forbidden triad, 293
  mobilization, 56
  weak ties, strength of, 54–56, 60, 120
Green, N., 33
Grim, B., 31, 192, 313
Gwin, C., 30

Hadden, J., 12
Hafez, M., 294, 299
Haidt, J., 254
Harary, F., 264
Hare Krishnas (International Society for
    Krishna Consciousness (ISKCON)),
    91, 138
Harnack, A., 198
Harris, F., 178
Harris, J., 112
Heider, F., 48, 263
Hentoff, N., 188
Herfindahl index, 25
Hinduism, 137, 334
Homans, G., 13
Hout, M., 9
Hunt, L., 133
Hunt, M., 133
Hybels, B., 114
hypernetwork sampling, 174, 192, 319
  suggested readings, 192

Iannaccone, L., xxii, 12, 13, 19, 24, 26, 124,
    132, 330
  religious freedom and violence, 192
  strict churches, 19–21
independent religious movement (IRM),
    208, 327
  and socioeconomic class, 208
  network density, 210, 211
indulgences, selling of, 145
INSNA (International Network for Social
    Network Analysis), 49
interaction rituals, 269
interdependence of actors, 52–54
*International Society of Christian
    Endeavor*, 161
isolates, 63

Jackson, M., 84
Johnson, A., 84
Johnson, B., 200, 220, 234
Johnson, J., 83, 314
Jones, J., 295
Judaism, xviii, 210, 334
  Diaspora, 142
  Orthodox, 222

Rabbinic, 142
Judge, E. A., 198
Juergensmeyer, M., 294

Kadushin, C., 84, 321
Kahneman, D., 15
Kanter, R., 261
Katz, E., 166
k-core, 68
  definition, 327
Keay, S., 167
Kelley, D., 19, 330
Kilduff, M., 297
King, Jr., M. L., 120, 169
King, M., 300
King, Sr., M. L., 178
Kinsolving, L., 297
Kivisto, P., 14, 44
Kleinberg, J., 84
Kliever, L., 288
Knoke, D., 59, 83, 84
Koenig, H., 250
Koresh, D., 300–301
Koskinen, J., 113
Krause, N., 250

Landau, D., 222
law of group polarization, 290
  risky-shift, 290
Leuba, J., 18
Levin, J., 250
Lewin, K., 48
Lewis, C. S., 87
Lewis, V., 173
liberation theology, 23
Lieberman, M., 43
Lim, C., 232
Lin, N., 84
Lincoln, E., 133
link analysis, 51
Lofland, J., xxii
  Moonies, 89
longitudinal networks, 58
  definition, 328
Lovin, L.-S., 220
Lundsgaarde, E., 13
Lusher, D., 113
Luther, M., 145
Lynd, H., 8
Lynd, R., 8

MacGregor, C. A., 173
MacIntyre, A.
  After Virtue, 254
Makowsky, M., 124, 132
Malherbe, A., 198
Mamiya, L., 133
Maoz, Z., 84

Index

Marsden, P., 167, 220
Martin, J. L., 287
Marx, K., 198, 199, 220
Masters, K., 224
Matthews, L., 168
maximal distance network (MDN). *See* archeological networks
Mayhew, B., 58
Mayo, E., 48
McAdam, D., 57
  Freedom Summer, 59, 91, 95, 125
McBride, M., 27, 33
McCauley, R., 42
McCleary, R., 30
McCulloh, I., xxii, 84
McFarland, D., 81
McGuire, M., 44
McPherson, A. S., 152
McPherson, M., 220
  Blau Space, 117, 131
  hypernetwork sampling, 174, 192
Meeks, W., 148, 198
Melton, G., 138
Menzel, H., 166
Meyer, J., 54, 150
Milgram, S.
  obedience to authority, 53
  small world studies, 64
Milk, H., 296
Mills, B., 142, 167
Mirola, W., 44
Mitchell, J. C., 48
modularity, 275
  definition, 328
Monahan, S., 44
Mondale, W., 296
Moreno, J., 48
Mormons (Church of Jesus Christ of Latter-day Saints (LDS)), 68, 208
  conversion, 90
  network density, 210
Moscone, G., 296
Mrvar, A., 83, 265, 266, 287
  Pajek, 287, 336
multi-agent modeling, 124, 132
Münster Rebellion, 302–304

Nadel, S., 48
National Association of Evangelicals, 152
Nepstad, S., 125–128
NetDraw
  description, 335
network closure, 111, 229, 290, 292, 295, 304, 305
  definition, 328
network data
  archeological networks, 139, 319
  counts of ties, 75

ego networks, 76
hypernetwork sampling, 174, 192, 319
one-mode networks, 62, 77, 328
simulated networks, 244, 319
two-mode networks, 62, 77, 331
whole networks, 77, 319
network size, 66, 306
  definition, 328
network topography, 66, 317
  definition, 331
Neuhaus, R., 193
new institutionalism, 54
  and women's ordination, 149–151
new religious movement. *See* independent religious movement (IRM)
Newcomb, T., 264
niche edge, niche overlap, 118–120
  and congregational racial homogeneity, 121–122
Niebuhr, H. R., 198, 203, 220
Nixon, E. D., 169
North, C., 28, 30, 33

Obama, B., 188
one-mode networks, 62, 77
  definition, 328
Organizational Risk Analyzer (ORA)
  description, 336

Pajek, 275, 287
  description, 336
Pargament, K., 250
Parks, R., 169
partition, 255, 265
  definition, 328
  medieval Christian philosophers, 274–284
  Sampson's monks, 266
path, 63
  definition, 328
  path distance, 63
    definition, 328
  walk, 63
    definition, 331
pendant
  defintion, 328
Peoples Temple, 295–298
  and the Symbionese Liberation Army, 297
  corrective fellowship, 296
  Guyana (Jonestown), 297
Perry, B., 221
Pescosolido, B., 221, 236–238
Pfaff, S., 167
Plowshares movement, 126–128
PNet, 104, 113
  description, 337
Podolny, J., 63
Polkinghorne, J., 3

Pope, W., 234
Popielarz, P., 118
Powell, W., 54, 149
Prell, C., 84, 314
Protestant Reformation
  suggested readings, 167–168
proximal point analysis (PPA). *See* archeological networks
Putnam, R., 173, 232
  social capital, 171, 187, 191, 192

QAP (quadratic assignment procedure), 74, 98, 318
  definition, 328

R
  description, 337
  EpiModel, 244, 337
  ergm, 337
  igraph, 60, 337
  RSiena, 337
  sna, 60, 337
  statnet, 104, 113, 337
  tnet, 337
Radcliffe-Brown, A., 48
Ramirez, F., 150
rational choice, 13, 317
  definition, 328
  rationality of religion, 15
  strictness, 19
  suggested readings, 46
Reagan, R., 254
regression to the mean, 204
religion and health
  suggested readings, 249
religion checklist, 334
religion, social networks, and group polarization, 293–295
religious economies, 22, 120, 317
  definition, 329
  empirical support, 25
  Herfindahl index, 25
  suggested readings, 46
  supply side, 24
    Consciousness Reformation, 25
    Japan, 24
    United States, 24
Richardson, K., 234
Roberts, K., 44
Robins, G., 84, 113
Robinson, J. A., 169
Roden, B., 299
Roden, L., 300
Rogers, E., 167
roles and positions, 73
  blockmodeling, 73, 318
  definition, 328

Romero, O., 23
Rowan, B., 150
Rubin, J., 167
Rushing, J., 234
Ryan, L., 298

sacred canopy, 34, 35, 230, 231
  definition, 329
sacred umbrella, 39, 231
  definition, 329
Sageman, M., 92
Sampson, S., 60, 263, 265
SAOMs (stochastic actor-oriented models), 74, 304, 314, 319
  co-evolution, 94, 310
  definition, 325
  definition, 330
  suggested readings, 314
Sawyer, M., 178
Scheitle, C., 18
Schelling T., 132
Schwartz, M., 48
Scott, J., 83, 84
Scroggs, R., 212
sect, 199
  and socioeconomic class, 203, 208
  definition, 329
secularization, 5, 42
  definition, 329
  empirical anomalies, 5
  suggested readings, 45
semi-involuntary thesis, 129
Sherkat, D., 129
Sikkink, D., 173
Simmel, G., 48, 254, 270
simulated networks, 244, 319
small world, 64, 82
Smilde, D., 93, 95, 96
Smith, C., xviii, 34, 44, 179, 223, 254, 333, 334
  adolescent health, 225–230
  congregational racial homogeneity, 120–122
  sacred umbrella, 39, 231, 329
  secularization, 12
  subcultural identity theory, 34, 46, 330
Snijders, T., 304, 314
Snow, D., 91
social capital, 171, 187
  definition, 329
  suggested readings, 191
social media, 50, 82
social network analysis
  assumptions, 52
  ethics, 319–321
  journals, 49
  suggested readings, 83

social networks, 60
social networks and group polarization, 290–293
social scientific study of religion
  suggested readings, 44
social structure, 56
  definition, 329
Stark, R., 12, 13, 21, 24, 26, 67, 89–90, 123, 145, 201, 206, 210, 220, 234, 262, 333
  Churching of America, 8, 24, 44
  epidemics, 238–244
    charity and differential survival, 240–243
    differential survival and network ties, 243–244
    explanations and effectiveness, 239–240
    simulated, 244–248
  Moonies, 89
  Protestant Reformation, 168
  The Rise of Christianity, xxii
Steffen, P., 224
Strang, D., 167
strictness, 19, 317
  definition, 330
  limits, 20
structural determinism, instrumentalism, and constructionism, 58, 330
structural holes, 71, 147
  definition, 330
structural location, 57
subcultural identity theory, 34, 121, 317
  definition, 330
  suggested readings, 46
  why religion survives, 37–38
  why some religions thrive, 38–40
subgroups, 68, 318
suicide, 232
  altruistic, 233
  anomic, 233
  Durkheim, 233
    critiques, 234
  ego, 233
  fatalistic, 233
  integration, 233, 238
  network centralization, 238
  network density, 236, 238
  Pescosolido and Georgianna, 236–238
  regulation, 233, 238
Sunstein, C.
  law of group polarization, 290
Swami Bhaktivendanta, 138
Swatos, W., 14, 44, 206, 220
Swift, M., 31

Tabor, J., 301
Tabory, E., 30

Tarrow, S., 57
Taylor, C., 8, 12
Tetzel, J., 146
Thalheimer, F., 18
Theissen, G., 198
Thomas, G., 150
Thomas, K., 6
Thumma, S., 132
ties, 54, 59
  definition, 331
  ties as conduits, 54
Tilly, C., 57, 189
Tolkien, J. R. R., 87
Tracy, P., 297
triad, 48
  definition, 331
Troeltsch, E., 198, 200, 220
Tsitsos, W., 181, 187
Tuma, N., 167
Tversky, A., 15
two-mode networks, 62, 77
  definition, 331

UCINET
  description, 337
undirected tie. *See* edge
  definition, 331

Valente, T., 167
Vance, J. D., 16, 223, 249

walk. *See* path
Wallace, A., 4, 239
Warner, W. L., 48
Wasserman and Faust, 58, 83
Wasserman, S., 58, 83
Weber, M., 44, 167, 199, 220
Welch, M., 123
Wellman, B., 48
White, H., xvii, 48, 58, 59
whole networks, 77, 212, 319
  definition, 331
Willow Creek Community Church, 114
women's ordination, 149–166
  and prior adopters, 151
  Pentecostal and Holiness traditions, 152
Wuthnow, R., 123, 132, 179

Yamane, D., 44
  secularization, 12
Yang, S., 83
Young, A., 178

Zablocki, B.
  urban communes, 255–263
Zimbardo, P., 128
  prison experiment, 53